Quakers and Abolition

QUAKERS AND ABOLITION

*Edited by Brycchan Carey
and Geoffrey Plank*

UNIVERSITY OF ILLINOIS PRESS
URBANA, CHICAGO, AND SPRINGFIELD

The Library of Congress cataloged the cloth edition as follows:
Quakers and abolition / edited by Brycchan Carey and Geoffrey Plank.
pages cm
Includes bibliographical references and index.
ISBN 978-0-252-03826-6 (cloth : alk. paper)
ISBN 978-0-252-09612-9 (ebook)
1. Quaker abolitionists—United States—History. 2. Antislavery movements—
United States—History. 3. Slavery and the church—Society of Friends—History.
4. Slavery and the church—United States. 5. Quaker abolitionists—History.
6. Antislavery movements—History.
I. Carey, Brycchan, 1967– editor of compilation. II. Plank, Geoffrey Gilbert,
1960– editor of compilation.
E441.Q35   2014
326.089'96073—dc23   2013045696

PAPERBACK ISBN 978-0-252-08347-1

Contents

Acknowledgments

THE EDITORS WOULD LIKE TO THANK Bryn Mawr College, Haverford College, Swarthmore College, and the McNeil Center for Early American Studies at the University of Pennsylvania for jointly hosting the conference that led to this volume. At the McNeil Center, we would in particular like to thank Dan Richter and Amy Baxter-Bellamy. At Haverford College, we would especially like to thank the staff at the Haverford College Quaker Collection—John Anderies, Diana Franzusoff Peterson, and Ann Upton—as well as Emma Lapsansky-Werner, Bethel Saler, the Office of Quaker Affairs, the Office of the Provost, the Margaret Gest Program, and the John B. Hurford '60 Humanities Center's Leaves of Grass Fund. At Swarthmore, we would like to thank Chris Densmore, Bruce Dorsey, Ellen Ross, and the William J. Cooper Foundation. We also gratefully acknowledge our own institutions—the Department of English and Creative Writing at Kingston University London, the Department of History at the University of Cincinnati, and the School of American Studies at the University of East Anglia—whose support has made this international collaboration possible. Finally, we thank Laurie Matheson, Dawn Durante, and Jennifer Clark at the University of Illinois Press for their help and support in seeing this volume into print, and Karen Hallman for her careful editing of the manuscript.

Quakers and Abolition

Introduction

BRYCCHAN CAREY AND
GEOFFREY PLANK

IN THE EARLY 1760S, WILLIAM BOEN was held as a slave under a Quaker master in western New Jersey. In 1762 or 1763, one of his neighbors, another Quaker, told him that his master was considering offering him his freedom. Boen had been legally owned by the same man since his birth in 1735. He said nothing in reply to his neighbor, not because he was hiding anything or trying to conceal his emotions, but because he had heard similar stories before, and he could not imagine that any of them were true. "I didn't think much about it," he later recalled. "Didn't expect there was anything in it, though I heard others say he talked of setting me free." Boen may have resented the neighbor's comment. He was deeply unhappy about his status, and assumed that everyone around him knew that he suffered as a slave. A few days later, Boen was walking alongside his master, "going to my work," when his master asked him, "William, wouldn't thee like to be free?" Again, Boen said nothing, this time because he thought the question was simple-minded and superfluous. "I didn't say anything to it. I thought he might know I should like to be free."[1]

These encounters illustrate several of the central themes of this volume. The Quakers are celebrated as leaders in the campaign against slavery in the eighteenth century, but they came to that position only because, for generations, many of them were slaveholders. Enslaved men and women made their unhappiness clear, but Quaker masters began to free them only in response to pleas from other white Quakers. The Quaker antislavery movement began as a conversation among whites. Many masters initially refused to free their slaves and, as Ellen Ross shows in chapter 1 of this volume, some abolitionists self-consciously excluded slaves from the discussion for fear that including them would seem incendiary. This may help explain why, even in 1762 or 1763, several years after the Society of Friends in the Delaware Valley formally renounced slaveholding, Boen was taken by surprise when his master indicated that he might free him. For many Friends, the process of turning against slavery was slow and painful because it involved renouncing a way of life that had permeated their own households and those of their neighbors for many years. For early Quaker abolitionists in America, the pervasiveness of slaveholding increased their sense of personal responsibility, instilling many with a strong sense of guilt but also energizing them with a passionate concern to make restitution and restore justice. At the same time, the process of emancipation in many ways reenacted and reinforced the unequal power relations that had been established in the context of slaveholding. In his subsequent relations with the Quakers, Boen was repeatedly reminded that most Friends continued to consider him inferior. He wanted to be a Quaker, but he was denied membership of the religious society until 1814.[2] Shortly after Boen died in 1824, American Quakers as a group withdrew from the forefront of antislavery action. In retrospect, given the politics of that era, their withdrawal from the political struggle seems predictable, since the abolitionist movement no longer stood for the ideals that animated the first wave of Quaker antislavery action, and Quakerism itself had changed.

The Society of Friends was intimately associated with slavery in the Americas almost from its inception. In 1655, shortly after the launch of the Quaker movement, Friends traveled from England to the English-ruled island of Barbados. The colony was in the midst of a demographic and legal transformation. Landowners were buying increasing numbers of slaves, and slavery was quickly becoming the dominant labor system on the island. Quaker missionaries found success among the planters of Barbados, and when the founder of Quakerism, George Fox, visited the island in 1671, it was home to the largest Quaker community outside the British Isles. At the time of the founding of Pennsylvania nine years later, there were already hundreds of Quakers living on Barbados, and others on the English-ruled Caribbean islands of Nevis, Antigua, and Jamaica. At least fourteen Barbadian Quakers owned plantations worked by sixty or more slaves.[3] When the Friends came to settle in New Jersey and Pennsylvania, they were familiar with the idea of slaveholding. Ships loaded with slaves began arriving in Philadelphia in 1684.[4] The demand for labor was high in the Delaware Valley, and the enslaved population grew rapidly.

In Barbados, Fox grew concerned about the condition of the slaves and pleaded with masters to treat their bondsmen well. He also told the slaves "to be sober and fear God, and to love their masters and mistresses, and to be faithful and diligent in their masters' service and business." Fox promised them that if they behaved well, "their masters and overseers will love them, and deal kindly and gently with them."[5] Fox hoped to introduce some slaves to the Society of Friends, and to advance that aim, the Quaker masters on Barbados held what Fox described as "meetings among your blacks" regularly, every two weeks.[6] Fox publicly denied, however, that he sought immediate freedom for the slaves or that he wanted to undermine the institution of slavery in the Caribbean.[7]

Fox's plea for benevolent slaveholding accorded with the official stance of Quaker meetings throughout the British Empire well into the eighteenth century. In Pennsylvania and New Jersey, Philadelphia Yearly Meeting expressed concern about the destabilizing influence of large slave imports and, as early as 1696, admonished Delaware Valley Quakers to "be careful not to encourage the bringing in of any more Negroes," but the meeting did not condemn slaveholding itself.[8] Indeed, between 1681 and 1730, slaveholders and occasional slave traders occupied most of the positions of leadership within the Delaware Valley's Quaker meetings.[9]

Against this background, individual Friends and small groups began denouncing slavery in the late seventeenth century. Fox's traveling companion William Edmundson may arguably have been the first Quaker abolitionist, but the first widely circulated antislavery protest was issued in 1688 by the Quaker meeting in Germantown, Pennsylvania. Long thought to have disappeared without trace or impact, the protest was in fact an influential event.[10] Over the next few decades, John Hepburn, Ralph Sandiford, Benjamin Lay, and others published essays denouncing slavery. With the exception of Elihu Coleman, a Quaker in Nantucket who managed to get approval from his meeting for the publication of his antislavery essay, none of the early Quaker abolitionists had their writings officially vetted or approved by Quaker meetings, and several abolitionists, particularly in the Philadelphia area, were formally denounced. An important shift came in 1752, when a number of future abolitionists, including Anthony Benezet, were appointed to Philadelphia Yearly Meeting's Overseers of the Press.[11] Early in 1754, the Overseers approved and helped circulate John Woolman's antislavery essay *Some Considerations on the Keeping of Negroes*, and later that year, Philadelphia Yearly Meeting issued a corporate statement, *An Epistle of Caution and Advice concerning the Buying and Keeping of Slaves*, which directed Quakers to avoid "being in any respect concerned in promoting the bondage" of "Negroes and other slaves."[12] The *Epistle of Caution and Advice* marshaled strong arguments against slaveholding, but it did not call on all masters to free their slaves, and it had little disciplinary force.

The year 1758 was pivotal for Quaker antislavery. London Yearly Meeting issued a strongly worded statement against participation in the Atlantic slave trade, admonishing Friends to "keep their hands clear of this unrighteous gain of oppression."[13] Borrowing language from the prophet Isaiah, London's statement was an early articulation of one of the most important spiritual and ideological arguments for Quaker abolitionism generally and more specifically for later boycott movements against slave-produced sugar and rum in the eighteenth century and against slave-produced cotton in the nineteenth. Additionally, in 1758, Philadelphia Yearly Meeting formally condemned slaveholding, although the meeting did not begin automatically disowning masters until 1776. London Yearly Meeting took a firmer line in 1761, issuing a "strong minute" that asked "Friends every where to discourage as much as in them lies a practice so repugnant to our Christian profession and to deal with all such as shall persevere in a Conduct so reproachful to the Society & disown them if they desist not therefrom."[14]

In America, the process of emancipation was slow by design. In the Philadelphia area, small committees visited slaveholders and struggled to convince them to free their slaves, but even at the end of the 1750s, 70 percent of Quaker masters in Pennsylvania refused to free their slaves.[15] One of the obstacles to immediate emancipation was the Quaker reformers' strong belief that there were ongoing, reciprocal obligations between the former masters and slaves. Prior to obtaining full legal freedom, slaves were forced into labor contracts binding them to the Quaker masters for terms of years. Quaker reformers such as Anthony Benezet, Joshua Evans, and John Woolman emphasized that before former slaves could be fully integrated into free society on a basis of equality, the Quakers owed them support, education, and perhaps (Woolman suggested) compensation for the injuries they had suffered and the uncompensated labor they had performed as slaves.[16] The Quakers struggled to gradually and peacefully disconnect themselves from slavery, but their efforts informed a wider American debate in the Revolutionary Era. Simply put, the Quakers inspired the project of gradual emancipation.

In 2011, in his Bancroft Prize–winning *Freedom Bound: Law, Labor, and Civic Identity in Colonizing English America, 1580–1865*, Christopher Tomlins wrote, "Those who celebrate the American Revolution and its aftermath as the beginning of slavery's end do history no favors."[17] He observed that the eighteenth-century abolitionists left much work undone. The statutory framework they supported called only for the gradual elimination of slavery and directly affected only the North, leaving the slavery regime in the South intact. Tomlins is right that celebrations distract us from the moral ambiguities and difficulties inherent in the gradualist program, but since the appearance of Jean Soderlund's *Quakers and Slavery: A Divided Spirit* in 1985, the scholarly literature on Quaker antislavery has not at all been uniformly celebratory.[18] On the contrary, scholars specializing in this field have paid increasing attention to the power of the Quaker slaveholders who worshipped alongside the early abolitionists. By the nineteenth century, those slaveholders were gone, but Ryan Jordan's *Slavery and the Meeting House: The Quakers and the Abolitionists Dilemma, 1820–1865* provides a further corrective to the old celebratory literature, by emphasizing widespread opposition within Quaker meetings to secular abolitionist efforts in the decades leading up to the Civil War.[19] By contrast, many Quakers in the United Kingdom remained active antislavery campaigners throughout the nineteenth century and were instrumental in the campaign that saw Britain outlaw slavery in its colonies in the 1830s. Even after this, British Quakers looked for ways, albeit with varying success, to reconcile their commercial activities with their opposition to slavery, for example, as Anna Vaughan Kett shows in chapter 4 of this collection, by buying clothes made from "free labor" rather than slave-produced cotton.

Edward Raymond Turner systematically surveyed the progress of Quaker antislavery more than a century ago and, in 1950, Thomas Drake produced a more detailed account that remains important to scholars today.[20] In their discussions of abolitionism in America and across the Atlantic World, David Brion Davis and Christopher Leslie Brown have highlighted the Quakers' influence in the early years of abolitionism.[21] More recently, many careful detailed studies by scholars who have contributed to this volume and others including Kristen Block, Brycchan Carey, Michael J. Crawford, Carol Faulkner, Larry Gragg, Katherine Gerbner, Vanessa Julye, Donna McDaniel, Geoffrey Plank, Jonathan Sassi, and Kirsten Sword have deepened our understanding of specific episodes and individuals involved in the development of Quaker slaveholding and abolitionism.[22] Still, outside of specialist circles, the Quakers' involvement in the debates over slavery is underappreciated. As Gary Nash argues in the closing chapter of this volume, pacifist Quakerism fits awkwardly within popular narratives of the history of the United States, which generally have found it easier to anticipate the Civil War and contrast the Puritans of New England and their descendants with the stubborn slaveholders of the South. Histories of British abolitionism neglect the Quakers because Britain has long revered an abolitionist pantheon dominated by non-Quakers such as Granville Sharp, Thomas Clarkson, and William Wilberforce. Concentrating on those figures slights not only the Quakers, but also early New World antislavery generally.[23] The recent attention paid to Olaudah Equiano, who was influenced by a variety of Quakers including his former master, Robert King, and the abolitionist Anthony Benezet, has only slightly altered this pattern of scholarly neglect.[24]

After 1772, when Granville Sharp argued and won the famous, though legally ambiguous, English law case of *Somerset v. Stewart*, abolitionism's most visible leaders would not be members of the Society of Friends. Quaker influence persisted, however, not only in America and Britain but, as Maurice Jackson and Marie-Jeanne Rossignol show us in chapters 7 and 12, respectively, in France and the French Empire as well. British and American Quakers were involved in several political debates relating to slavery in the late eighteenth and nineteenth centuries, including Revolutionary-era bans on slave imports into the United States; later debates over the transatlantic slave trade, which was formally outlawed by the United States and the British Empire in 1807; colonization schemes proposing to settle freed slaves in the western United States, as well as in Africa; the abolition of slavery in the British Empire in 1838; and the persistent debate over the future of slavery in the American South.

As the essays in this volume show, the Quaker response to the problem of slavery was deeply affected by their shared religious tenets, formal structures, disciplinary procedures, and decision-making process. For this reason, a few key terms should be defined here. The *Inward Light* is the Quakers' source of inspiration and personal knowledge. Although Quakerism is rooted in Protestant Christianity and deeply informed by the Bible, the Quakers have always believed that God can speak to each of them personally and directly by way of the Inward Light, and they value knowledge obtained through experience of the Inward Light above other authority. The *sense of the meeting* is the judgment of a Quaker meeting. Meetings make decisions by seeking divine guidance through a process combining discussion and worship. Unanimity is not required, but members are expected to defer to the sense of the meeting after it has been declared by the meeting's clerk. *Monthly meetings* make decisions for Quakers within a particular region or county. *Quarterly meetings* make decisions for a group of constituent monthly meetings, and *Yearly meetings* preside over several quarterly meetings. There has never been any formal hierarchy among yearly meetings. London Yearly Meeting, Philadelphia Yearly Meeting, New England Yearly Meeting, and others made decisions independently during the debates over slavery, though they often listened to each other's advice. In America, Quaker discipline was shattered in 1827, when disagreements over the inerrancy of the Bible led meetings to denounce one another, and rival monthly, quarterly, and yearly meetings were formed. The *Orthodox* Quakers revered the Bible and in some ways came to resemble other evangelical Protestant groups, while the Quakers known as *Hicksites* (after the preacher Elias Hicks) placed more emphasis on silent worship and the importance of waiting for the Inward Light. Even after the 1827 schism, there were many beliefs that

Quakers generally shared. As J. William Frost reminds us in this volume, the Quakers' *testimonies* have evolved over time and have never been codified in any definitive, permanent sense, but certain values described as testimonies have informed Quakerism since its early years. These include commitments to simplicity, integrity, and peace.

Although Quakers were deeply engaged in political controversies, as a group the Friends had been uneasy about resorting to legal remedies for social conflict since the time of the religious society's founding. In America, Friends became more wary of participating in formal politics as a consequence of their experiences during the Seven Years' War and American Revolution. Seeking to distance themselves from the violence of politics, Quakers increasingly pursued other means for affecting social change, by exhibiting exemplary behavior and declaring their trust in Providence. As J. William Frost and Thomas D. Hamm argue in chapters 2 and 3, respectively of this volume, Quaker opposition to the abolitionist movement in the antebellum period drew on well-established Quaker principles. The rift in American Quakerism in 1827 was not primarily about slavery, but it occasioned a great deal of soul-searching and a reexamination of all elements of Quaker discipline. Most Quakers became wary of cooperating with religious outsiders in general and non-Quaker evangelical abolitionists in particular. Like virtually all other Protestant denominations in antebellum America, the Quakers were split by the politics of slavery, but it was a far from even split. The politically engaged abolitionist meetings were a small minority. Quakerism produced antislavery heroes in this period, including Lucretia Mott, but most Quakers fighting slavery did so quietly, sometimes, as Christopher Densmore reminds us in chapter 8, completely stealthily, acting to aid escaped slaves fleeing from the South.[25]

There are a number of reasons why the Quakers' engagement with slavery needs more scholarly attention. The old celebratory literature concentrating on antislavery heroes still distracts many of us from the complexities of the Quaker response to slavery. Furthermore, many of those Quakers who were most engaged in antislavery work deliberately concealed themselves, and there is detective work still to be done to bring their work to light. A further difficulty stems from a lazy scholarly habit of retrospective thinking, analyzing abolitionism as a step toward the creation of liberal capitalist economies. Tomlins is only the latest in a long line of scholars who have analyzed abolitionism teleologically, confident in the knowledge that the end result of the campaign against slavery was the establishment of markets for wage-earning laborers. At least since the publication of Eric Williams' *Capitalism and Slavery* in 1944, scholars have debated whether abolitionists were serving economic interests.[26] Many have argued against Williams, that the abolitionists were campaigning against a profitable institution, but that formulation does not adequately change our frame of reference. In order to understand the Quaker abolitionists, we need a more appropriate vocabulary. To start, we need to examine the Quakers' language and literature closely and study the ways they themselves analyzed and discussed their religious life, internal social relations, material circumstances, and their interactions with a wide range of non-Quakers, including freed people and slaves. This is a topic that demands interdisciplinary investigation.

The essays in this volume were first presented at a conference held in November 2010 sponsored by Bryn Mawr, Haverford, and Swarthmore Colleges, as well as the McNeil Center for Early American Studies at the University of Pennsylvania. Conducted over three days at the McNeil Center, Swarthmore, and Haverford, the meetings brought together 205 registered participants, who gathered to discuss twenty-four papers from specialists in history, literature, and religious studies. The fourteen essays included in this volume are drawn from these papers and are organized into three sections.

Part I of this volume, "Freedom within Quaker Discipline: Arguments among Friends," examines debates among Quakers over slavery from the seventeenth century to the outbreak of the American Civil War. This section, and the book, opens with Ellen Ross's examination of the eighteenth-century Quaker Joshua Evans, who regarded self-reformation as a means for achieving social transformation. Evans visited almost every Quaker meeting in America and urged Quakers to free their slaves. Like Woolman and later Quaker abolitionists Elias Hicks and Lucretia Mott, he described and condemned the intertwined practices that perpetuated slavery. In the next chapter, examining a longer period of Quaker history, J. William Frost asks why, after the Quakers began directly addressing the problem of slavery in the 1670s, there was only one period, between 1758 and 1827, during which they achieved any kind of consensus among themselves on the issue. The answer lies, Frost suggests, in changes within Quakerism itself. Thomas Hamm's chapter focuses on the antebellum era, a critical period of transformation and dissension. Concentrating on the prominent minister George F. White, Hamm reveals how White's opposition to abolitionists such as Lucretia Mott was rooted in his experience as a supporter of Elias Hicks, whose controversial teachings helped fracture American Quakerism in the 1820s. In chapter 4, Anna Vaughan Kett shows how one Victorian Quaker family—the famous Clark family of Somerset—attempted to balance their commercial lives with their commitment to antislavery by promoting "free labor cotton," believing that "their individual and collective acts could create an alternative economy, end the slave system, and rid society of an evil." This section closes with Nancy Hewitt's analysis of Amy Post, an antislavery Quaker who quit her meeting in the mid-1840s to pursue "worldly" efforts to end slavery. Hewitt traces Post's complex spiritual development. Hundreds of abolitionists like Post left the Society of Friends in the antebellum period, but many continued to express Quaker values in the fight against injustice.

Part II, "The Scarcity of African Americans in the Meetinghouse: Racial Issues among the Quakers," examines the predominantly white Quaker meetings and the ways white Quaker slaveholders and opponents of slavery understood race and interacted with blacks. This section begins in seventeenth-century Barbados. Kristen Block attempts to tackle the paucity of documentary evidence about Africans on the island by urging historians to consider if it is always appropriate to maintain an adherence to "strict empiricism." Instead, she suggests, "we can recreate an unknown past by examining the cultural and social milieu both of Africans brought forcibly to the island and their ostensible masters." In the next chapter, moving to the eighteenth century, Maurice Jackson examines the global impact of Anthony Benezet's antislavery ministry, including Benezet's influence on black abolitionists outside the Society of Friends. Olaudah Equiano, Ottobah Cugoano, and Ignatius Sancho relied on Benezet's writings for their knowledge of Africa. Blacks such as Richard Allen, Lemuel Haynes, Absalom Jones, and James Forten were deeply influenced by Benezet's educational and antislavery activities. Addressing related themes on a more local scale in the nineteenth century, Christopher Densmore examines escapes from slavery and settlement patterns in and around Pennsylvania. Conscious of the present-day resonance of the history he is discussing, Densmore analyzes the mundane interactions of white Quakers and African Americans as well as their sometimes heroic collaboration in the fight against slavery. Such a collaboration is explored in the following chapter. In his study of the correspondence between Samuel McGill, a black emigrant to Liberia, and Moses Sheppard, a white Quaker supporter of the American Colonization Society, Andrew Diemer casts light on the vexed role of the American Colonization Society in abolitionist thought of the 1850s, as well as on Quaker notions of interracial communication and friendship. James Emmett Ryan, by contrast, asks how an ordinary Quaker not involved in the abolition campaign might have considered the matter of slavery and answers this by reading the memoir of Charles Pancoast, a Philadelphian Quaker whose time on the frontier in the 1840s and 1850s was marked by a cautious response to the problem of slavery.

Part III, "Did the Rest of the World Notice? The Quakers' Reputation," examines legacies left by the Quaker abolitionists in the wider antislavery movement and in historical memory. It opens with James Walvin's assessment of the Quaker impact on the early British anti–slave trade campaign and, in particular, the influence Quaker writings and networks had on the early career of Thomas Clarkson. Via Clarkson, Walvin argues, the Quakers exercised "a profound influence out of all proportion to their numbers." Dee Andrews and Emma Jones Lapsansky-Werner examine this in more detail by reading what they call Thomas Clarkson's "Quaker Trilogy": his history of the abolition movement, biography of William Penn, and a "Portraiture" of the Quaker movement. Looking both at the printed texts and Clarkson's manuscripts, they conclude that Clarkson's "glorification of Quaker life and antislavery leadership permitted him to produce an abolitionist history acceptable to both British and American readers." Quaker abolitionists had influence beyond Britain and America as well, something Marie-Jeanne Rossignol demonstrates in her investigation into the friendship between J. Hector St. John de Crévecoeur and French abolitionist Jacques-Pierre Brissot. In Rossignol's analysis, the Quaker example was an important influence on French abolitionism. Finally, this section, and the book, concludes with Gary Nash's account of how the story of Quaker abolitionism has been hidden from the general public. Nash surveys American middle school, high school, and university textbooks, monuments, and film and suggests that most Americans know little about Quaker antislavery. He ends by proposing a partial remedy: a campaign to draw attention to the career and legacy of Anthony Benezet.

Taken together, the essays in this collection attest to both the depth and complexity of Quaker engagements with slavery over more than two centuries. These essays illuminate many previously unconsidered aspects of Quaker history and the history of slavery and abolition, but it is clear that there remains much both for historians and for literary scholars to uncover. The editors of this collection hope that the essays offered here will raise as many questions as they answer and encourage further research into the relationship between Quakers and slavery in the seventeenth, eighteenth, and nineteenth centuries.

NOTES

1. *Anecdotes and Memoirs of William Boen* (Philadelphia, 1834), 6.

2. *Anecdotes . . . of William Boen*, 17.

3. See Larry Gragg, *The Quaker Community on Barbados: Challenging the Culture of the Planter Class* (Jefferson City: University of Missouri Press, 2009), 64.

4. Gary B. Nash and Jean R. Soderlund, *Freedom by Degrees: Emancipation in Pennsylvania and Its Aftermath* (New York: Oxford University Press, 1991), 10.

5. Quoted in Brycchan Carey, *From Peace to Freedom: Quaker Rhetoric and the Birth of American Antislavery, 1657–1761* (New Haven: Yale University Press, 2012), 46.

6. Henry J. Cadbury, "Negro Membership in the Society of Friends," *Journal of Negro History* 21 (1936): 151–213, 151.

7. For more on Fox's stance see Jerry Frost, "Why Quakers and Slavery? Why Not More Quakers?," chapter 2 this volume.

8. J. William Frost, ed., *The Quaker Origins of Antislavery* (Norwood, Pa.: Norwood Editions, 1980), doc. 7; Jean R. Soderlund, *Quakers and Slavery: A Divided Spirit* (Princeton, N.J.: Princeton University Press, 1985), 20–21, 25; Carey, *From Peace to* Freedom, 98–99.

9. Soderlund, *Quakers and Slavery*, 34

10. Carey, *From Peace to Freedom*, 72–86.

11. See Jonathan Sassi, "With a Little Help from the Friends: The Quaker and Tactical Contexts of Anthony Benezet's Abolitionist Publishing," *Pennsylvania Magazine of History and Biography* 135 (2011): 33–71, 39.

12. See Geoffrey Plank, *John Woolman's Path to the Peaceable Kingdom: A Quaker in the British Empire* (Philadelphia: University of Pennsylvania Press, 2012), 105–10; Carey, 177–95.

13. *Epistles from the Yearly Meeting of Friends* (London, 1818), 330–31. See Isaiah 33:15.

14. Quoted and discussed in Carey, *From Peace to Freedom*, 213–14.

15. Nash and Soderlund, *Freedom by* Degrees, 65.

16. See Maurice Jackson, "Anthony Benezet: Working the Antislavery Cause inside and outside of 'The Society,'" chapter 7 this volume; Ross, "Liberation Is Coming Soon," chapter 1 this volume; Plank, 173.

17. Christopher Tomlins, *Freedom Bound: Law, Labor, and Civic Identity in Colonizing English America, 1580–1865* (Cambridge: Cambridge University Press, 2010), 504.

18. Soderlund, *Quakers and Slavery*; see also especially Nash and Soderlund, *Freedom by Degrees*.

19. Ryan P. Jordan, *Slavery and the Meetinghouse: The Quakers and the Abolitionist Dilemma, 1820–1865* (Bloomington: Indiana University Press, 2007).

20. Edward Raymond Turner, *The Negro in Pennsylvania: Slavery-Servitude-Freedom* (Washington, D.C.: American Historical Association, 1911); Thomas E. Drake, *Quakers and Slavery in America* (New Haven, Conn.: Yale University Press, 1950). See also Sidney V. James, *A People among Peoples: Quaker Benevolence in Eighteenth-Century America* (Cambridge, Mass.: Harvard University Press, 1963), which places abolitionism in the context of other Quaker reform efforts.

21. David Brion Davis, *The Problem of Slavery in Western Culture* (Ithaca, N.Y.: Cornell University Press, 1966); Davis, *The Problem of Slavery in the Age of Revolution, 1770–1823* (Ithaca, N.Y.: Cornell University Press, 1975); Christopher Leslie

Brown, *Moral Capital: Foundations of British Abolitionism* (Chapel Hill: University of North Carolina Press, 2006).

22. Kristen Block, *Ordinary Lives in the Early Caribbean: Religion, Colonial Competition, and the Politics of Profit* (Athens: University of Georgia Press, 2012); Carey, *From Peace to Freedom*; Michael J. Crawford, *The Having of Negroes Is Become a Burden: The Quaker Struggle to Free Slaves in Revolutionary North Carolina* (Gainesville: University Press of Florida, 2010); Carol Faulkner, *Lucretia Mott's Heresy: Abolition and Women's Rights in Nineteenth-Century America* (Philadelphia: University of Pennsylvania Press, 2011); Katherine Gerbner, "Antislavery in Print: The Germantown Protest, The 'Exhortation,' and the Seventeenth-Century Quaker Debate on Slavery," *Early American Studies* 9 (2011): 552–75; Gragg, *Quaker Community on Barbados*; Donna McDaniel and Vanessa Julye, *Fit for Freedom Not for Friendship: Quakers, African Americans, and the Myth of Social Justice* (Philadelphia: Quaker Press of Friends General Conference, 2009); Plank, *John Woolman's Path to the Peaceable Kingdom*; Sassi, "With a Little Help from the Friends," Sassi, "Africans in the Quaker Image: Anthony Benezet, African Travel Narratives, and Revolutionary-Era Antislavery," *Journal of Early Modern History* 10 (2006): 95–130; Kirsten Sword, "Remembering Dinah Nevil: Strategic Deceptions in Eighteenth-Century Antislavery," *Journal of American History* 97 (2010): 315–43.

23. Marcus Rediker's narrative in *The Slave Ship: A Human History* (London: Penguin, 2007), 308–42, implicitly perpetuates this view. See also Adam Hochschild, *Bury the Chains: Prophets and Rebels in the Fight to Free an Empire's Slaves* (Boston: Houghton Mifflin, 2005).

24. On Equiano, see Vincent Carretta, *Equiano the African: Biography of a Self-Made Man* (Athens: University of Georgia Press, 2005).

25. On Mott, see Faulker, *Lucretia Mott's Heresy*.

26. Eric Williams, *Capitalism and Slavery* (Chapel Hill: University of North Carolina Press, 1944).

PART I   *Freedom within Quaker Discipline*
Arguments among Friends

1 "Liberation Is Coming Soon"

The Radical Reformation of Joshua Evans (1731–1798)

ELLEN M. ROSS

EIGHTEENTH-CENTURY QUAKER REFORMER Joshua Evans, although little known today, was an important voice in Quaker antislavery, Indian rights advocacy, and American peace history. Recent transcriptions by Jon Peters and Aaron Brecher of all known extant manuscripts of Evans's journals provides an opportunity to reexamine this figure, a friend and sometime neighbor of John Woolman, and a "beloved friend" of Elias Hicks. Evans was a critic of the developing capitalist economy. He perceived that people were increasingly implicated in the exploitation and oppression of enslaved people, the poor, Indians, even animals, and the land itself. For Evans, war was the fundamental symptom of humans' alienation from God and the most potent catalyst for the ills afflicting eighteenth-century society. He objected to an interconnected market system that perpetuated war: an economy increasingly dependent upon slavery and overreliant on tariffs and foreign trade, the oppression of Indians, the export of grain to import rum, the cultivation of tobacco, and the production and consumption of luxury goods.

Evans labored to bring to reality an alternative vision of America, one that would hold all people in equal regard. The divine injunction to "do unto others as one would have others do unto one" was for him the fundamental principle guiding the formation of the new society. The means to the transformation was a "regeneration," a "reformation," inspired by the "ancient testimonies" of Friends. The vision Evans articulated included a critique of particular Quaker practices that he thought manifested degeneration within the Society of Friends, and it moved beyond that to a critique of American society, and, at times, to a critique of the universal state of humankind.

Evans's life and work provides a rendering of the American ethical lineage in which the cultivation of personal transformation is prescribed as the most critical strategy for promoting social transformation. He sought to make the new America a reality in his own life. His hope was that as others were persuaded of the need for personal reformation, the pernicious and misguided war-based economy would give way to a harmonious world in which "the hungry would be fed & the Naked Cloathed, no hard thinking against another, nothing would hurt or destroy."[1] For reformers like Evans antislavery advocacy was a part of a larger and overarching concern about the disposition of the Quaker community and society in general.

The location of the concern about slavery within a wider theological perspective helps explain the tenacity and influence of people such as Evans. Obedience to God yielded freedom in the world. The power of visionaries like Evans was in their willingness to stand over and against the customs of their day in order to bring to reality another way of being. At times, this reformation of the mid– and late eighteenth century is depicted as signaling Quaker withdrawal from society. The story of Evans offers an alternative narrative. Rather than separating himself from society, he made a claim about what the center of society could be and sought to bring that to reality in his own life and, through his public ministry, to call others to walk with him. Scholars often underestimate the power of religious faith to sustain movements for reform. Consideration of Evans's life sheds light on the critical connection, common to many Quaker antislavery advocates, between personal religious convictions and methods of social transformation.

In 1756, during the French and Indian War, Evans refused to join the militia or to participate in the common practice of paying another person to go in his place. In his journal he wrote, "I cannot reconcile War with Christianity nor the devouring spirit with the Lamb's nature, No More than Murther [murder] and theft with the Royal Law of doing to others as [we] would they should do unto us."[2] Eventually he also refused to pay property taxes that would have been used to finance war. He observed in his journal that he was "much reproached," but, he concluded, "I could not pay my money to defray the expense of sheding blood."[3] Evans's journal is a window onto the world of eighteenth-century Quaker activism. Although at times he described himself as a lone voice crying out in the wilderness, he emerged among other Quakers who were similarly awakened to the unified agenda that drove his ministry. Jack Marietta's *The Reformation of American Quakerism, 1748–1783* locates Evans and Woolman in a spectrum of Quaker reformers and in particular within what Marietta aptly calls the ascetic and prophetic branch of the reformation.[4] Freed from the constraints of social custom by the command to obey God, Evans and other Quakers were empowered to disregard many sacrosanct practices of their day. Evans urged Quakers and non-Quakers to free their slaves. He called for all people to desist from using the products of slave labor, because to use anything produced by slaves was to be implicated in the institution of slavery. He also advocated for Native

American rights and warned people not to buy imported goods, the taxes on which were used to support war against Indians. Although scholars often place Quakerism among the less theological Christian traditions, the late-eighteenth-century movement for reform had a practical, prophetic theology that, its practitioners claimed, was rooted in early Quaker life and thought. The themes of this reformation were knit together by what Evans called the "capstone," the divine command to "have love to God and one to another."[5] Like the early Quakers, reformers such as Evans and Woolman believed that as the kingdom of God was realized in the lives of individuals, it would come to be a reality on earth.

Evans lived by the divine directive to "do unto others as you would have others do unto you."[6] This command ran like a plumb line through the heart of his life and work. He used it to distinguish good customs from evil customs and to distinguish the godly course of action from other, human-centered paths. Living in accord with this precept was, Evans and his peers believed, the means of bringing God's realm to earth, and literally re-forming the world into a "harmonious whole." His vision was shared by contemporaries such as Woolman, Hannah Foster, Anne Emlen Mifflin, Warner Mifflin, Samuel Allinson, and John Hunt, Quakers who embraced the reformation agenda, and who themselves invite further study.

Evans's journal chronicles his own spiritual growth and delineates the process of religious transformation with a transparency rare in religious literature of this period. He offered his journal to mark the way for those who would come after him. The cornerstone of his personal spiritual practice, as well as of his public teaching, was his call for people to conform their wills to the will of God. His starting point was that "God is Love, and those who dwell in God must dwell in Love saith the Apostle."[7] Echoing the early Quaker George Fox's vision, Evans articulated the hope that God's love would cover the earth as the waters cover the sea.[8] His journal is the narrative of his own growth in love "to God the Brethren and my Neighbours & fellow Creatures throut the World."[9] His life was a pilgrimage of deepening compassionate response to the world, in which awakening to one kind of injustice led to awakening to others. By 1791, after almost forty years of spiritual journeying, he wrote: "I love the Brethren and Mankind Uneversally."[10]

Evans understood himself to be an instrument, a ram's horn, through which God became manifest to the world: "I sometimes feel it [love] flow from the inexhaustible fountain thro me to the whole world, wishing all to harmonize in singing his praise who made all things good."[11] Evans narrated many tales of his painful journey to accept God's will. He frequently described the Quaker progression from the early stages of spiritual transformation, when humans perceived their sinfulness, to the stage when they were sustained by the light and mercy of God.

Like many biblical prophets, he was often without honor in his own country. Oscillating between agonizing and yearning, his journal frequently witnesses his struggles to bear the reproaches of the world as he strives for the peace that comes from doing God's will.[12] At times Evans's prophetic voice thunders from the pages of his journal: "Some day their will be an overturning . . . the land is Stained with the blood of negros & indeans and the Crie of the Slain no doubt hath reached the holy ear."[13] He carried this message for thousands of miles, visiting all but four Quaker meetings in the colonies and Canada and speaking in meetinghouses, Baptist churches, courthouses, homes, schoolhouses, in meetings with individuals and families, ministers, political leaders, enslaved and free, Quakers and non-Quakers, in small groups and in large assemblies. While preaching the way to harmony, he lamented the suffering he perceived around him, most poignantly in witnessing the ill treatment of enslaved peoples, and the oppression of Indian peoples through the seizing of their lands.

Evans asked repeatedly, "How can I be clear of the blood of the poor innocent ones"?[14] His rhetoric evoked the story in Genesis of Cain's murder of Abel: "And the Lord said to Cain, 'What have you done? Listen; your brother's blood is crying out to me from the ground. And now you are cursed from the ground, which has opened its mouth to receive your brother's blood from your hand. When you till the ground, it will no longer yield to you its strength'" (4:9–12). Human disorder caused cosmic disorder, because for Evans all creation was interconnected. "The opreshon of the black people couseth a Cloud of dearkness to hang over this land yet the Lord has a little remnant that Cryeth against this Crying Sin of Slavery."[15] When he traveled in North Carolina, he wrote that he was not surprised that the land was barren. Spiritual disorder was written onto the natural landscape as well as onto the bodies of the suffering Indian and black peoples.[16] Natural disasters and political and social unrest were signs for Evans that humans were not right with God. Nonetheless, he retained unwavering confidence that God was on the side of the oppressed: "way will be made for theire liberation."[17]

When Evans's journals were edited, first by his son-in-law Abraham Warrington, and then by George Churchman in 1804, prophetic passages were excised, toned down, and often stripped of their power to evoke the world of the biblical prophets and the early Quakers. In the edition of the journal published by John Comly in 1837, Evans's prophetic voice was almost entirely erased.[18] Just as earlier generations of Friends had expressed discomfort with the apocalyptic worldview of the Quakers of the 1650s and 1660s, the silencing of Evans's prophetic voice was an indication of the later Society of Friends's discomfort with the apocalyptic confidence of some eighteenth-century reformers.

Evans proffered the joy and "Sweetness of God's peace" as possible for all persons, but attainable only by those who passed through the flames of relinquishing self-will in obedience to God. The joy of the "indwelling of the peaceable spirit of Jesus" was for Evans, as for all of the ascetic and prophetic reformers, the measure of the rightness of his actions in the world. He lived his life in the confidence that, as more and more people experienced God's peace, God's kingdom would come, and the world would be transformed:

> Come taste and see how good the Lord is . . . his Sweet Peace for obedience . . . has been sweeter than the Honey-comb. . . . Then might they come to know the in-dwelling of the peaceable Spirit of holy Jesus; This would put an end to quarrelling & [w]ars, to hard thoughts and hard Speeches, and introduce in us the coming of his kingdom. Men would thus be taught and enabled to love enemies, & to bear reviling for Christ's sake: without reviling again; They would find no better way to gain victory, than by overcoming evil with good.[19]

Evans was aware that he was "led in a way very uncommon in this age," but he sought to let the experience of God's peace outweigh the discomfort caused by the misunderstanding of the world. As a young man, beginning in 1752, Evans underwent a series of dramatic life changes. Like many other Quakers, including Woolman, he began to reform his frivolous ways after an illness (pleurisy) and thereafter resolved to live more fully engaged with his Quaker roots, his early experiences of the light of God, and the power of Quaker meetings for worship. His escalating opposition to war was one of the earliest manifestations of his willingness to challenge social customs.

Another of Evans's early convictions was that he should wear undyed clothing, because the dying process caused cloth to be wasted, and because hiding dirt was analogous to spiritually hiding sins. At first, he decided to wear white stockings and a white hat. Over the course of four trips (at least three of them to Philadelphia) to buy a white hat, his resolve completely failed, and he bought a black hat. Then, when he was "finally willing to be accounted a fool," he bought a white hat and white wool stockings. At last, he returned to "sweet peace and joy." Evans's decision to wear all undyed clothes was an action he believed to be in accordance with God's will, "but much in the cross to my own." In this instance and throughout his writings he expressed concern that he might not be able to bear the "reproach" of those who criticized him for being "singular."[20]

Evans first mentions his growing concerns about slavery in journal entries in 1761, three years after the condemnation of slavery at the 1758 Philadelphia Yearly Meeting.[21] In the company of like-minded Friends, he visited Quaker families in order to persuade them to free their captives. "As wise as Serpents and as harmless as Doves" (as Evans put it, echoing Matthew 10:16), they met with all of the household at first, and then addressed their antislavery witness only to the holders of the enslaved persons so as not to be perceived as inciting armed rebellion. Evans was increasingly haunted by the specter of the mistreatment of human beings in the institution of slavery: "It seemed as tho the Cries of the Slaves in the West Indes reached my ears day & night for some months, and in a special manner when partaking of their labor." He began to refuse items produced by slave labor, although people initially told him that he was going "too far" in this. Eventually others began to imitate him, and he lived in the hope that the concern to end slavery would "spread thro all Opposition of men."[22]

Once, at a time of sickness, Evans dreamt that he was in a dreary land trying to make his way home. People slowed him down, directing him toward worldly pleasures; although feeble and weak, he pushed on. He came to a town inhabited by "widows and fatherless the poor, the Lame and the halt," a beautiful place with simple buildings and a central green, where everyone lived "in sweet harmony and love without respect to Circumstance." Passing an aged and sorrowful black man, Evans inquired about the cause of the man's dejection. He replied that he had a hard master. When Evans offered to talk with the master, the old man appeared to be taken up to heaven, and Evans awoke. In the dream, it was those who were often overlooked by society who lived in harmony and love. The dream compelled Evans to "take an Ancient Black Woman to my house who had been turned [out] in Old Age to shift for herself." She stayed with Evans for three or four years until she died. He commented that some people thought she was a burden to him, but it felt light to him "for the peace of my mind so far outbalanced it."[23]

In journal entries in 1762, Evans recorded that God required him "to be cautious of taking life, or eating any thing in which life had been." Like others before him, he believed that meat eating arose only after the fall and signaled the breakdown of the original harmony in creation. "Life in all is sweet the taking of which has been for some time a tender point with me." The meat-eating habit was not easily broken: "my appitite seem'd to crave flesh more than ever." Evans acknowledged that at first some of his friends stood aloof from him, and some people even treated him with disdain. He was "evilly spoken of by many." Evans was cautious about censuring those who did not agree with him, acknowledging that they might be attending to the business God called them to, but he wanted to be accorded the same respect by his detractors.[24]

With the exception of a short journal noting seven dreams for the period from 1765 to 1798, we do not have any records for the interim between 1763 and 1771. When the journal picks up in 1772, Evans's transformation is still ongoing. In that year, he decided not to provide rum to his workers during the harvest. On his travels, he had witnessed widespread hunger, and, in particular, a shortage of bread, despite flourishing crops. He found that the best flour and corn from America was shipped to the West Indies, much of it in exchange for rum. Not only was the source of people's sustenance marred by the export of grain, but the workers' rum drinking also brought about rioting and waste. "An answer intilegable to mind came thus, use no more Rum for it is a great evil in the Cuntry and thou shalt have peace in so doing."[25] Evans undertook this change with trepidation since he was defying not only a "deep-rooted" social practice, but also his own practice of using rum liberally during harvest time. Further, he was afraid of endangering his workers' health since he had heard stories of workers "dying instantly by drinking Water for want of Rum."[26] Even his friends counseled him not to forgo rum, although he noted that his wife Priscilla supported him. Certain that God required this of him, he went forward, "trembling" at what might happen to those working in the heat without rum. And as he often did, Evans remarked that many who opposed him were eventually convinced.[27]

Evans objected to the growing practice of the cultivating of large quantities of tobacco to be traded for imported goods subject to duties, which were then used to finance wars, "to hire men to go out to war & maintain them whoile destroying the poor indeans to make room for us."[28] He emphasized that time and energy should be spent raising crops to provide food and clothing for those close to home. He also believed that locally produced food was healthier for the constitutions of people living in America. As with the exportation of grain for rum, he protested against the importation of foreign goods and the pursuit of international trade. "I believe the Vast extensive Trade that has and now is carried out in this once favor'd Land has and will prove a Curse instead of a blessing."[29] "Money is the sinnues [sinews] of war," he wrote. He urged people to "be content with the natural products of our country." People who used imported goods were implicated in the war economy, and their hands were stained with innocent blood.

Tea from India, Evans maintained, was a luxury often indulged in by people who could not even afford regular meals. He objected to extravagance in "eating, drinking, wearing, using, etc.,"[30] and he opposed "many worldly concerns . . . fine houses and rich furniture . . . Sumptuous living, rich Tables, many dishes, great attendance, and a lordly way of getting thro' the world."[31] He protested against extravagant clothes and home decorations, and decried the appearance of painted and elaborately carved carriages.[32] Evans urged Quakers and society in general to observe plainness and resist worldly customs.[33] Correspondents such as Charity Rotch of New Bedford testified to the impact of his ministry: "many minds have been deeply united and dipped with him into a sense of the great degenerency of the present day and though such revolting and devia- tion was conspicuous to many of us before; yet moved I was not aware of the dangerous situation we were in until it was so clearly set forth; both in precept and example by my much valued and truly beloved friend."[34]

For more than forty years, Evans's journals expressed distress about the treatment of Native Americans. His generation remembered their fathers' stories of Indians' kindness, and he remembered a time when "we loved them as Brothers for our kindness was to each other as Brethren which makes me love the Indians to this day." The Indians sold lands "for a trifle not know- ing our improvements would spoil their hunting." He often thought of the Indians as he traveled, remembering that the lands had once been theirs until they were "driven of [sic] by white people." He urged Quakers to respect the law of "doing as we would be done by" and to "keep the Indians in greatful remembrance."[35] Though he provided no details, he recorded that two Indians lived with him for many years. Evans lamented white people's greed for land and protested against Quakers who were swept up in the desire to acquire more land at the expense of the Native Americans: "this was trying to behold that friends did not Stand Cleare but was following on aftor & Setling the land thus obtained [the Indians] being voiantly forsed of [violently forced off] their lands."[36] During a visit to Gunpowder, Maryland, in 1797, he spoke with Moses Dilwyn, who had traveled to land newly purchased from Indians beyond the Ohio River. Dilwyn discovered that the Indians felt they had been wronged and more land taken from them than they anticipated, so he returned and settled in Maryland.[37]

Sometime after 1772, Evans was compelled by the "requiring of [his] Lord & Master," to give up shaving. As with choosing vegetarianism, he believed that while shaving had become a custom, it was not the original, more perfect state. Although at times his friends and traveling companions worried that his singularity might drive people away from him, Evans himself recognized that his beard brought him notoriety, which in turn drew audiences to him. Letters to his second wife, Ann, reassure her that he was well received on his travels. In 1794, William Brown of Nantucket wrote to her that "news of his singular appearance gave rise to fears . . . but the fears vanished and the way opened to admiration."[38] Nevertheless, his "singularity" led to the meeting's refusal to grant him a traveling certificate to go to England. He was, as he put it, a "prisoner for Conscience sake."[39] Evans's journal records yet a further transformation in 1791. For some years, he had not used imported goods, but he had partaken of salt because it was so commonly used. As his opposition to any participation in war-related activity grew more nuanced, and as he lived more fully the dictum to "do unto others as we would wish them to do unto us," he reached the point where he wanted to live on bread and water so that he could live his testimony consistently.

Evans's principle objection to slavery was that to own slaves or to use goods produced by slave labor was a fundamental abrogation of the divine injunction to "do unto others as we would be done by."[40] Quakers such as Warner Mifflin and Woolman laid out more detailed arguments about the evils of slavery, but Evans was implacable in his focus on the golden rule as the standard for human conduct. All humans, equally beloved by the Creator, are created to love God and one another. So, for Evans, humans were to resist anything that degraded one person's life or attained something at a cost to another. On his journeys through Virginia, Tennessee, and the Carolinas between 1794 and 1798, he regularly held meetings that included both black people and white people. Later, in language evocative of his prophetic predecessor Benjamin Lay, an antislavery activist who chronicled the conditions of the enslaved in Barbados, he described with horror and indignation what he saw on his travels through the South.[41]

Evans described conversations in which black people told him about their hardships with respect to food, clothing, and treatment by their overseers: "My mind was touched with Sympathy and a tender feeling for their Condition."[42] Slaves frequently had only rags to wear, and young children often had no clothes. Food was often only a peck of Indian corn a week or sometimes corn and a few herring or a pound of beef. Evans observed that, surely, the wealthy white women who wore trailing gowns could spare some of their cloth for the poorly clothed enslaved.[43] In Padgetts Creek, South Carolina, he was told about a slave badly beaten by his owners. When his dead body was found in the woods, the owners refused to let him be buried. Evans wrote that people who would do this were the "devil's children" and unless they repented would "be in torment it being the Just reward of their works."[44] His awareness of the sexual oppression of enslaved women appears repeatedly in his journal entries. "Some of their cruel heard taskmastors will be gilty of fornication & adultrey with those they use So Crewely when maney of those poor black women however modest deare not Say nay for Some of them have received a hundred Stripes for So doing."[45] He wrote: "A sight and sense of such oppressions seemed almost more than I could bear."[46] His indignation is as palpable as his certainty that God was on the side of the oppressed. Just as the earth carried Abel's cries to God, so would the innocent cry of slaves reach God's ear. "Wo Wo will be the lot of Such heard taskmastors unless they repent of their wickedness. . . . Their will be a mighty over turning in this land So that the oppresed will go free and the opresor will be the oppresed."[47]

Evans observed repeatedly that slave-keeping hardened the hearts of the oppressors and thus put them at odds with the God of peace. He wrote that seeing black people dressed in rags, and children "naked as they was born" with their arms loaded with wood they were carrying to their master's house more than a mile away, or living in conditions worse than dogs, or being whipped, or having so little to eat was enough to "tender the heardest heart," but slave keepers, whose hearts were hardened by "Custom & wickedness," were unmoved.[48] Evans expressed concern for the children of slave owners who were taught to tyrannize black people and speak to them in disdainful language that appalled him.[49] He further questioned whether Friends who employed free blacks paid and clothed them as well as justice demanded. He wrote, "I believe friends Hands not Clear anough to plead their Couse . . . but will have them Sum way in their families because they Can be had at lower rate to do the drudgery then the whites."[50] He insisted that children should be taught to work hard for both their spiritual and physical well-being, "for eydolnes produses luxury & luxery many diseases both of body & Soul."[51] In Little Creek, Maryland, he was troubled by the distinction of dress, bedding, and meeting attendance between the Quaker children and the poor white and black children who were under the care of the meeting: "they are the Cildren of Somebody & have Souls to Save or loose as well as our one Children."[52]

Evans knew that he was called "in a way different from most," and his absolute commitment to live in accordance with the golden rule, and to draw others to that path, made him appear a radical to the world of which he was a part. He wrote, "tho my part might appear as a drop in the Ocean yet it is made up of many drops."[53] The reformation for him was radical in its most fundamental sense of going back to the roots of Quaker traditions. His work was to teach people to "wash their hands in innocency." His goal was to build God's house by making God's love present in the world. The influence of his witness to God's love is attested to in John Hunt's record that Evans's burial in 1798 was attended by "a vast concourse of people . . . of different colours, Negroes and Indians, for whom he had been a great advocate . . . as well as white people."[54]

Late-eighteenth- and nineteenth-century reformers such as Elias Hicks, John Jackson, and Lucretia Mott were like Evans in that their opposition to slavery grew within a theologically connected network of commitments centered on opposition to war and advocacy for Indian rights and the rights of free black persons. Within this ethical lineage, concerns for reform are not generally focused on any single issue, because the source that gives rise to the passion for reform is a spiritual vision of creating a new and universal society with the "do unto others" ethic at its center. Consumption was a moral act for such reformers, from early Quakers such as Fox and William Edmundson through Lay, Ralph Sandiford, and Evans. Carol Faulkner's work on the free produce movement of the 1820s observes that, in that period: "Their calls for socially responsible commerce were rooted in contempt for slavery, not a broader critique of the market economy, wage labor, and industrialism."[55] This is not the case, however, for those at the origins of the free produce movement. The likes of Evans, Woolman, and Hicks were adamantly opposed to the growing market economy, which was fueled in part by the acquisition of land acquired through oppression of Indians, by the exporting of grain, the importing of rum, and by the purchasing of luxury goods.

In 1811, Hicks published the brief *Observations on the Slavery of the Africans* and set out a series of arguments for the equality of all persons. Hicks argued that slaves were captured in a state of war, the war itself caused by "an avaricious thirst after gain." [56] Anyone who expressed opposition to slavery and yet used the products of slave labor was "strengthen[ing] the hands of the oppressor" and participating in a state of war.[57] Hicks argued for a boycott of the products of slave labor, as well as luxuries and, in particular, rum.[58] The articulation of the intertwining issues of slavery and war is a significant trajectory in the history of American social reform. For Evans and others such as Hicks, objections to slavery arose out of an overarching concern for "reformation" that included a critique of a spectrum of human interactions that were "warlike" and a commitment to cultivating a society that recognized the equality of all people. The fundamental strategy in the consistent call for a reformation, not only of Quakers, but at a national level, was the cultivation of personal transformation as the most critical means for promoting social transformation. The implacable commitment to the simple precept "do unto others as you would have others do unto you" was offered as the antidote to an increasingly oppressive society and led this lineage of reformers to challenge the status quo and to protest against the systemic oppression produced by war, greed, and slavery.

NOTES

1. Evans MS Journal, 1731–1793, Joshua Evans Papers, RG 5/190, Friends Historical Library of Swarthmore College, transcribed by Jon Peters (hereafter MS A), [1762], 19. (My thanks to Christopher Densmore, curator, Friends Historical Library of Swarthmore College, Swarthmore, Pennsylvania, for bringing the Joshua Evans manuscripts to my attention.) Born in New Jersey, Joshua Evans lived his life in and near Haddonfield, Mt. Holly, Newton Township, and Evesham, including living for some period of time around 1757 on property "near John Woolman's" (MS A [1757], 9). He was the son of Rebekah Owen, appointed an Elder for Evesham Monthly Meeting in 1748, and Thomas Evans, a well-known Quaker minister. At age fourteen, Joshua Evans was apprenticed to a bricklayer, and Haddonfield Monthly Meeting records describe him as a bricklayer at the time of his marriage in 1753 to Priscilla Collins (Haddonfield Monthly Meeting Marriages L.13 a, pp. 76, 77). He writes that in 1761 he purchased a farm in Newton Township. Priscilla and Joshua had ten children. After Priscilla's death (1774), in 1777, he married Ann Kay (Joshua Evans Papers, Private Collection, Debby Hadden. I am grateful to Esther Cope for providing me with access to these sources.) Evans was recorded as a minister in 1759 at Haddonfield Meeting. During his lifetime, Evans traveled extensively in the ministry, including journeys north to New York, through New England, and to Nova Scotia, as well as south into Virginia, Georgia, and the Carolinas.

2. MS A [1761], 12–13.

3. MS A [1761], 11.

4. Jack Marietta, *The Reformation of American Quakerism, 1748–1783* (Philadelphia: University of Pennsylvania Press, 1984), 91, 110.

5. MS A [1772], 24; MS A [1762], 19.

6. MS A [1791], 24.

7. MS A [1762], 9.

8. MS A [1762], 9.

9. MS A [1762], 6.

10. MS A [1791], 25.

11. MS A [1762], 19.

12. Evans MS Journal 10/4/1796–6/29/1798, Joshua Evans Papers, RG 5/190, Friends Historical Library of Swarthmore College, transcribed by Aaron Brecher (hereafter MS C) 19th 2 month–23rd 3 month 1798, 64.

13. MS C, 18th 4 month 1797, 23.

14. E.g., MS C, 5th 5 month 1797, 25.

15. MS C, 23rd 2 month 1797, 17.

16. "The Country is poor baron as is the people poorly Cultyvated there Crops have failed & to me no mearvel" (MS C, 17th 11 month 1796, 6); MS C, 4th 9 month 1797, 46.

17. MS C, 8th 12 month 1796, 8.

18. Joshua Evans, *A Journal of the Life, Travels, Religious Exercises, and Labours in the Work of the Ministry* (Byberry, N.J.: J. & I. Comly, 1837).

19. Evans MS Journal 7/29/1795–12/17/1796, Joshua Evans Papers, RG 5/190, Friends Historical Library of Swarthmore College, transcribed by Aaron Brecher (hereafter MS E), 31st 8 month 1796, 185–86.

20. MS A [1762], 13–14.

21. Marietta, *Reformation of American Quakerism*, 116.

22. MS A [1761], 11.

23. MS A [1755], 28–29.

24. MS A [1762], 16–19.

25. MS A [1772], 20.

26. MS A [1772], 20.

27. MS A [1772], 22.

28. MS C, 5th 5 month 1797, 25; MS C, 29th 6 month 1797, 33.

29. MS A [1793], 25; Evans, MS C, 18th 7 month 1797, 38.

30. MS E, 3rd 9 month 1796, 187.

31. MS E, 31st 8 month 1796, 184.

32. MS C, 9th 1 month 1798, 61.

33. MS E, 24th 11 month 1796, 196; MS C, 9th 1 month 1798, 61.

34. Charity Rotch to Ann Evans, 28th 8 month 1794, Joshua Evans Papers, RG 5/190, Friends Historical Library of Swarthmore College.

35. MS Journal 4/2/1794–6/13/1796, Joshua Evans Papers, RG 5/190, Friends Historical Library of Swarthmore College, transcribed by Jon Peters and Aaron Brecher (hereafter MS D), 26th 3 month 1795, 38.

36. MS C, 18th 4 month 1797, 23.

37. MS C, 22nd 10 month 1797, 53.

38. William Brown to Ann Evans, 12th 8 month 1794, Joshua Evans Papers, RG 5/190, Friends Historical Library of Swarthmore College.

39. MS A [1772], 23.

40. MS A [1772], 24.

41. MS C, 11th 4 month 1796, 4; MS C, 27th 11 month 1796, 8; MS C, 12th 7 month 1797, 37; MS E, 3rd 11 month 1790, 192.

42. MS E, 25th 10 month 1796, 189.

43. MS E, 17th 11 month 1796, 195.

44. MS C, 13th 3 month 1797, 26.

45. Ms C, 7th 3 month 1797, 25; Ms C, 17th 11 month 1796, 7.

46. Evans MS Journal 12/18/1796–7/7/1798, Joshua Evans Papers, RG 5/190, Friends Historical Library of Swarthmore College, transcribed by Aaron Brecher (hereafter MS F), 8, 9, 10, 12th 1 month 1797, 208.

47. MS C, 29 & 30th 5 month 1798, 79.

48. MS C, 10th 11 month 1796, 4.

49. MS C, 24th 7 month 1797, 37.

50. MS C, 25th 12 month 1796, 10.

51. Evans MS Journal 4/20/1794–2/16/1796, Joshua Evans Papers, RG5/190, Friends Historical Library of Swarthmore College, transcribed by Aaron Brecher (MS B), 24th 11 month 1794, 21.

52. MS C, 27th 11 month 1797, 57.

53. MS A [1761], 12.

54. John Comly, ed., *Journals of the Lives, Religious Exercises, and Labours in the Work of the Ministry of Joshua Evans and John Hunt*, vol. 10 of *Friends Miscellany* (Philadelphia: William Sharpless, 1837), 277.

55. Carol Faulkner, "The Root of the Evil: Free Produce and Radical Antislavery, 1820–1860," *Journal of the Early Republic* 27, no. 3 (2007): 389.

56. Elias Hicks, *Observations on the Slavery of the Africans* (New York: Wood, 1811), 7.

57. Hicks, *Observations*, 15.

58. Hicks, *Observations*, 7.

2 Why Quakers and Slavery?
Why Not More Quakers?

J. WILLIAM FROST

QUAKERS HAVE HAD A GOOD PRESS for their responses to slavery in spite of the pervasive racism within and outside the meeting.[1] Nevertheless, before 1750 and after 1830, a Friend could be disowned for vigorous, public opposition to the meeting's position on slavery. Neither Quakerism nor slavery remained the same between the 1670s and 1865. While there were common features, the institutions of slavery evolved over time in different regions. Major changes also occurred among Friends. Early Friends would have recognized a similarity in styles of worship, the practice of discipline, and the plain style of life among pre–Civil War Friends. They would have found the language Friends used to describe their religious life familiar and would not have been surprised that there were additional schisms. Still, they would have been disturbed, even appalled, at the bitterness and enormous differences in beliefs among American and, to a lesser extent, British Friends. So historians need to be careful to recognize the diversity of Friends over time and not assume that the source of the Quaker concerns and responses to slavery were essentially the same over two centuries.

Historians are in agreement that American Quakers were the first church to grapple with the morality of slavery, to require members to free their slaves, to found manumission societies seeking general emancipation, and to defend the rights of freed blacks.[2] Still, it was only between the 1760s and the 1820s that Quakers enjoyed what they termed *a sense of the meeting* or what we would call essential agreement on slavery. British Quakers showed little interest in slavery during the first half of the eighteenth century, but they took the lead in agitation after the American Revolution. They aimed to end the slave trade and then to abolish slavery, although there is no consensus about the influence of popular opinion on the decisions of Parliament in 1807 or 1833.[3] The slogan "immediate abolition," popularized by William Lloyd Garrison, originated with English Quaker Elizabeth Heyrick. Nonetheless, after 1831, British Friends had only limited influence in persuading Orthodox American Friends to join antislavery societies. Instead, American Friends closed meetinghouses to abolitionist lecturers and, on occasion, disowned those Friends who criticized the meetings for timidity.

It is easy for historians to ignore Friends' influence on the antislavery movement on the eve of the Civil War, except as a symbol of moral rectitude as portrayed in Harriet Beecher Stowe's *Uncle Tom's Cabin*. Here the Halliday family, who seem to have no theology, by kindness and morality can aid fugitive slaves, reform slave traders, and turn a desire for vengeance into love.[4]

The thesis of this chapter is that to understand Quaker antislavery, scholars need to understand how the beliefs and practices in the Society of Friends from the 1670s until the Civil War evolved, because these affected Friends' perspectives and actions on slavery. A few Quaker beliefs and practices influenced the variety of stances Friends took on slavery: the Inward Light, progressive revelation, the authority of the Bible, the nature of the church, the "Holy Experiment," the antiwar stance, and the Quaker family. This essay will discuss those themes in turn because they first facilitated and then hampered antislavery activities.

Friends in all periods have proclaimed the central and defining essence of their religion as the experience of the Inward Light of Christ. Some historians have argued that this belief led to antislavery, yet what I find most striking in the literature of the first men publicly to oppose slavery is the scarcity of references to this doctrine. Certainly, one can find this emphasis in Lucretia Mott and the Progressive Friends of the pre–Civil War period, but in the seventeenth and early eighteenth centuries, Friends did not believe there was any natural godliness in men, women, or children, except that within each person's conscience was a receptacle that, once touched by God, could awaken him or her to unmediated insights and messages from God. The Inward Light vindicated God from what Friends believed was the cruel deity of the predestinationist Calvinists.[5] The first Friends proclaimed that all had the ability to still the will so that God could act within, but in adults, the first experience of that of God would be traumatic—a sense of sin or evil that had previously dominated the person. The universality of the availability of the Christ Within meant that all peoples, not God, bore responsibility for their sinful acts. So early Friends did not arrive at a judgment against slavery because they saw Africans as noble. This helps to explain why George Fox, the authors of the 1693 "Exhortation," John Hepburn, John Bell, Elihu Coleman, or John Woolman (in the 1754 tract only) never explicitly invoked the doctrine of the Inward Light.[6]

This neglect need not mean that the doctrine was unimportant to antislavery, because the Inward Light undergirded the entire Quaker method of biblical exegesis and epistemological certainty in religious matters. When authors referred to Bible verses, they could gain assurance that they had understood God's meaning correctly. They also could receive inward confidence that their moral stance was correct, even if other Friends disagreed. In their antislavery writings, they generally do not tell us how they came to their judgments, whether by reason, observation, or inward meditation. The audience of the early antislavery writers was predominantly Quaker, but they wanted to persuade others who did not share their confidence in knowledge gained through direct personal revelations.

Directly linked to the experience of the Inward Light was the belief in progressive revelation—that God could still speak to his chosen servants with the same authority as in biblical times and that new knowledge could be gained into the nature of God and his wishes for humanity. Because historians have demonstrated that few had previously concluded that slavery was evil, a reasonable assumption is that to gain the confidence to break established patterns, Friends should have asserted progressive revelation as revealed by the Inward Light to justify their novel assertions. Nonetheless, such statements rarely appear in the Quakers' antislavery arguments. The unpublished papers of Cadwalader Morgan in 1696 and Robert Piles in 1698, probably submitted to the meeting, are two sources to consider. Morgan argued that he could find no satisfaction by discussions with others, so he "desired" knowledge from the Lord who "made it known unto me, that I should not be Concerned with them."[7] Piles engaged in the same kind of intellectual search until he had a dream that persuaded him not to buy a black man. Note that the revelation in these two cases is personal: A Friend who is debating a course of action with others finds no certainty in seeking for knowledge of right and wrong behavior. The language of the yearly meeting on slavery is similar in seeking clearness in response to concerns from individuals.

The primary significance of progressive revelation for the yearly meetings was that they could, after years of temporizing, change the testimony on slavery. The Bible showed the Jews and early Christians over time gaining new understandings. Friends had long insisted that Christian "perfection" meant perfect obedience but allowed for a growth in the demands of discipleship. So late-eighteenth-century Friends could at the same time revere their ancestors when complaining about declension and repudiate the decisions of the first settlers of Pennsylvania and New Jersey on slavery. They could choose to remember those who opposed slavery in the meeting, or who had refrained from purchasing slaves, and see the cautions and strictures on importing Negroes as showing incipient abolitionist sentiments. In his journal, Woolman declared that in "infinite love and goodness," God had "opened our understandings from one time to another concerning our duty" toward the slaves.

In reading the published antislavery authors before Anthony Benezet, most striking is their intense Biblicism. Friends saw no need to invoke progressive revelation because they had another source of certitude: the Bible. Fox began this process in his 1671 sermon, delivered in Barbados and printed in England five years later. Confronting for the first time a new form of labor, he cited a tremendous range of verses from the Old and New Testaments designed to remind masters of their obligations to their families, servants, and "bought" servants. Fox never condemned slavery as evil, but he was so ambiguous that all other early Quaker writers against slavery, except the authors of the "Exhortation," cited him. By 1715, the Quakers had mined both Testaments for verses against slavery. In addition to the prohibition against manstealing and God's deliverance of the Israelites from Egyptian slavery, there were additional verses from Exodus, Leviticus, Kings, and the prophets. The New Testament verses cited were the Golden Rule, Christ's dying for all men and women, Philip and the Ethiopian, and Paul's claim in Acts that all peoples were of one blood.

Fox's concern in Barbados was the conversion or convincement of people and the institution of "gospel family order," that is, the way Friends organized the life of meetings and of members. Fox did not condemn slavery and explicitly denied to the governor that he sought a slave rebellion. He wanted to convert the enslaved and planters and to foster a moral life among both. So he invoked Abraham's family nurture as a way of exhorting the planters to bring the blacks to meetings, provide them with decent food and clothing, and protect the sanctity of their marriages. He also suggested, in a short passage hidden in the middle of a long sermon, that a modified form of the Hebrew's jubilee year custom of freeing Jewish servants be applied to blacks after they had served a term of years. When Fox's sermon was published in England in 1676 and in Philadelphia in 1701, the definite term of years Fox had suggested was made more vague.[8] William Edmundson, who accompanied Fox, returned from Barbados in 1676 and to him goes the honor of attempting to end slavery. He wrote antislavery letters to Friends in North Carolina and New England, but there is little evidence that these letters circulated widely, and his thoughts would not have been well known until his *Journal* was published in 1715. The conversion of the enslaved, however, would remain a theme for those Quakers who condoned and those who condemned slavery.

Friends' identification of themselves with ancient Israel and the early church could be a cause for self-satisfaction but also for worry, because they knew that Israel had sinned and had been conquered and that the purity of the early church had given way to the compromises under Constantine and the rise of Roman Catholicism. While there had been good men and women in all periods, thanks to the Inward Light, the institutions of the church had been corrupted. Was the same happening to Friends? For John Hepburn, Ralph Sandiford, and Benjamin Lay, Friends' involvement with the slave trade and slavery was a sign of declension that might prompt a just God to cut off his new chosen people. Sandiford and Lay directed their complaints primarily at Quaker ministers who owned slaves, because a false prophet would lead the people to destruction.[9] The chosen people motif was combined with a search to understand God's providences. So it was no coincidence in the eighteenth century that antislavery agitation became most intense and the meetings most responsive just before wars, because wars were God's judgment upon a sinful people.

The chosen people motif reinforced the "Holy Experiment" ideal that Friends applied not just to Pennsylvania, but also to the entire Delaware River Valley. Pennsylvania and New Jersey were new lands, and the settlers were establishing a pattern that would endure if they remained godly. So Quakers wished to be able, if not to impose their beliefs, at least to mold the character of the entire society. William Penn welcomed Baptists, Presbyterians, and Anabaptists because they did not threaten Quaker control of the assembly. The Old Testament showed that the rulers had special responsibilities for the morality of the people, and Quakers in the government would see that at least the laws fostered, though they could not guarantee goodness. Under Penn's 1701 charter, Pennsylvania became a land of prosperity and peace symbolized by the state house's Liberty Bell, but Quaker prophets saw wealth as a mixed blessing that could lead to declension and the removal of God's protection. We know that some Friends worried about the character of their new land if Pennsylvania and New Jersey should become slave societies like Virginia, South Carolina, and the West Indies.

Fox, Edmundson, Sandiford, and Lay visited the South and West Indies and observed the effects of slavery on planters, their families, and the enslaved. It is striking that none of the early antislavery advocates were Friends converted in the West Indies, New England, or the South. Rather, Quakers in those areas, some of whom migrated to Pennsylvania and became some of the wealthiest merchants in Philadelphia, provided strong support for slavery, and their presence in the meetings stymied the so-called radicals for seventy years. Slave owners allowed compromises that allowed the meeting repeatedly to advise against bringing slaves into Pennsylvania or engaging in the slave trade, although violation would not be a disownable offence. The

Pennsylvania Assembly even attempted to place stiff duties upon imported slaves. In supporting these partial measures, colonists who opposed slavery joined with many who disliked blacks because they were allegedly uncivilized and prone to crime and revolt.

Like the limitation of slave imports, colonization schemes did not divide Friends until the 1830s. During the early colonial period, antislavery Friends believed that colonization could be a blessing in two senses: it would end the cruelty of slavery in America and could introduce Christianity and civilization to Africa. The number of the enslaved at first was small enough that this seemed an easy solution. The need to bring true religion and Western culture to Africa remained a constant theme in Quaker discussions of colonization up to the Civil War.

What later Friends would call the "peace testimony" and which colonial Quakers called their "war" teachings could prompt or reinforce the antislavery beliefs in two ways. If Friends were called to govern Pennsylvania as a holy commonwealth and remain a peaceful people, what would happen in case of a slave revolt? Keeping the slave population nonexistent would allow Pennsylvania to be peaceful, which was a necessity because the Quaker-dominated Pennsylvania Assembly would not create a militia. We do not know how much early antislavery Friends were aware of the effects of the slave trade on Africa, but they knew enough to realize that the Africans sometimes waged war to gain men and women to sell to Europeans. They also knew that Europeans did not enslave other Europeans if they became captives during a "just" war.

Some weighty Friends, including Robert Barclay and Penn, allowed that a professedly Christian magistrate who was not a Quaker could wage a just war of self-defense. However, the wars in Africa to gain slaves were not just wars and the European slave traders did not care about or investigate the causes of these conflicts. In addition, even in a just war, noncombatant immunity should apply to nonwarrior men and to all women and children. So for Quakers, there could be no just war defense of slavery.

During the eighteenth century, Friends began to expand the meaning of the antiwar stance into the peace testimony, a belief that family life should reflect a nonviolent, nonthreatening, gentle attitude. Loving kindness would characterize the Quaker family. The result was an emphasis upon the family as a "garden enclosed" where a distinct pattern of what Barry Levy termed "holy conversation" would prevail. Parents had to practice self-discipline and so did children, learning patience and submission to the will of God. Absolute submission, quietness of will before God, was required, but power over other human beings tended to destroy humility. How would having virtually absolute power over other human beings and their offspring affect the master, his wife, their children, and the enslaved? The children who grew up ordering slaves would not grow up to be servants of God and defer to the meeting.[10] It was only natural that Friends who were concerned for their own families would extend that scrutiny to the effects of wars in Africa, the Middle Passage, and servitude on the families of the enslaved. Fox was the first to complain about the destruction of marriage bonds in slavery, and Hepburn pictured the plight of husbands separated from wives and children taken from their parents. Quakers could not rest easily with an institution that destroyed family bonds, in whites as well as blacks.

Finally, Quakers had an ambivalent attitude toward wealth. From Penn's "No Cross, No Crown" to Woolman's "Journal" and "Plea for the Poor," Friends rejoiced in a moderate prosperity but feared the effects of money on piety. Slavery intensified those misgivings by intensifying suspicions of its effects. All the published attacks on slavery focus on the foundation of the institution: inordinate greed. George Grey, a West Indian immigrant and minister, published the only explicit defense of slavery written by a Quaker in the entire colonial period. He argued, based upon selective biblical verses and distorted quotes from prominent Friends, that Quaker masters strove for the welfare of the enslaved.[11] Although probably submitted to the meeting, Grey's manuscript was not published.

Beliefs in the Inward Light, progressive revelation, the nature of the church, the Holy Experiment, peace, family, and wealth created a persistent critique of slavery, but success in cleansing the meeting of slavery required two new stimuli: a reform movement tightening discipline and war. Friends might have viewed the events from 1750s through 1780 as a "perfect storm," consisting of the French and Indian War, the march of the so-called Paxton boys on Philadelphia, the battle over repealing Penn's charter, the agitation over British imperial policy and taxation, the Revolution, and the new Pennsylvania government that overturned the colonial charter, disenfranchised Friends, and exiled many of their leaders. At the same time, a movement for reform occurred within Quakerism, tightening the exercise of discipline, disowning those who fought or who married out of unity, and questioning Friends' participation and ultimately requiring withdrawing from governing. Through refusing to endorse the new revolutionary governments by affirming their loyalty or paying war taxes, Friends embraced suffering as a mark of their obedience to God. Their quest for purity led to abolition, as Friends sought to understand the reasons for God's chastisement from war and the failure of the Holy Experiment. Colonial American meetings began a process of disciplining those who engaged in the slave trade and eventually forced all slave owners to free their slaves.[12]

In requiring members to abstain from politics and renounce power, to refrain from fighting and renounce patriotism, and to end slavery and make economic sacrifice, the yearly meetings showed the efficacy of their form of organized religion. At the same time, the meetings' failure to control the dissenters meant many would be disowned. Recognizing that disowning slave owners would not help the enslaved, the meetings moved more slowly and showed more tolerance here than in enforcing other aspects of the discipline. And although slavery was evil, the process of emancipation could be gradual—particularly for children. The Quakers not only did not compensate owners for their ex-slaves, they required that owners provide for elderly freedmen and women.

Friends assumed that the same kind of gradual processes by which they had freed their slaves could work for the rest of the country. After all, during the Revolutionary Era, by various means, the states had provided to gradually eliminate slavery in the North, and many Southerners complained about the institution. In the New Republic, Quakers would found manumission societies in the North and South, petition state legislatures and Congress to end the slave trade, defend the rights of freedmen and women, and seek to educate and make blacks respectable so that the Southerners would see that abolition would bring no threat and that free labor by white and black would bring prosperity. For those who saw no future for blacks in America, such as Quaker Paul Cuffee, colonization of Africa would be good for all concerned. When North Carolina Friends found that their legislature would not allow newly freed men and women to stay in the state, the yearly meeting took ownership until they could ship the blacks to Indiana or Pennsylvania or, later, to Liberia or Haiti.[13] In the New Republic, many Friends supported colonization, but the Pennsylvania Abolition Society, dominated by Friends, refused to endorse the work of the American Colonization Society and insisted that those who were to leave America had to agree. Neither Pennsylvania nor North Carolina Friends would support forced exile of unwilling slaves or freedmen. Before 1830, even the most radical antislavery Friends including Elisha Tyson in Baltimore, Thomas Garrett in Wilmington, and Edward Hopper in Philadelphia, who openly distorted or defied the law to help runaway slaves, remained in unity with their meetings.[14]

In 1827, the Society of Friends, as a series of autonomous yearly meetings in Great Britain and America who shared religious beliefs, social concerns, and visiting ministers, ceased to exist.[15] Not only between but also within each yearly meeting, conflicting groups laid claim to the mantle of true Quakerism and charged their opponents with betraying the heritage of Fox, Penn, and Woolman. The Orthodox charged the Hicksites with being unduly influenced by Unitarians and rationalists; the Hicksites countered that the Orthodox had surrendered to evangelical Methodists and Presbyterians. The quietists in both meetings accused their opponents of abandoning the traditional Quaker emphasis on stilling the will. All claimed to be preserving the essence of Quakerism and sought to hold together the remnant of those who agreed with them while engaging in ecclesiastical billingsgate and disowning opponents. The result was that every fundamental belief and practice of the Society of Friends was now open to being reinterpreted: the Inward Light, sense of the meeting proceedings, the practice of discipline, the peculiar customs of dress and speech, and the social testimonies including antislavery.

Garrisonian abolitionism posed an additional threat to the unity of Friends. Like Friends, Garrison wanted moral suasion, not political action, and was less interested in the economic consequences of slavery than the evil of the institution.[16] There might have been close cooperation between radical abolitionists and some Friends, particularly Hicksites, who at first supported the creation of the American Abolition Society in 1834. Yet by 1840, all the major yearly meetings, except for the emerging Progressive Friends, had closed their doors to abolition lectures, and soon several prominent abolitionists had either been disowned or resigned from meeting. In 1843, Indiana Yearly Meeting divided with the minority of activist antislavery Friends forced out.[17]

Garrison's tone and content went against Quaker practices. He sounded more like Lay than Woolman, strong on denunciation rather than persuasion, a prophet rather than a healer. Even though his motto, "immediate emancipation" had originated with a British Quaker, Friends advocated gradual emancipation—preparing the enslaved for freedom. Samuel Janney, a Virginia Hicksite, who published his thoughts on abolition in newspapers throughout the 1840s, laid out the steps that should be taken: free discussion in the South, repeal of laws requiring manumitted slaves to leave Virginia, education of blacks, prohibiting the domestic slave trade, beginning a postnatal emancipation plan, a period of adjustment between slavery and total freedom, and compensation for slaveholders to be derived from the sale of Western lands.[18] In addition, Garrison addressed his tracts to the North, and when the South stopped debating the subject, advocated disunion. Most Friends did not believe disunion would help the slaves and thought that such a disruption would lead to a war that would violate the Quakers' antiwar testimony and create more animosity without improving the lives of the enslaved.

To quietist Orthodox and Hicksite Friends, Garrisonian abolition was a creaturely activity, based upon human intelligence and activism rather than silent waiting for God's prompting. Quakerism required isolation from the world's people; it was primitive Christianity revived, not another denomination, and its traditions were not human discoveries but insights from God. Not just abolition societies, but Bible societies, higher education, missionary organizations, and political parties should be shunned by Friends. Long before the schism, Elias Hicks had voiced displeasure at Friends joining outside organizations. Quietist Friends constituted a substantial minority, perhaps a majority, of both Philadelphia Yearly Meetings. The initial decisions to close meetinghouses to abolitionist lectures came from both Philadelphia organizations and then were seconded by other American Yearly Meetings.[19]

Quietist weighty Hicksite Friends correctly saw abolitionists such as Lucretia Mott as undermining traditional Quakerism.[20] Mott seems more romantic than either evangelical or quietist.[21] She claimed Penn was a Unitarian, saw humans as perfectible, spoke in Unitarian churches, and read the Bible for insights rather than as God's truth. Her pacifism was a combination of Quaker sectarianism and Garrisonian nonresistance, but unlike Garrison, she remained consistent during the Civil War. Even if women had gained the suffrage, she would not have voted. She preached abolitionism in meetings for worship and, in letters, denounced the quietist ministers and elders as attempting to resurrect Orthodoxy among the Hicksites. Her religion was an immanent Christ wedded to reform. Yet as a weighty Friend, she continued to wear plain dress and speak plain language, supported the free produce movement, defined abolition as a moral rather than a political movement, did not vilify slave owners in her speeches, and supported educational reform. She counseled Abby Kelley not to resign from Quakerism and complained that the radicals who left meetings became narrow.[22] As clerk of the Hicksite Philadelphia Yearly Meeting women's meeting and with the support of the members of Cherry Street Meeting, she had sufficient authority and followers to resist attempts to disown her. She was untouchable, but the quietists in Philadelphia and elsewhere had sufficient support among ministers to close meetinghouses to abolitionist lecturers, and the reforms she advocated, except for the founding of Swarthmore College, did not occur until long after the Civil War.

Mott thought New York quietist minister George Fox White was insane, but White's preaching attracted a large and receptive crowd who filled the Cherry Street Meeting house to capacity even in the heat of a Philadelphia summer. In his sermon—so long that even the perspiring scribe taking down his words had to stop in the middle—White denounced Quakers' joining with outsider organizations, including antislavery groups. Yet White also endorsed the free produce movement and saw himself as favoring abolition.[23] White and Mott saw each other as promoting a disunity that would lead to another schism among Friends.

Orthodox Friends in Philadelphia and New England had similar reservations about John Greenleaf Whittier's support of Garrison. Whittier remained a Friend in good standing, but one would not know from his writings that he was a Gurneyite Quaker. The outward atonement, virgin birth, inerrancy of the Bible—these Orthodox doctrines play no role in his published prose writings, poetry, or his letters. His essay on the Bible and slavery insisted that if the Bible had supported slavery, then it would be in error but, of course, it did not. In his published work, he was careful not to criticize Orthodox Quaker beliefs, but there is considerable evidence that he regarded all religious dogmas and language as symbolic—pointing to deeper truths. He wanted to be a Quaker, but not a "sectarian Quaker."

Whittier shunned religious disputes. His criticism of New England Friends' decision to close meetinghouses to abolitionists remained in private letters sent to close friends. He was so reticent in person that his biographer records that he made only three public speeches in his life—none in Quaker meetings. He associated with antislavery Hicksites, including the Motts; wrote a positive letter to the Progressive Friends; and deplored the breakup of the antislavery societies, for which he blamed Abby Kelley and Garrison. Like Mott, he supported many reforms including women's rights and working men's rights, but unlike Mott, he wanted them kept separate from antislavery, which he argued had enough difficulties by itself. Even after New England Friends opposed antislavery societies, Whittier worked with Joseph John Gurney and Joseph Sturge, who advised Orthodox Friends that they should join such organizations and work for immediate abolition. Associating with such weighty English Friends protected Whittier from censure from other Friends. Like Mott, he had serious disagreements with the conservatives in meeting, and like her, he never criticized them in print, but often in private letters. Unlike others, Mott and Whittier observed the letter of the Quaker testimony against exposing differences among Friends in print. They both refused to choose between Quakerism and abolition. As Whittier phrased it, "I mean to be a Quaker as well as an abolitionist."

Unlike Mott and Garrison, Whittier was always interested in politics. He began as a strong Whig and a fan of Henry Clay, but antislavery ended his political career, and from then on, he made abolition the sine qua non for his support. Whittier's endorsement of the Liberty Party in 1840 and later denunciations of Clay and Daniel Webster and maneuverings for the election of Charles Sumner reveal the consistency of his politics. In meeting for worship, Whittier was a quietist stilling the will and experiencing God directly, but his quietism ended at the meetinghouse door.[24]

In the aftermath of the 1827 schism, Friends' views of abolition societies depended upon their understanding of the experience of the Inward Light, the nature of the church, and the enclosed garden life. The response of all bodies of Friends to the fear that they might be wrong was to become more rigidly assertive that they had not outrun their gift. If the Light could be known only through a long period of silence and could be easily overcome by worldly activity, then associating with others for religious or moral reform glossed over the inherent corruption in all purely human endeavors. So Friends should separate from such worldly activity, make their perspective on slavery known, and trust God to convince others of the truth. The religious foundations of Quaker antislavery before 1755 were used against the radical abolitionists after 1830—the peace testimony, a way of living marked by "peculiar" customs, the purity of the meeting as the only true church, the way one experienced the Light.

In retrospect, their various reactions to antislavery crusaders show the difficulty the Friends continue to face in seeking a way to oppose and reform entrenched social systems that are radically evil and seemingly not susceptible to quiet spiritually inspired discourse. In the 1850s, Quakers stood apart from the violence of Bleeding Kansas and Harper's Ferry. Northern racism and Southern intransigence made the future appear bleak. Because of their religious beliefs, the normal response of Friends to extreme evil they cannot stop is to offer help to the victims: supporting the Underground Railroad, aiding the freedman in the Civil War, war victims in World War I, Jews in the 1930s, and draft resisters over Vietnam. Quakers as individuals and organizations still advocate following Penn's advice: "Let us see what love can do," and if love does not succeed, they have no alternative strategy but to trust in the providence of God.

NOTES

1. See Donna McDaniel and Vanessa Julye, *Fit for Freedom, Not for Friendship: Quakers, African Americans and the Myth of Racial Justice* (Philadelphia: Quaker Press, 2009).

2. Thomas Drake, *Quakers and Slavery in America* (New Haven, Conn.: Yale University Press, 1950); Jean R. Soderlund, *Quakers and Slavery: A Divided Spirit* (Princeton, N.J.: Princeton University Press, 1985); Ryan Jordan, *Slavery and the*

Meetinghouse: The Quakers and the Abolitionist Dilemma, 1820–1865 (Bloomington: Indiana University Press, 2007).

3. Judith Jennings, *The Business of Abolishing the British Slave Trade, 1783–1807* (London: 1997); Roger Anstey, *The Atlantic Slave Trade and British Abolition, 1760–1810* (London: Macmillan, 1975); Christine Bolt and Seymour Drescher, eds., *Anti-Slavery, Religion and Reform* (Folkstone: W. Dawson, 1980); Christopher Leslie Brown, *Moral Capital: Foundations of British Abolitionism* (Chapel Hill: University of North Carolina Press, 2006); David Brion Davis, *The Problem of Slavery in Western Culture* (Ithaca, N.Y.: Cornell University Press, 1966) and The *Problem of Slavery in the Age of Revolution, 1770–1823* (Ithaca, N.Y.: Cornell University Press, 1975).

4. Glenn Cummings, "Exercising Goodness: The Antislavery Quaker in American Writing 1774—1865" (Ph.D. diss., University of Virginia, 1996), ch. 4.

5. Robert Barclay, *Apology for the True Christian Divinity* (first English edition, London, 1678), Prop. I, II, IV.

6. Roger Bruns, ed., *Am I Not a Man and a Brother: The Antislavery Crusade of Revolutionary America 1688–1788* (New York: Chelsea House, 1977); J. William Frost, *The Quaker Origins of Antislavery* (Norwood, Pa.: Norwood Editions, 1980). On the 1693 "Exhortation," see Katharine Gerbner, "Antislavery in Print: The Germantown Protest, The 'Exhortation,' and the Seventeenth-Century Quaker Debate on Slavery," *Early American Studies* 9 (2011): 552–75.

7. Frost, *Quaker Origins of Antislavery*, 70–72.

8. George Fox, "Gospel Family Order," reprinted in Frost, 35–55. J. William Frost, "George Fox's Ambiguous Antislavery Legacy," in *New Light on George Fox*, ed. Michael Mullett (York, U.K.: Ebor Press, 1991), 69–88; Brycchan Carey, "'The Power That Giveth Liberty and Freedom': The Barbadian Origins of Quaker Anti-Slavery Rhetoric," *ARIEL* 38, no. 1 (Jan. 2007): 27–47.

9. J. W. Frost, "Quaker Antislavery: From Dissidence to Sense of the Meeting," *Quaker History 101* (Spring, 2012): 12–33, contains an analysis of the published writings of these men.

10. Barry Levy, *Quakers and the American Family: British Settlement in the Delaware Valley* (New York: Oxford University Press, 1988), 80–82, 130–32; Frost, *Quaker Family in Colonial America: A Portrait of the Society of Friends* (New York: St. Martins, 1973), ch. 4–5.

11. Printed in *New Light on George Fox,* 82–84.

12. Jack Marietta, *The Reformation of American Quakerism, 1748–1783* (Philadelphia: University of Pennsylvania, 1984); Sydney V. James, *A People among Peoples: Quaker Benevolence in Eighteenth-Century America* (Cambridge, Mass.: Harvard University Press, 1963); Arthur Mekeel, *The Relation of Quakers to the American Revolution* (Washington, D.C.: University Press of America, 1979). On antislavery in general in Pennsylvania, see Gary Nash and Jean Soderlund, *Freedom by Degrees: Emancipation in Pennsylvania and Its Aftermath* (New York: Oxford University Press, 1991).

13. H. M. Wagstaffe, ed., "Minutes of North Carolina Manumission Society 1816–1834," special issue, *The James Sprunt Historical Studies* 22, nos. 1 and 2 (1934): 86–88,

95, 103; Beverly Tomek, "Seeking a Manageable Population: Limitation, Colonization, and Black Resistance in Pennsylvania's Antislavery Movement" (Ph.D. diss, Houston, 2006), 130–37; Emma Lapsanky and Margaret Hope Bacon, eds. *Benjamin Coates and the Colonization Movement in America 1848–1880* (University Park: Penn State University Press, 2005).

14. Leroy Graham, "Elisha Tyson, Baltimore and the Negro" (M.A. thesis, Morgan State College, 1975), 36; James McGowan, *Station Master on the Underground Railroad: Life and Letters of Thomas Garrett* (Jefferson, NC: McFarland, 2005).

15. H. Larry Ingle, *Quakers in Conflict: The Hicksite Reformation* (Knoxville: University of Tennessee Press, 1986).

16. Henry Mayer, *All on Fire: William Lloyd Garrison and the Abolition of Slavery* (New York: St. Martin's Press, 1974).

17. Thomas Hamm, April Beckman, Marissa Florio, Kirsti Giles and Marie Hopper, "'A Great and Good People': Midwestern Quakers and the Struggle against Slavery," *Indiana Magazine of History* 100, no. 1 (March 2004), 3–25, and Thomas D. Hamm, David Dittmer, Chenda Fruchter, Ann Giordano, Janice Mathews and Ellen Swain, "Moral Choices: Two Indiana Quaker Communities and the Abolition Movement," *Indiana Magazine of History* 87, no. 28 (June 1991), 117–54; Ryan P. Jordan, "The Indiana Separation of 1842 and the Limits of Quaker Anti-Slavery," *Quaker History* 89 (Spring 2000), 1–27.

18. Gail McPherson, "Samuel Janney: Quaker Reformer" (M.A. thesis, University of Utah, 1977), 74; Jordan, *Slavery and the Meeting House*, 29.

19. *Review of "An Address" Respecting Slavery Issued by the Yearly Meeting of Friends, Held at Lombard Street, Baltimore, 11th Month, 1842*, 1–8.

20. Edward Hicks, *Memoirs of the Life and Religious Labors of Edward Hicks* (Philadelphia: Merrihew & Thompson, 1851), 136, 175, 181, 190, 228, 231, 242, 251.

21. *Lucretia Mott: Her Complete Speeches and Sermons,* ed. Dana Greene (New York: Mellen Press, 1980), on the Bible, 123–34, on worship, 271–81; Margaret Hope Bacon, *Valiant Friend: Life of Lucretia Mott* (New York, 1980).

22. *Selected Letters of Lucretia Coffin Mott,* ed. Beverly Wilson Palmer (Urbana: University of Illinois, 2002), on Garrison's language, 51–53; on Abigail Kelley and leaving meeting, 47–48, 106; on reforming discipline, 106, 136; on Bible, 107, 233; on her religious beliefs, 108; on abolitionists, 21, 281, 35–36, 153; on Unitarians, 92, 107, 179; on Whittier, 39, 72, 75, 110.

23. *Selected Letters of Lucretia Coffin Mott,* 22, 59–61, 67, 72, 91–94, 103, 109; *Sermon by George F. White . . . Delivered 12 Mo. 19th 1843 . . . at Cherry Street Meeting* (Philadelphia: King & Baird, 1843).

24. *Letters of John Greenleaf Whittier,* ed. Samuel Thomas Pickard (Cambridge, Mass.: Harvard University Press, 1975), 3 vols. quotations, 1: 343, 2: 277; on strong language, 180; on closing meeting houses to abolitionists, 237, 617; on nonresistance, 250, 393; on Hicksites, 295; on Lucretia Mott, 135, 345; on being eldered, 425; on Wilburite split, 596; on beliefs, 1: 388, 2: 196, 277, 416–17; *The Writings of John Greenleaf Whittier,* 7 vols. (Boston, Mass: Hougton Mifflin 1889), "The Bible and Slavery," 7: 96–99. "William Ellery Channing," 6: 283.

3 George F. White and Hicksite Opposition to the Abolitionist Movement

THOMAS D. HAMM

ON MARCH 25, 1839, Deborah Ferris Bringhurst, a weighty Hicksite Friend, was sitting in meeting in Wilmington, Delaware, when she heard an unfamiliar voice break the silence. "I listened to one of the most extraordinary sermons I ever heard. It was 'glorious in holiness' & lucidly clear in opening the Scriptures and the most powerful logical reasoning on *divine truths* under divine authority. My soul rejoiced in the evidence that Infinite Goodness is still raising up instruments to proclaim the *great truths* of the Gospel."[1] Two years to the day later, the *National Anti-Slavery Standard* carried an article about the same minister. Entitled "Rare Specimen of a Quaker Preacher," it scored this particular Friend. The writer described how the preacher "delivered a discourse, (if we may call it by that name) which, for incoherency of argument, misrepresentation and caricature of the sentiments of others, abusiveness of style, and passionate ferocity of manner, exceeded any thing which we had ever heard from a man professing to be a minister of the gospel." "Painful surprise" was far too weak a term to describe the writer's feelings. "Our emotions were those of utter astonishment—nay, almost of horror! . . . But for the outward peculiarities of the Quaker assembly, which we saw about us, we should have been ready to conclude that we had missed our way and gone to a political caucus, and that we were listening to the harangue of some unscrupulous demagogue."[2]

The minister who spoke so effectively to Bringhurst's condition, and so horrified the abolitionist editor, was a Hicksite Friend from New York City named George Fox White. In the 1840s, White was the most controversial, polarizing figure in Hicksite Quakerism. He felt it his duty to use his unquestioned talents to warn Friends, in the most forceful terms, against participating in antislavery, temperance, nonresistance, and other reform movements that many, most notably Lucretia Mott, saw as advancing Quaker testimonies. The controversy over his crusade against reform movements would ultimately help fracture every Hicksite yearly meeting except Baltimore and change the course of Hicksite Quakerism.

White was, as his full name suggests, a birthright Friend. He was born in New York City in 1789. In 1820, he was disowned by his meeting after his mercantile business failed to fully pay its debts, but in 1832 he rejoined the meeting. Four years later, he became a minister, and he soon began to travel among Hicksite Friends. By 1840, he had established himself as a major force in Hicksite Quakerism. Benjamin Swayne, a Chester County, Pennsylvania Friend who heard him in 1839, described White as "a man of very amiable disposition, agreeable and cheerful in his intercourse among his fellow beings and I think the most obedient in attending to the requisitions of duty of anyone I ever met with." Swayne wrote, "the few days spent in his society were among the most beautiful and happy of my life." A year later, a New York Friend concluded that White was "thought by some to be the greatest preacher in our society and even put him before Elias Hicks. . . . I know of no one that I like to hear as well." Rachel Hicks, herself an influential minister from Long Island, publicly described White as a "modern Paul."[3] By then, however, as a result of the slavery controversy, White had also become one of the most embattled Hicksite Friends in North America.

The 1830s saw the transformation of the antislavery movement in the United States. Before that time, organized antislavery had been disproportionately a Quaker movement. After 1830, a new generation of abolitionists, drawing their energy largely from a sometimes uneasy alliance of free blacks and zealous young Northern evangelical Protestants, repudiated older themes of moderation to advocate the immediate abolition of slavery. The abolitionist movement divided Friends, both Orthodox and Hicksite. On the one hand, from the 1830s through the Civil War, Friends of both persuasions continued to be visible in antislavery work. Of the sixty-two delegates who formed the American Anti-Slavery Society in Philadelphia in 1833, twenty-one were Friends, mostly Hicksites. Popular perceptions put Friends at the center of the movement.[4] Nonetheless, many Friends had doubts about the activities of the American Anti-Slavery Society; by 1842, nearly every yearly meeting, Hicksite and Orthodox, had cautioned members about participating in abolitionist activities, and many had ordered that meetinghouses be closed to traveling abolitionist lecturers and the meetings of antislavery societies. No more public and articulate advocate of opposition to abolitionism could be found than White. Why were he and other Friends so opposed to a movement that was seemingly consistent with three generations of Quaker activism?[5]

In the case of White and like-minded Hicksites, the answer lies in their experiences in the 1820s, particularly their perception of American society and the role and power of the evangelical Protestant clergy in it. Convinced that Friends were called on to preserve and keep before the world certain testimonies about the nature of true Christianity, Hicksite Friends engaged in public controversies with non-Quaker clergy to a degree not seen since the seventeenth century. Hicksite opposition to the trends in Quakerism that they labeled Orthodox—the Bible as final authority and Trinitarianism—was driven in large part by a conviction that these were the inroads of a grasping, power-hungry evangelical clergy. These clerics would not be content simply with overthrowing Quakerism—indeed, they would not stop until they had control of the United States and had united their church with the powers of the state.[6] "It is a serious matter to marshall one Religious Society against another," wrote William Poole in 1822. Yet Friends had no choice. Poole thought them likely to be "the *only stumbling block* that *seems to stand in the way of the splendid schemes* carrying *on by the Presbyterians*." Opposition might well bring persecution, but it was "necessary that some persons or Society shall stand in the Gap—or Clerical Tyranny may overturn all our Religious liberties."[7]

At the heart of this critique was the conviction that all paid ministers were by definition hirelings, who were at best subject to the prejudices of the congregations that paid their salaries and at worst seekers after wealth and power. Elias Hicks himself argued, "You might search the kennels of any great city, and take soldiers, sailors, and the very worst of mankind, and they would be more likely to enter into the kingdom of heaven than the hireling priest." Joseph Foulke, a minister from Gwynned, Pennsylvania, apocalyptically described clergymen as "an hireling mercenary and bigoted priesthood . . . the locusts that came out of the smoke of the bottomless pit and covered the earth." The Wilmington Hicksite controversialist Benjamin Ferris similarly condemned "the universal and insatiable begging of missionary and other societies, organized by 'ministers of the Gospel,' and the Jesuitical means and *holy* cunning practiced by them to get money."[8]

Hicksites saw in the aggressive proselytizing and reforming fervor of the Second Great Awakening a threat to religious liberty. "I long for the time to come when the Highly favored people of this land may be delivered from this cruel yoke of bondage Priest Craft," wrote New York minister Eleazar Haviland in 1815. Edward Hicks agreed—pastors and missionaries were "enemies to civil and religious liberty." William Gibbons, another Wilmington Hicksite, saw Calvinist clergy in a conspiracy "to establish Calvinism as the national religion in this country, by making our civil magistrates the 'nursing fathers of the church.'" Hicksites thus took a strict view of separation of church and state, opposing legislative chaplains, federal incorporation of the American

Sunday School Union, and the evangelical campaign against Sunday mail delivery. Significantly, they saw Orthodox Friends as allies of evangelicals in their efforts to unite church and state; a Hicksite in Richmond, Indiana, predicted, "it would occasion no surprise, if the *orthodox* should become extinct in a few years, and be amalgamated with those charitable institutions, as they call them."[9]

By associating with non-Friends within reform movements, Friends endangered their own testimonies and undermined their faith. According to Jesse Kersey, reformers acted "under the guidance of the natural understanding." Thus, "when Friends join with them and attend their meetings, they cease to maintain a state of humble dependence upon the gospel power, and expect to be sufficiently wise of themselves." Elias Hicks thought that "familiarity with those who did not rely on the Divine light to call and qualify for good work, tended to lead to a dependence on other means of instruction." The Hicksite Philadelphia Yearly Meeting summed up this view in 1830:

> This is a day, wherein many schemes and plans are in operation, calculated to ensnare the unguarded mind; although professedly designed to enlarge the borders of the Redeemer's kingdom. Beware, dear friends, of joining with any of these, lest you mar our testimonies, and be led back into the very state, out of which our ancient Friends were called. If we, as a society, so far depart from the teachings of the spirit of truth, as to mingle with other professors in what is called religious concerns,—though professedly to promote the cause of Christ . . . our individuality, as a people, will be lost, and our excellent testimonies, as it respects us, will fall to the ground.

Misguided participation in outwardly good causes endangered the very existence of Friends as a peculiar people.[10]

Thus, when White launched his critique of reformers, every argument he offered was consistent with positions that leading Hicksites had already taken. His antireform argument was a logical and consistent outgrowth of the Hicksite Reformation of the 1820s. Its roots lay in a quietism that eschewed undertaking any action without a clear divine leading, in worries about the impact that joining with non-Friends even in good causes would have on Quakers, and in fear of the ambitions and influence of evangelical Protestant reformers, especially the clergy, in American society. During White's visit to Ohio Yearly Meeting in 1836, a Friend recorded that he "spoke largely on the disadvantages of us as a people associating with others & especially with hireling teachers, let the object be ever so good to be accomplished."[11] By 1838, he was becoming notorious for this view. In October 1838, Mary R. Post, a

Long Island Hicksite, heard White preach in New York City. "He said he was commissioned to declare against the popular associations of the day." White, alluding to the controversies dividing the antislavery movement, "said their bands were growing weaker, that we should soon hear of war abolitionists, peace abolitionists and of woman rights abolitionists." If Friends were willing to wait, White predicted, "they would soon see [abolitionists] like the Babel builders be confounded." In the fall of 1839, in Pennsylvania, one non-Friend described how White condemned reformers as "worse than so many pick-pockets, likening them to the jaws of that monstrous bear which is trying to hug Quakerism to death."[12]

In 1840, White preached that all "hirelings," "both individually and collec-tively . . . were emesarrys of satan." Their sole interest was money. "Where the carcase is, there will the fowls of the air be gathered together. Where money is, there can always be found hireling preachers." Much of their power, he said, came from assuming the prerogative of God in judging fellow humans as sin-ners. "Judgment, in the matter of sin, is the prerogative of God; and sooner than attempt its assumption, may my tongue cleave to the roof of my mouth, my arm drop from my shoulder blade." "I believe the most powerful weapon, and which has been most destructive to the temporal happiness of man, *is the usurped prerogative to designate sinners*. O! how often, in the hands of a corrupt hierar-chy, it has fattened the land with blood! The power and influence of hirelings the world over, and throughout all ages, have produced more suffering to the human race, than the aggregate from war, famine, pestilence, and slavery."[13] In White's mind, professional abolitionists were indistinguishable from hirelings. Preaching in Chester County in 1843, he told Friends, "Whoever undertakes to do God's work, in the capacity of an editor, a lecturer, or any other, and receives money for it, is a *base hypocrite*." They were "traders in benevolence," and in White's judgment "the meanest beings on earth—they were the very scum— . . . they were more *degraded than the Devils in hell*."[14]

White believed that reformers tended toward self-esteem. They were "puffed up like toads till they were big as a barrel," he preached in 1842, and "he often wondered they did not burst."[15] Nonetheless, White himself was a determined opponent of slavery who could, when he felt led, denounce it in terms that even the most fervent abolitionists praised. For example, in 1842, he followed the denunciation just quoted with what an abolitionist called "the most powerful gospel sermon." Taking slavery as his theme, "he portrayed it in the most vivid colors from the capturing of the victims on the coast of Africa to the dealing & condemning of their products & said in plain terms if there was any one more guilty than another in this chain, it was he who upheld the system. I never heard such a picture of slavery from a Friends' gallery before, not even by the most stern opposers of the evil." White abstained from the use of any product of slavery, and when traveling in the South, like John Woolman, tried to compensate any slave who served him.[16]

Opponents accused White of saying that if a slave, he would not try to escape. That is unclear, but White did say, "I had a thousand times rather be a slave, and spend my days with slaveholders, than to dwell in companionship with abolitionists." White clearly thought that slavery might be a part of "bearing the cross"—the sufferings and baptisms that, under the guidance of the Inward Light, all people must experience in order to be fitted for heaven.[17] In his opinion, abolitionists were presumptuous in usurping divine prerogative. He asked one abolitionist, "Is it not apparent if thou wert introduced into the counsels of the Almighty that thou wouldst cause discord there?" Abolitionists verged on blasphemy when they held up the antislavery movement as the best hope of the slave.[18]

Like most Hicksites at the time, White feared doing anything that originated in his own will. He called himself "a worm of the dust" and told Friends, "in my flesh dwelleth no good thing." His preaching was not his own work; therefore, "in proceeding in it, I depend not upon my own wisdom nor upon my own power." He took this to an extreme unusual even for a Hicksite. "*All power is of God*, and *consequently that of ourselves we can do nothing*," he wrote. "When this truth has been so often confirmed that we lose all confidence in the flesh, we become first, *quiet*, then *watchful*; after this our natural senses, especially the eye and the ear, seldom transmit anything to the soul which will induce us to engage in a work of righteousness." White took this to the point of being wary even of offering advice to individuals about their actions. "He believed that every man had his own particular law, written in his own mind; and it was to the fulfilling of this law that he desired to encourage them."[19]

In practical terms, White questioned the efficacy of immediate abolition. In 1845, he wrote, "There are, interwoven with the framework, or texture of Society, evils, of a magnitude too great for man, unaided by Deity, to grapple with successfully; and which may produce in their suppression, as well as in their continuance, consequences too important and too baneful for the human mind, unaided from above, to appreciate." He compared abolishing slavery to nursing a starving man. Giving too much food too quickly to the patient would kill him. So it was with slaves—to give them unrestricted freedom immediately would likely bring devastation. For proof, he pointed to abolition in the British West Indies, which he believed was a failure. The former slaves refused to work and were being replaced with other workers;

he feared that they would be "exterminated." To make matters worse, White was convinced that the slave trade had increased since West Indian emancipation.[20] He also objected to abolitionist tactics. He condemned abolitionist firebrands such as Stephen S. Foster, who interrupted religious services to respond to what they considered proslavery, unchristian sermons. "Such an act is as gross an outrage of justice, as that of entering the residence of a private family and obtruding advice at the hearth or the board." He emphatically rejected any comparison to the similar actions of early Friends, whose attacks on hirelings were in his mind clearly different. He worried further about the disunionism of Garrisonians, the branch of abolition with which Hicksites tended to identify. Such abolitionists professed commitments to peace, he wrote, but were "mustering under the crimson banner of treason, and loudly preaching rebellion against the government under which they live."[21]

One possibility that must be considered is that an element of sexism drove White. Mott was certainly a favorite target. As early as 1838, a New York Friend noted their "collision of sentiment," and in 1842, Isaac T. Hopper wrote that White "in his public communications frequently aims blows at Lucretia Mott." Mott herself the same year approvingly quoted an Irish Friend that "oil and water would unite as readily as G. F. White and L. M." At times, he appeared to travel with the clear mission of pursuing Mott and refuting her errors. In 1838, when New York Yearly Meeting considered a proposal to appoint women to its Meeting for Sufferings, White was opposed. He dismissed the idea of equality of men and women as "a very silly matter," since a woman was one with her husband. In Chester County in 1839, his contempt was acerbic: "What did woman want in the name of rights, but liberty to roam over the country from Dan to Beersheba spurning the protection of man? For himself, before he would submit to the dictation of an imperious woman, he would traverse the earth." On the other hand, some of White's most visible and fervent supporters were women ministers, such as Rachel Hicks and Rachel Barker in New York Yearly Meeting and Rachel Rogers and Mary Pike in Philadelphia.[22]

It is vital to keep in mind that fears about the impact of ties with non-Quakers were not confined to conservative, quietist Hicksites. In 1837, one of the most active Hicksite abolitionists, Charles Marriott, wrote to a fellow abolitionist Hicksite: "In regard to our associating with others in Anti Slavery Societies, I am apprehensive that many of us might insensibly lose ground by so doing, unless more watchfully attentive to our best guide, than I fear we should be." Although Marriott concluded that Friends should take the risk, his fears show how seriously Friends took the question. "A Hireling Mercenary Priesthood," Marriott insisted, was a terrible evil, as bad as slavery or intemperance. John

Jackson, one of Mott's favorite ministers, wrote in 1841, "a hireling ministry has done and is doing more harm to the cause of truth and righteousness than all the open infidelity that has ever been promulgated." Even as staunch an abolitionist as Mott conceded that many abolitionist Hicksites were suspicious of the influence of the clergy in the antislavery movement. Even Isaac T. Hopper, considered the leading Hicksite abolitionist in New York City, was as late as 1839 warning Friends against "the mixture" in reform activities. Hopper and Marriott took such fears so seriously that in 1839 they actually organized an exclusively Quaker antislavery society in New York.[23]

It was inevitable that White's attacks would attract attention from non-Quaker abolitionists, always alert for indications of temporizing with the sin of slavery in the churches. White's most persistent, and public, critic was Oliver Johnson, the editor of the *National Anti-Slavery Standard*, the organ of the American Anti-Slavery Society. Late in 1840, Johnson began an exchange of letters with White, taking him to task for failures ranging from his denunciations of abolitionists and other reformers to an obscure controversy over whether a lecturer on nonresistance had obtained the key to a meetinghouse in eastern Ohio under false pretenses. In February 1841, Johnson published the exchange with editorial comment that concluded by mourning Friends' "want of fidelity to truth." Hopper printed it and predicted, "When it makes its appearance it will create a volcano." Then in March 1841, Johnson published "Rare Specimen of a Quaker Preacher," an even more scathing attack.[24]

Johnson's assault had tragic consequences. Three Hicksite Friends—Hopper, Marriott, and James S. Gibbons—were members of the board of directors of the American Anti-Slavery Society. Within a week of the article's publication, the overseers of New York Monthly Meeting charged them with "being concerned in the support and publication of a paper calculated to excite discord and disunity among us." All three steadfastly refused to concede that they had done anything wrong, and so the monthly meeting disowned them. Badly divided quarterly and yearly meetings upheld the disownments. The case reverberated beyond New York. As far away as Indiana, the difficulties led directly to a radical abolitionist secession in Indiana Yearly Meeting and would be a major force in the eventual formation of new yearly meetings of reform-minded Congregational or Progressive Friends from Ohio, New York, Genesee, and Philadelphia Yearly Meetings.[25]

Many, then and since, assumed that White was the force behind the disownments. Hopper complained that White had "been for some time past using all his efforts to 'screw up' his disciples to the sticking point, and he has at last accomplished his object." Certainly, he helped create the atmosphere, but in fact nothing links him to the complaint itself. There is strong evidence that he had been on good terms with Marriott and Hopper. Marriott was his brother-in-law, married to one of White's sisters. And as late as 1839, Hopper wrote thus of White: "George F. White made me a very pleasant visit this morning—he generally comes several times a week and notwithstanding he and I differ very widely on some points, I love the man and have nearer unity with his spirit than almost any other friend in this city." A year later, even as White had become notorious for his attacks on abolitionists, he and Hopper were close enough for Hopper to carry some papers to Philadelphia for him. This closeness ended with the disownments.[26]

It is possible that White made a good faith effort to resolve the conflict. In August 1841, as the monthly meeting united in disowning Hopper and Gibbons, White submitted a letter of resignation to it. The clerk decided not to read it, and so it was not recorded in the minutes. Mott saw it as a maneuver to sway the monthly meeting when it appeared that Hopper and Gibbons were gaining sympathy. Post chortled, "I believe all were astonished to hear that the great *would be* champion of Quakerism had faltered." Hopper's daughter Abby Gibbons, James's wife, wrote that White's supporters were "fairly frightened. I never knew greater consternation in a camp." More-sympathetic Friends saw it differently. One wrote that the substance of the letter was that "if the truth should suffer by his retention he wished the meeting to release him." It is possible that he really was willing to leave Friends in order to restore peace. But once the monthly meeting had decided to proceed, he supported it as in good order.[27]

By 1841, many of White's critics more or less openly questioned his sanity. Hopper's daughter in Philadelphia, Sarah Palmer, spoke for them when she told her sister Abby, "Geo. White is either very crazy or very wicked." Mott tried to be kinder. Writing in 1842, she said that she was "ever hoping—even against hope, that he would be restored to his right senses." One physician Friend from Chester County, Ezra Michener, told another Friend that "one of two things was certain—either Lunacy would develop itself in Geo. White, or he would leave the Society." But even otherwise sympathetic Friends had worries. When John Comly, perhaps the most respected Hicksite Friend in Philadelphia Yearly Meeting, made cautious moves to make peace in New York, White responded angrily, to Comly's consternation. And in 1846, even the previously supportive Rachel Barker accused White of being divisive.[28]

The disownment of Hopper, Gibbons, and Marriott polarized Hicksite Friends. Some meetings, such as Peru Monthly Meeting in upstate New York, sent letters of condemnation. Abolitionist Friends argued that White was the true cause of disunity and division because of his defamation of abolitionist Friends. "Our religious meetings, instead of being seasons of quiet and useful meditation, affording means of spiritual refreshment," were instead "arenas for exciting and violent communications, in which the most unprovoked insult, wholesale denunciation, abuse, irony, sarcasm, bitterness and misrepresentation seemed to vie with each other for pre-eminence." Mott concluded that White had "sowed more discord than we shall soon be able to root out and destroy." She branded New York Friends "pseudo-Quakers" and compared them with the Orthodox fifteen years before, as did Isaac T. Hopper.[29]

Most observers, however, including even abolitionists, thought that White had the upper hand in the dispute. A New York Friend wrote that White was "an instrument raised up by the hand of Providence, and fitted for these peculiar times." Another saw White as the victim of an abolitionist "conspiracy" that had fortunately failed. Foulke wrote of White: "I think that the Spirit that opposes him is the same spirit that opposed the Prophets and Apostles of old and will in the end bring down the same judgment on itself that they seek to bring on him." An admirer in New York City told another Friend that Elias Hicks himself never stood higher there than White. By 1847, Hopper thought that White's views were gaining ground even in Philadelphia. And in 1852, Mott herself mourned: "No corner of our Heritage . . . is not suffering under a blighting, sectarian conservatism."[30]

White died in Poughkeepsie, New York, in 1847. Responses were predictable. Sympathetic Friends shared his deathbed words and the judgment of his physician: "I had never known a more striking case of resignation and submission to the Divine will." Mary S. Lippincott, a supporter in Philadelphia Yearly Meeting, wrote that he was "one who loved his master more than the world, and therefore was not ashamed of his gospel, tho' rejected by man! Society has lost one of its brightest ornaments." Less kind was Post. "There is no one to fill his place," she wrote to her brother and sister-in-law. "No one else has the power he had to say all manner of absurd things and still be the cherished idol of *his congregation*."[31] Post's evaluation would set the tone for subsequent evaluations of White. "Lucretia has outlived her persecutors," was the judgment of one Friend in 1880, and it is largely accurate. After the Civil War, Hicksites not only idealized abolitionist Friends such as Mott and largely embraced her vision of Quakerism, but they also cast aside the old strictures against forming ties with "the world." Mott's assessment of White as essentially aberrant became orthodoxy. Yet two things are clear about White. One is that his views of abolition and reform were fully consistent with those of many, perhaps most, of the Hicksites of the 1820s. And in the

1840s, when Hicksites had to choose between those views and those of the radical reformers, most found White's more congenial. White was one of Elias Hicks's legitimate heirs.[32]

NOTES

1. Deborah Bringhurst Diary, 3rd Mo. 25, 1839, box 2, Bringhurst Family Papers, Special Collections, University of Delaware Library.

2. "Rare Specimen of a Quaker Preacher," *National Anti-Slavery Standard*, March 25, 1841, 167.

3. Benjamin Swayne Journal, 10th Mo. 21, 1839, 10th Mo. 17, 1847, box 5, Swayne Family Papers, Friends Historical Library; John Willis to Amy Post, 11th Mo. 26, 1840, box 2, Post Papers; Mary R. Post to Isaac and Amy Post, n.d., box 1, ibid.

4. Thomas E. Drake, *Quakers and Slavery in America* (New Haven, Conn.: Yale University Press, 1950), 140; James Emmett Ryan, *Imaginary Friends: Representing Quakers in American Culture, 1650–1950* (Madison: University of Wisconsin Press, 2008), 77, 159–62.

5. Ryan P. Jordan, *Slavery and the Meetinghouse: The Quakers and the Abolitionist Dilemma, 1820–1865* (Bloomington: Indiana University Press, 2007), 24–62.

6. See Bruce Dorsey, "Friends Becoming Enemies: Philadelphia Benevolence and the Neglected Era of American Quaker History," *Journal of the Early Republic* 18 (Autumn 1998): 395–428.

7. William Poole to Eli Hilles, 8th Mo. 2, 1822, Poole Letters.

8. *The Cabinet; or Works of Darkness Brought to Light* (Philadelphia: John Mortimer, 1825), 17; Joseph Foulke to George Hatton, 4th Mo. 26, 1830, box 2, Foulke Family Papers, Friends Historical Library.

9. Eleazar Haviland memorandum, 4th Mo. 1815, in Eleazar Haviland Journal, Friends Historical Library; Benjamin Hallowell to Charles Farquhar, 3rd Mo. 24, 1830, Charles Farquhar Papers, ibid.; *Memoirs of the Life and Religious Labors of Edward Hicks* (Philadelphia: Merrihew and Thompson, 1851), 352–53; [William Gibbons], *Truth Advocated* (Philadelphia: Joseph Rakestraw, 1822), 125; "The Herald of Truth," *The Friend; or, Advocate of Truth* 3 (12th Mo. 15, 1830), 422; Robert Morrison letter, ibid., 2 (2nd Mo. 1829), 38–39; "Sunday School Union," *Berean*, 1 NS (4th Mo. 1828), 164–67; Editorial, *Delaware Free Press*, Jan. 23, 1830; George Washington Banks, *Orthodoxy Unmasked* (Philadelphia: G. W. Banks, 1829), 46–51.

10. *A Narrative of the Early Life, Travels, and Gospel Labors of Jesse Kersey* (Philadelphia: T. E. Chapman, 1851), 133; Rachel Hicks, "Elias Hicks," *Friends' Intelligencer*, 8th Mo. 18, 1866, 372; *Journal of the Life and Religious Labors of Elias Hicks* (New York, 1832), 383; *Extracts from the Minutes of the Yearly Meeting of Friends* [Hicksite] *Held in Philadelphia* (Philadelphia: William Sharpless, 1830), 7–8.

11. *Memorials concerning Deceased Friends* (New York: W. J. Banner, 1848), 29; "Address of the Board of Managers of the New-York Society for the Promotion of Knowledge and Industry," *American Railroad Journal and Advocate of Internal*

Improvement, June 8, 1833, 356–57; Joseph S. Walton Diary, 8th Mo. 28, 1836, box 1, Margaretta Walton Papers, Friends Historical Library.

12. James Mott to Joseph A. Dugdale, 9th Mo. 11, 1841, Joseph A. Dugdale Papers, Friends Historical Library; Mary R. Post to Isaac and Amy Post, 10th Mo. 9, 1838, box 2, Post Papers; C. C. Burleigh to J. M. McKim, Oct. 26, 1839, box 1, Lucretia Mott Papers, Friends Historical Library; Beverly Wilson Palmer, ed., *Selected Letters of Lucretia Coffin Mott* (Urbana: University of Illinois Press, 2002), 59.

13. Abby Kimber to Elizabeth Pease, 3rd Mo. 3, 1841, Antislavery Manuscripts, Rare Books Department, Boston Public Library; Mary R. Post to Isaac and Amy Post, 10th Mo. 26, 1840, box 2, Post Papers; George F. White, *Discourse at the Friends' Meeting House, Rose Street.* (New York, n.d.), 8; George F. White, *Sermon Delivered by George F. White, in Friends' Meeting House, Cherry Street, Philadelphia* (New York: Baker and Crane, 1843), 17; *Sermon Delivered by George F. White*, 5.

14. White, *Discourse*, 8; R.A.L., "G. F. White—Reforms—Women's Rights—Slavery—'Patient Waiting,'" *National Anti-Slavery Standard*, Nov. 16, 1843, 94; Nathaniel Potter to Amy Post, 7th Mo. 10, 1845, box 2, Post Papers.

15. *Sermon Delivered by George F. White*, 20; Mary R. Post to Isaac and Amy Post, 10th Mo. 26, 1840, 11th Mo. 23, 1841, box 2, Post Papers; [?] Fussell to Graceanna Lewis, 11th Mo. 1842, box 3, Graceanna Lewis Papers (Friends Historical Library); Abby Kimber to Richard D. and Hannah Webb, 1st Mo. 15, 1842, Antislavery Manuscripts.

16. [?] Fussell to Lewis, 11th Mo. 1842, box 3, Lewis Papers; *Memorials*, 34; William Adams, "Reminiscences. No. 42," *Journal*, 9th Mo. 2, 1874, 242.

17. E., "To George F. White, a Preacher in the Society of Friends," *Pennsylvania Freeman*, 11th Mo. 10, 1841, 2; L. Maria Child, *Isaac T. Hopper: A True Life* (Boston: J. P. Jewett, 1854), 389; Moses Pierce to George F. White, 7th Mo. 31, 1845, White-Pierce Correspondence (Friends Historical Library).

18. White to Pierce, 8th Mo. 17, 1845, White-Pierce Correspondence; Isaac T. Hopper, *Narrative of the Proceedings of the Monthly Meeting of New-York* (New York: H. Ludwig, 1843), 88–90.

19. *Sermon by George F. White, of New York* (n.p., 1843), 3; "A Letter of George F. White," *Friends' Intelligencer*, 3rd Mo. 1, 1890, 133; *Memorials*, 33.

20. White to Pierce, 8th Mo. 17, 1845, 6th Mo. 2, 1846, White-Pierce Correspondence.

21. *Sermon Delivered by George F. White*, 21–22; White to Pierce, 5th Mo. 4, 1842, White-Pierce Letters.

22. Isaac T. Hopper to Sarah H. Palmer, 1st Mo. 5, 1842, Sarah H. Palmer Papers, Friends Historical Library; Mary Pike to Benjamin Ferris, 9th Mo. 27, 1840, box 2, Ferris Family Papers (ibid.); Palmer, ed., *Selected Letters*, 59, 109; John Ketcham to Isaac Post, 9th Mo. 1838, box 2, Post Papers; R.A.L., "G. F. White," 94; Albert John Wahl, "The Congregational or Progressive Friends in the Pre-Civil-War Reform Movement" (Ed.D. diss., Temple University, 1951), 32; Marriott to Robinson, 11th Mo. 23, 1838, box 1, Robinson Papers; Margery Post Abbott, *Post, Albertson, and Hicks Family Letters* (2 vols., Portland, Ore.: Margery Post Abbott, 2010), I, 265–66; Esther Lewis to Graceanna Lewis, 5th Mo. 15, 1842, box 1, Lewis Papers.

23. Marriott to Robinson, 3rd Mo. 2, 1837, Box 1, Robinson Papers; Marriott to William Lloyd Garrison, 12th Mo. 31, 1837, Antislavery Manuscripts; John Jackson to Rachel Jackson, 2nd Mo. 10, 1841, Jackson Mss., Friends Historical Library; Lucretia Mott to James M. McKim, 3rd Mo. 15, 1838, box 1, Mott Papers; Sarah Hopper Emmons, ed., *Life of Abby Hopper Gibbons,* 2 vols. (New York: G. P. Putnam, 1897), 1:106; Drake, *Quakers and Slavery,* 160–61.

24. *Correspondence between Oliver Johnson and George F. White* (New York: O. Johnson, 1841), esp. iii–iv, 7, 17, 28–30, 48; "Rare Specimen," 167; Hopper to Palmer, 2nd Mo. 13, 1841, box 1, Palmer Papers.

25. See Hopper, *Narrative;* Thomas D. Hamm, *God's Government Begun: The Society for Universal Inquiry and Reform, 1842–1846* (Bloomington: Indiana University Press, 1995), 66–69; and Jordan, *Slavery and the Meetinghouse,* 92–103.

26. Marriott to Robinson, 3rd Mo. 2, 1837, 12th Mo. 18, 1841, box 1, Robinson Papers; Hopper to Palmer, 6th Mo. 29, 1839, box 1, Palmer Papers; Hopper to Thomas McClintock, 3rd Mo. 31, 1841, Isaac T. Hopper Papers, Friends Historical Library; White to Ferris, 4th Mo. 18, 1840, box 2, Ferris Papers.

27. New York Monthly Meeting (Hicksite) Men's Minutes, 8th Mo. 4, 1841; Robert Hicks to Samuel Griffith, 2nd Mo. 18, 1842, Hicks Papers; Marriott to Robinson, 12th Mo. 18, 1841, box 1, Robinson Papers; Joseph S. Walton Diary, fragment, ca. 1842, box 1, Walton Papers; Mary R. Post to Isaac and Amy Post, 11th Mo. 23, 1841, box 2, Post Papers; Palmer, ed., *Selected Letters,* 109.

28. Emmons, ed., *Life of Abby Hopper Gibbons,* I, 103–5; Palmer, ed., *Selected Letters,* 102; George Truman to Catherine Truman, 12th Mo. 20, 1841, vol. 2, Truman Papers; Hopper to Palmer, 10th Mo. 13, 1846, box 1, Palmer Papers; Robert Hicks to Griffith, 2nd Mo. 18, 1842, Hicks Papers; Emmons, ed., *Life of Abby Hopper Gibbons,* 1:110–11.

29. Hopper, *Narrative,* 11–12; Palmer, ed., *Selected Letters,* 93, 108; M. M. Davis to E. M. Davis, Dec. 10, 1843, box 1, Mott Papers; Hopper to Palmer, 10th Mo. 11, 1841, box 1, Palmer Papers.

30. Robert Hicks to Griffith, 2nd Mo. 18, 1842, Hicks Papers; Foulke to Hatton, 6th Mo. 13, 1842, box 2, Foulke Papers; Isaac Hicks to David Evans, 10th Mo. 14, 1844, box 1, Evans Family Papers, Ohio Historical Society; Thomas Wright to David Seaman, 1st Mo. 26, 1843, David Seaman Papers, Friends Historical Library; Hopper to Palmer, 6th Mo. 15, 1847, box 4, Palmer Papers; Palmer, ed., *Selected Letters,* 222.

31. *Memorials,* 38; "Extracts from a Letter from Dr. Barnes dated Poughkeepsie, Oct. 16, 1847," Blake-Henley Papers (Friends Historical Library); Mary S. Lippincott to Foulke, 12th Mo. 10, 1847, box 2, Foulke Papers; Mary R. Post to Isaac and Amy Post, 9th Mo. 22, 1847, box 1, Post Papers.

32. Maria Mott Davis to Sister, May 17, 1880, box 5, Mott Papers. See Thomas D. Hamm, "The Hicksite Quaker World, 1875–1900," *Quaker History* 89 (Fall 2000): 17–41; Julie Roy Jeffrey, *Abolitionists Remember: Antislavery Autobiographies and the Unfinished Work of Emancipation* (Chapel Hill: University of North Carolina Press, 2008).

4 "Without the Consumers of Slave Produce There Would Be No Slaves"

Quaker Women, Antislavery Activism,
and Free-Labor Cotton Dress in the 1850s

ANNA VAUGHAN KETT

THIS CHAPTER DEMONSTRATES THE WAYS in which dress can be used as a powerful interpretative tool, in understanding how the Quaker family, and especially women, engaged with antislavery activism in the 1850s. It takes as a point of departure a pair of unique photographs, dubbed here the "free-produce photographs," one of which is shown (see figure 4.1).[1] The photograph shows the Quaker Clarks of Street, Somerset, in the West Country of England: Eleanor Stephens Clark, her husband James Clark, and their twelve children. The Clark family is famous for the prosperous shoemaking company, C. & J. Clark, founded by brothers, James and Cyrus, in 1825. The photograph was taken in 1858, by John Aubrey Clark, the Clarks' nephew, and importantly it shows the women, boys, and girls of the family dressed in extraordinary clothes. These are made from "free-labor" cotton cloth, made from cotton, grown by free, or waged, labor, rather than the labor of slaves, which can be matched to manufacturer's samples of free-labor cotton cloth (figure 4.2).

The photograph references the Clark family's antislavery activism and, in particular, the largely forgotten transatlantic strategy known as the free produce movement, which took place from the 1820s to the 1860s. The movement mounted two campaigns to persuade consumers to reject goods made by slaves: the first against slave-grown sugar (1791–1792 and in the 1820s) and the second against slave-grown cotton (from the 1830s to 1865). To date, no other photographs have been found that have been proven to show people wearing free-labor cotton. This image (and its partner) is therefore of great significance in understanding free-produce activism, forms of antislavery clothing, and what free-labor cotton looked like. Free-produce activists, dubbed here "the free-produce community," used their clothing to demonstrate a simple "free-produce rationale." In the words of the poet of the movement, American Quaker Elizabeth Margaret Chandler (1807–1836), "Without the consumers of slave produce there would be no slaves."[2] The community accordingly

Figure 4.1. The Clark family of Street, 1858, dressed in free-labor clothing, LRSF, London, box C. 2 909.7, copy of the original, exhibited in the Museum of Shoemaking, C. & J. Clark, in Street. A similar image is held in the AGT at C. & J. Clark, HSHC 55. Left to right: Eleanor Clark (1812–1879), Mabel (1857–1872), James Clark (1811–1906), Amy Jane (1837–1906), William (1839–1925), Frances (1840–1930), Mary (1842–1920), Ann (1844–1924), Eleanor (1846–1915), Florence (1847–1882), Sophia (1849–1933), James (1850–1944), Edith (1852–1943), and Francis (1853–1938). Courtesy of the Religious Society of Friends in Britain.

argued that if consumers avoided slave-goods, the market would disappear, immediate emancipation of the enslaved would follow, and "there would be no slaves." Commitment to the rationale was exemplified by the Free Labor Cotton Depot in Street, a small shop, founded by Eleanor Clark, which between 1853 and 1858, supplied free-labor cotton to the village.[3]

Drawing on materials in the Alfred Gillett Trust at C. & J. Clark in Street and the Library of the Religious Society of Friends in London (hereafter known as the AGT and LRSF), and especially the collection held by family member, "HSHC" or Helen Sophie Horn Clark, this chapter discusses how dressing in free-labor cotton clothes embedded antislavery consumption practice into everyday life, as an embodiment of individual political belief. It presents new research on the Clarks' involvement in the antislavery cause; it discusses the British free produce movement and its campaign against slave-grown cotton; it examines Quaker attitudes to dress; and it compares dress in the photographs to surviving examples. These include unique samples

Figure 4.2. Card of four manufacturer's samples, showing free-labor cotton, large-checked gingham cloth, LRSF, London, MS box 8:3. The samples were probably made by John Wingrave of Carlisle, and in 1853, they were sent to Eleanor Clark at the Free Labour Cotton Depot in Street by Josias Browne of Manchester. Courtesy of the Religious Society of Friends in Britain.

of free-labor gingham cloth, sent to the Street Depot (figure 4.2). It draws upon the small body of literature discussing the movement in Britain and America, particularly by Ruth Nuermberger, Clare Midgley, Julie Roy Jeffrey, and Carol Faulkner.[4] It also uses contemporary sources, notably the Quaker press, the *British Friend* and *The Friend,* the antislavery press, the *Anti-Slavery Reporter,* and the British community's own newspaper, *The Slave; His Wrongs and Their Remedy.* The latter was published by Newcastle Friends, Anna and Henry Richardson, who were leaders of the movement in Britain.

Since Nuermberger's pioneering text, published in 1942, and until the 1990s, history has not been altogether kind to the free produce movement. Notably, in 1972, Howard Temperley assessed the campaigns of the 1850s, including free produce, as "marginal" to antislavery history.[5] The recent ongoing reassessment has, however, established that it merits closer examination and, above all, it is now understood that this was an important instance of a market-based strategy, enacted by consumers, primarily women, at a time when they were discouraged from public-sphere activity and were excluded from formal positions of power. This left important legacies in establishing female agency and political activism, which assisted women's pathway into public life. Historians of consumer activism also recognize that boycotting or avoidance of slave-made goods undoubtedly paved the way for the myriad of subsequent "ethical consumption" initiatives, including those seen today.[6] It should nevertheless be pointed out that while activism against slave-sugar has been extensively discussed, the campaign against slave-cotton remains less well explored.[7]

The Clarks are renowned for their substantial contribution to British industrial history as pioneers in the mass production of high-quality boots and shoes; these are still produced today. They became the dominant family in their locale, bringing great social change, and significantly remodeling the village of Street according to their Quaker, evangelical principles.[8] Less well known is the family's participation in the transatlantic antislavery movement, which included active support in a number of campaigns. It should be pointed out that, although the campaign against slave-grown cotton attracted ardent support from a close-knit group of Friends, it failed to stem the burgeoning British cotton industry's dependence on American, raw, slave-grown cotton. Between 1840 and 1860, Britain became entirely reliant on American plantations for up to 90% of its raw cotton needs. Imports of American slave-grown cotton tripled, and Britain bought over 75% of America's crop—which accounted for nearly 90% of American exports.[9] By the 1850s, cotton manufacturing became synonymous with Britain's commercial success, and the city of Manchester, dubbed "Cottonpolis," underpinned the British economy.[10] This presented an enormous challenge to the movement, for unlike the campaign against slave-sugar, no single alternative "free" source could be found. Slave-cotton was everywhere in British society and, as detractors of the campaign liked to note, it was even present in the paper used to print antislavery tracts.

Free-produce activity was instigated, enacted, and disseminated by women, primarily Friends, as a practical solution or "remedy" to slavery. As custodians of the domestic sphere, women were responsible for provisioning the home, and they oversaw the buying and consumption of all articles across household departments. Abstinence came naturally to Quaker consumers, and the free-produce rationale was quickly disseminated; it spread efficiently through the "Quaker networks" of kinship, friendship, and commerce in Britain and America. From the 1820s, a network of free-produce societies was established, attached to ladies' antislavery societies. These were followed by a small number of warehouses, or "depots." It should be pointed out that obtaining free-labor goods required considerable commitment. Except in the largest cities, articles were difficult to find and, by the admission of *The Slave*, they lacked variety, their quality varied, and they were "a trifle dearer to buy."[11] Like many of their Quaker kin, the Clarks bought free-labor cotton and foodstuffs, and the home of Joseph Sturge in Birmingham was entirely "slave free," a fact that greatly impressed Harriet Beecher Stowe during her visit to Britain.[12] Free-produce originated with Quakers, who since their foundation were familiar with the practice of abstaining from any aspect of "the world" that offended their moral or religious codes. From the early eighteenth century, some Quakers had objected to both the trade and the holding of slaves. Significantly, their practical support included the refusal of slavery's products, such as indigo, coffee, rice, tobacco, sugar, and later, cotton. Abstinence flourished in the 1770s, when John Woolman demonstrated that it was possible to live without recourse to the products of slavery. Significantly, his clothing became an expressive medium. As Geoffrey Plank points out, Woolman's homespun, woolen garb was "freighted with moral significance," for it operated as a powerful sign of his critique of the "unquiet world."[13] Subsequently, Woolman was often referenced, for example by Chandler, who was widely read by the free-produce community.[14] Abolitionist concern found a practical expression during the famous Sugar Boycott (1791–1792), when numbers of Britons refused to buy West Indian sugar. The campaign was hugely successful in persuading society to view slave-grown sugar as "tainted" by slavery, and women adopted the vital role of ridding the home of the "polluted" product.[15] Abstention arguments again crystallized with Elizabeth Heyrick's visionary pamphlet *Immediate Not Gradual Abolition* (1824), which proposed abstinence as the "shortest means" to achieve immediate manumission for the enslaved. As imports of slave-cotton grew, from the 1830s, abolitionist attention was directed to cotton and the affecting trope of tainting was revisited. For example, in her poem "Slave Produce," Chandler described the "shriek and groan" of the slave, "lingering" in cotton cloth.[16] Frederick Douglass wrote evocatively that slavery's invisible traces "floated amid the folds of our garments . . . in its warp and woof."[17] In framing cotton as polluted by the "dark red stain" of slavery, consumers were forced to see it as soiled, repulsive, and "haunted" by the misery of the slave.[18]

It is important to emphasize the centrality of the "Quaker network" and, especially, the strong link between the Clarks and the family of Joseph Sturge. James Clark and Joseph Sturge were cousins, with a joint business trading corn conducted with their brothers. They and their wives shared interests in philanthropy and antislavery, and the cousins were part of the reforming, progressive group at London Yearly Meeting known as "the Moderates."[19] The Clarks were drawn into the heart of antislavery activity, for Sturge was a leading abolitionist who founded the British and Foreign Anti-Slavery Society in 1839 and the British Free Produce Society in 1849. Eleanor Clark's friendships with Sturge's sister, Sophia Sturge, and his second wife, Hannah Dickinson Sturge, connected her to the foremost women's antislavery society in Britain: the Birmingham Ladies' Negro's Friend Society.[20]

Eleanor Clark was extremely industrious with a strong commitment to public service, as established in her strict, Quaker upbringing. Her parents were successful drapers, and weighty Friends, in the Quaker community in Bridport, Dorset. It was especially her mother, Amy Metford Stephens, who embedded in her seventeen offspring the traditional testimonies, as well as evangelical principles.[21] Clark's passion for the antislavery cause was kindled by her parents, who made the home a hub for visiting activists from Britain and America, including Thomas Clarkson.[22] Clark replicated the milieu of domestic-based antislavery activism at Netherleigh, her home in Street, after her marriage to James Clark in 1835. The house became a core for philanthropic activities, involving her extended family and a cohort of approximately twenty Quaker kinswomen, who gathered regularly to support an impressive range of campaigns. Brokered by personal letters from Sophia Sturge, Clark's group corresponded with the Massachusetts Female Emancipation Society in Boston, sending parcels of goods to their antislavery fairs.[23] Their support was part of a thriving transatlantic female economy that saw British and Irish women supplying roughly half of all goods sold at New England fairs during the 1840s and 1850s.[24] Through a personal introduction from Sturge, the family became involved with Connecticut campaigner, Elihu Burritt, who in 1846 founded the League of Brotherhood. This peace organization was financed through female auxiliaries, known as Olive Leaf Circles, which raised funds from the sale of sewn articles. In 1851, Clark opened one in Street. Burritt was a staunch supporter of free-produce, holding free-produce fairs, and encouraging circles to use only free-goods. Thus, circles exerted a considerable demand for free-labor cloth, making Clark's decision to open the Street Depot highly pragmatic. Through connections with the Richardson family, Clark and her group raised funds for the enslaved family of John Weims, who were close friends of the African-American abolitionist, Henry Highland Garnet. The group also expressed their admiration of *Uncle Tom's Cabin* by collecting pennies for the national Tribute to Mrs. Stowe, set up by the Birmingham Ladies.[25] The Clarks' commitment to antislavery continued, for in the 1870s, Eleanor, her daughter Sophia Clark, and her niece Catherine Impey coordinated shipping parcels to ex-slaves in Kansas, organized by the Freedmen's Aid Society.[26] As well as practical contributions, Clark also expressed her antislavery sentiments through the many poems and essays she wrote for Village Album, the local literary society that she ran with John Aubrey Clark.[27]

Above all, Clark and her cohort were highly productive needlewomen who attended the village sewing circles to sew for a range of charitable causes, including antislavery fairs. Women's needle skills were utterly indispensable, for until readymade and machine-made items became commonplace in the last quarter of the century, women sewed and maintained by hand all textile articles used by the entire household.[28] Philanthropic sewing was seen as a "natural" extension of women's domestic role, and sewn and worn items provided the primary expression for their antislavery sentiment. As Alice Taylor has noted, sewing was crucial to women's political identities, firmly establishing them as valued contributors, using their needles as "social, economic and political weapons."[29] Antislavery sewing circles also fulfilled social functions, for here women could read works of literature and share views. As William Lloyd Garrison observed, "sewing-parties" were also a "means of social improvement."[30]

Despite growing popularity in Britain, achieved substantially by American abolitionist visitors, by the mid-1850s free-produce remained a controversial strategy in the antislavery movement.[31] Substantial criticism came from William Lloyd Garrison, who viewed it as both completely ineffective and a dangerous distraction from the push for the emancipation of slaves.[32] Free-produce was subjected to great hostility, particularly from Garrisonian antislavery societies, for example in Bristol. Here, John Estlin completely disparaged the work of the Richardsons, Garnet, and their supporters as: "Nonsense about freeing slaves by Quaker ladies giving up the use of dresses made with American cotton."[33] In addition to ideological disagreements, the manufacture of free-labor cotton was beset with a myriad of practical difficulties. Free-cotton had to be segregated throughout the manufacturing processes and as it was indistinguishable from slave-grown cotton, this led to suspicions that the cloth could never be fully slave-free. Sources of raw free-cotton remained exceedingly limited, and it was impossible to maintain continuous production of cloth in order to satisfy demand. Shipments of raw cotton came from free farms in America, as well as India, the West Indies, and West Africa. In order to make up quantities, types had to be mixed during the spinning process, which affected the quality of the finished cloth. At times, the economies of small-scale production and distribution were reflected in the finished price and customers had to pay a little more for their textiles. This increased the price of the cheapest cotton textiles from three pennies to four or five pennies a yard, a fact that caused some consternation in the community.[34]

In the absence of the records of the British Free Produce Association, it is difficult to ascertain precise quantities of raw cotton imported into Britain.[35]

According to reports in the antislavery press, during the period January 1849 to January 1850, three large shipments of raw free-cotton arrived, and others are mentioned, at least 1,500 bales.[36] When seen in comparison to American imports of one million bales, this makes free-labor cotton but a fraction of a percentage of the total.[37] Despite its difficulties, however, the campaign was tenacious and enduring. Robustly undeterred by detractors, the community was determined to continue their attack on "the root of the evil." When Clark opened the depot in 1853, there was considerable optimism that free-cotton could become a commercially viable alternative.

The Street Depot provides a useful case study through which to understand the campaign. It was a modest and unassuming "shop," comprising a temporary stall set up in the village Temperance Hall. As stated in the advertising flyer, "Calicoes, Ginghams, Colored Linings, Check Muslins, Stockings, Knitting and Sewing Cottons &c. &c" were for sale, which suited plain and traditional tastes.[38] Accounts show that it traded for two years, selling roughly twenty-five to thirty pounds worth of goods per annum. Overheads were minimal, prices were very low, and it neither made a profit nor operated at a loss. In 1858, it disposed of unsold stock, including to Clark. Sales ranged enormously, but repeated was the purchase of one yard of muslin and six yards of checked gingham.[39] According to a contemporary dressmaking guide, these would make, respectively, a Quaker lady's scarf and a slim-skirted gown.[40] It was clear that the depot was part of antislavery activism, because the flyer proclaimed that it was opened, "when the subject of Slavery is exciting so much attention in the public mind, through the reading of 'Uncle Tom's Cabin.'" This was a buoyant moment in British antislavery, for Stowe's novel attracted phenomenal support, chiefly among women, and it galvanized them to "do what they could for the slave."[41] *Uncle Tom's Cabin* attracted a strong following in Street, and Clark was an ardent reader, even using the pen name "Eva," in reference to the character Little Eva in the novel.

Clark was knowledgeable about cloth and took a special interest in cotton, as seen in her informative essay written for Village Album. This included her passionate views on the horrors of the plantation.[42] She corresponded at length with her two principal suppliers: the Quaker agent, Josias Browne of Manchester, and the handloom weaver, John Wingrave of Carlisle. Browne was integral to the free-cotton supply chain; he liaised with the Philadelphia Free Produce Society, who shipped raw cotton from America, and distributed it for spinning and weaving in the North West of England. Browne stocked his warehouse in Manchester with the best goods he could find, the majority of which were manufactured by Friends. Wingrave's company, the Free Cumberland Weavers'

Co-Operative, was a small and highly specialized weaving manufactory, using warranted free-labor yarn, woven on handlooms, to customers' specifications. As reported in press, the firm was also deeply philanthropic, offering work, accommodation, and education to the workforce.[43]

The free-produce photographs thus record a specific period in the lives of the Clarks: one of deep commitment to the free-produce cause and a desire to "go public" in this respect. It is perhaps surprising that they were taken at all, for Quakers were reticent about indulging in the "vanity" of portraiture, which they believed transgressed the testimony of Truth.[44] The late 1850s were, however, changing times in British Quaker culture, which saw significant liberalization of the very restrictions, such as traditional dress, that had established Quakers as "peculiar." Progressive Friends such as the Clarks embraced change and became fascinated by photography, which they viewed as "scientific," rather than "artistic."[45] The AGT contains many different types of photographs, including formal studio portraits taken by professionals as well as these informal, spontaneous pictures, taken by a keen amateur practitioner and member of the family. They permit the viewer to glimpse the Clarks dressed in free-produce clothing as habitually worn in their private and domestic worlds. It should also be remembered that the Clarks are also dressed for the camera, where they display and memorialize particular aspects of their political identities.

Material culture such as clothing is highly expressive of our social and political worlds. As Leora Auslander has noted, the objects with which we surround ourselves perform a multitude of simultaneous tasks: as "modes of communication, or memory cues, or expressions of the psyche, or extensions of the body."[46] This is especially true of dress, which, Lou Taylor explains, operates at multifaceted levels within any society and any culture; hence it "provides a powerful analytical tool, across many disciplines."[47] The family's religious identity is clearly marked through their use of relatively plain dress, demonstrating a broad Quaker refusal to indulge in the fashions of the day. "Plainness" developed early in Quaker culture, with George Fox advising followers to "shun gaudy apparel."[48] By the nineteenth century, it embraced a wide-ranging set of aesthetic and moral values, governing the lifestyle, appearance, and visual culture of Quakers.[49] Above all, Friends used plain dress to construct a metaphorical "hedge," which maintained religious and moral difference and established a highly mediated relationship with society. At the time of the photographs, moral aspects of clothing were at the center of controversy, as the Religious Society of Friends struggled to reform faith and practice. The old condemnation of fashion as a vice was reiterated in 1856: "To gratify the lust of the flesh, of the eye and the pride of fallen man."[50] By 1860, however, progressives sought ways to modernize the faith, and "plainness" developed into the more moderate "simplicity," which signaled the demise of traditional forms of clothing.[51] The change in attitude can be read in the Clarks' clothing, for as stated by James Clark in 1856, a "liberality of feeling" was in alignment with liberalizing culture, and this included the freedom to express one's antislavery sentiment.[52]

Comparisons of the free-produce photographs, surviving Quaker garments, and photographs of Friends put the dress of the Clarks into wider context. Examples of clothing in LRSF confirm that, in the late 1850s, some plain Friends still wore traditional garb: for women, "drab" silk gowns, caps, kerchiefs, shawls, aprons, and bonnets. These were devoid of fashionable embellishments. As Frederick Tolles has put it, they were typically made from woolen and silken cloth, of "the best sort, but plain."[53] The small, photographic visiting cards held by the Friends Institute, archived in LRSF, show that while traditional garb was retained by older and conservative Friends, younger and progressive members all but abandoned it. In its place, they wore varied, patterned, and expressive styles, in what was known as "gay," or "wet," rather than "plain" style.[54] Some cards show Friends dressed in checked gingham gowns, very bold, broad stripes, and some with fashionably full skirts, supported on hoops (see figure 4.3).[55] Eleanor Clark's card is in the collection, showing her dressed in a pale, spotted gown, with a lace collar, decorative brooch, and worn with a dressy, frilled cap.[56] This confirms that although Clark dressed modestly, her outfit shares many characteristics with mainstream fashions—which brings us back to the clothing in the free-produce photographs.

The clothes show an engagement with debates on plainness, and in addition, they signify personal conscience, or "witness," to antislavery. It is highly likely that the vibrant, large-checked cloth was made by Wingrave; a hypothesis that is supported by the fact that close visual matches can be made with Wingrave's samples, used in conjunction with a note from Browne discussing the samples and receipts for Clark's purchase of his cloth. These also match descriptions given by George Washington Taylor, the proprietor of the Philadelphia Free Produce Depot, who bought from Wingrave.[57] Taylor wrote to complain that the gingham was "a little on the heavy side" and "if they had been finer, they would have sold better." He also requested that in the future, smaller checks should be sent, for "small plaids . . . suit Friends best."[58] Specifically, the bold-checked gown worn by Ann (in figure 4.1) closely resembles sample 2 (in figure 4.2) and the gowns worn by the daughters Eleanor and Frances, closely resemble fabric samples 1 and 3.

Figure 4.3. Photographic visiting card for Margaret Bright of Rochdale, sister of John Bright MP, ca. 1860. Bright is dressed in a full-skirted, heavy, bold striped cotton gown. Friends' Institute Collection, the archive of Friends' Institute, LRSF, London. Courtesy of the Religious Society of Friends in Britain.

Although no surviving Clark garments have been identified to match the striking clothing worn in the photographs, the gown worn by the infant Mabel can be compared to one held in the AGT: a hand-sewn, white, checked cotton muslin gown, with a triangular insert of lace at the breast.[59] Mabel's dress may also be compared to another surviving example of an infant's gown held in the Philadelphia History Museum. This is the *only* known example of a surviving garment, made from free-labor cotton, with the accompanying provenance to verify it as genuine.[60] It survives complete with two original paper labels, pinned to the garment, which read, "Free Labour Cotton" and "12." The first label identifies it as genuine, but the meaning of the second label is unclear. The museum understands that the gown was previously kept by the Friends' Historical Library; it dates to the 1840s or 1850s; it was owned by Friends; and it was probably sold at a New England antislavery or free-produce fair.

The free-produce photographs also raise some issues concerning the act of wearing free-labor cotton. These include tensions between public and private support for antislavery and the emotional aspects of wearing slave-free cloth. The photographs are private images, yet they have made public the event of wearing free-labor cotton. The public identity of free-cotton was complex, for it was identical to slave-cotton, and therefore it was necessary to label it, or to know it as such, in order to appreciate it. The free-cotton trade struggled to persuade the public that its products were genuine, and customers worried that cloth might be tainted by slavery. Although a paper ticket was used by the American Free Produce Association, and a stamp or "mark" may have been applied, no records for British equivalents have been found.[61] The stamp was declined by Browne on the grounds that it offered a "false assurance," or even an invitation to forgery, and Browne's advice was simple: to shop only from Quakers, "upon whose word we can rely."[62] The invisibility of free-cotton's "special" qualities suggests another paradox, for while Browne flagged up its purity, he was eager to dispel any idea that it was different from slave-cotton in terms of price, style, and quality.[63] Although the clothes in the photograph were not visibly labeled as free-cotton, the "label" may be present in the design of the cloth. The vibrant patterns are bold and confidant, and it is clear that, although made into modest gowns, they are not "quiet"; in this way, the Clarks are highly visible embodiments of belief. As Helen Bradley Foster argues, "The clothing one puts on one's corporeal self helps to mark one's place in humanity."[64] The Clarks' place in humanity was a very public one, and few members of the community could have been unaware of their antislavery commitment. A close connection among dress, humanity, and public display had already been successfully employed in antislavery. From the 1780s until

1807, Josiah Wedgwood's ceramic "slave medallion" was specifically worn to show support for the cause. Thomas Clarkson famously observed, "Fashion which usually confines itself to worthless things, was seen for once in the honorable office of promoting the cause of justice, humanity and freedom."[65] Clarkson's words could be applied to the free-produce photographs, for here worn reminders of the enslaved are on display.

It was feasible to incorporate free-produce into everyday life, and it is clear from the two photographs that the Clarks owned several outfits made from free-labor cotton. The experience of wearing them, however, was a complex one, for even though the clothes appeared to be free from slavery, in reality, this was far from the case. In the emotive rhetoric of *The Slave,* wearing free-labor clothing was "a silent but impressive act of conscience," but it was not "comfortable." Importantly, it acted as a constant "remembrancer" of the enslaved, specifically intended to recall the misery of "bleeding, torn humanity."[66] Free-labor dress became a powerful means to unify supporters and to express their shared values. As stated by *The Slave,* "Every man, woman and child in their ranks should wear a *uniform,* not distinguished by cut or color, but by one fundamental quality—by being completely *free* from the *stain* of slavery." The "uniform" would represent a "determination of purpose, a depth of conviction, a force of moral will," sending a message to the slaveholders of the world.[67] Thus, the wearing of free-labor cotton operated in different ways: affirmation of conscience, desire for "clean hands," and painful sympathy with the enslaved.

This chapter has examined how the free-produce photographs demonstrate the free produce movement in action, through the free-labor cotton clothes of the Clark family. Taken at a time when clothing was at the center of a heated debate within British Quaker culture, the photographs chart the tensions between traditional and progressive attitudes, which were highly symbolic of growing engagement with the world of reform. The Clark "liberality of feeling" permitted the family's dress to express engagement with the world, and this encompassed antislavery. The campaign against slave-grown cotton was a seemingly impossible task, given the British reliance on American slave-grown cotton. However, for the Clark family and others in the free-produce community, this was a matter of moral principle, which could not be ignored. Free-produce also offered rich, spiritual rewards for supporters, for its use was sacralized as a form of Christian worship. In the words of Chandler, writing on free-labor cotton, "Whilst the Master she adored, what she *could,* that she hath done."[68] These words could be applied to Eleanor Clark, whose Quaker, evangelical duty compelled her to "do what she could" for the enslaved, and whose engagement with free-labor cotton offered her a practical and respectable place in the antislavery movement. This established her as part of the transatlantic sisterhood of women activists, the "great army of silent workers, unknown to fame, and yet without whom the generals were powerless."[69]

NOTES

1. The original caption by C. & J. Clark: "The family of James Clark. The daughters are dressed in free labour cotton."

2. Elizabeth Margaret Chandler, "Consumers," in *Essays. Philanthropic and Moral, by Elizabeth Margaret Chandler: Principally Relating to the Abolition of Slavery in America,* ed. Benjamin Lundy (Philadelphia: Lemuel Howell, 1836), 113.

3. This refers to my Ph.D. research: "Quaker Women, the Free Produce Movement and British Anti-Slavery Campaigns: The Free Labour Cotton Depot in Street 1853–1858" (unpublished Ph.D. thesis, University of Brighton, 2012); materials relating to the Street Depot are in LRSF, MS box 8:3; the depot is briefly discussed in Louis Billington, "British Humanitarians and American Cotton 1840–1860," *Journal of American Studies* 11, no. 3 (1977): 326–27.

4. Ruth Ketring Nuermberger, *The Free Produce Movement: A Quaker Protest against Slavery* (1942; repr., New York: AMS, 1970); Clare Midgley, *Women against Slavery: The British Campaigns 1780–1870* (London: Routledge, 1992); Julie Roy Jeffrey, *The Great Silent Army of Abolitionism: Ordinary Women in the Antislavery Movement* (Chapel Hill: University of North Carolina Press, 1998); Carol Faulkner, "The Root of the Evil: Free Produce and Radical Antislavery 1820–1860," *Journal of the Early Republic* 23, no. 3 (2007): 377–405.

5. Howard Temperley, *British Antislavery 1833–1870* (London: Longman, 1972), 246.

6. Monroe Friedman, *Consumer Boycotts: Effecting Change through the Marketplace and the Media* (London: Routledge, 1999); Lawrence Glickman, *Buying Power: A History of Consumer Activism in America* (Chicago: University of Chicago Press, 2009).

7. Midgley, "Slave-Sugar Boycotts, Female Activism and the Domestic Base of British Anti-Slavery Culture," *Slavery and Abolition* 17, no. 3 (1996): 137–62; John Oldfield, *Popular Politics and British Anti-Slavery: The Mobilisation of Public Opinion against the Slave Trade 1787–1807* (Manchester: Manchester University Press, 1995); Charlotte Sussman, *Consuming Anxieties: Consumer Protest, Gender, and British Slavery, 1713–1833* (Stanford: Stanford University Press, 2000).

8. Roger Clark, *Somerset Anthology: Twenty-Four Pieces by Roger Clark of Street 1871–1961* (York: Sessions, 1975); Michael McGarvie, *The Book of Street: A History from the Earliest Times to 1925* (Buckingham: Barracuda, 1987); George Barry Sutton, *C. & J. Clark 1833–1903: A History of Shoemaking in Street, Somerset* (York: Sessions, 1979); Edward Milligan, *Biographical Dictionary of British Quakers in Commerce and Industry 1775–1920* (York: Sessions, 2007).

9. Douglas Farnie and Jeremy David, *The Fibre That Changed the World: The Cotton Industry in International Perspective 1600–1905* (Oxford: Pasold Research Fund and Oxford University Press, 2004).

10. Beverly Lemire, *Fashion's Favourite: The Cotton Trade and the Consumer in Britain 1660–1800* (Oxford: Oxford University Press, 1991); Mary Rose, ed. *The Lancashire Cotton Industry: A History since 1700* (Preston: Lancashire County Books, 1996).

11. *The Slave; His Wrongs and Their Remedy* (Newcastle, Jan. 1851): 3.

12. Harriet Beecher Stowe, *Sunny Memories of Foreign Lands* (London: Sampson and Low, 1854), 141.

13. Geoffrey Plank, "The First Person in Antislavery Literature: John Woolman, His Clothes, and His Journal," *Slavery and Abolition* 30, no. 1 (2009): 67–91.

14. Chandler, "John Woolman," in Lundy, *Essays, Philanthropic and Moral*, 25–26.

15. Sussman, 110–29.

16. Chandler, "Slave Produce," in Benjamin Lundy, ed., *The Poetical Works of Elizabeth Margaret Chandler: With a Memoir of Her Life and Character* (Philadelphia: Lemuel Howell, 1836), 111.

17. *The Slave* (Sep. 1855): 35.

18. Faulkner, 398–99.

19. Edwin Bronner, "Moderates in London Yearly Meeting, 1857–1873: Precursors of Quaker Liberals," *Church History* 59 (1990): 357–71.

20. Materials relating to Birmingham Ladies' Negro's Friend Society are in LRSF, MS box 8:4.

21. Morwenna Stephens, *The Stephens Family* (n.p., n.d.,), LRSF.

22. Rebecca Stephens Thompson, "Journal," in M. Stephens, 113; William Stephens, "Diary," (1788–1836) in J. E. Clark, "From an Old Quaker Diary, William Stephens 1788–1836," *The Friend* (30 Oct. 1931): 991–93.

23. Letters, Martha Ball to EC, on pamphlets, LRSF, MS box 8:4 (7) and box 8:4 (8).

24. Debra Gold Hansen, *Strained Sisterhood: Gender and Class in the Boston Female Anti-Slavery Society* (Amherst: University of Massachusetts Press, 1993), 66–75; Deborah van Broekhoven, "'Better than a Clay Club': The Organization of Anti-Slavery Fairs, 1835–1860," *Slavery and Abolition* 19, no. 1 (1998): 24–45; Jeffrey, 108–26.

25. LRSF, MS box 8:4, and 8:1.

26. LSRF, MS box 8.

27. R. Clark, 1–7.

28. Rozsika Parker, *The Subversive Stitch: Embroidery and the Making of the Feminine* (London: Women's Press, 1984); Clare Rose, *Clothing, Society and Culture in Nineteenth Century England*, 3 vols. (London: Pickering and Chatto, 2011).

29. Alice Taylor, "'Fashion Has Extended Her Influence to the Cause of Humanity': The Transatlantic Female Economy of the Boston Anti-Slavery Bazaar," in Beverly Lemire, ed., *The Force of Fashion in Politics and Society* (London: Ashgate, 2010), 119.

30. *Liberator* (4 Dec. 1846).

31. Especially Frederick Douglass, Henry Highland Garnet, and Harriet Beecher Stowe.

32. Temperley, 245; Richard Blackett, *Building an Anti-Slavery Wall: Black Abolitionists and the Atlantic Abolitionist Movement, 1830–1860* (Baton Rouge: Louisiana State University Press, 1983), 122.

33. Letter, JE to Maria Weston Chapman (1 Mar. 1851) in Blackett, 122.

34. *The Slave* (Feb. 1852): 55.

35. Billington estimates only a "few hundred bales" arrived overall.

36. *Anti-Slavery Reporter* (Jan. 1849–Jan. 1850).

37. James Mann, *The Cotton Trade of Great Britain: Its Rise, Progress and Present Extent* (1860; repr., London: Cass, 1968 [1860]), appendix.

38. LRSF, MS box 8:4(1).

39. LRSF, MS box 8:5 (25).

40. A Lady [pseud.], *The Workwoman's Guide Containing Instructions to the Inexperienced in Cutting Out and Completing Those Articles of Wearing Apparel etc. Which Are Usually Made at Home; Also Explanations on Upholstery, Straw-Plaiting, Bonnet-Making, Knitting etc. "A Method Shortens Labour"* (London: Simpkins, Marshall and Co., 1835), chap. 6.

41. Audrey Fisch, *American Slaves in Victorian England: Abolitionist Politics in Popular Literature and Culture* (Cambridge: Cambridge University Press, 2000); Marcus Wood, *Blind Memory: Visual Representations of Slavery in England and America 1780–1865* (Manchester: Manchester University Press, 2000); Sarah Meer, *Uncle Tom Mania: Slavery, Minstrelsy, and Transatlantic Culture in the Nineteenth Century* (Athens: University of Georgia Press, 2005).

42. EC, "Cotton," "Village Album" (1861), AGT, VA XIV.

43. *The Slave* (May 1853): 17.

44. Marcia Pointon, "Quakerism and Visual Culture 1650–1800," *Art History* 20, no. 3 (1997): 397–431.

45. "Scientific Notes," *The Friend* (Sep. 1861).

46. Leora Auslander, "Beyond Words," *American Historical Review* 110, no. 4 (2005): 1015–45, 1015.

47. Lou Taylor, *The Study of Dress History* (Manchester: Manchester University Press, 2002), 1.

48. Joan Kendall, "The Development of a Distinctive Form of Quaker Dress," *Costume* 19 (1985): 58–74.

49. Emma Jones Lapsansky and Anne Verplanck, eds. *Quaker Aesthetics: Reflections on a Quaker Ethic in American Design and Consumption* (Philadelphia: University of Pennsylvania Press, 2003).

50. *British Friend* (7th Mo 1856): 187.

51. Kendall, 71.

52. *The Friend* (6th Mo 1856): 97.

53. Frederick Tolles, "'Of the Best Sort, but Plain': The Quaker Esthetic," *American Quarterly* 11, no. 4 (1959): 484–502.

54. Kendall, 58.

55. Cards, Ellen Barrett, Margaret Bright, Mary Cudworth, Anne Pike, LRSF, "Friends Institute Collection," vols. A–Z.

56. Card, EC, LRSF, "Friends Institute Collection," vols. A–C.

57. Nuermberger, 88–89.

58. Letters, GWT to JW (5th mo. 9th and 9th mo. 2nd 1853), *Taylor Letterbooks,* volume, 1852–1854, Haverford Library Quaker Collection.

59. AGT, Costume Collection, box 33: 2.

60. Philadelphia History Museum, cat. no. 87.35.368.

61. *Anti-Slavery Reporter* (Jan., Apr., Dec. 1846).

62. Josias Browne, *To the Members of the Anti-Slavery Societies:* And All Friends of the Slave (Manchester: n.d., ca. 1853), 2.

63. Ibid.

64. Helen Bradley Foster, *"New Raiments of Self": African American Clothing in the Antebellum South* (Oxford: Berg, 1997), 69.

65. Thomas Clarkson, *The History of the Rise, Progress and Accomplishments of the Abolition of the African Slave-Trade by the British Parliament,* 2 vols. (1808; repr., London: Cass, 1968), 2: 192.

66. *The Slave* (Mar. 1851): 10; (Jun. 1855): 23.

67. *The Slave* (Jun. 1855): 23.

68. Chandler, "Free Labour Cotton," *British Friend* (4th Mo 1849).

69. *Liberator* (19 Oct. 1847), in Jeffrey, 1.

5 The Spiritual Journeys of an Abolitionist: Amy Kirby Post, 1802–1889

NANCY A. HEWITT

CLEARLY QUAKERS AS A GROUP WERE AMONG the most commit-ted advocates of abolition in the eighteenth and nineteenth centuries. They were also well represented in the woman's rights movement, prison reform, campaigns for Indian rights, and a host of other efforts aimed at progressive social change. But the Society of Friends, like other religious denominations, embraced a diverse constituency. Not all Friends were abolitionists; indeed, some individuals, mainly merchants, benefited from slavery and the slave trade. Among those who advocated antislavery in some form, many only testified to their beliefs within Friends' meetings. Others came to abolition via Quakerism but ultimately broke with the Society of Friends in order to pursue more worldly forms of activism. For these individuals, the ten-sion between spiritual and political commitments often raised deep conflicts and concerns. The spiritual journeys of one such abolitionist—Amy Kirby Post—can contribute to a broader understanding of both Quakerism and abolitionism in the nineteenth-century United States.

Amy Kirby was raised a Quaker on Long Island, and she embraced the Hicksite meeting after her marriage to Isaac Post in 1828. She remained an active Hicksite until the mid-1840s, when she withdrew from Genesee Yearly Meeting. But she did not reject the religious teachings of her youth. Instead, she continued to embrace the concept of the Inner Light and Quaker testi-monies against social injustice even as she sought a spiritual path that allowed her to act more directly in the world. Thus in 1848, Amy Kirby Post helped to found the Congregational Friends, and she continued on as a Progressive Friend and then a Friend of Human Progress into the 1850s. Participants in these meetings pursued social reform—including abolition, woman's rights, racial equality, prison reform, peace, and Indian rights—as part of a faith-based effort to rid the world of oppressive institutions and practices. Yet at the very same time, Post participated in spiritualist circles, hosting—with her husband Isaac—meetings and séances in their Rochester, New York, home. Later in life, she attended Unitarian meetings with her youngest son Will, and when she died in 1889, her funeral was held at Rochester's First Unitarian Society. Some of Amy Kirby Post's great-grandchildren, including Will's granddaughter Amy Foster Post, only discovered their Quaker heritage when the Post Family Papers were donated to the University of Rochester archives in the late 1970s.

Such spiritual journeys could indicate uncertainty about one's religious commitments. Some Quaker historians have questioned especially the rationale behind activists' embrace of spiritualism, arguing that the concept of the Inner Light provides much the same understanding of the individual's relationship to God. Yet questions of faith run far deeper than logical relationships between belief and practice. As British historian Phyllis Mack has argued in *Heart Religion in the British Enlightenment*:

> Secular historians need an angle of vision that allows them not only to accept [individuals'] spiritual concerns as sincere and legitimate, but to . . . stand with individual men and women as they worked to shape their own subjectivity, not in a single cathartic moment . . . but over a lifetime.[1]

My purpose, then, is not to argue that the spiritual journey Amy Kirby Post followed was the only means of bringing together her spiritual and political commitments, or that her commitment to spiritualism and then Unitarianism offered a superior religious experience to that enjoyed by those who remained Friends. Instead, I want to explore what led an individual whose Quaker coworshippers already accepted the wrongs of slavery to seek nonetheless a different path, one that she felt offered her a deeper bond between faith and action.

What is clearest in examining the life of Amy Kirby Post is that she was committed to finding a spiritual home that not only *allowed* her to pursue social justice on this earth, but also *required* her to do so. For her, faith had to demand, not simply permit, efforts to build a better world on earth as well as beyond it. During the first four decades of her life, witnessing against social ills in Quaker meetings seemed to satisfy her need to improve the world. But beginning in the 1840s, she embraced a more active sense of religious and political agency, which drew her into the Progressive Friends, spiritualism, and Unitarianism, as well as into an astonishing range of movements for social change.

For those not familiar with her story, you might think of Amy Kirby Post, in one sense, as a "local Lucretia," that is, an individual wholly engaged with a universalist campaign for equality and rights in every arena of life—the family, the community, the meeting, the larger society.[2] She was an ardent abolitionist and cofounder of the Western New York Anti-Slavery Society (WNYASS) in

1842; a confidante of Frederick Douglass, William C. Nell, and Harriet Jacobs; an organizer of antislavery petition campaigns and fundraising fairs; and a conductor on the Underground Railroad. Post also advocated woman's rights, fought for the rights of American Indians, cofounded a Working Women's Protective Union in Rochester with two local seamstresses, protested against the U.S. war with Mexico and capital punishment, and supported various health reforms from Graham diets to campaigns against tobacco. Like Lucretia Mott, she believed that "all these subjects of reform are kindred in their nature."[3] And like Mott, she was for many years a committed Quaker. During the 1830s, she served on the meeting for sufferings and on committees to assist Indians and develop vocational education programs. She also helped write epistles to other meetings from Rochester Monthly, Farmington Quarterly, and Genesee Yearly meetings. And in 1836, she participated in discussions at Genesee Yearly Meeting that led to the appointment of a committee to consider changes in the *Discipline,* including women's full equality in the Society of Friends, the role of Friends in the antislavery cause, and the role of ministers and elders in the meeting.[4]

Also like Mott, who joined the mixed-race and interdenominational Philadelphia Female Anti-Slavery Society, Post began working alongside non-Quakers in the 1830s. She signed her first worldly antislavery petition in 1837, setting her name alongside those of several hundred Methodist, Baptist, Presbyterian, and Unitarian neighbors. Yet she went further than Mott over the next decade, breaking with the Society of Friends over a variety of disciplinary issues. In the 1840s, Amy and Isaac Post, with a circle of like-minded Friends in western and central New York, challenged the structure of Hicksite meetings. One important aspect of this challenge involved the right to work with people from other denominations. In 1841, for instance, she and Isaac queried antislavery Friends about the effects of excluding non-Quakers from abolitionist meetings. John Ketcham, a Long Island friend and Friend, agreed with their "sentiment that our light (if we have any) would be more likely to shine where it would do good by uniting with all without distinction of Sect or creed."[5]

A year later, the Posts became founding members of the WNYASS, which was inspired in part by the appearance in Rochester of former Quaker Abby Kelley and the young Frederick Douglass. They were touring the region as agents of the American Anti-Slavery Society (AASS). Kelley suggested the need for an AASS branch in Rochester, and area abolitionists created the WNYASS, which attracted evangelical Presbyterians and Baptists, as well as two dozen Hicksites and a number of blacks from the local African Methodist Episcopal

Zion church. Amy Kirby Post and three Quaker coworshippers immediately joined Kelley in drafting "an address to the abolitionists of Western New York," suggesting a series of fundraising fairs, the first to be held on February 22, "the birth day of the great, good, pious, immortal, slaveholding Washington!"[6]

Having moved from testimony to direct action, Amy Kirby Post was soon subject to a visit from a committee appointed by the overseers of Rochester Monthly Meeting. Their purpose, in part, "was to advise her in regard to her duty towards her family," but they could find no sign of domestic neglect, and, in fact, found several members of the household joining Amy in her questionable activities.[7] Refusing to be deterred from her abolitionist efforts, Post wrote to Kelley on stationary embossed with an antislavery logo and noted, almost with regret, that the overseers had "taken no further notice of my case." Yet she suspected "they will have a fresh charge against me soon as I yesterday transcribed Epistles for the Preparataive meetings on such paper as this, and have little doubt but that the imploring image [of a slave in chains] will disturb their quiet."[8]

Over the following three years, debates in Rochester Monthly and Farmington Quarterly meetings over women's equality, worldly activism, and "church" hierarchy extended to Michigan Quarterly Meeting. Genesee Yearly Meeting set up a committee to discuss the issues, but it continually postponed action. In response, the Posts and like-minded Friends pushed harder to change Quaker discipline, including the elimination of men's and women's separate meetings, the diminution of the power of ministers and elders, and the acceptance of women's independent action on the dismissal of female members. Yet when some changes were implemented in Rochester Monthly and Michigan Quarterly meetings, it only led to further conflict. In 1843, a few Hicksites began withdrawing from the yearly meeting rather than continue in the old ways. By February 1845, Amy and Isaac Post joined this group, although they asked to be released from Rochester Monthly Meeting rather than simply withdrawing. Their requests were granted the following month. Their daughter Mary Hallowell was disowned two years later for "neglect of duty," and her husband William stopped attending meeting although he did not withdraw for several years.[9]

Individual disownments, releases, and withdrawals continued over the next three years. Then on June 6, 1848, the crisis came to a head with Genesee Yearly Meeting dismissing a sizeable number of dissidents for their "disregard of the injunctions of the discipline and the authority of the church."[10] A week later, a large group of disaffected Hicksites met in Waterloo, New York, to found the Yearly Meeting of Congregational Friends (YMCF). Amy and Isaac

Post, other Rochester Friends from the Burtis, Fish, and Hallowell families, and Waterloo Quakers such as the McClintocks were among the founding members. Lucretia Mott attended the inaugural meeting of the YMCF and was supportive of their efforts, although she did not relinquish her membership in the Hicksite Philadelphia Yearly Meeting. But other dissident Quakers in Chester, Pennsylvania; central Michigan; and Greenplains, Indiana, formed Congregational meetings, creating a network of former Hicksites who combined spiritual commitment with worldly activism. Largely rural, committed to abolitionism and social equality more broadly, and deeply religious, these Congregational Friends sought to establish what they viewed as a purer and more perfect form of Quakerism. Yet they also eagerly opened their meeting to non-Quakers who shared their spiritual and political vision.[11]

Still, the division was painful on all sides, especially for those families whose religious allegiances were split. Although the members of the Post family in Rochester all joined the Congregational Friends, their relatives on Long Island remained committed Hicksites. In early 1845, Mary Kirby pled with her "dear children"—daughter Amy and son-in-law Isaac—to "stand and wait patiently" rather than provoke a dismissal. Surely, she wrote, the meeting's leaders "will be overcome by your good and consistant [sic] lives."[12] But others viewed dismissal as a badge of honor. Thus Nathaniel Potter, a dissident Hicksite abolitionist from Buffalo, wrote to the Posts after their release, quoting the Bible: "Blessed are they who are persecuted for righteousness' sake, for theirs is the kingdom of Heaven."[13] It is intriguing that Potter viewed the Posts as persecuted even though they had asked to be released.

The Posts like most of their coworshippers believed that in forming the Congregational and then Progressive Friends, they were carrying on the best traditions of the Society of Friends. Amy, for example, was even more active in the YMCF than she had been in her final years with Genesee Yearly Meeting. The Congregational/Progressive Friends invited reform-minded Hicksites such as Lucretia Mott to attend their yearly meetings along with antislavery activists including Frederick Douglass, William Lloyd Garrison, Gerrit Smith, Elizabeth Cady Stanton, and others. Women and men met together for worship and to discuss the critical issues of the day. There was no committee of ministers and elders who ruled over the meeting, and individuals were admitted based on their spiritual commitments rather than a set discipline. There were no limits on worldly activity and no tolerance for sexual or racial discrimination.[14] Amy served on a number of YMCF committees, including the one that drafted "An Address to the Women of the State of New York" in 1850. The address drew on examples of women's wrongs and women's rights from around the world to insist on the need for sex equality in all realms of life and for women of all races and nationalities.[15] Their claim—"When we speak of the Rights of Women, we speak of Human Rights"—went significantly beyond the resolutions passed at the Seneca Falls Woman's Rights Convention two years earlier.

Despite the upheavals in Quaker circles and the efforts to launch a new yearly meeting of progressive Friends, Amy did not lessen her commitment to abolition or other worldly reform efforts. In fact, between 1848 and 1850, she was more engaged with antislavery and woman's rights than at any previous time. She helped organize fourteen antislavery fairs in 1848 alone, along with a major abolitionist convention in Rochester. The surge in activity was inspired in part by Frederick Douglass's decision to settle in the city, a decision reinforced by the kind reception he received from the Posts on earlier visits. And Douglass's presence ensured that local efforts to assist escaped slaves via the Underground Railroad would multiply. In addition, with the publication of the *North Star* in Rochester, activists from Boston, New York, and Philadelphia, as well as abolitionists from England and Canada visited the city more often. And the Posts regularly hosted antislavery lecturers in their home and also befriended fugitive slaves in the area.[16] At the same time, Amy became more involved in the nascent movement for woman's rights, attending the July 1848 convention in Seneca Falls and helping to organize a second in Rochester two weeks later. That second convention spawned the Rochester Working Women's Protective Union, which Amy cofounded with her friend Sarah Owen and two local seamstresses. Thus, her work on the YMCF address to New York women was a logical extension of her reform activities, just as her refusal to buy slave-produced goods or serve alcohol brought her religious and political commitments into the intimate domain of the household. She had created an apparently seamless world in which daily life, social activism, and spiritual beliefs merged.

Yet in the midst of her seemingly nonstop efforts on behalf of antislavery, woman's rights, and progressive Quakerism, Amy Kirby Post embraced spiritualism. And this step on her religious journey was likely the result of more than her experiences in Friends' meetings or her commitments to social justice. For in the years just before Amy added spiritualism to her religious and activist repertoire—from roughly 1844 to 1848—she dealt with a series of personal tragedies and upheavals. In the summer of 1844, Sarah Hallowell, Amy's sister, was suddenly widowed at the age of 26. Soon after her husband Jeffries' death, she was shocked to discover that he was deeply in debt, a debt that Isaac and Amy agreed to repay. To do so, the Posts were forced to move from their home in Rochester to a less expensive house on the city's edge. There Amy and Sarah worked the farm, while Isaac labored to maintain his small pharmacy in the city. Just a year earlier, Amy's other sister, Elizabeth Mott, had been abandoned by her husband, leaving her in desperate financial straits as well. The impact of the two events lingered for years. They may have inspired Amy to scribble notes to herself on a prospectus for the *North Star* in 1848, noting that while the husband legally controls the purse strings, the family's money "as rightfully belongs to her as to him—she either recev'd [*sic*] it from her inheritance or contributed her full share of labour to produce it."[17]

Amy Kirby Post was forced to deal with a more traumatic event as well. In 1840, at age 38, Amy gave birth to a daughter Mathilda. At some point in the midst of their move to the farm, Mathilda took ill, and after a painful wasting away, died in January 1845. In the same letter in which Mary Kirby lamented her daughter's growing separation from the Hicksite meeting, she also sent condolences on the loss of her "darling and only *little* daughter." Three months later, Amy finally penned a letter to her 12-year-old son Joseph who was living with his aunt and uncle on Long Island. She wrote of "the loss of thy little interesting sister." And though she claimed, "We must submit [to God's will]," she admitted that "the repressed tears often become too potent to obey the check, when reflecting on her loveliness and our disappointed hopes."[18] Amy had faced tragic loss before. In the spring of 1825, her fiancé had died suddenly just as wedding plans were being finalized, and two years later, her older sister Hannah, Isaac Post's first wife, died of a fever. Amy was then swept up in the care of Hannah's and Isaac's two young children, Mary and Edmund, and in 1828 married Isaac. In September 1830, Edmund died, less than a year after Amy gave birth to her first son, Jacob. Another son, Henry, born in July 1834, died just before his third birthday, less than a year after the Posts had moved to Rochester. When misfortune struck again in 1844–1845, Amy seemed less resilient. She took ill and did not fully recover for at least a year.[19] And this time she did not turn to the Quaker meeting for comfort. Instead, Amy continued to push against what she saw as meaningless formalities that stood in the way of a true godly life and found solace in antislavery activities.

Just a month after Mathilda's death, Amy returned to the worldly fray. She served on the resolutions committee for the WNYASS annual convention, over which Isaac presided. Perhaps committing themselves to abolitionist work was a way to offset the economic crises and personal tragedies that had marked the previous months. Later in 1845, Frederick Douglass stayed with the Posts while visiting western New York, at least his third trip to the city in three years. By October 1847, he had decided to move to Rochester and launch the *North Star* there. A year earlier, he had written to Amy, "your family was always Dear, dear to me, you loved me and treated me as a brother before the world knew me as it now does, & my friends were fewer than they are now."[20] He no doubt hoped that that friendship would ease his move from Boston to Rochester, a move that angered many of his old allies, including William Lloyd Garrison. Douglass was accompanied by his partner Martin Delaney and soon after by William C. Nell, a free black abolitionist and journalist who commuted back and forth between Boston and Rochester for several years. The presence of Douglass and Nell, both of whom became close friends and confidantes of Amy Kirby Post, transformed her world.

Despite having a new baby—Willett, born in 1847—and still recovering from the upheavals of 1844–1845, Amy was busier than ever. In her mid-forties, she eagerly took on the work of organizing antislavery fairs and lectures, hiding fugitives, and befriending a host of newcomers to Rochester. In the summer of 1848, she and Isaac hosted the wedding of William Nell's sister Frances to ex-slave Benjamin Cleggett and "caused great dissatisfaction in the Rochester community" by inviting whites and blacks to celebrate together.[21] She also helped organize the celebration of British Emancipation Day on August 1. During that summer, she became engrossed in woman's rights efforts in Seneca Falls and Rochester. She also continued her efforts to assist Seneca Indians on the Cattaraugus Reservation near Buffalo, where tribal members were disputing land cessions and attempting to forge their first written constitution. And she remained an active participant in the YMCF, serving on committees and writing addresses and epistles.

Yet despite all this activity, Amy Kirby Post was searching for some deeper way to engage, or perhaps after the loss of her daughter, to re-engage her faith. And in June 1848, she found at least part of what she sought. A family friend and Rochester neighbor, Leah Fox Fish, invited the Posts to her house during a visit from her younger sisters Margretta and Kate Fox, who lived with their parents in nearby Hydesville, New York. That spring, either as part of an effort to trick their parents or as the result of some felt communication from the beyond, the Fox sisters began receiving messages from the dead. In June, they displayed their extraordinary skills to Amy and Isaac Post and their friends Abigail and Henry Bush. The Posts quickly became ardent believers in the Fox sisters' spiritual abilities. Séances with the Fox sisters were regularly held in Rochester homes that summer, including the Posts', and the group of local converts included large numbers of Methodists, some ex-evangelicals, and several other Quakers. Indeed, among local Congregational Friends, the Hallowell, Willetts, Burtis, and Kedzie families included several believers. Some early skeptics were won over when investigating committees could find no physical means by which the Fox sisters created their "rappings," though a public performance of their spirit communication at Rochester's Corinthian Hall in November 1849 led to a near riot.[22] Frederick Douglass was invited to a spiritualist evening at the Posts' in fall 1848, but he left unconvinced. But some African American friends, most notably William C. Nell and the fugitive slave Harriet Jacobs, did embrace spiritualism, ensuring that the Posts' religious, as well as political, circles remained interracial and mixed-sex.[23]

It was Isaac Post who became the most ardent spiritualist in the family, leading séances and publishing *Voices in the Spirit World* (1852), a collection of letters from the beyond he had been directed to write by spirits who had contacted him. Yet Amy also found a deep connection to the spirit world that lent a new power to her faith and her campaigns for social justice. In part, she may have been drawn to spiritualism by the loss of Mathilda and the sense of the fragility of life that surrounded her in the years immediately preceding 1848. She also knew Leah Fox Fish and no doubt found it impossible that the young Fish girls Maggie and Kate—just twelve and fourteen—could be involved in fraud of any kind. But she may also have embraced the interdenominational appeal of spiritualism. The yearly gatherings of Congregational Friends certainly attracted a wide array of participants, but most of the non-Quakers seem to have attended to promote reform campaigns rather than spiritual growth. Indeed, Elizabeth Cady Stanton criticized established religions for their part in oppressing women. But spiritualist meetings brought together a diverse group of Rochesterians who were focused on faith. Methodists appear to have been especially well represented among the believers in the city, but so too were former evangelical Presbyterians and a few women and men from a scattering of other churches. Here was a religious movement that reached across denominations as well as across that great divide between the living and the dead.

Moreover, Amy quickly recognized the ways that spiritualism reinforced her efforts on behalf of social justice, especially woman's rights, for it eliminated the need for any intermediary between the individual and those in the next world. A number of progressive Quaker women shared Post's spiritualist beliefs as did a range of woman's rights advocates.[24] Even as the veracity of the Fox sisters' rappings became more widely contested, these believers did not reject their belief either in the existence of spirits or in the ability of at least some ordinary women and men to communicate with them. Of course, Amy lived with Isaac Post, who regularly communicated with spirits, both those of friends and family members and those of prominent political figures such as George Washington and John C. Calhoun. But she also shared with women activists a sense that spiritualism widened the reach of female faith in particular. Thus, her friend and antislavery coworker Sarah Thayer wrote her in 1853 that a woman "ought to be better qualified to direct the spiritual life of her own sex than any belov'd disciple or even Jesus himself as a man and a brother."[25]

For the next two decades, Amy Kirby Post continued to pursue spiritualism, progressive Quakerism, abolition (and the rights of free and freed blacks), woman's rights, and a host of other social justice campaigns. Just as she imagined that all these reforms were "kindred in their nature" and should be pursued at once, she also accepted that distinct religious beliefs and practices could be kindred in *their* nature and embraced simultaneously.

Nonetheless, sometime in the 1860s, while she still embraced spiritualism, Post also joined the Unitarian Society of Rochester, whose leaders had been among the critics of the Fox sisters in the 1840s. By then the Progressive Friends–turned–Friends of Human Progress had begun to fade from the scene as well, and the Fox sisters had become increasingly erratic in their behavior and their spiritual claims. Maggie Fox gave up her spiritualist career upon her engagement to Dr. Elisha Kane in 1856. Although she dabbled in spirits again after his death in 1860, she never resumed her career as a medium and, finally, in the 1880s, denounced spiritualism as a fraud.[26] Perhaps more importantly, the practice of spiritualism had taken a strange turn, with women—often young, attractive women—serving as passive mediums for voices from the beyond. Indeed, the movement gained more and more adherents as it distanced itself from early supporters who were bent on linking faith to social justice and focused instead on the simpler pleasures of allowing individuals to communicate with relatives and friends who had passed away.[27]

As spiritualism gained a wider and wider audience during and following the Civil War, when the horrendous toll of young men drew many to private and public séances, the Posts pulled back. Even after Isaac Post died in 1872, Amy does not seem to have sought solace through communicating with his spirit, or at least no evidence of such efforts exists. Instead, she attended services at the Unitarian Society, where she worshiped until her death in 1889. Her daughter Mary Hallowell had joined the Unitarians at least by the 1860s, and Amy and Isaac's son Willett regarded himself as a Unitarian his whole life and raised his children in that church. When Amy Kirby Post died, her funeral and burial were conducted by Unitarians.[28] The rich ties that bound together her faith in progressive Quakerism, spiritualism, abolition, and woman's rights had frayed.

Amy Kirby Post's embrace of Unitarianism was due in part, no doubt, to the fading power of the Friends of Human Progress and early spiritualists.

But she may also have been drawn to Unitarianism because by the 1860s and 1870s it attracted a wide array of Rochester reformers, drawing together as Congregational Friends once did calls to combine faith with justice. Unitarians in Boston and elsewhere had long been tied to the antislavery cause, and from the 1850s on, it was also home to many woman's rights advocates. In Rochester, Emily Collins and Laura Ramsdell, both of whom advocated abolition as well, joined the Unitarians, and Susan B. Anthony attended First Unitarian Society services for decades even though she never relinquished her membership in the Society of Friends. The younger members of many progressive Quaker families adopted Unitarianism as well, including the sons and daughters of Sarah Burtis, Sarah Fish, Lemira Kedzie, and other coworkers in the WNYASS and the woman's rights movement. Mary Hallowell and her husband William thus sat among old friends when they started attending Unitarian services. Indeed, William seems to have joined the Unitarian Society in 1849, five years before he was released from Genesee Yearly Meeting. Clearly, for at least some former Quakers, Unitarianism served the same function as spiritualism did for Amy and Isaac Post, complementing a Quakerism that was a source of frustration and contention as well as faith and community.

Although Amy Kirby Post embraced Unitarianism, she still considered herself a progressive Quaker at heart and also continued her friendships with former spiritualists, many of whom now advocated free love or at least an end to Victorian sexual standards through the National Liberal League. Amy was invited to attend their annual meeting in 1879, but she declined for reasons of health, though she supported their efforts to liberalize government and advocate a single standard of sexual behavior.[29] At the same time, she became a staunch advocate of women's suffrage, a goal that she had considered less significant in the 1840s and 1850s when the U.S. government embraced slavery and war and many Quaker men refused to vote even though they could. By the early 1870s, she tried to register and vote in Rochester alongside Anthony and several of her Unitarian coworshippers.[30] Thus even in the last decade of her life, she continued to combine support for myriad reforms with a religious faith that was both broadly accessible to women and men and driven by some interior sensibility.

Amy Kirby Post did not pursue her spiritual or political journeys alone. She was part of a vibrant circle of Friends in Western New York that over time expanded to include free and fugitive slaves and other non-Quaker abolitionists as well as woman's rights advocates, utopian communalists, spiritualists, and Unitarians. In all of these endeavors, she joined efforts to push both religious and reform societies to live out their principles. Thus, she expected

Quakers, spiritualists, abolitionists, and woman's rights advocates to engage free and fugitive blacks on equal terms with whites and women on equal terms with men. As historian Judith Wellman has suggested, these radical activists insisted—in every area of their lives—on the absolute equality of individuals, blurring distinctions between black and white, male and female, Quaker and non-Quaker. Because "physical distinctions were not very important to them," it may have been easier for those like Amy Kirby Post to also blur distinctions between spiritual and physical worlds, crossing the boundary between the living and the dead.[31] Although we may find this last belief hard to grasp, as scholars we must, as Phyllis Mack argues, "accept [individuals'] spiritual concerns as sincere and legitimate, . . . [and] stand with [them] . . . as they work[ ] to shape their own subjectivity . . . over a lifetime."[32] Amy Kirby Post's journey illuminates a path followed by hundreds of women and men in the mid-nineteenth century who left the Society of Friends, but who continued to build on the values and visions they first learned in Quaker meetings, testifying against injustice, including slavery and racism.

NOTES

My thanks to Phyllis Mack, Carol Faulkner, Ellen Ross, and especially to Judith Wellman and Christopher Densmore for their critiques, assistance, and inspiration on this chapter.

1. Phyllis Mack, *Heart Religion in the British Enlightenment* (Cambridge: Cambridge University Press, 2008), p. 7.

2. "Local Lucretia" refers to Quaker preacher Lucretia Mott. On Mott's religious and political vision, see Carol Faulkner, *Lucretia Mott's Heresy: Abolition and Women's Rights in Nineteenth-Century America* (Philadelphia: University of Pennsylvania Press, 2011).

3. Lucretia Mott to Edmund Quincy, printed in *Liberator,* 6 October 1848.

4. Genesee Yearly Meeting of Women Friends (hereafter GYMWF), Minutes, June 1836, Quaker Collection, Swarthmore College, Swarthmore, Pennsylvania. (Hereafter, Quaker Collection, Swarthmore.) I originally examined these papers at the Haviland Record Room, New York City. The report of the committee and discussions about their suggestions for changes in the *Discipline* can be found in GYMWF Minutes, June 1837, 1838, 1839, and 1840.

5. John Ketcham to Amy and Isaac Post, 11 March 1841, Isaac and Amy Post Family Papers, Rare Books and Manuscripts Room, University of Rochester Library, Rochester, New York. (Hereafter IAPFP.)

6. Proceedings of the Western New York Anti-Slavery Society (WNYASS), in *Liberator,* 6 January 1843; and E[lizabeth] McClintock to Abby Kelley, 10 January 1843, Abby Kelley Foster Papers, American Antiquarian Society, Worcester, Massachusetts.

7. Lucy N. Colman, *Reminiscences* (Buffalo, N.Y.: H. L. Green, 1891), 84. The other family members who were activists likely included Amy's stepdaughter Mary Hallowell, sister Sarah Kirby Hallowell, and husband Isaac Post. In addition, Amy and Isaac's sons Joseph and Jacob may have been living in the household and their infant daughter Mathilda certainly was. Amy and Isaac's son Henry had died in 1837, and the youngest child, Willett was not born until 1847.

8. Amy Post to Abby Kelley, 4 December 1843, Abby Kelley Foster Papers.

9. For records of numerous dismissals, releases, and withdrawals, see GYMWF and Genesee Yearly Meeting of Friends, Minutes, for the 1840s and 1850s, Quaker Collection, Swarthmore College, Swarthmore, Pennsylvania. For Isaac and Amy Post's request for release and approval of that request, see Rochester Monthly Meeting Minutes, Men's Minutes, 21 February 1845 and 18 March 1845; and for Amy Post, see Rochester Monthly Meeting, Women's Minutes, 21 February 1845 and 18 March 1845, Quaker Collection, Swarthmore. The minutes of these meetings do not contain information explaining the requests or the Posts' release. Indeed, in January 1845, Isaac Post had been appointed to a Rochester Monthly Meeting committee; see Men's Minutes, 24 January 1845.

10. There is no mention of the dissension in the June 1847 or June 1848 GYMWF Minutes, but for a discussion of the controversy, see Yearly Meeting of Congregational Friends (YMCF), *Proceedings of the Yearly Meeting of Congregational Friends, held at Waterloo, New York, from Fourth to the Sixth of Sixth Month, Inclusive, 1849* (Auburn, N.Y.: Oliphant's Press, 1849), 32–35. Those who withdrew voluntarily included close friends and abolitionist coworkers of Amy Kirby Post, such as Sarah Fish, Sarah Burtis, and Rhoda DeGarmo.

11. For early discussions of the creation of the Congregational/Progressive Friends, see A. Day Bradley, "Progressive Friends in Michigan and New York," *Quaker History* 52 (1963): 95–103; Carlisle G. Davidson, "A Profile of Hicksite Quakerism in Michigan, 1830–1860," *Quaker History* 59 (1970):106–12. For the most important recent discussions of this development, see Christopher Densmore, "The Quaker Origins of the Women's Rights Convention," *Friends Journal* (July 1998): 26–28; Christopher Densmore, "'Be Ye therefore Perfect': Anti-Slavery and the Origins of the Yearly Meeting of Progressive Friends in Chester County, Pennsylvania," *Quaker History* 93 (2004): 28–46; and Christopher Densmore, "From Hicksites to Progressive Friends: The Rural Roots of Perfectionism and Social Reform among North American Friends," *Quaker Studies* 10 (2006): 243–55.

12. Mary Kirby to Amy and Isaac Post, 9 January 1845, IAPFP.

13. Nathaniel Potter to Isaac Post, 18 September 1845, IAPFP.

14. See "Basis of Religious Association," in YMCF, *Proceedings*, 1849, appendix.

15. "An Address to the Women of the State of New York" in YMCF, *Proceedings of the Yearly Meeting of Congregational Friends, held at Waterloo, New York, 1850, with an appendix* (Auburn, N.Y.: Oliphant's Press, 1850), 13–18, quote on human rights on p. 14.

16. For a detailed discussion of Douglass's time in Rochester, see William S. McFeeley, *Frederick Douglass* (New York: W. W. Norton, 1991), chaps. 13–15. On Nell

and other black abolitionists, see Stephen Kantrowitz, *More than Freedom: Fighting for Black Citizenship in a White Republic, 1829–1889* (New York: The Penguin Press, 2012), esp. chap. 4.

17. Speech, Rochester Woman's Rights Convention, 2 August 1848, IAPFP. There is no signature on this note, but it appears to be the writing of Amy Kirby Post and it was mixed in with other Post papers for 1848.

18. Mary Kirby to Amy and Isaac Post, 9 January 1945; and Amy Post to Joseph Post, 11 April 1845, IAPFP. Mathilda was Amy's only "*little* daughter" because step-daughter Mary Hallowell was already an adult.

19. On earlier losses see, Amy Kirby to Isaac and Hannah Post, July 28, 1825; P[hebe] K. Carpenter to Amy Post, June 24, 1837; and Mary W. Willis to Amy Post, August 1, 1837, IAPFP. Of the seven children Amy Kirby Post mothered—5 boys and 2 girls—her stepson Edmund, son Henry, and daughter Mathilda died at five years of age or younger.

20. Frederick Douglass to Amy Post, 28 April 1846, IAPFP.

21. Mary Robbins Post to Isaac and Amy Post, [1848/49?], IAPFP.

22. On Fox sisters and early spiritualism, see Nancy Rubin Stuart, *The Reluctant Spiritualist: The Life of Maggie Fox* (New York: Harcourt, 2005), especially chaps. 1 and 2. On Rochester and the Posts' connections to spiritualism, see Blake McKelvey, *Rochester, the Water Power City* (Cambridge: Harvard University Press, 1945), 289–90; Nancy A. Hewitt, *Women's Activism and Social Change: Rochester, New York, 1822–1872* (Ithaca, N.Y.: Cornell University Press, 1984), 142–43, 169; and Margery Post Abbott, ed., *Post, Albertson and Hicks Family Letters,* vol. 1 (Portland, Ore.: Margaret Post Abbott, 2009), 164, 184–86, 188–90, 193, 198–200, 205, 214–18, 225, 234, 237–38.

23. On Harriet Jacobs and spiritualism, see Jean Fagan Yellin, *Harriet Jacobs: A Life* (New York: Basic Books, 2004), 131–32.

24. On spiritualism and woman's rights, see Ann Braude, *Radical Spirits: Spiritualism and Women's Rights in Nineteenth-Century America* (Boston: Beacon Books, 1999).

25. Sarah [Thayer] to Amy Post, 9 March 1853, IAPFP.

26. See Stuart, *The Reluctant Spiritualist,* esp. chaps. 8, 10, 13.

27. See Braude, *Radical Spirits,* chap. 20.

28. First Unitarian Society, Membership lists and burial notices, First Unitarian Church, Rochester, New York.

29. Amy Post to A. L. Rawson, 9 September 1879, IAPFP.

30. *Democrat & Chronicle* (Rochester, N.Y.), November 1, 1872; and Ida Husted Harper, *The Life and Work of Susan B. Anthony* (Indianapolis: Bobbs-Merrill, 1899), vol. 1: 423–29.

31. Email communication with Judith Wellman, [April 10, 2010].

32. Mack, *Heart Religion,* 7.

PART II   *The Scarcity of African Americans*
in the Meetinghouse
Racial Issues among the Quakers

6 Quaker Evangelization in Early Barbados
Forging a Path toward the Unknowable

KRISTEN BLOCK

MANY HISTORIANS OF THE SOCIETY OF FRIENDS are now aware that the island of Barbados was the Quakers' first American "Cradle of Truth." Beginning in 1656, and throughout the 1660s, missionaries such as Mary Fisher, Anne Austin, Henry Fell, and Richard Pinder brought their simple faith in the Truth and Inward Light to the island, where significant numbers of wealthy slaveholding planters and merchants were "convinced," lending the Society legitimacy and status in Barbados.[1] We also know that Friends first began to engage with the moral problems of slavery in Barbados, as George Fox initiated a serious challenge to patriarchs on the island to think of the enslaved Africans and Indians among them as members of a universal spiritual family, reminding them that "Christ dyed for the Tawne[y]s and for the Blacks, as well as for you that are called whites."[2]

Certainly, Fox's call marks an important moment in the history of Quakers and slavery. Scholars have often judged the subsequent campaign for evangelization a Quaker success story.[3] However, this effort was clearly a secondary issue. Only sparse references remain of missionaries holding meetings with "the negroes in several plantations"; only three instances are recorded of leading planters being prosecuted for including slaves in religious gatherings.[4] Might there have actually been a complete lack of enthusiasm for this mission? Certainly, it would stimulate fear and unease among local slaveholders. I hoped that wills—the one body of evidence that still exists in fairly complete form for this time period—would offer some more indirect clues that some enslaved individuals may have been considered converts by their ostensible masters. Even after a broad prosopographical investigation of nearly eight hundred Quakers who had lived in or visited Barbados (including roughly 150 wills from the island's registers), however, I could not find any "smoking gun," no references to blacks as "Christians" or "Friends." In the end, only a handful of examples seemed to suggest—and by no means conclusively—that *some* Barbadian Friends felt compelled to follow Fox's suggestion to evangelization. Nonetheless, something happened beyond that great void of evidence, and

I felt compelled to draw from the deep well of imagination, waters that can stagnate when historians only trust in strict empirical mirrors of the past.

To conjure up the past, and to inhabit, however imperfectly, those spaces rendered dark by the passage of time, I first draw on historical context to explore how the nascent evangelization movement would have connected to Quakerism's evolving trends in theology and spiritual symbolism: from personal revelation to communal consensus, from the supremacy of the Inward Light to the supremacy of scriptures. Such context next considers a general overview of Africanist literature on religious and communal life, an exploration of the shared cultural constructs that might have drawn potential converts to their masters' society. Finally, I put this knowledge to practice by imagining the circumstances that would have led to everyday spiritual interactions between enslaved members of Quaker households and their masters.

First, examining the debates and subtle shifts in Quaker ideals and practice during the decades just prior to and after Fox's call for evangelization suggests ways in which identifying a new target group for conversion might have played into ongoing theological discussions. Fox, Penn, Whitefield, and others who had emerged as leaders of the movement worked ceaselessly throughout the latter decades of the seventeenth century to counter charges that members of the Society did not believe in the Bible, or were immoral, "disorderly" people.[5] Various schismatic movements also forced leaders to "purify" the movement from within and force greater conformity on the Society's members. These two efforts led to a tempering of the mystical and visionary tone that marked the movement's early days—and would have been reflected in evangelization efforts.

Before the conservatism, however, there was idealism, best embodied by the missionary activity of those who traveled to the furthest reaches of the English world and beyond: to Constantinople, to Catholic strongholds such as Rome, and to the West Indies. Early converts spoke of spiritual authority as emanating from an Inward Light, a basic and universal human impulse that could be sparked by personal interaction between those who had discovered their own Light and those still languishing in the darkness of wrong teaching or ignorance. Spiritual Truth could be held by men or women, educated and "plain" folks alike, and was not limited to those of the English nation (or even to Protestants). This belief in a universal Light in all humanity featured prominently in Fox's *Gospel Family Order*. Citing numerous examples of "Ethiopians" and "Black-Moors" who had converted to Christianity or been of service to prophets and apostles in the Old and New Testaments, Fox's argument in *Gospel Family Order* was meant to build irrefutable evidence that members of his own Society must themselves follow the example of the biblical Joshua and declare firmly, "As for me and my house, we will serve the Lord."[6] Shortly after his return from his American sojourn, Fox wrote and published another small tract, *The Heathens Divinity*, in which he again built a biblical argument supporting the inner righteousness and spiritual perception of "heathens." His central point was that "both Papists and Protestants" were hypocritical to deny the capacity for Christian understanding from those who had never known Christian doctrine.[7]

On this and many other issues where Quaker leaders tried to explain novel parts of their Society's practical theology, they had to appeal to outsiders' sense of propriety—the scriptures were *not* expendable parts of their faith and, as such, the Bible needed to be referred to as *confirmation* of a person's inner spiritual experiences.[8] The arrival of one charismatic Public Friend banished to Barbados in 1661 had already led Quaker leaders such as Fox to accentuate the Society's stance on biblical supremacy. John Perrot, the "hat heretic," is now widely considered a schismatic for preaching the preeminence of individual conscience and the irrelevance of "forms"—that is, outward rules—as a sign of fidelity to God. But the weight of biblical tradition aided Fox and others in their campaign to ostracize Perrot and his followers as "Ranters"—called so for their cavalier dismissal of Friends' efforts to set strict standards, their early fame stained by tales of backsliding and poverty.[9] Quaker women, some of the most ardent of Perrot's followers, had been similarly labeled unruly, and although the new settlement of the Quaker Meeting structure gave unprecedented authority to women, after the 1660s, leaders emphasized women's nurturing and educational roles as "Mothers in Israel" over prophesy, public preaching, or missionary travel.[10] One early advocate of slave evangelization wrote an epistle in 1695 lauding the early Christians who had kept "Disorderly, Unruly Women" from leadership, putting "Qualified Men" in charge of the fledgling sect.[11]

Thanks to the many conflicts and controversies that occupied the Society in the second half of the seventeenth century, consolidating authority within the Society came to be a matter of highest importance. Fox and his wife Margaret Fell began pushing for more regular ordering of meetings, a major concern during his 1671 sojourn in Barbados. Unlike Perrot, most Barbadian Friends seemed in agreement with the new plan—in December 1680, at the home of Ralph Fretwell, a former judge and notable convert, thirty-nine men and forty-three women signed a letter promising to "give up their whole Concern if required, both Spiritual & Temporal, unto the Judgement of the Spirit of God in the Men & Women's Meetings: as believing it to be more according to the Universal Wisdom of God, than any particular measure in my self."[12] London Separatist circles who leaked the document claimed Fox and his followers were corrupting the Quaker principle of individual conscience, but stability and order were more highly valued in Barbados.[13]

The same tensions would have played out between those Barbadian Quakers inspired by the "stirrings of the Spirit" to bring "pagan" Africans into the fold. Most early Quakers, like other Protestants of their time, were adamant that Christians must read and know the Bible by heart. However, inculcating that sort of deep knowledge must have been difficult for an enslaved population that had neither literacy nor time to become literate. Only those who grew up in close proximity to the slaveholder's children and family would have had any opportunity to absorb the moral messages of the Bible in any holistic way. They might have glimpsed, however, that Friends believed one should submit their inner, spiritual journey to the guiding hand of established leaders, lest those with an incomplete, or "immature," knowledge of the Bible's teachings destabilize the Society's claims to Truth (in line with traditional Protestant orthodoxy). Prevailing sentiments on Africans' alleged lack of reason were in tension with Quakers' universalizing impulses.[14] Even Fox was forced to yield to the lack of agreement: Shortly after his visit to Barbados, he had asked Barbadian Quakers to send him a black youth to prove that he might be made a "free man." West Indians seemed reluctant to follow up on such a provocative request, but Fox knew that when it came to forging a strong community, he could not be too overbearing. He later wrote, "(it is no matter) I did it but to try them."[15] Given the turmoil of recurring separatist movements, West Indian Friends would have been reticent about expressing either support for or discomfort with slave evangelization, making the silence palpable, for they knew that if the group could not be unified in their stance (or lack thereof), their denomination would look weak, exposing them to ridicule when so many hoped to improve the Society's standing in the world.

These fairly well-known social and theological trends within the Society of Friends, including in Barbados, all hint at ways in which transcultural conversations with the enslaved—although they had the potential to flourish—may have been cut short by a reluctance to destabilize social hierarchies by preaching on spiritual equality and individual revelation, as well as the social pressure on individual Friends to elevate Unity over personal idealism. Scholars have traced the Society of Friends' conservative shift in the decades following the restoration of Charles II; as we have seen, similar patterns held true in Barbados, leading to a conservatism that doubtless pulled Quakers more in line with the "reasonable" Christian majority of English settlers in the Caribbean—who demurred from any kind of large-scale mission work to the enslaved.

Careful attention to shifts in Quaker theology and practice is useful but can only explain one side of the story. Enslaved Africans and their descendants helped to determine the potential for Quakerism's successful expansion beyond the cadre of European settlers attracted to the denomination's community and message. Scholarship on West and West-Central African religions and society provides one lens through which to examine potential intersections and points of conversation. Although terms such as *shaman* or *cult* can unnecessarily exoticize and "primitivize" Africans, I propose that we repurpose this language and replace familiar labels usually applied to Christian groups (such as *priest* or *missionary*, *sect* and *denomination*). By "othering" our own perspective on Quakerism, we can take on the role of curious and observant outsiders—a distance of "strangeness" that might approximate how enslaved Africans saw the Society of Friends and their religious practices.

Historical scholarship on early West African religiosity, informed by anthropological studies, has developed tremendously, with nuanced discussions covering both time and space. One insight that almost every Africanist scholar seems to agree upon is that what have come to be called "traditional" religions are marked by their flexibility and adaptability. Many note that in oral cultures, faith practices change continually with the needs of the community. Joseph Miller describes the broader cultural *mentalité* as follows:

> Africans thought of themselves on multiple levels: as blacks/Africans (their master's definition), as part of communities defined by "country marks," by intimate affiliations. . . . These collectivities were supple groupings that people created, often by intense experiences of personal conversion, to pursue many strategies, from primary affective bonds of family to economic collaboration, social reproduction, personal clientage, political factions, or—for Muslims—affiliation with faith-based communities of worship . . . people in Africa claimed as many different connections as their means and interests allowed. The more their memberships, the greater the personal autonomy and advancement they might achieve by playing loyalties claimed in one against challenges or constraints imposed by others.[16]

We know that such flexibility and mutually beneficial social contacts with Portuguese traders and arms dealers during the sixteenth through eighteenth centuries allowed Christian missionaries to reach a relatively large segment of the population in the Kingdoms of Angola and Kongo.[17] Similarly, Islam expanded into many areas of West Africa, linking communities within a larger

regional system of influence and trade, coexisting alongside many other local spiritual practices.[18] Such a tradition of flexibility makes it unlikely that
Africans and their American-born families in Quaker households would
have immediately scorned the "white man's god" (despite the trauma of the
Middle Passage), for many would have looked for aspects of commonality
with their masters' communal traditions and rituals, understanding religious
integration as part of the search for a patron, for stability, and for community.
Their knowledge of and interaction with various forms of slavery in their
homelands, most of which stressed incorporation and fictive kinship, would
have also conditioned an attitude of some openness.

Given the religious pluralism in seventeenth-century Barbados and Quakers' highly developed sense of their difference from (and superiority to) other
faiths, Africans may have understood the Society of Friends as a secret society
open only to the initiated.[19] Such an interpretation may have been strengthened by the meeting structure for which Fox had begun to advocate; a large
portion of his time in Barbados was devoted to the formation of ordered
men's and women's meetings, a quarterly meeting attended only by the Society's leading men, allowing Quaker surgeons, midwives, and schoolmasters
to institute other smaller "committee"-like meetings. Each branch played a
role in members' social interactions—some disciplining wayward Friends,
others vetting proposed marriage partners, still others monitoring the ap-
prenticeships of youths into a profession or trade, guiding each in the ways of
comporting themselves in a "godly" fashion. Indeed, Fox's sermon advocating
evangelization had taken place at the newly established Men's Meeting at the
home of his father-in-law, Lt. Col. Thomas Rous, a major sugar planter and
one of the earliest to embrace Quakerism. Fox instructed those already used
to control and management to implement evangelization as a top-down policy
directed by "Masters of Families" (mistresses were later added to the policy,
but it was clear that a hierarchy of age, rank, and gender would structure the
incorporation of members). Certainly, they would have preached, as in so
many colonial plantation societies, the virtues of submission, suffering, and
the joys of the afterlife.

Or perhaps the enslaved understood their masters' faith as a possession
cult, given that Quakers' "silent" meetings were (especially in the early years)
punctuated by spirit-filled speeches and prototypical trancelike "quaking" that
gave the cult its common name. Scholars have noted how people of African
descent were drawn to the more emotive religiosity of Protestant evangelicals
in the eighteenth- and nineteenth-century transatlantic Great Awakenings.[20]
The same may have been true for early Quakers: William Penn's report of his

first religious stirrings as an adolescent came after listening to a sermon so evocative that "a black servant of the family could not contain himself from weeping aloud."[21] Elizabeth Webb, an early Quaker missionary to America, attested that she was at first disconcerted by the "great Numbers of black people that were in slavery" in Virginia, but at a New England meeting where slaves were in attendance, she said that she "felt a stream of Divine love run to them . . . One Young man a Black was so reached to by the love of God through Jesus Christ that his heart was so broken that the tears did run down like Rain."[22] The Quaker ethos of bodily religious experience in a space of spiritual equality might have offered Africans a way to interact with their masters in a way that temporarily suspended the hierarchies of colonialism.

Perhaps African observers of the Society of Friends saw the spiritual organization as akin to the healing cults that sprung up in areas of Western Africa where instability and violence disrupted social cohesion. Kongolese Christians such as Beatriz Kimpa Vita had adapted European mythologies into a powerful cult of hope and revelation in a time of war. After being possessed by Saint Anthony, Doña Beatriz led a religious movement to heal a kingdom in a state of moral breakdown.[23] For Quakers worked to break down social barriers, whether policing everyday language or simply encouraging Friends to hold themselves apart from the world around them (a world that delighted in "Pride, Drunkennesse, Covetousnesse, Oppression and deceitful-dealings"[24]). They espoused an early modern philosophy of "loving kindness," a direct response to the "hardness of heart" and cruelty that inhabitants and visitors to the West Indies regularly denounced. Like Kongolese healing cults, Quakerism emerged to promote the restoration of public morality, a process that involved the healing of the society as well as the individual.[25] Quakers' intensely silent gatherings and their repeated denunciation of sin and immorality might have strengthened slaves' attraction to their masters' rituals, designed to purge the Society from the poison of greed and alienation. The important role of missionaries and visits by Public Friends in the early organization of the Society in Barbados may have made them into traveling shamans whose charisma and personal mystical experiences of spiritual enlightenment was so contagious as to spark spiritual stirrings in others.

Nuances, both place- and time-specific, are bound to be lost in this rather schematic look at what are often considered "traditional" elements of African religion. What we lose in historical certainty, we gain in a more holistic sense of the opportunities for transcultural engagement between enslaved Africans and Quaker slaveholders in seventeenth-century Barbados. We can be certain that the enslaved—those who wished, or were compelled, to be initiated into the Quaker community—used their preexisting knowledge to make sense of slaveholders' religious characteristics. They would have observed a clannish group whose banding together in the face of local ostracism and institutional persecution justified their strong sense of superiority and embattlement. Those brought into Quaker meetings would have observed the unwritten rules that governed behavior (who spoke and when) and would have recognized the aura of leadership that surrounded a select few. They may have watched others (including women) experience trancelike "dissociative" states and would have felt the energetic alterations that accompanied the Society's conservative shift. That this shift took place during the same decades that Fox promoted slave evangelization would have quite certainly diminished Quakerism's attractiveness to Africans, whose multiple and synchronic forms of religious organization upheld spirit possession and healing cults as a way for marginalized peoples to seek relief from the social and psychic pressures of their world. (I do not presume that religious practices focused on ecstatic rituals would have been "naturally" more appealing to Africans, but merely that marginalized individuals identified as "mystics" or "possessed" have often been able to exercise special spiritual power in the process.) Even if Africans sought initiation into the Quaker "secret" Society, expecting to follow its necessarily hierarchical modes, they would have known that in the British colonial world, racialized thinking meant that African initiates would forever remain at the bottom of the organizational hierarchy.

We can go beyond these contextual musings by imagining the personal interactions behind specific incidents mentioned in the surviving archive. I will focus here on a few references to manumission of slaves in Quaker wills held in Barbadian archives, for they are perhaps the fullest expression of the generosity Fox imagined that Quakerism's perfect, universal Christianity would produce. His *Gospel Family Order* sermon challenged slaveholders to consider freeing the black members of their family "after a considerable Term of Years, if they have served them faithfully." According to Thomas Drake, Fox's original sermon specified seven years as a fitting term of service for freedom, but Friends who edited the sermon before its 1676 publication altered his text to allow slaveholders more leeway in their judgment. Indeed, one surviving manuscript version of the sermon mentions thirty years' service "more or less" as deserving reward, a period of time directive borne out by two specific testators in Barbados.[26] And indeed, although only a tiny fraction (about 2 percent) of the population at large manumitted slaves in their wills during the seventeenth century, nearly 10 percent of slaveholding Quaker testators in my sample (8 of 76) included manumission clauses.[27] This may not be an overwhelming response, but it is a suggestive deviance from the island's larger norms, one we might see as derived from Friends' sense of evangelical responsibility.

One of these was the widow Elizabeth Barnes, whose allegedly "shameful Miscarriages" might have created the means by which religious connection was experienced between black and white. Elizabeth Barnes (Brumes) was a charismatic and powerful widow who died in Barbados ca. 1681, but she had been active in the Bridgetown Women's Meeting for more than five years prior to her death. Yet ten years earlier, it seems she had grown frustrated with the turn from pure Spirit to a more fastidious recourse to scripture, and as a result was labeled by William Penn as one "of that backsliding Spirit." He remembered that Barnes had called the scriptures "the Pope's Idol, the Professors Idol, and the Quakers Idol," and "in a height of Rage . . . offered to burn them." Apparently, Barnes found a way back into the fold, for in her will she divided her substantial widow's portion among several young Friends, including a bequest of money for an almshouse to support "poor and aged friends men and women." She also directed her team of Quaker executors to free "my negro boy Callabarry" within a year after her decease.[28] What did she hope to gain by this range of civic-minded bequests, and how might her slaves and coreligionists have seen the decisions? Quaker men such as Penn might have disapproved of her "Ranterish" charisma and presumption (her will contained the rather vulgar request that her Quaker executors should all receive £10 worth of silver plate "with these words engraven on it Elizabeth Barnes gave this peece of Plate"). If the forty slaves who lived on her estate saw her performances of spirit-possessed defiance, did they speak of religion with one another? Why single out Callabarry alone as deserving his freedom? Was he among the slaves hailed by William Edmundson after his second trip to Barbados, as among those several "convinc'd . . . [who] confess to Truth"?[29] How did slaves such as Callabarry interact with Barnes's executors and other blacks who remained slaves after her death? We cannot narrate the full story, but the fragments of evidence seem to fit some of the theological shifts and controversies of her age.

Though no surviving cases allow us to plumb the depths of modern historians' questions, speculating on the ways in which religious interactions happened in more mundane settings allows us to "see" moments where the breach between cultural practices prompted intervention. The everyday life of work and family management were the two areas of greatest interaction between enslaved blacks and Barbadian Quakers, and so are the best ways to forge a path toward the unknowable, imagining what very well *may* have been. Work was the most prevalent area of interaction between masters and slaves, and it is not surprising that we see here the most tangible evidence for relationships based on a mutual understanding of the spiritual value of diligence in labor and excellence in craftsmanship. I have written elsewhere about how the Protestant work ethic, so valued by early modern Friends and other Protestants, informed interactions between the enslaved and Quaker slaveholders.[30] Missionaries to Barbados such as William Edmundson would have doubtless spoken during his travels about the moral virtues of hard work: "all [should] labor, for he that will not work, must not eat."[31] But did the same maxims get repeated outside the meetinghouse, when field laborers nearly fainted from the blistering sun and long exertion, when cooks and scullery maids sweated in the sweltering kitchens over feasts for their masters and guests, or during the frantic, round-the-clock efforts to precisely manage the sugar harvest so that planters would see a rich return on their investments?

Barbados wills show us that Friends made this spiritual mandate central to interactions with those they held as slaves. Martha Hooten, a widow living in Bridgetown in the early 1700s, may have used her wealth to comply with God's mandate to value labor, by providing an annual stipend to the eight slaves who labored in her home, a practice that would continue after her death. Writing her will, she required that "within one month after my decease [my executor should] Pay and deliver unto Every one of the negroes that I shall be Possesst of at the time of my decease as well them that I have Leased to Clayborne Hasleword . . . Twenty shills: yearely and Every year to each and every of these negroes following Dureing their & Every one of theire Naturall Lives." Hooten recognized, however, that there might be some resistance to her wishes that Tony, Cesar, Cuffy, Abraham, Nanny, Bussie, Andre, and Besse receive this allowance (she would have known that most Friends did not do the same, nor did many approve of her largesse, imagining the possible deleterious consequences of such generosity), and so she stipulated that if her first named executor refused to honor the clause that he should be deprived of the entire management of her estate.[32]

Quakers who aspired to evangelization by example may have also encouraged African initiates into their society to first develop a trade, a "calling." Therefore, enslaved men living in close proximity to their masters who wished to capitalize on that privilege would have to perform their diligence as workers devoted to their masters' business. "One Negroe Mann named Ockro, a Smith by Trade," may have been one who spoke of spiritual matters with his master Thomas Foster after he admired Ockro's workmanship. After all, blacksmiths were held in high esteem in many parts of West Africa for their mysterious ability to create swords and tools from earth, air, and fire. Smiths such as Ockro, trained as "craft specialists," were routinely set apart from other members of the community and were expected to operate their own cults of spiritual leadership, controlling rules of kinship and initiation.[33] Foster's regard for his blacksmith can be seen in the codicil he added to his will in 1684, protecting Ockro from being sold off as part of his general estate. Perhaps as part of an earlier agreement, Foster promised Ockro that he and "his tooles . . . [would] belong to the Plantacon whereon I now reside dureing his Life."[34] We must assume that he and others discussed similar proposals with Quaker planters or merchants, repeating their masters' words on the value of their work and their wish for a life worth living. We must also imagine the expressions of disappointment when Ockro learned he would not be freed in recognition of his work ethic. How would have Martha Hooten's slaves reacted if they were in fact denied their annual twenty shillings, if their mistress' fears came to pass that her financial arrangement with them would not be honored by her executor? Quakers' own profit motives would have conspired against the best efforts to put faith into action where work was concerned.

Family and child-rearing was another area in which the lives of enslaved and free in Quaker households would have overlapped, especially for women designated as cooks or wet nurses, as well as for those of both sexes who managed and maintained plantation households. At the core of Quaker conceptions of family lay the marital relationship. Fox's own remarks in his sermon on Gospel Family Order ordered Quaker masters that "if any of your Negroes desire to marry, let them take one another before Witnesses, in the Presence of God, and the Masters of the Families . . . [vowing] not to break the Covenant and Law of Marriage (nor defile the Marriage-Bed) as long as they lived . . . and so to record it in a Book"—the same way that they were to keep careful records of white births, marriages, and deaths.[35] If these records ever existed, their demise is yet another tragic loss to historians. Yet the prevalence of crude references to "breeding" among early travelers to Barbados suggests a pattern of thinking that Africans from polygamous cultures were hypersexual and animalistic by nature.[36] In both Fox's address to Quaker patriarchs and island authorities, indeed, he focused on the evils of polygamy, instructing planters to hold the enslaved to their promise not to "defile the Marriage-Bed" with any extramarital relations.[37] Later, William Edmundson lambasted Barbados leaders for failing to "restrai[n] [Negroes from] this filthy Liberty in the Lust of the Flesh, which fills your Island with Confusion, and makes it like a Sodom."[38] One of his main concerns was always that "there be a Godly care upon yor minds & Spirits to prevent & keep out all Debauchery, & uncleanness out of yor Familyes."[39] Admonishments of a similar nature appear in several Quaker epistles that mention the purpose of "family" meetings with blacks. A manuscript copy of Fox's exhortations at a Barbados Women's Meeting asks plantation mistresses to "endeavour to break ym off of yt Evil Custome among ym of runing [sic] after another Woman w[he]n married to one already."[40]

But even these sources cannot reveal how sexual unions were discussed between Quaker masters and their slaves. Certainly Quaker parents warned their children against too close contact with the opposite sex as they reached adolescence and marriageable age, and when a union was approved, celebrated the marriage with a ritual recognition of the new partnership. These ceremonies would have been times to discuss the "godly" procedures for joining a man and woman in marriage—solemnized rituals that Fox at least hoped would become the norm among enslaved people too. Reading extant wills, however, it would appear that few official unions were recognized. For example, Quaker Dennis Dynyne bequeathed both a male and female slave "with their increase" to each of his seven children, but never used the words "husband" and "wife."[41] Wealthy Friends almost never recognized marital bonds among their enslaved labor force and only occasionally made a real effort to keep mothers and children together. Quakers' silence on the issues of monogamy and marriage tells us much about the realities of separation in the black family under slavery.[42]

Did enslaved men and women turn to recriminations against masters who separated their families, making it impossible to maintain marital ties? Did they try to explain the purpose of polygamy once they learned that the Old Testament patriarchs also had multiple wives?[43] We are locked out of those heated arguments, the subtle coercions that would have characterized Quaker and enslaved interactions in Barbados. Their engagement at the spiritual level may have provoked arguments about what constituted "filthy uncleanness" in sexual relations, and resentments over how their cultures and traditions were so blithely dismissed. Many may have rejected the idea that their grueling labor was a spiritual discipline, their suffering a virtue. No doubt they resisted efforts to make blacks model their lives after European family structure when the stability and unity of enslaved families depended on the mercurial benevolence of those they would always have to call "master."

We should, nevertheless, entertain the idea that these concepts gave the enslaved a sense of purpose, stability, and hope. African and European interactions may have inspired agreement on the idea of work as a spiritual "calling," sacralizing occupations and turning industry into divine commandment. The enslaved man named Peter had no doubt negotiated with his master Henry Feake, a merchant, to make sure that he, his wife Bess, and their boy Paralie would all be manumitted together at Feake's death. Peter had earned the right to maintain possession of the "Chest, box, cloathes, [and] bedding" that Feake counted among *his* belongings, as well as "my carpenter, Masons and Coopers Tooles, [and] my Iron Vice and the musquett that is now in his custody." With these tools at Peter's disposal, his family could make the transition to freedom and self-sufficiency easier than most.[44] Those former slaves of Elizabeth Hooten, if they were indeed paid their bequests, likely bargained their social and spiritual capital into a way to join together to build homes for their families and produce crops that would provide for their sustenance, perhaps even buying the freedom of their wives or children from the inheritors of their master's estate, pointing to her idealism when faced with resistance.

By putting our imaginings and historical musings on the page, we feel more embedded in a world only very imperfectly represented in archival documents. Suddenly the occasional appearance of an enslaved family or person in Quaker wills—a young boy named Callabarry; a blacksmith named Ockro; Peter, a husband and father hoping to provide for his wife and their boy—allows us to think of the specific moments in which each interacted with the writer, creating a relationship that went beyond the mundane into spiritual, moral, and philosophical realms. We also become aware how rarely such interactions produced truly transformative understandings. It is clear from wills that Quakers' idealism was not enough to sympathize with black men and women more easily incorporated into account ledgers than the meetinghouse—this despite (today's) oft-quoted philosophical challenge by early missionary William Edmundson: "And many of you count it unlawfull to make Slaves of the Indians, and if soo [*sic*], then why the Negroes?"[45] It is equally unlikely that the Quaker way of seeing the world proved very tempting to many enslaved people. For most, as Karen Fog Olwig wrote of later Moravian involvement with the enslaved in the Danish West Indies, such evangelization efforts stimulated little more than a "resistant response."[46]

Historians should not replicate the creeping conservatism of the Society of Friends in the seventeenth century by adherence to strict empiricism—we can recreate an unknown past by examining the cultural and social milieu of both Africans brought forcibly to the island and their ostensible masters. We can reasonably surmise that religious/cosmological preconceptions may have led to flashes of spiritual connection—and that the underlying falsity of such cognates played a large part in reinforcing the dynamics of racialization and labor hierarchies already so strong among the population at large. Even if these questions rise out of modern scholarly (and political) dilemmas, they are issues that give history relevance, that allow us to think about the past anew, to rediscover something lost. Seeing Fox's iconic *Gospel Family Order* as the first step toward a heroic overthrow of slavery and racial prejudice has been a narrative planted and compacted by generations of Quaker scholarship. A close reexamination of the evidence suggests, I believe, a much less heroic reality, of the pitifully small gains he reaped with that effort in Barbados. But that reexamination should till up a whole new field of questions, for we cannot dismiss the reality that Fox found a few others who shared his concerns about the consequences of promoting an inescapable, lifelong servitude based on little more than a presumed difference in Africans' "nature" or their capacity or unwillingness to adopt Christianity. The glimpses we get in Quaker wills of the engagement with individual enslaved men and women, however limited, hint at much deeper conversations and struggles over questions of independence and moral obligations to one's community. By taking up a more imaginative exploration of these issues, historians must become more comfortable with crossing disciplinary boundaries such as religion and anthropology, fields that do not always privilege the nuances of change over time. They do, however, allow us to draw a bit closer to the human psyche and the recovery of historical realities.

NOTES

1. The most comprehensive recent study of Quakerism in Barbados is Larry Gragg, *The Quaker Community on Barbados: Challenging the Culture of the Planter Class* (Jefferson City: University of Missouri Press, 2009).

2. George Fox, *Gospel Family Order, Being a Short Discourse concerning the Ordering of Families, Both of Whites, Blacks, and Indians* ([London], 1676), 14.

3. Gragg, *Quaker Community*, chap. 7; Barbara Ritter Dailey, "The Early Quaker Mission and the Settlement of Meetings in Barbados, 1655–1700," *Journal of the Barbados Museum and Historical Society* 39 (1991): 24–46.

4. Joseph Besse, *A Collection of the Sufferings of the People Called Quakers*, 2 vols. (London: L. Hinde, 1753), 2:310, 349; *A Short Account of the Manifest Hand of God That Hath Fallen upon Several Marshals and Their Deputies: Who Have Made Great Spoil and Havock of the Goods of the People Called Quakers in the Island of Barbadoes* . . . (London, 1696), 18–19; Joan Vokins, *God's Mighty Power Magnified* (London, 1691), 43; William Edmundson, *A Journal of the Life, Travels, Sufferings and Labour of Love in the Work of the Ministry* . . . (London, 1715), 98.

5. William C. Brathwaite, *The Second Period of Quakerism* (Cambridge: Cambridge University Press, 1961), 280.

6. Fox, *Gospel Family Order*, 4–5; Joshua 24:15.

7. F[ox], G[eorge], *The Heathens Divinity Set upon the Heads of All Christians, That Say, They Had Not Known That There Had Been a God, or a Christ, unless the Scripture Had Declared It to Them* ([London], 1672/1673).

8. James L. Ash, Jr., "'Oh No, It Is Not the Scriptures!' The Bible and the Spirit in George Fox," *Quaker History* 63, no. 2 (1974): 94–107.

9. Kenneth L. Carroll, *John Perrot: Early Quaker Schismatic* (London: Friends' Historical Society, 1971).

10. Phyllis Mack, *Visionary Women: Ecstatic Prophecy in Seventeenth-Century England* (Berkeley: University of California Press, 1992), esp. chaps. 8, 9.

11. Edmundson, *Journal*, 310–11.

12. Thomas Crisp, *Babel's Builders Unmasking Themselves: As Appears by the Following Paper from Barbadoes, (Promoted by George for His Party, and Subscribed by Eighty Two of Them)* (London, 1681), 4.

13. Brathwaite, *Second Period*, 348–49.

14. Brycchan Carey, *From Peace to Freedom: Quaker Rhetoric and the Birth of American Antislavery, 1658–1761* (New Haven, Conn.: Yale University Press, 2012), chap. 1. [Alice and Thomas Curwen], *A Relation of the Labour, Travail and Suffering of That Faithful Servant of the Lord Alice Curwen* ([London], 1680), 18.

15. Thomas Edward Drake, *Quakers and Slavery in America* (New Haven, Conn.: Yale University Press, 1950), 7. Drake notes that this comment was only found in 1939, a segment of Fox's personal papers that had not been published—likely another example of later generations of Friends' discomfort with their leaders' ambivalent attitude regarding abolition.

16. Joseph Miller, "Retention, Reinvention, and Remembering: Restoring identities through enslavement in Africa and under slavery in Brazil" in *Enslaving Connections: Changing Cultures of Africa and Brail During the Era of Slavery*, ed. José C. Curto and Paul E. Lovejoy (New York: Humanity Books, 2004), 81–121.

17. John Thornton also emphasizes shared notions of continuous revelation as aiding Africans' adaptation of Christianity; *Africa and Africans in the Making of the Atlantic World, 1400–1800*, 2d ed. (Cambridge: Cambridge University Press, 1998), 257–61.

18. See Walter Rodney, *A History of the Upper Guinea Coast, 1545–1800* (Oxford: Clarendon Press, 1970), 110–11, 224–39; Sylviane A. Diouf, *Servants of Allah: African Muslims Enslaved in the Americas* (New York: New York University Press, 1998), 1–41.

19. Adam Jones, *From Slaves to Palm Kernels: A History of the Galinhas Country (West Africa), 1730–1890* (Wiesbaden: Steiner, 1983), 179–82.

20. G. P. Makris, "Historicising Possession," in *Changing Masters: Spirit Possession and Identity Construction among Slave Descendants and Other Subordinates in the Sudan* (Evanston, Ill.: Northwestern University Press, 2000), 1–20; Ann Taves, "Knowing through the Body: Dissociative Religious Experience in the African- and British-American Methodist Traditions," *Journal of Religion* 73, no. 2 (1993): 200–222; Sylvia R. Frey and Betty Wood, *Come Shouting to Zion: African American*

Protestantism in the American South and British Caribbean to 1830 (Chapel Hill: University of North Carolina Press, 1998).

21. Harry Emerson Wildes, *William Penn* (New York: Macmillan, 1974), 322.

22. Quoted in Carla Gerona, *Night Journeys: The Power of Dreams in Trans-Atlantic Quaker Culture* (Charlottesville: University of Virginia Press, 2004), 87–89.

23. John K. Thornton, *The Kongolese St. Anthony: Dona Kimpa Vita and the Antonian Movement, 1684–1706* (Cambridge University Press, 1998).

24. John Rous, *A Warning to the Inhabitants of Barbadoes: Who Live in Pride, Drunkennesse, Covetousnesse, Oppression and Deceitful Dealings; and also to All Who Are Found Acting in the Same Excess of Wickedness, of What Country Soever, That They Speedily Repent . . .* ([London, 1657]).

25. John M. Janzen, *Lemba, 1650–1930: A Drum of Affliction in Africa and the New World* (Garland Publishing, 1982); Miller, "Retention, Reinvention, and Remembering," 90.

26. Fox, *Gospel Family Order*, 16; Drake, *Quakers and Slavery*, 6; Haverford Library Special Collections, Richardson MSS, 86;Will of Rebecca Ormunt (d. ca. 1684–1685), BDA, RB6/10, 353–54; Will of Edward Parsons (d. 1700), BDA, RB6/43, 165–68.

27. Population estimates for Quakers in Barbados sit at well over one thousand for the seventeenth century. My prosopographical database of nearly eight hundred Barbadian Quakers allowed me to search for wills in the Barbados Department of Archives, resulting in a total of 181 wills, 76 of those for slaveholders, only 8 of which carried manumission clauses. Jerome S. Handler and John T. Pohlmann's island-wide statistical survey of manumission patterns found that 80 out of 3,777 Barbados testators (about 2%) manumitted one or more slaves "Slave Manumissions and Freedmen in Seventeenth-Century Barbados," *William and Mary Quarterly* 41, no. 3 (1984): 405.

28. William Penn, *Judas and the Jews Combined against Christ and His Followers . . .* (London, 1673), 51–52; Library of the Society of Friends (London), Box Mtg MSS, no. 30, 35; Will of Elizabeth Barnes (Brumes), d. 1681, BDA, RB6/8, 566–70.

29. Edmundson, *Journal*, 297.

30. Kristen Block, "Cultivating Inner and Outer Plantations: Property, Industry, and Slavery in Early Quaker Migration to the New World," *Early American Studies* 8, no. 3 (2010): 533–41; see also Katherine Carté Engel's contribution to the same issue of *Early American Studies*, "Religion and the Economy: New Methods for an Old Problem," 482–99.

31. Edmundson, *Journal*, 311.

32. Will of Martha Hooten (d. 1704), BDA, RB6/16, 188–89.

33. George E. Brooks, *Landlords and Strangers: Ecology, Society, and Trade in Western Africa, 1000–1630* (Boulder: Westview Press, 1993), 40, 290; Robert M. Baum, *Shrines of the Slave Trade: Diola Religion and Society in Precolonial Senegambia* (New York: Oxford University Press, 1999), 6, 33.

34. Will of Thomas Foster (d. 1685), BDA, RB6/10, 349–52. See also Block, "Cultivating Inner and Outer Plantations," 534–36.

35. Fox, *Gospel Family Order*, 17–18.

36. Jennifer L. Morgan, "'Some Could Suckle over their Shoulders': Male Travelers, Female Bodies, and the Gendering of Racial Ideology, 1500–1770," *William and Mary Quarterly* 54, no. 1 (1997): esp. 170–73, 183–86.

37. Fox, *Gospel Family Order*, 17–18.

38. Edmundson, "To the Governour and Council, and All in Authority, in This Island of Barbados" in Besse, *Sufferings*, 2:306–8.

39. W[illiam] E[dmundson], "For Friends in Maryland, Virginia, and other parts of America." HLSC, Richardson MSS epistle book, 43. See a transcript of this letter in *The Friend*, 61 (1887): 68.

40. "For the General Monthly, Quarterly, and Six Months Meetings in Barbadoes," HLSC, Richardson MSS epistle book, 111.

41. Will of Dennis Dynyne (d. 1697), BDA, RB6/1, 7–10.

42. Like in the will of Hester Foster (d. 1686), who named her slaves "Hagar and her three children by name, Mingoe, Bell and Man" (RB6/40, 343–345), John Grove (d. 1717) bequeathed his daughter a "negro woman named Rose & her three children Vizt. Maribah, Mercy & Judy." (RB6/4, 151–52).

43. Kristen Block, *Ordinary Lives in the Early Caribbean: Religion, Colonial Competition, and the Politics of Profit* (Athens: University of Georgia Press, 2012), 173–74, 185, 188.

44. Will of Henry Feake (d. ca. 1713–1716), BDA, RB6/4, 95–101.

45. J. William Frost, ed., *The Quaker Origins of Antislavery* (Norwood, Pa.: Norwood Editions, 1980), 68.

46. Karen Fox Olwig, "African Cultural Principles in Caribbean Slave Societies: A View from the Danish West Indies," in Stephen Palmié, ed. *Slave Cultures and the Cultures of Slavery* (Knoxville: University of Tennessee Press, 1995), 36.

7 Anthony Benezet
Working the Antislavery Cause inside and outside of "The Society"

MAURICE JACKSON

MORE THAN ANY OTHER INDIVIDUAL'S WORK in the eighteenth century, that of Anthony Benezet served as a catalyst, throughout the Atlantic world, for the initial organized fight against slave trade and the eventual ending of slavery. His written work, which combined Quaker principles and Enlightenment thinking with knowledge gained through a deep study of Africa and her history, and his own contacts with black people as a teacher and philanthropist influenced men from Benjamin Franklin to John Jay and Patrick Henry in North America; from Thomas Clarkson, Granville Sharp, and William Wilberforce in England; to Condorcet and the Abbé Raynal in France. His words helped inspire African-born Olaudah Equiano and Ottabah Cugoano to write, and students at his Quaker schools such as American-born blacks Richard Allen and Absalom Jones to organize.

Anthony Benezet was born to Huguenot (Protestant) parents in St. Quentin, Picardy, France, on January 31, 1713. His parents had braved a generation of intensifying religious persecution, during which they were forced to join the Roman Catholic Church, into which Anthony was baptized the day after he was born. His father Jean Etienne Benezet belonged to a nonviolent Huguenot resistance group called Inspires de la Vaunage, but in 1715, he finally fled with his young family to Holland and then to England. Anthony would later tell his friend François Barbé-Marbois, Marquis de Barbé-Marbois, of his family's oppression by French persecutors: "one of my uncles was hung by those intolerants, my aunt was put in a convent, two of my cousins died in the galleys, and my fugitive father was hung in effigy for explaining the gospel differently from the priests, and the family was ruined by the confiscation of his property."[1] Such a family history might have led Anthony in various directions; whether for this reason or not, he came to have a deep sympathy for other oppressed and exiled people, particularly enslaved Africans.

Although moderately successful during sixteen years in England, Jean Benezet moved his family in 1731 to Philadelphia. While Quakers associated with them during their first years in Philadelphia, the Benezet family was not yet Quaker; Anthony's father and several of his sisters soon joined the Moravian Brethren. Jean also admired the great English evangelist George Whitefield and revealed his own sympathy for blacks by contributing to Whitefield's unsuccessful attempt to start the Nazareth training school for blacks on 5,000 acres of land near the Delaware River.

Anthony had been apprenticed to a Quaker merchant in London. As a merchant in training, he was not a success, but he was attracted to his master's religion and eventually he became a Quaker. In Philadelphia, on May 13, 1736, he married Joyce Marriot, granddaughter of prominent Quaker physician and "ministering Friend" Griffith Owen. Both the children born to Joyce and Anthony died in infancy. Joyce, like her grandfather, became a "ministering Friend," a public spiritual figure in a religious community that allowed women to address religious meetings and did not believe in a "hireling ministry."

Even though he was the eldest son of a versatile father who had now become a successful Philadelphia dry goods importer, Anthony Benezet had no desire to join his brother in business. He wrote to a friend, "I find being amongst the buyers and sellers rather a snare to me."[2] He had a small frame and a "frail constitution," and because of this, he sought what he thought would be a less strenuous vocation. Equally importantly, his love of books, his mastery of several languages, his love of children, and his passion for the truth led him to become a teacher. In 1742, he took charge of the Friend's English School in Philadelphia (later renamed the William Penn Charter School). He also founded a school for Quaker girls in 1755. Nonetheless, what most distinguished Benezet from his Quaker contemporaries was his free association with blacks.

Benezet began teaching blacks in his home in the evenings in 1750; after two decades of private tutoring, he established the Friends School for Black People, later called the African Free School, which opened its doors in the summer of 1770. Benezet later wrote, "having observed the many disadvantages these afflicted people labor under in point of educations and otherwise, a tender care has taken place to promote their instruction in school learning, and also their religious and temporal welfare." He reverted uncharacteristically to the third person in the epilogue to his *Short Observations on Slavery*:

A. Benezet teacher in a school established by the private subscription, in Philadelphia, for the instruction of the Black children and others of that people, has for years, had the opportunity of knowing the temper and genius of the Africans; particularly of those under his tuition, who had many, of different ages . . . and he is bold to assert, that the notion entertained by some, that the Blacks are inferior to the Whites in their capacities, is a vulgar prejudice, founded on the Pride of Ignorance of their lordly masters who have kept their slaves at such a distance, as to be unable to form a right judgment of them.[3]

Students at the school included Absalom Jones, the first priest of African descent in the Protestant Episcopal Church. Richard Allen, the founder of the African Methodist Episcopal Church, also greatly appreciated Benezet's work as teacher and abolitionist. Together they founded the Free African Society in 1797. Another student at what became known as Benezet's School was James Forten, the sail maker and entrepreneur. These three free blacks had petitioned Congress to repeal the Fugitive Slave Act of 1793, and Allen and Jones assisted Dr. Benjamin Rush during the yellow fever epidemic in 1793. Forten would also lead the opposition to the American Colonization Society and its efforts to send free blacks back to uncertain lives in unfamiliar Africa.

Linking his Quaker beliefs with his growing hatred of slavery, Benezet began his career as a teacher, writer, and activist with the purpose of freeing enslaved Africans as well as educating them. There were several intellectual, religious, and social links between Benezet's Quakerism and abolitionism. The first was "that all people were equal in the sight of God" and carried an "inner light" within them. A second important influence was the Quaker doctrine of nonviolence, and a third Quaker rule was "that Friends should avoid ostentation and sloth in their daily lives" as that "made both masters and children lazy." Benezet believed that greed, luxury, and vanity corrupted human beings and that the quest for wealth was the root of the evils of his time, including the burgeoning Atlantic slave trade. One of his early anti-slavery tracts argued: "Thus an insatiable desire for gain hath become the principal and moving cause of the most abominable and dreadful scene that was perhaps ever acted upon the face of the earth."[4] Tying the slave trade to a worldwide drive for profits, Benezet wrote to his friend Samuel Fothergill, "it is frequent to see even Friends, toiling year after year, enriching themselves, and thus gathering fuel for our children's vanity and corruption." He believed that anyone "who is not blinded by the Desire of Gain"[5] should recognize that "the right by which these Men hold the Negro in Bondage is no other than what is derived by those who stole them."[6] In 1758, the Philadelphia Yearly Meeting seemed poised to defeat a motion requiring Quakers to disavow slavery and free their slaves. Benezet, who had been silent throughout the meeting, solemnly rose. Weeping profusely, he walked to the front of the meeting and recited a well-known passage from the Book of Psalms 68.31:

"Ethiopia shall soon stretch out her hands unto God." His message was that the children of Africa were God-fearing, God-loving, and worthy of God's grace. Benezet's message, backed by his life of service, carried the day.

Although the Quakers had finally taken their initial stand on religious grounds, slavery continued to flourish among a much larger group of people who could not be converted by religious arguments alone. In his unending campaign against the slave trade and slavery, Benezet incorporated secular arguments from an impressive array of reading. He was a founding contributor to the Library Company of Philadelphia, and his library was full of current scientific studies, and he read from the libraries of prominent Philadelphia gentlemen including James Logan, Benjamin Rush, and Benjamin Franklin. Benezet used every available source to add rational support for his religious, moral, and ethical arguments against slavery.

Like many writers of the time—particularly Dissenters in the English-speaking world—Benezet relied heavily on biblical citations to buttress his arguments, but he found rational endorsement for his crusade in the writings of enlightened philosophers and jurists. Charles Louis Secondat, Baron de Montesquieu clearly denounced slavery in his *The Spirit of the Laws* (1748). Montesquieu wrote, "the state of slavery is in its own nature bad. It is neither useful to the master or to the slave; not to the slave because he can do nothing through a motive of virtue; nor to the master, because by having an unlimited authority over his slaves he insensibly accustoms himself to the want of all moral values." This caused man to become "fierce, hasty, severe, choleric, voluptuous and cruel."[7] Benezet endorsed Montesquieu's argument that slavery had a destructive effect on both the state and free men therein; he noted that slavery destroyed both the white soul and the black body.

The gentle Quaker was deeply influenced by the Scottish moral philosophers. The first of these men he quoted from was Francis Hutcheson, who in his *System of Moral Philosophy* (1755) declared, "no endowments natural or acquired, can give a perfect right to assume power over others, without their consent."[8] Hutcheson reasoned, "all men have strong desires of liberty and property, have notions of right, and strong natural impulses to marriage, families, and offspring, and earnest desires of their safety."[9] Hutcheson insisted that slaves who were sold into far away countries had never legally forfeited their freedom, and he argued for universal liberty, happiness, and benevolence. Benezet generally agreed with Hutcheson, except on the right of the enslaved to use violence in resistance. As a pacifist Quaker, Benezet hoped to avoid violence through black education and white renunciation of slavery.

Benezet was also fond of Scottish jurist George Wallace's *A System of the Principles of the Law of Scotland* (1760), especially his idea that there could never be any legal title for the possession of one human being by another, and thus all transactions for human flesh were legally void. Wallace wrote, "Men and their liberty are not '*in commercia*'; they are not either saleable or purchasable. . . . For every one of those unfortunate men are pretended to be slaves, has a right to be declared free, for he never lost his liberty; he could not lose it; his Prince had no power to dispose of him."[10] At another point, Wallace went a step further in his beliefs. He wrote, "property, that bane of human felicity is too deeply rooted in Society, and is thought to be too essential to the sustenance of it, easily to be abolished. But it must necessarily be banished out of the world, before an Utopia can be established."[11] Benezet embraced natural law theory to insist that every human was born free by a right based in the law of nature. Yet the political remained religious. Government was an "ordinance of God," and "no legislature on earth can alter the nature of things, so as to make that to be right which is contrary to the law of God."[12] He argued, "liberty is the right of every human creature, as soon as he breathes the vital air. And no human law can deprive him of the right, which he derives from the law of nature."[13]

Like Adam Smith, Benezet argued that slavery diminished the productive capacity and corrupted the morals of both blacks and whites. History can be a powerful aid to revolution, and he studied African history with a clear purpose and remarkable care. In seeking to understand African folkways and customs, he read all the available English, French, and Dutch sources, consulting an impressive number of the narratives of adventurers, factors, and accountants of the Royal African Company, as well as those of the surgeons and crewmen of the slave ships. His most important works on Africa were *Observations on the Inslaving, Importing and Purchasing of Negroes* (1759), *A Short Account of That Part of Africa Inhabited by the Negroes* (1762), and *Some Historical Observations of Guinea* (1771). This third, ambitious study was divided into twenty-one chapters discussing "the different parts of Africa, from which the Negro is brought to America." Benezet laid out several premises that directly contradicted prevailing European notions of Africa. He insisted, "scarce a country in the whole world is better calculated for affording the necessary comforts of life to its inhabitants" that the Africans "still retain a great deal of innocent simplicity: and when not stirred up to revenge from the frequent abuses they have received from the Europeans in general, manifest themselves to be a human, sociable people, whose faculties are as capable of improvement as those of other men." Finally, he asserted that their economy and government was in many ways commendable, and "it appears that they might have lived happy, if not disturbed by the Europeans." His wide-ranging study included a description of southernmost Africa, a country "settled by Caffers and Hottentots: Who have never been concerned in the making or selling of slaves." He explored in detail what was known of the Kongo and Old Benin, in present-day Nigeria. Later in the work, he described the lives of the "Jalofs, Fulis, and Mandingos" of West Africa.[14] He directly confronted the myth of the natural inferiority of Africans and the superiority of the Europeans who came to save the supposedly "feeble race." He described an abundant Africa, inhabited by people who produced only what they needed. Rare for his era, Benezet distinguished between those Africans who collaborated with slave traders and those who were victims. His understanding of the societies, tribal structures, and social geography of eighteenth-century Africa were remarkably accurate for a writer of his time. *Some Historical Account* became a first school textbook on Africa (and was later assigned in Reconstruction schools).

Benezet entered the debate over the number of blacks forcibly taken from Africa, the number perishing during the Middle Passage, and the number reaching the New World. He started by extracting from the printed *Liverpool Memorandum-Book* a list of that port's slave trade, which he estimated carried thirty thousand Africans a year into American slavery. Adding an estimate for the London and Bristol trades, he concluded that "at least One Hundred Thousand Negroes [are] purchased and brought on board our ships yearly from the coast of Africa."[15] He knew that millions of enslaved Africans did not reach western shores due to disease, maltreatment, and resistance, mainly by leaping overboard during the Atlantic crossing.

Benezet was primarily addressing English-speaking audiences, and he paid special attention to the English colonies of Jamaica and Barbados. He described the white indentured servants of Barbados and argued that Europeans were as suitable as Africans for labor in the tropics. He quoted the rector of St. Lucy parish in Barbados, who believed that if there were any inadequacies among blacks in the arts or in the "common affairs" of life, it was due to lack of education and the "depression of their spirits by slavery" rather than any lack of natural ability. Benezet's evaluation of the situation for the blacks in the West Indies was confirmed by the unnamed author of *An Account of the European Settlements in America,* who wrote, "the Negroes in our colonies endure a slavery more complete, and attended with far worse circumstances, than what any people in their condition suffer in any other place in the world, or have suffered in any other period of time." In *A Short*

Account, Benezet had already documented the treatment of the slaves in Barbados. Using the account of Sir Hans Sloane, the well-known English author of the *History of Jamaica,* Benezet detailed the atrocities against the blacks. As he made note of the disproportionate number of blacks to whites in South Carolina, Benezet used Sloane to describe Jamaica as having three times as many blacks as whites and to indicate that, because the slaves made frequent attempts to revolt, blacks were never trusted or left idle. Benezet believed that once the enslaved Africans realized their own strength, they would try to "get their Liberty, or to deliver themselves out of the miserable slavery they are in."[16]

Benezet closely collaborated with the Quaker leader John Woolman. He also had a tremendous influence on Benjamin Franklin, who credited his pamphlets and antislavery petition efforts with the decision of the Virginia House of Burgesses to petition the king for an end to the slave trade in 1772. Benezet brought the Philadelphia physician Benjamin Rush, who later wrote anonymous tracts condemning slavery, into the struggle for black freedom. Benezet wrote many hundreds of letters, corresponding with religious leaders such as George Whitefield, John Wesley, and Moses Brown and secular leaders such as Franklin and Rush about his views on slavery and the slave trade. Wesley's *Thoughts upon Slavery* (1774) is based almost entirely on Benezet's *Some Historical Observations of Guinea,* and the Quaker thanked the founder of Methodism for using his work. Upon receiving one of Benezet's pamphlets, sent to him by the Virginia Quaker Robert Pleasants, the future Patriot firebrand Patrick Henry wrote on January 18, 1773: "I take this Opportunity to acknowledge ye receipt of Anthony Benezet's book against the slave trade. I thank ye for it." Henry added ruefully, "would anyone believe that I am a Master of Slaves of my own purchase? I am drawn along by ye general Inconvenience of living without them; I will not, I cannot justify it."[17]

As the American Revolution approached, Benezet readily exploited the obvious irony of the rhetoric of revolutionaries railing against tyranny and the threat of their own "enslavement" while holding slaves themselves. In the wake of the Stamp Act crisis, he had already asked "how many of those who distinguish themselves as the Advocates of Liberty, remain insensible and inattentive to the treatment of thousands and tens of thousands of our fellow man," the enslaved Africans. Benezet refused to accept the hypocrisy of many of his peers such as Benjamin Franklin and Patrick Henry who said they opposed slavery yet owned slaves.

When kidnapped blacks were transported through Philadelphia on their way south, Benezet intervened to obtain their freedom; his actions helped lead to the formation of the Society for the Relief of Free Negroes Unlawfully Held in Bondage on April 14, 1775. Throughout the Revolutionary War, he sought to extend to the blacks the rights that the American revolutionaries had won for themselves. He wrote in *Notes on the Slave Trade*:

It cannot be that either war, or contract, can give any man such a property in another as he has in his sheep or oxen. Much less is it possible, that any child of man ever be born a Slave. Liberty is the right of every human creature, as soon as he breathes the vital air. And no human law can deprive him of that right; he derives from the right of nature.[18]

As a pacifist, Benezet had not believed in the American revolutionaries' right to use violence in resisting George III's government; surprisingly, Benezet was able to publish antiwar pamphlets in Philadelphia repeatedly during the American Revolution. He was also concerned throughout his writings with the danger that slavery would provoke violent uprisings. In a letter to his friend Joseph Phipps, Benezet wrote:

With respect to the Danger of the Southern Colonies are exposed to from the vast disproportion there is between the number of Negroes, the whites, but it was too tender a point to expose to ye view of such of the blacks, as can read. In the treatise, the Proportion in South Carolina is said to be fifteen Blacks to a white, but by their own account, the difference is rather twenty to one. In Georgia and South Carolina the Negroes are not hemmed in by the some hundreds of miles, as they are in the Islands, but have a back Country uninhibited for some hundreds of miles, where the Negroes might not only retire, but who expect to be supported & assisted by the Indians.[19]

He realized that in places such as South Carolina, where blacks outnumbered whites significantly, the potential for violent revolution existed. Benezet saw the potential of African and Native American unity in the face of white rule.

Benezet was much more tolerant of the propensity of the Africans, in the words of the old Negro spiritual, to "Steal Away." Running away seemed legitimate resistance. In numerous publications, he denounced laws that encouraged the murder of runaways. In his letter to Phipps, he had referred approvingly to the Maroons, escaped slaves who established their own runaway communities. In South Carolina, this occurred near the Sea Islands of the Atlantic Coast, but maroonage was much more common in the mountainous areas of the West Indies, in Latin America, and especially in Brazil. Benezet alluded to the necessity to make plans for the "freedom of those amongst us, after a reasonable period of time." He later called for some reparations to the freed blacks in the form of communally shared land. This land-sharing plan was amazingly similar to African forms of communalism, or primitive communism, which existed before European conquest, and which Benezet knew from his reading. His idea of giving land to the newly freed blacks proceeded the Reconstruction dream of "forty acres and a mule" by almost a century.[20]

In preparing *An Essay on the Slavery and Commerce of the Human Species, particularly the African, (1786),* the British abolitionist Thomas Clarkson wrote of Benezet's *Some Historical Account of Guinea* that "in this precious book, I found almost all I wanted."[21] Benezet's descriptions of Africa proved to be so central that William Wilberforce quoted Benezet at length in the great 1792 Parliamentary debates on ending the slave trade. At that time, a motion was forwarded in favor of abolishing that trade—the first such action taken in any parliamentary body in the world. Although it did not win passage, it is credited with having brought about the beginning of the end of the international slave trade. Benezet corresponded with the founders of the Société des Amis des Noirs (Society of the Friends of the Blacks) in Paris, who initially authorized the translation of works on Africa. Among these men were Jean-Pierre Brissot; Nicolas Caritat, Marquis de Condorcet, a politician and defender of human rights, especially for women and blacks; Étienne Clavière, a peer of Brissot's in the Girondist movement; Honoré Gabriel Victor Riqueti, Comte de Mirabeau, who was imprisoned because of his revolutionary activities; Abbé Guillaume-Thomas Raynal, a Jesuit priest who left the order to devote his life to politics; and Bishop Henri Grégoire, the leading antislavery figure during the French Revolution.

Charles Ignatius Sancho wrote in 1778 about "the Christian, the learned author of that most valuable book *Some Historical Account of Guinea,*" Anthony Benezet.[22] The Quaker's work also greatly influenced the famed African-born abolitionists Quobna Ottabah Cugoano and Olaudah Equiano. Both of these men were kidnapped as children from Africa and relied on Benezet's writings to enhance their knowledge of their homelands. Formerly enslaved Cugoano, whose account *Thoughts and Sentiments on the Evil and Wicked Traffic of Slavery and Commerce of the Human Species* was first published in London in 1787, referred his readers to "the worthy and judicious" Benezet as giving "some very striking estimations of the exceeding evil occasioned by that wicked diabolical traffic of the African slave trade."[23]

Some Historical Account of Guinea was praised two years later by Olaudah Equiano. Kidnapped as a child, Equiano relied upon Benezet when telling of his native Nigeria. Equiano's dramatic kidnapping scene in *Interesting Narrative of the Life of Olaudah Equiano or Gustavus Vasa, the African* (1789) is remarkably similar to a description printed by Benezet eighteen years earlier. He advised his readers in his *The Interesting Narrative* to "see Anthony Benezet throughout" to bolster his own description of the Africa of his youth, before the "arrival of the Europeans."[24] In depicting his Igbo culture and homeland, in what later became Nigeria, Equiano closely followed Benezet's geographical and physical accounts.

Like other opponents of slavery in the 1780s, Benezet came to focus on the abolition of the slave trade as the practical first target in the abolition of slavery. In 1783, he wrote to Britain's Queen Charlotte, urging her to help end the British slave trade. His *Notes on the Slave Trade* exclaimed the "inconsistence of slavery with every right of mankind, with every feeling of humanity, and every precept of Christianity; not to point out its inconsistency with the welfare, peace and prosperity of every country, in proportion as it prevails." He described the sufferings the trade brought upon the blacks, and then confronted the whites directly. First, he addressed the "captains employed in the trade." He described the kindness of the African people whom the slavers separated from their loved ones, then:

> forced them into your ships, like a herd of swine . . . You have stowed [them] together as close as they ever could lie, without any regard to decency . . . Such slavery . . . is not found among the Turks at Algiers, no, nor among the heathens in America.

Benezet begged the slave-trading captains to quit their horrid trade immediately. He then turned his attention to the slave merchant, telling him, "it is your money, that is the spring of all." He challenged the morality of the slave sellers and urged them to promise hypothetically that "I will never buy a slave more while I live." Moving in on the conscience of the reformed merchant and his readers, Benezet asserted, "Oh let his resolution be yours! Have no more any part in this detestable business."

Benezet appealed to the plantation owner who might claim, "I pay honestly for my goods, and am not concerned to know how they are come by." The goods referred to were, of course, his chattel slaves, whom the plantation owner viewed merely as part of his property. Benezet accused the planter of not being as honest as a pickpocket, housebreaker, or highwayman. He indicted him for fraud, robbery, and murder and told him that it was his "money that pays the merchant, and through him the captain and the African butchers" before concluding that he was "the spring that puts all the rest in motion." Thus no one who had any part in slavery, from the "man stealer," to the ship captain, to the merchant, to the plantation owner, to the men or women who proclaimed innocence because they inherited the homeless slave, was truly innocent.

Benezet repeatedly confronted those who claimed, "that if the English were to drop this Trade entirely, it would be immediately thereupon carried on by other Nations, to a much greater Degree than it is now." He also challenged those who asserted that an end to slavery "would lessen if not ruin, some other considerable branches of our commerce, especially the Sugar and Tobacco Trades, because of the Difficulty in getting Hands enough, in the room of the Blacks, to work and labor in those plantations."[25] Characteristically, he answered in moral terms, reinforced with facts about the ability of white labor to perform adequately in tropical weather. He ended by alerting whites to the "impending catastrophe" of slave revolt if the trade continued.

In early 1787, a number of free blacks including Richard Allen and Absalom Jones met to discuss forming a religious society. Feeling that their numbers were too small and their religious sensibilities too many, they instead formed, in April 1787, the Free African Society, at the home of Richard Allen. Its articles of incorporation were written under the aura of Benezet and indeed specified, "It is always understood that one of the people called Quakers . . . is to be chosen to act as Clerk and Treasurer of this useful institution."[26] Beginning in early 1789, the society held its meetings at the Quaker building known as Benezet's African School House. The society began circulating petitions that were modeled in part on Benezet's earlier ones, and James Forten's opposition to colonization schemes was similar to Benezet's. In voicing his opposition to colonization, Benezet was an early advocate of giving land to free blacks.

The educator wrote to his friend Benjamin Franklin on March 5, 1783, one year before he died, about his life teaching blacks: "I know no station in life I should prefer before it."[27] Friend Anthony Benezet died on May 3, 1784. His last will and testament began with the words "Be it remembered that I, Anthony Benezet, a teacher of the Free School for the Black People of Philadelphia." In death, as in life, Benezet served as a symbol to those who fought against slavery. He usually led by quiet example and devout work. He had lived modestly and plainly, preferring to use his meager salary as a teacher to help defray the cost of his writings and to run the Quaker schools. *The Pennsylvania Gazette* as well as *Watson's Annual Journal* wrote of Benezet's death on May 13, 1784, and noted that hundreds of blacks followed his coffin in the streets. The *Gazette's* obituary provided more details of his bequests to educate blacks: "in his last will and testimony [he] bequeathed the annual; income of his whole estate, forever (after the decease of his wife), for the instruction and education of Negroe and Mulattoe children."

Although Benezet said upon his deathbed, "I am dying and feel ashamed to meet the face of my maker, I have done so little in his cause," the blacks who followed and wept at his funeral procession felt otherwise. He need not have uttered his deathbed fear that he had not done enough. The enslaved African men, women, and children whom he fought to free viewed him as a saint among sinners, a healer amid the wounded, and a godsend among infidels. That is why the largest gathering of blacks in Philadelphia, up until that time, and a comparable number of whites, followed his casket along the city streets to the burial grounds of the Society of Friends. Of his funeral, Benezet's first biographer wrote:

> never had the city on such an occasion seen a demonstration in which persons of all classes participated. There were the officials of the city, men of all trades and professions, various sects and denominations, and hundreds of Negroes testifying by their attendance, and by their tears, the grateful sense they entertained of his pious efforts on their behalf.[28]

What set Benezet apart from others was his great imagination in using every available resource to develop new methods in the arena of antislavery politics. Guided by his Quaker religion, he universalized the belief that all human beings were equal in God's sight. At the very root of his thinking was the belief that black men, women, and children were human beings. Summing up the general feeling about the passing of Benezet, Jean-Pierre Brissot, the famed French writer and revolutionary, wrote for humanists everywhere:

> What author, what great man, will ever be followed to his grave by four hundred Negroes, snatched by his own assiduity, his own generosity, from ignorance, wretchedness, and slavery? Who then has a right to speak haughtily of this benefactor of men? . . . Where is the man in all of Europe, of whatever rank or birth, who is equal to Benezet? Who is not obliged to respect him? How long will authors suffer themselves to be shackled by the prejudices of society? Will they never perceive that nature has created all men equal, that wisdom and virtue are the only criteria of superiority? Who was more virtuous than Benezet? Who was more useful to society, to mankind?[29]

Long after Benezet's death, antislavery advocates continued to invoke his name, and antislavery newspapers and periodicals of the early nineteenth century, time and again, resurrected his legacy. African American leaders continued to pay homage to the gentle Quaker decades after his death. A half century after he died, James Forten Jr., the eldest son of the famed black abolitionist and student at the Benezet School, spoke before the Philadelphia Female Anti-Slavery Society in April 1836: "You are called fanatics. Well what if you are . . . There is eloquence in such fanaticism for it whispers hope to the slave; there is sanctity in it, for it contains the consecrated spirit of religion; it is the fanaticism of a Benezet, a Rush, a Franklin, a Jay."[30] That the descendant of a slave invoked the name of Benezet first among those in the antislavery crusade shows the depth of black admiration for the man who dedicated his life to their cause and internationalized the struggle for their freedom.

NOTES

1. François, Marquis de Barbé-Marbois, *Our Revolutionary Forefathers: The Letters of François, Marquis de Barbé-Marbois: During His Residency in the United States as Secretary of the French Legation,* trans. and ed. Eugene Parker Chase (1969; repr., Freeport, N.Y.: Books for Library Press, 1990), 139.

2. *Friends' Miscellany,* vol. 3, no. 3, tenth month, 1832.

3. Anthony Benezet, *Short Observations on Slavery, Introductory to Some Extracts from the Writing of the Abbé Raynal on that Important Subject* (Philadelphia: 1781), 11–12.

4. Anthony Benezet, *A Caution and a Warning to Great Britain and Her Colonies in a Short Representation of the Calamitous State of the Enslaved Negroes in the British Dominions. Collected from Various Authors, and Submitted to the Serious Considerations of All, and More Especially of Those in Power.* (Philadelphia: Henry Miller, 1766), 16.

5. Anthony Benezet to Samuel Fothergill, November 27, 1758, Haverford College Quaker Collection.

6. Anthony Benezet, *A Short Account of that Part of Africa . . . and the Manner by Which the Slave-Trade Is Carried On* (Philadelphia: 1762), 64.

7. Montesquieu, Charles de Secondat, Baron de, *The Spirit of the Laws* (Cambridge: Cambridge University Press, 1989; first edition Paris, 1748), bk. 15, chap. 1, p. 246.

8. Francis Hutcheson, *A System of Moral Philosophy* (Edinburgh: 1755), bk. 2, chap. 5, sec. 2, p. 301.

9. Hutcheson, *A System of Moral Philosophy,* bk. 1, chap. 1, sec.1.

10. George Wallace, *A System of the Principles of the Laws of Scotland* (Edinburgh, 1760), 95–96. Benezet first used this quote in *Short Account of Africa.*

11. Wallace, *A System of the Principles of the Law of Scotland,* 90.

12. Anthony Benezet, *The Plainness and Innocent Simplicity of the Christian Religion* (Philadelphia:1782), 14.

13. Anthony Benezet, *Notes on the Slave Trade* (Philadelphia: 1781), 8. Benezet did not accept the Aristotelian notion that some men were born to be slaves or Hobbes's view that the powerful had the right to enslave the weak.

14. Anthony Benezet, *Some Historical Account of Guinea, Its Situation, Produce, and General Disposition of Its Inhabitants, with an Inquiry into the Rise and Progress of the Slave Trade, Its Nature and Lamentable Effects* (Philadelphia: 1771), ii, 1, 4, 8.

15. Benezet, *A Caution and a Warning*, 30.

16. Benezet, *A Short Account of That Part of Africa*, 57.

17. Patrick Henry to Robert Pleasants, January 18, 1773, Haverford College Quaker Collection.

18. Benezet, *Notes on the Slave Trade*, 8.

19. Anthony Benezet to Joseph Phipps, May 28, 1763, Haverford College Quaker Collection.

20. Maurice Jackson, *Let This Voice Be Heard: Anthony Benezet. Father of Atlantic Abolitionism* (Philadelphia: University of Pennsylvania Press, 2009), 212–14.

21. Thomas Clarkson, *The History of the Rise, Progress and Accomplishments of the Abolition of the African Slave-Trade by the British Parliament*, 2 vols. (London: Longman, Hurst, Rees, and Orme,1808), 1, 208–9.

22. Ignatius Sancho, "Letter LVII to Mr. F[isher] Charles Street, January 27, 1788," in Vincent Carretta, ed., *Letters of the Late Ignatius Sancho an African* (New York: Penguin Books, 1989), 111–12.

23. Quobna Ottabah Cugoano, *Thoughts and Sentiments on the Evil and Wicked Traffic of Slavery and Commerce of the Human Species,* ed. Vincent Carretta, (New York: Penguin Classics, 1999), 75.

24. Olaudah Equiano, *The Interesting Narrative of the Life of Olaudah Equiano or Gustavus Vassa, the African*, ed. Robert J. Allison (New York: Bedford, 1995), 39.

25. Benezet, *Notes on the Slave Trade*, 1, 3, 6–7, 7.

26. William Douglass, *Annals of the First African Church in the United States of America, now Styled the African Episcopal Church of St. Thomas* (Philadelphia, 1862), 17–18.

27. Anthony Benezet to Benjamin Franklin, March 5, 1783, Haverford College Quaker Collection.

28. Roberts Vaux, *Memoirs of the Life of Anthony Benezet* (Philadelphia, 1817), 134.

29. Jacques-Pierre Brissot, Extracts from a Critical Examination of the Marquis De Chasellux's Travels in North American in a Letter Addressed to the Marquis, dates July 1, 1786. Trinity College, Atkinson Library, Hartford, Connecticut.

30. Philip S. Foner and George E. Walker, eds. *Proceedings of the Black State Conventions, 1840–1865*, Vol. 1: *New York, Pennsylvania, Indiana, Michigan, Ohio* (Philadelphia: Temple University Press, 1979), 125.

8   Aim for a Free State and Settle among Quakers
African-American and Quaker Parallel Communities in Pennsylvania and New Jersey

CHRISTOPHER DENSMORE

The confluence of the history of slavery and the politics of race suggest that slavery has become a language—a way to talk about race—in a society in which black people and white people hardly talk at all.
—Ira Berlin

OVER THE PAST SEVERAL YEARS, I have given a fair amount of "public history" talks to local historical societies, cultural organizations, conferences, and meetings. With public audiences, the questions and discussions inevitably turn toward contemporary concerns about race relations. The discussions are not always comfortable because when the issue is race, people care a great deal about how the issues are presented and interpreted. My own interests have shifted from a focus on Quaker antislavery to an interest in how African Americans and Quakers interacted. The story presented here focuses on Chester County, Pennsylvania, and Greenwich Township, Cumberland County, New Jersey, ca. 1820 to 1860. What does this history tell us about who we are as people and as Americans?

The African American abolitionist Samuel Ringgold Ward wrote in his autobiography that when his family escaped from the Eastern Shore of Maryland in 1820, their objective was to "go to a free state and live among Quakers." They were headed toward Greenwich Township, in Cumberland County, New Jersey, "where they had learned slavery did not exist . . . [and] Quakers lived in numbers, who would afford the escaped any and every protection consistent with their peculiar tenets—and where a number of blacks lived, who in cases of emergency could and would make common cause with and for each other."[1] Ward's characterization of New Jersey as a "free state" needs qualification. According to the 1820 census, New Jersey had 20,017 people of color, and 7,557 of those remained enslaved. The populations of free and enslaved were not evenly distributed across the state. In Bergan County, in the north of the state, the majority of African Americans remained enslaved, and the enslaved were more than 9 percent of the population. But the Wards were going to Cumberland County, in the southern part of the state, where the 1820 census reported only 18 slaves, 0.1 percent of the population. Slavery was not dead in Cumberland County, but 97 percent of its African American population was free.[2] Greenwich, with its free black communities of Springtown and Othello, was one of a number of "parallel communities" in New Jersey where African Americans and Quakers lived in proximity.[3]

In 1824, eleven members of the Trusty family escaped from the Eastern Shore. They traveled by night until reaching the home of Quaker Thomas Garrett in Wilmington, Delaware. After leaving Wilmington, the party split up, some going to New Jersey and the others to New York City. In freedom, the family adopted the surname Garnet. One member of the family was a nine-year-old who was to become the well-known abolitionist Henry Highland Garnet.[4] How the Ward family in 1820 and the Trusty/Garnet family in 1824 knew of the existence of a small, rural New Jersey community is a mystery. It may be significant that when the Trusty family reached New Jersey, they encountered other African Americans already there who had been free for a generation or more and who bore the name of Trusty.[5] Samuel Ringgold Ward, whose family escaped in 1820, and Henry Highland Garnet, whose family escaped in 1824, were not only both from Eastern Shore of Maryland, but they were also second cousins, having common great grandparents.[6] Thus, a multigenerational kinship network stretching back three generations may have connected the free Trusty family in New Jersey with their enslaved cousins in Maryland.

Chester County, Pennsylvania, was home to a significant, though unknown, number of freedom seekers. Thomas Mitchell was one. About midnight on August 22, 1849, the slave-catchers came for him. He was then a twenty-seven-year-old farm laborer living north of Kennett Square with his wife Elizabeth and their infant daughter Louisa. The attackers pointed a pistol at Elizabeth, overpowered Thomas, dislocating his shoulder in the process, and took him away. Mitchell's neighbors were awakened by Elizabeth's screams and organized a pursuit to rescue Mitchell. They believed, or at least claimed to believe, that Mitchell was a native Pennsylvanian and therefore a free person. They set off in pursuit of Mitchell and his abductors at about four o'clock in the morning. They did not blunder around in the darkness. They reasoned that the abductors were heading for the railroad line running from Philadelphia through Wilmington, Delaware, to Baltimore, and that Mitchell was likely to be taken to the slave pens of Baltimore. Therefore they split into two parties, one headed for Wilmington, about fourteen miles to the southeast, the other party headed to Elkton, Maryland, some twenty miles southeast.[7]

The Wilmington contingent went to the house of Thomas Garrett, the man who had assisted the Trusty family in their escape in 1824. Garrett sent a telegram to Baltimore asking John Needles, a fellow Quaker, to go to the train station and wait for the expected appearance of Mitchell and his kidnappers. Needles was not available and so his family sent Dr. J. E. Snodgrass to meet the train. In the meantime, the other party of rescuers had reached Elkton, where they found Mitchell in chains in the custody of one Thomas McCreary, a sometime Elkton police officer and now the leader of the party that abducted Mitchell. McCreary and Mitchell boarded the train for Baltimore, and the rescuing party rode on the same train. They arrived in Baltimore the morning of Thursday, August 23, 1849, and were met at the train station by both Dr. Snodgrass and the Baltimore police. After some discussion, the police arrested George Martin, Mitchell's employer, on the grounds that Martin should have been paying Mitchell's wages to his Maryland owners.

The rescuers believed, or at least asserted, that Mitchell was a free-born resident of Pennsylvania, and they had anticipated a legal battle to restore his freedom. Unfortunately, Mitchell had confessed to his captors that he was indeed the fugitive slave from Elkton and that he had escaped from his owners twelve years earlier. George Martin was jailed for not having paid for Mitchell's services, but he was released after a few days. Mitchell was in a great deal of trouble. He was not merely facing a return to slavery in Maryland. His likely fate, unless he could be freed, was to be sent to the Deep South to work on one of the cotton or sugar plantations where work was long and hard and life expectancy short. Mitchell's Chester County neighbors arranged to purchase his freedom for $600.[8] With the exception of Dr. Snodgrass of Baltimore, who was on good terms with Friends, the rescuers were largely, and possibly exclusively, Quakers.

At the time of his capture, Thomas Mitchell was living a little more than twenty miles from the place where he worked as a slave in Maryland. He was living about five miles north of the border of Delaware, a slave state. He was not the only "fugitive from labor" in his neighborhood. Isaac Mason had escaped with others from Chestertown, Maryland, about sixty miles south, in December 1846, and found temporary shelter among the free people in Chester County. Mason's host took him to church, probably the African Union Church known locally as Timbuktu. "After the service was ended, he announced in the church that he had with him three travelers, and wanted some of the brethren to care for them. A woman by the name of Mary Jackson arose and said that her employers wanted a man, and if one of them could go home with her, she thought she could get him a place." It worked, and Mason reported, "just two weeks from the time we started from the land of slavery for that of freedom, we were settled down, independently working for our own bread, and choosing our own employers." At the time of the kidnapping of his neighbor, Isaac Mason was working for a Quaker farmer who gave him "fifty cents a day, a house to live in and two acres of planting land for my own use, six months firewood, with the use of a horse and team, and a horse to plough the ground" and was planning to get married.[9]

After Mitchell's kidnapping, Isaac Mason decided he was no longer safe living there and left for Massachusetts. Others held their ground. In Chester and Lancaster Counties in Pennsylvania, we have clear evidence of organized African American resistance to slave catchers and kidnappers. In December 1850, a party of six to ten men, led by a federal deputy marshall, attempted to enter a home near Gum Tree, south of Coatesville, in search of fugitives. One of the occupants of the house, a man named Green, defended his home with an axe, and though he was wounded, he bought enough time for his African American neighbors to arrive. The resistance was successful. According to one newspaper account, the slave-hunters rode off, being pursued by fifteen to eighteen men, and it was only the speed of their horses and the darkness of the night that saved them from harm.[10] R. C. Smedley's *History of the Underground Railroad* records several examples of organized resistance among African Americans.[11] At Christiana, Pennsylvania, in September 1851, a similar attempt by federal marshals and slave-catchers to recover fugitives resulted in an exchange of gunfire, leaving one slave catcher dead and another sorely wounded. The skirmish took place at a tenant house owned by the Quaker Pownall family but occupied by William Parker, the acknowledged leader of the resistance. A number of local African Americans along with two Quakers were subsequently arrested for treason. Local Quakers, including the Pownalls, helped the leaders of the resistance escape to Canada.[12]

There were clearly overlaps between Quaker and African American Underground Railroad networks in Chester County. In the Mitchell case and the Christiana Resistance, and probably the Gum Tree affair, the African American leaders of the resistance were tenants of Quaker farmers. Quakers pursued the abducted Mitchell to Baltimore and paid for his freedom. Quakers were arrested after the Christiana Resistance for refusing to aid the federal marshals. Thomas Garrett was closely associated with African Americans William Still, Harriet Tubman, and Samuel D. Burtis.[13] In his reminiscences of New Jersey in the 1820s, Samuel Ringgold Ward said that when slave-catchers came prowling, "Quakers threw all manner of *peaceful* obstacles in their way, while the Negroes made it a little too *hot* for their comfort."[14]

Those people who followed Mitchell into Maryland were white. His abduction was accomplished before an alarm could be given. It took some time before Mitchell's neighbors could mount their pursuit, by which time, the kidnappers were undoubtedly across the state border. For African Americans to have pursued the kidnappers into Maryland would have been a risky business. What the reaction would be to the arrival of an aroused and possibly armed rescue party in Maryland can be imagined. By Maryland law, any person of African descent entering the state from outside would be fined twenty dollars for the first offense and sold into slavery on the second offense.[15] There were at least two such cases in Elkton, involving the arrest, jailing, and fining of African American visitors from Delaware in the months surrounding the kidnapping. In responding to criticism of this treatment, the Elkton newspaper commented that such laws were enacted by the slaveholders of Maryland to prevent "the colored emissaries of abolitionists . . . from interfering with their slaves."[16]

How could someone like Mitchell consider himself safe living within a day's walk of the place where he had been enslaved? More generally, what created a place of safety for freedom seekers associated with the Underground Railroad? First, there had to be a significant free African American population. *Significant* does not mean large or necessarily visible to outsiders. According to the 1860 census, 2 percent of the population of Pennsylvania was African American. Looking at the county-level data, about 4 percent of the population of Philadelphia was African American, but the county with the highest proportion of African Americans was Chester with 8 percent. In Chester County, the African American population in the townships ranged from a single individual to 561 in West Chester, or expressed as a percentage of the population, from 0.1 to 29.3 percent. The Mitchell family lived in East Marlborough Township, which according to the census was 15 percent African American, which was more than seven times the state average.[17]

Within five miles of Mitchell's house were no less than seven Quaker meetinghouses (Marlborough, Unionville, Old Kennett, Kennett Square, London Grove, Parkerville, and New Garden). Within that same radius of five miles were at least four black churches: Ebenezer (African Methodist Episcopal), Timbuktu (African Union), Red Lion, and Denton Hollow (African Union). Without making the claim that every African Union or African Methodist Church was an active station of the Underground Railroad, at the very least, they represented a visible, interconnected, and widespread support network for African Americans.

The existence of independent African American institutions, particularly churches, was a clear marker for communities, with the caveat that people who associated with a particular church may have been distributed over a wide geographical area. As with Quaker networks, ties of both family and religion were significant. Many of the local churches were part of the African Union Methodist denomination founded by Peter Spencer in Wilmington, Delaware. This body had churches scattered through rural southern Pennsylvania and New Jersey as well as the slave states of Delaware and Maryland. Quarterly meetings and other gatherings at these churches were occasions not just for prayer, but also socializing.[18]

A place of safety required a significant portion of the white population to be ideological (politically or religiously) antislavery. This was often a minority. In Chester County, the antislavery movement was largely a Quaker concern. In Delaware, Chester, and Lancaster Counties, the areas of greatest reported Underground Railroad activity had both a significant African American and a significant Quaker presence. In areas of those same counties where there were few or no African Americans, or few or no Quakers, there is little or no evidence of Underground Railroad activity.[19] That Quakers were always and everywhere the backbone of the Underground Railroad is a myth, but it does appear to hold true for Chester County.

Safety also depended on access to the courts and the legal system. Pennsylvania by the 1820s had strong antikidnapping laws. African Americans' direct access to legal redress was hampered by custom and economic conditions, if not by law, but abolitionists and Quakers were able to step in. The intention of those Chester County Quakers who were trying to rescue the kidnapped Mitchell was not, presumably, to have a violent confrontation, but rather to institute legal proceedings with the assistance of Friend Needles in Baltimore. The final phase of the Christiana Resistance was not the battle but the treason trial of the alleged participants that ended in acquittal.

Jobs were essential. Thomas Mitchell and Isaac Mason found employment among the Quaker farmers of Chester County. By 1849, both had established households, though as tenants rather than owners. Mitchell had established a family and Martin was anticipating beginning a family. We should not necessarily believe the assertions of Mitchell's neighbors that they thought he was a free man. Quakers in the area probably had a "don't ask, don't tell" policy about whether the man who showed up looking for work on the farm was or was not a fugitive.

In Mitchell's Chester County, the area of greatest interracial contact was on the job, but there was an unequal relationship of white employers and black employees. Most African American men were landless farm laborers. It was difficult to move up the economic ladder. In his autobiography, Samuel R. Ward writes of the "great kindness" shown to him by one of his Quaker teachers in New York City, but he also describes how he and his fellow students were unable to find employment. "The idea of employing a black clerk was preposterous—too absurd to be seriously entertained. I never knew but one coloured clerk in a mercantile house . . . but he was never advanced a single grade . . . [I]f I sought a trade, white apprentices would leave if I were admitted."[20] Though Ward does not specifically criticize Quakers in this passage, it seems inescapable to observe that New York Friends may have been good about providing education to African American children, but they do not appear to have been forward in providing advanced employment opportunities.

What of education? Samuel R. Ward named his schoolmates in New Jersey, and the names were those of local Quaker families. At the local level, in rural districts, apparently white and black children did go to the same schools. At the higher levels, the story was quite different. In a letter to *Frederick Douglass's Paper* in 1855, Ward gave a more critical assessment of Quakers: "They will give us good advice. They will aid in giving us a partial education, but never in a Quaker school, beside their own children. Whatever they do for us savors of pity, and is done at arm's length."[21]

There were a few exceptions. According to her family, Mary Ann Shadd Cary, daughter of Abraham D. Shadd, and later the first African American woman to edit a newspaper, entered a Quaker school in West Chester, Pennsylvania, at the age of ten, and she remained there for six years. Several researchers have attempted to find written or printed documentation to identify the school and verify Mary Ann's attendance, but with no success.[22] However, the Shadds had numerous Quaker connections. Smedley's *History of the Underground Railroad in Chester County* reports a route on the Underground Railroad connecting Chandler Darlington in Kennett to "the Darlington sisters and Abraham D. Shadd, West Chester."[23] Another private school operated by Quakers and located at Hamorton, four miles from Mitchell's home, advertised in 1846 in the *Pennsylvania Freeman* that it accepted students regardless of color.[24] With a tuition of $100 per year it was beyond the reach of the Mitchell family.

In 1832, the Clarkson Anti-Slavery Society was established for the area along the border of Chester and Lancaster County. Its original constitution explicitly stated that membership was open to all without regard to color or gender.[25] In the next several years, numerous local antislavery societies were established, and the area around Kennett Square, a mile south of Mitchell's home, was particularly noted for its persistent antislavery and Underground Railroad activity. These local societies were in turn heavily dominated by Quakers. But the organized antislavery movement, despite the rhetoric of racial equality, did not succeed, if it even tried, to become racially inclusive. In an analysis of the leadership of the local societies in Chester County, I have yet to identify a person of color. Several well-known African American abolitionists from outside the area, including Frederick Douglass and Robert Purvis, certainly participated in antislavery meetings in the area, but there is scant evidence of biracial interaction within the abolitionist movement at the local level. Even Abraham D. Shadd of West Chester, who had been a founder of the American Anti-Slavery Society in 1833, never held an office in any of the local antislavery organizations, though he is listed occasionally in the pages of the *Pennsylvania Freeman* as a financial contributor. It is possible that lack of visible African American participation was due to economic as much as racial factors. To be an active reformer after the model of Lucretia Mott required discretionary time to travel and attend meetings, and the financial resources to do so. Isaac Mason, making fifty cents a day as a laborer, was simply not in the same social and economic class as the well-to-do Robert Purvis.

Harriet Beecher Stowe's *Uncle Tom's Cabin* includes a chapter on "The Quaker Settlement," where Quaker Rachel Halliday addresses Eliza Harris as "daughter" and both the Quakers and African Americans eat at the same table. According to Stowe's *Key to Uncle Tom's Cabin*, the Hallidays were modeled in part on Thomas Garrett.[26] It is unlikely that Stowe had ever met the Garretts, and her portrayal of them should be seen as an element of her literary idealization of Quakers. There is reason to inquire further into the question of whether Quakers and African Americans shared meals. Who could sit at the table was a matter of considerable importance.

Two semifictional accounts of Quakers in Lancaster County, adjacent to Chester County, speak to this issue. Ellwood Griest's *John and Mary: Or the Fugitive Slaves* (1873) is presented as fiction, though the locations are clearly identifiable as the region in southeastern Lancaster County, closely adjacent to Chester County to the east and Maryland to the south. The main Quaker family, the Browns, appear to be modeled on Griest's own family. Griest was an active abolitionist before the Civil War and certainly knew people who were active in the Underground Railroad if he was not himself a participant. Though the story is told largely from the perspective of a Quaker family, it is clear that the business of the Underground Railroad was largely carried out by African Americans, though with the assistance, when asked, of white Quakers. One of the African American characters is Neddy Johnson, a former

slave who lived in "the Barrens" and worked for the Browns during thresh-
ing season. On these occasions, the Browns and their "negro" hired workers
ate the same food, but "following the custom of those days in that section"
at separate tables. According to Griest, Johnson accepted this as the custom
and "therefore considered it no degradation."[27]

Phebe Earle Gibbons tells a different story in *The Pennsylvania Dutch and
Other Essays* (1882). In a chapter titled "The Friend," the Quaker abolitionist
is named Samuel Wilson but is a transparent description of her father-in-
law, Daniel Gibbons of East Leacock, Lancaster County, Pennsylvania. The
description of "The Friend" is almost certainly based on family stories if not
firsthand observation. In this version, the Gibbons family was accustomed
to eat at the same table with their hired men, mostly African Americans, and
when a newly hired white man objected he was shown to a separate table,
and left to eat his dinner in solitude.[28]

Both Griest's and Gibbons's accounts describe environments similar to
Mitchell's neighborhood in nearby Chester County. Quakers were the land-
owning farmers there, while people of African descent were the hired men
working for those farmers. They usually did not own either property or
homes, but lived, as did Mitchell, in houses owned by Quakers. On Sunday,
those of African descent went to the African Union Methodist Church, while
Quakers went to their meetinghouses. People of African descent were buried
in Quaker burial grounds, but usually in separate sections. Did Neddy Johnson indeed feel no degradation? Did the hired men on the Gibbons farm feel
themselves to be socially, if not economically, equal? Unfortunately, finding
direct contemporary testimony is difficult.

There are more than thirty contemporary newspaper accounts of Thomas
Mitchell's abduction, but none speaks with the voice of Thomas Mitchell.
Mitchell did speak at an "Indignation Meeting" held shortly after his return
to Chester County, where he gave his account "in a plain, simple, straight forward style, which would have done no discredit to many a man of higher pretensions and greater prominence." The accounts of the Indignation Meeting
published in the *Pennsylvania Freeman* describe, but do not quote, Thomas
Mitchell.[29]

Thomas Mitchell and his family remained in East Marlborough Township, Chester County, until his death in 1880. According to the manuscript
census for 1850, his household included his wife and two children. He was
employed as a laborer. In the manuscript census for 1870, Thomas was still a
farm worker, and the Mitchell family had ten children living at home, and all
those of school age and above were literate.[30] When he died in February 1880,

he owned a small parcel of land, a modestly furnished two-story house, two cows, and two pigs.[31] Mitchell was a member of that charter generation who had passed from enslavement to freedom, and after 1849, no one disputed that he owned himself. One wonders what Mitchell would have said about his life in Chester County. Would he have looked back and been comforted by a life of modest but very real accomplishment, or would he have felt frustrated or betrayed by the limited opportunities for African Americans?

There is little in the modern landscape to mark the antebellum African American population of Mitchell's neighborhood. Although the eighteenth- and nineteenth-century Quaker meetinghouses in Mitchell's neighborhood still stand and house modern congregations, the nineteenth-century African Union and African Methodist Episcopal church buildings are now gone with little or nothing to mark their sites. Hosanna African Union Methodist Protestant Church, near Lincoln University, is the only extant example of an antebellum African American church still standing in Chester County.

The failure of Quakers to be racially inclusive in the eighteenth and nine-teenth century is hardly a new story. Henry T. Cadbury's frank "Negro Membership in the Society of Friends" grew out of a course at the Quaker study center at Pendle Hill in 1934, and was published in the *Journal of Negro History* in 1936. Thomas Drake's *Quakers and Slavery in America* (1950) and Larry Gara's *Liberty Line: The Legend of the Underground Railroad* (1961) are useful correctives to anyone who has made the assumption that all Quakers were radical abolitionists in the model of John Woolman, Isaac T. Hopper, Levi Coffin, or Lucretia Mott. Most recently, *Fit for Freedom, Not for Friendship: Quakers, African Americans and the Myth of Racial Justice* (2009), by Donna McDaniel and Vanessa Julye, provides a critical look at Quaker failures.[32] All of these books were written by active Quakers.

I presented a public lecture to a Chester County audience on the Mitchell case. The first question following the lecture was from a local Quaker about Quaker involvement in slavery and the lack of African American Quakers. The follow-up was a comment by an African American woman whose family had resided in Chester County for generations. This woman took exception to the first question. "Maybe we [meaning African Americans] did not want to be Quakers. We have our own churches, thank you very much." I presented a similar lecture at Buxton, Ontario, a community founded by former enslaved people from the United States. The first question was "why so few black Quakers," followed by a comment from an African American man in the audience, who said "I have been to a Quaker meeting and I know why there aren't many black Quakers." Was the religious divide in southern

Chester County between white Quakers and black Methodists a sign of racial exclusion or an indication of the desire for creating independent organizations? Clearly exclusion, whether deliberate or unintentional, is part of the story. The creation of autonomous African American churches is another.

When I first began speaking to public audiences about the Underground Railroad and related topics, I was uncomfortable with discussions turning as they almost inevitably did to present-minded concerns on race and race relations. Since then, however, I have come to the conclusion that we are best served as a society by having those present-minded conversations. Perhaps setting the discussion about race relations in a historical context provides a bit of distance and therefore an ability to be a bit more candid on these troubling subjects.

Within the context of the popular, and to some extent, the scholarly understanding of the role of Quakers, we seem to have a conflict between the image of the good Quaker, as fictionalized by Harriet Beecher Stowe or exemplified in the lives of Lucretia Mott, Levi Coffin, or Isaac T. Hopper, and the useful correctives, often from the pens of Quaker historians, reminding us that not all Quakers were Lucretia Mott or John Woolman, that many Quakers played no active role in antislavery, that the flip side of benevolence could be paternalism and a desire for social control, and that Quaker institutions and meetings have not been free of racism.

More importantly, the mythology of the good Quaker in the antislavery movement and in the Underground Railroad often underplays African American agency. Smedley's *History* includes only scattered references to African American involvement in the Underground Railroad. In contrast, Elwood Griest's 1873 *John and Mary*, though told from the perspective of (white) Quakers, shows local African Americans in control of the business of aiding fugitives, with Quakers acting as their assistants. At the dramatic point in the novel when the fugitives John and Mary are captured by the slave-hunters, the rescue is organized by Davy McCane, an African American. As McCane sets off to rescue John and Mary, he encounters two Quakers. "Follow me now and ask no questions" he tells them, and without hesitation they obey.[33]

Griest presents a fictionalized account of Quaker and African American relations in the Pennsylvania borderlands in the antebellum period, but it seems to correspond largely with the realities. He presents African Americans as living among Quakers but separated from them by class and religion as well as race. From the perspective of our own times, one can fault these Friends for failing to become themselves racially inclusive or to ensure a route to upward economic and social mobility for the free people. However, they

130   CHRISTOPHER DENSMORE

also provided, at least in some areas, an opportunity for building African American communities and providing a space for the development of African American institutions. These parallel communities of Quakers and African Americans were not equal. They were divided by race, class, and religion, but they remained connected.

I recently spoke at Old Kennett Meetinghouse in Chester County, only a few miles from Mitchell's residence. One of the attendees was an African American woman who told me about all of her relatives who were buried at the meeting, and she expressed a sense of affection for and connection to the meeting, even though her family's religious home was the African Methodist Episcopal Church. Her family stories were about people who had worked as laborers or domestics for white people in the area and, in her words, the previous generations were "brought up hard."

A reunion of the descendants of the Payne family was held at the Menallen Friends Meetinghouse in Adams County, Pennsylvania. The family had been released from slavery in Virginia in 1843 and moved to Pennsylvania. In 1845, Kitty Payne was kidnapped and taken back to Virginia by persons who claimed that she was still legally a slave. She was released after a lengthy court battle in Virginia, where several Quakers from Menallen participated in her defense.[34] The modern descendants of the Payne family came to Menallen from as far away as California. During the afternoon, the descendants walked to a wooded area that was the approximate site of the Payne residence in 1845. Many of the children came with remembrances—a small stone, a tree leaf, or a bit of wood. This was their Plymouth Rock, the place where the charter generation of the Payne family began to live as free people.

This reflects an attitude expressed in a number of local studies of African American communities that, while not ignoring the poor economic conditions and hardships of the early nineteenth century, choose instead to tell the story of the beginnings of autonomous communities and institutions. I return here to the opening quotation from Ira Berlin about slavery being a way we talk about race. People do care about how we tell the story of enslavement and freedom. People often feel "ownership" of the story because this is the story of who we are and how we came to be who we are.

NOTES

Ira Berlin, "American Slavery in History and Memory," in *Slavery, Resistance, Freedom*, ed. Gabor Boritt and Scott Hancock (New York: Oxford University Press, 2007), 8.

1. Samuel Ringgold Ward, *Autobiography of a Fugitive Negro* (London: John Snow, 1855), 22.

2. Census figures derived from Historical Census Browser. University of Virginia, Geospatial and Statistical Data Center. Available at: http:mapserver.lib.virginia.edu/collections.

3. Dennis Rizzo, *Parallel Communities: The Underground Railroad in South Jersey* (Charleston: History Press, 2008), 81–94; Emma Marie Trusty, *The Underground Railroad Ties that Bound Unveiled* (Philadelphia: Amed Literary, 1999), 142–62; Christopher P. Barton, "Antebellum African-American Settlements in Southern New Jersey," *African Diaspora Archaeology Network Newsletter*, December 2009. Available at: http://www.diaspora.illinois.edu/news1209/news1209–4.pdf.

4. Henry Highland Garnet, *Memorial Discourse* (Philadelphia: Joseph M. Wilson, 1865), 17–20.

5. Trusty, *Underground Railroad Ties*, 234–64.

6. Garnet, *Memorial Discourse*, 25.

7. The Mitchell kidnapping story is based on contemporary newspaper accounts. See "Alleged Case of Abduction," *Baltimore Sun*, August 24, 1849; "Daring Outrage," *Cummings' Telegraphic Evening Bulletin* (Philadelphia), August 25, 1849; "A Slave Case," *Daily Republican and Argus* (Baltimore), August 24, 1849; "The Slave Case," *Baltimore Sun*, August 25, 1849; "A Mistake," *Baltimore Sun*, August 25, 1849; "Slave Case," *American and Commercial Advertiser* (Baltimore), August 25, 1849; "Baltimore, Friday, Aug. 24—AM," *New-York Daily Tribune*, August 25, 1849; "Baltimore, Friday, Aug. 24—A.M.," *Liberator* (Boston), August 31, 1849; "The Slave Case," *Daily Republican and Argus* (Baltimore), Saturday evening, August 25, 1849; "Discharged from Custody," *American and Commercial Advertiser* (Baltimore), August 27, 1849; "The Case of Martin," *Baltimore Sun*, August 27, 1849; "Arrest of a Slave-Excitement," *Village Record* (West Chester, Pa.), August 28, 1849; "The Slave Kidnapping Case," *New-York Daily Tribune*, August 29, 1849; "The Baltimore Abduction Case—An Authentic Statement of the Facts," *New-York Daily Tribune*, August 29, 1849; "Slave Case," *Daily Republican and Argus* (Baltimore), August 29, 1849; "More Kidnapping in Pennsylvania," *Pennsylvania Freeman* (Philadelphia), August 30, 1849; "Letter from Baltimore," *National Era* (Washington, D.C), August 30, 1849; "Letter from Baltimore," *North Star* (Rochester, N.Y.), September 7, 1849; "Letter from Baltimore," *National Anti-Slavery Standard* (New York), August 30, 1849; "Letter from Baltimore, *Jeffersonian* (West Chester, Pa.), September 4, 1849; "Outrageous Slave Abduction Case," *Blue Hen's Chickens* (Wilmington, Del.), August 31, 1849; "The Slave Case," *Blue Hen's Chickens* (Wilmington, Del.), August 31, 1849; "An Outrageous Case—The Operation of the Slave System," Liberator (Boston), August 31, 1849; "Officer McCreary, *Cecil Whig* (Elkton, Md.), September 1, 1849; "The Slave Albert," *Village Record* (West Chester, Pa.), September 4, 1849; "Row among the Blacks," *Evening Bulletin* (Philadelphia), September 5, 1849; "A Delegation from the Union Anti-Slavery Society . . .," *Pennsylvania Freeman* (Philadelphia), September 6, 1849; "The Chester County Abduction Case," *Pennsylvania Freeman* (Philadelphia), September 6, 1849; "Indignation Meet-

ing—Grand Rally!!," *Pennsylvania Freeman* (Philadelphia), September 6, 1849; "The Following Account of the Seizure of Thomas Mitchell . . .," *Friends Weekly Intelligencer* (Philadelphia), September 8, 1849; "We Publish in Another Part of this Paper . . .," *Friends Weekly Intelligencer* (Philadelphia), September 8, 1849; "Excitement in Chester County," *Cecil Democrat* (Elkton, Maryland), September 9, 1849; "Indignation Meeting," *Village Record* (West Chester, Pa.), September 11, 1849; Davis, George B., "Scraps from the County, No. 39: Negro Catchers," *Blue Hen's Chickens* (Wilmington, Del.), September 14, 1849; Davis, George B. "Scraps from the Country, No. 40: Abolitionism," *Blue Hen's Chickens* (Wilmington, Del.), September 21, 1849; "Indignation Meeting— General Rally, *National Anti-Slavery Standard* (New York, N.Y.), September 20, 1849; "Meetings in Neighboring Counties, *Pennsylvania Freeman* (Philadelphia), September 30, 1849; "Proceedings of the Chester County Indignation Meeting," *Pennsylvania Freeman* (Philadelphia), September 30, 1849; "The Chester County Abduction," *The Non-Slaveholder* (Philadelphia), 10th Month 1, 1849; Thomas, Amos, "To the Editors of the Pennsylvania Freeman," *Pennsylvania Freeman* (Philadelphia), November 15, 1849.

8. "Buying a Slave: How Enoch Swayne and His Neighbors Freed a Kidnapped Slave," *Daily Local News* (West Chester, Pa.), May 3, 1889.

9. Isaac Mason, *Life of Isaac Mason as a Slave* (Worchester, Mass., 1893), 50–51.

10. "Shameful Outrage," *Pennsylvania Freeman* (Philadelphia), January 2, 1851; "An Interesting Letter from Gum Tree," *Pennsylvania Freeman* (Philadelphia), January 2, 1851; "Letter from Chester County," *Public Ledger* (Philadelphia), January 10, 1851.

11. R. C. Smedley, *History of the Underground Railroad in Chester and the Neighboring Counties of Pennsylvania* (Lancaster, Pa.: The Era, 1883), 92–93, 97, 112–14, 133.

12. Recent scholarship on Christiana includes Thomas P. Slaughter, *Blood Dawn: The Christiana Riot and Racial Violence in the Antebellum North* (New York: Oxford University Press, 1991); and Ella Forbes, *But We Have No Country: The 1851 Christiana, Pennsylvania Resistance* (Cherry Hill, N.J.: Africana Homestead Library, 1998). Resistance leader William Parker's personal account appeared in the *Atlantic Monthly* 17 (Feb.–March, 1866): 152–66, 276–95.

13. James A. McGowan, *Station Master on the Underground Railroad: Life and Letters of Thomas Garrett* (Jefferson, N.C.: McFarland and Company, 2005).

14. Ward, *Autobiography*, 25.

15. *Laws Made and Passed by the General Assembly of the State of Maryland at Session . . . 1839–1840* (Annapolis, Md.: William M'Neir, 1840), 36–39.

16. *Pennsylvania Freeman* (Philadelphia), October 18, 1849, November 23, 1849; *Liberator* (Boston), September 14, 1849; *Cecil Whig* (Elkton, Md.), August 25, 1849.

17. Chester County township level data calculated from United States. Census Office, *Population of the United States in 1860* (Washington, D.C.: Government Printing Office, 1864), 418–19.

18. Lewis V. Baldwin, *"Invisible" Strands in African Methodism* (Philadelphia: American Theological Library Association, 1983); Dorothy E. Willmore, *Peter Spencer's*

Movement: Exploring the History of the Union American Methodist Episcopal Church (Wilmington, Del.: Village Printing, 1991).

19. Based on a comparison of African American population as reported in the 1860 Census and the location of Friends Meetings.

20. Ward, *Autobiography*, 29.

21. *Frederick Douglass's Paper* (Rochester, N.Y.), April 13, 1855.

22. Jane Rhodes, *Mary Ann Shadd Cary: The Black Press and Protest in the Nineteenth Century,* (Bloomington: Indiana University Press, 1998), 17, 231.

23. Smedley, *History of the Underground Railroad,* 33.

24. *Pennsylvania Freeman*, November 6, 1845, advertisement for the Kennett Boarding School for Girls "irrespective of color."

25. *Genus of Universal Emancipation* (Philadelphia, Pa.), July 3, 1833, 143–44.

26. Harriet Beecher Stowe, *A Key to Uncle Tom's Cabin* (Boston: John P. Jewett, 1853), 54–55. Stowe misnames Thomas Garrett as John Garet.

27. Ellwood Griest, *John and Mary; Or, the Fugitive Slaves* (Lancaster, Pa.: Inquirer, 1873), 40–41.

28. Phebe Earle Gibbons, *Pennsylvania Dutch and Other Essays* (Philadelphia: J. B. Lippincott, 1882), 246–47.

29. *Pennsylvania Freeman*, September 30, 1849.

30. U.S. Census. Manuscript Schedules, East Marlborough Township, Chester County, Pennsylvania, 1850 and 1870.

31. *Daily Local News* (West Chester, Pa.), March 30, 1880.

32. Henry J. Cadbury, "Negro Membership in the Society of Friends," *Journal of Negro History* 20 (1936): 151–213; Thomas E. Drake, *Quakers and Slavery in America* (New Haven, Conn.: Yale University Press, 1950); Larry Gara, *The Liberty Line* (Lexington: University of Kentucky Press, 1960); Donna McDaniel and Vannesa Julye, *Fit for Freedom, Not for Friendship: Quakers, African Americans and the Myth of Racial Justice* (Philadelphia: Quaker Press of Friends General Conference, 2009).

33. Griest, *John and Mary,* 111.

34. Mary Gandy, *Guide My Feet, Hold My Hand* (Canton, Mo.: M. G. Gandy, 1987); Debra Sandoe McCauslin, *Reconstructing the Past: Puzzle of a Lost Community* (Gettysburg: For the Cause Productions, 2005), 51–53.

9 The Quaker and the Colonist

Moses Sheppard, Samuel Ford McGill, and Transatlantic Antislavery across the Color Line

ANDREW DIEMER

IN FEBRUARY 1849, IN A LETTER to a man named Samuel McGill, a Baltimore Quaker named Moses Sheppard shared his thoughts concerning slavery, the law, and individual conscience. Sheppard asserted his belief in the validity of the law of slavery, provided that an individual may be allowed to keep himself free of the institution. A man must not be forced to own a slave, nor should he be compelled to "arrest fugitive slaves," but he insisted that one may not "annul a law that he dislikes," which would produce a state of chaos.[1] Sheppard was personally opposed to slavery, yet like many who felt as he did, especially those who lived in the Upper South, he maintained that respect for the law and the Constitution was paramount; violation of either would produce worse evil than even slavery itself.

A few months later, McGill responded to this contention with a stern rebuke. He challenged the very notion that a man could be legally enslaved.

> Let the slave determine the question, he is a living, sentient, immortal being, and would proclaim that those do him an injustice who debar him from his freedom. It is only by force that he is held, by blows that he is forced to unrequited toil. . . . Upon finding and establishing our claim to stolen property, it is restored to us, in this case is the true owner bound to indemnify him who is dispossessed, even although he had purchased it of the thief?[2]

Such disagreements were not uncommon in these years. What makes this particular exchange more interesting than many others like it is that McGill was a black emigrant to Liberia while Moses Sheppard was a white colonizationist.

The American Colonization Society (ACS) had been founded in 1816 by a coalition of northern reformers and southern slaveholders. Its stated goal was to establish a colony in Africa that was to be populated by American free blacks. The ACS would also help to promote the growth of that colony by assisting free blacks who consented to become colonists. Many of its northern supporters (and some of its southern supporters as well) hoped that these efforts would help make possible the gradual end of slavery in the United States. All of the supporters of the ACS agreed, however, that nothing should be done to forcibly emancipate the enslaved. The property rights of slave owners were to be respected.[3] The majority of northern free blacks vigorously opposed the ACS and African colonization, denouncing it as a proslavery plot to remove American free blacks from the land of their birth.[4]

Historians have had widely divergent understandings of the African colonization movement. For much of the twentieth century, colonization was deemed "quixotic," though even its detractors in general considered it a mild form of antislavery. In the late 1960s, however, historians, especially those who began to take the words and actions of free blacks more seriously, helped to advance the argument that the ACS was a functionally proslavery organization.[5]

More recently, some historians have made the case that the antislavery claims of the colonization movement need to be reconsidered. In an influential essay, the historian William Freehling argued that colonization posed a genuine threat to slavery. It was possible, he insisted, that colonization could indeed have served as a part of a larger political effort to extinguish slavery in the Border South, which in turn would have threatened the institution in the Lower South. The fear that a Republican president might promote just such a course of events was a crucial factor on the road to the secession crisis.[6] Other historians, often looking at local- or state-level colonization societies, have argued that whatever the intentions of their white supporters, such organizations were used by enslaved and free African Americans as a means of promoting emancipation.[7]

In weighing these conflicting assessments of colonization, it is important to consider both the local-level negotiations over emancipation and colonization as well as the role of colonization in the larger, political struggle over slavery. It is clear that colonization *could* be used for antislavery ends, but this possibility does not prove that colonization was, on balance, antislavery. Even the most vehement immediate abolitionists recognized that in certain instances, African colonization could lead to the emancipation of the enslaved. These instances, however, needed to be weighed against the larger claims of abolitionists that colonization undermined support for more effective antislavery strategies. Even accepting Freehling's argument that it was reasonable for slaveholders to see colonization as a *future* threat to slavery, we still might ask what effect colonization *did* have on slavery. To put it another way, Lower South slave owners may have been right to fear that colonization would ultimately tip the balance in favor of gradual emancipation, but did colonization actually undermine slavery in the years before the Civil War?

Within the Society of Friends, Moses Sheppard was not alone in his support for colonization. African colonization struck many Quakers as the best solution to America's slavery and race problems. While some prominent Friends did become advocates of immediate abolition, many were troubled by the violent conflicts provoked by Garrisonian abolition, not to mention the violent rhetoric of Garrisonians themselves. Some pointed to the peaceful religious tradition of the Society of Friends as a means of creating a common ground in the violent conflict between abolitionists and colonizationists.[8]

Others were more forthright in their support of colonization as the ideal means of ending slavery gradually. The December 1816 meeting that gave birth to the ACS called for the organization of a national society "to assist in the formation and execution of a plan for the colonization of the Free People of Colour, with their consent, in Africa or elsewhere."[9] Through the subsequent years, the word *consent* appears again and again in the public and private discourse of colonization; in print it was often italicized; in private correspondence, it was commonly underlined.[10] The supporters of colonization saw the consensual nature of their project as crucial to its success. Quaker colonizationists could point to the ACS's rhetoric of consent as perfectly in line with the traditions of the Society of Friends, and at colonization as the best means of promoting emancipation without recourse to conflict or coercion. This was especially true in the Border South state of Maryland.[11]

Moses Sheppard can provide us with insight into the antislavery potential of African colonization, especially as it functioned within the Society of Friends. Although the colonization movement had its share of cynics who merely sought to use colonization as a means of diffusing the sectional tension over slavery, Sheppard was not one of them. He seems to have been genuinely devoted to the gradual end of slavery. Sheppard sincerely grappled with the notions of race that legitimated the system of slavery and that challenged those who would call for immediate emancipation. Perhaps just as important, he was not a marginal figure. Prosperous, respectable, and well-connected, with contacts to the North and to the South, Sheppard was caught in the middle of the national discussion of the institution of slavery. His correspondence with the Liberian emigrant Samuel McGill, in particular, can help us understand what sort of role colonization might have played in a political fight against slavery in the Border South. That correspondence also points to the ways in which Liberians hoped to shape colonization and to influence the struggle against slavery in their native United States.

Sheppard was born into a prosperous Quaker family settled just north of Philadelphia. Fearing the coming violence of the American Revolution, they departed for Nova Scotia, where they lived for a time. After the end of the war, they returned to the United States, this time settling in Maryland. By the early years of the nineteenth century, young Moses had established himself in the bustling city of Baltimore, where he prospered in business. He also devoted himself to philanthropic causes and was an early supporter of African colonization. In 1832, he was instrumental in the organization of the Maryland auxiliary of the ACS, which increasingly acted independently of the national organization, even establishing its own colony, Maryland-in-Liberia.[12]

The vehemence of black opposition to colonization, and later the opposition of white abolitionists (most famously William Lloyd Garrison), presented a dilemma to those supporters of colonization who genuinely saw their movement as a means to gradually end slavery. Answering the challenges of Garrisonians by arguing for colonization as a form of antislavery ran the risk of alienating Southern slaveholders and therefore gutting the movement's strength and organization in the Southern states. Without Southern support, the potential of colonization to actually remove emancipated slaves (rather than just blacks who were already free) would be seriously limited.[13]

Moses Sheppard was among those who were troubled by the accusations of Garrison and other critics of colonization. The accusation that seems to have most troubled Sheppard was the claim that the promoters of colonization sought only to remove free blacks from the United States. Colonizationists, claimed these critics, either cared little for enslaved blacks or actually hoped to strengthen slavery by removing its chief antagonists, free blacks. While some colonizationists may have dismissed these claims out of hand, Sheppard recognized that they contained a germ of truth. In a letter to Robert Finley, Moses admitted that there were some colonization supporters who hoped that the removal of free blacks would increase the value and security of their own investment in slavery. He insisted, though, that such men were unwittingly supporting the work of emancipation.[14]

Critics also mocked African colonization as a visionary scheme that would never be able to remove African Americans at a rate necessary to even match the natural growth of America's black population; colonizationists generally advocated a more modest goal. Their organizations, they insisted, should focus on establishing stable and prosperous colonies. Once these colonies were established and thriving, they reasoned, free blacks would emigrate of their own free will and (they hoped) on their own dime. Benevolent masters, then, would feel free to emancipate their slaves, knowing that they would be removed to one of these new, prosperous colonies.

This logic assumed that masters genuinely wanted (or would want) to emancipate their slaves and were only held back by the fear of a growing free black population in the United States. This claim seems dubious, especially in the Lower South where slavery was expanding dramatically. It makes a certain amount of sense, however, if one focuses, as Sheppard did, on conditions in his home state of Maryland. Even though it is clear that manumissions were not primarily the result of masters' benevolence, over the course of the 1830s, Maryland saw a decrease in its enslaved population (in raw numbers and as a percentage of total population) and a corresponding rise in its free black population.[15] Sheppard saw Maryland as the place where slavery could be most effectively attacked, and African colonization as the tool most suited to promoting this assault.

He also held that his responsibility to free blacks who chose to emigrate did not end once they departed for Liberia. In addition to his contributions to various colonization societies, Sheppard acted as a patron for a number of Liberian settlers over the years. He maintained a correspondence in which he offered guidance, and he sent along to them items he felt would be of use. His advice could be gentle, as when he encouraged Stephen Tippet to use the books and writing paper he had sent in order to learn to read and write. Often it could be condescending, and no doubt helped to reinforce the obvious imbalance of power inherent in the relationship. When he was informed that one of the men whom he supported was drinking excessively, Sheppard wrote that while the man had a right to drink, Sheppard had "a right to withhold from him my aid."[16]

If this correspondence could often emphasize the inequality of the relationship of white patron and black colonist, it could also provide an opportunity for Sheppard to imagine a different sort of relationship. "The laws of a nation make men free in that nation," Sheppard wrote to Thomas Jackson, a Liberian colonist, "The United laws of nations make men free throughout the world, but Christianity confers liberty in all the World and proclaims a man free throughout the works of God."[17] Paradoxically, the distance that lay between him and his correspondents seems to have allowed Sheppard the opportunity to develop a kind of intimacy that would have been nearly impossible in the United States.

Such an opportunity presented itself when Sheppard received a letter from Samuel Ford McGill, the son of one of his correspondents. McGill expressed his desire to become a physician and inquired as to whether one of the colonization societies might provide him assistance in doing so. The Young Men's Colonization Society of Baltimore pledged $250 a year, provided that McGill returned to Liberia when his education was complete. Moses Sheppard was empowered to work out the specifics of McGill's training.[18]

In January 1836, Sheppard wrote to McGill's father, seeking to reassure him concerning the conditions his son would encounter in the United States. The son, Sheppard insisted, "will be regarded as a white man by a very numerous and respectable circle," though he admitted that "the habits and usages of society, alias our prejudices, will prevent his being treated as such in our public and common intercourse."[19] He later noted that he had initially hoped to send the younger McGill to a medical school in Philadelphia, but he was unable to do so because of resistance to enrolling a black student. He commented that among those to the "Eastward," the likelihood that a man would "clamor for the rights of our 'colored brethren' is greater and the inclination to admit them to personal equality less."[20]

The contrast between racial attitudes in Baltimore and those to the north is one that Sheppard frequently mentioned, especially in his correspondence with black Liberians. He was aware that African Americans were the most skeptical of colonization's critics and that demands for racial equality were a key part of the immediate abolitionists' program. Yet Sheppard insists that it is border-state colonization that provides the best example of racial egalitarianism. Such depictions of the (admittedly private) racial attitudes of colonizationists are, for him, a crucial means of countering the claims of abolitionists to represent the best interests of African Americans.

Quite often, Sheppard's correspondence with black Liberians served as a means of reinforcing the arguments of colonizationists. He recognized that colonists were an essential means of promoting future emigration, and Liberians continued to communicate with friends, family members, and former neighbors back in the United States. The firsthand accounts of emigrants constituted a crucial element of colonizationist propaganda.[21] Liberians needed to be reassured that they were better off in Africa than they ever would have been in the United States.

Yet it seems that Sheppard's depictions of these racial dynamics were not simply a means of persuading blacks of the virtues of colonization. They also served as a way for him to struggle with his own conflicted feelings, as a Friend and as a colonizationist, with questions of race. Quakers were not immune to the influence of the wider American culture of race, and even among those who actively opposed slavery, many felt uncomfortable with the prospect of racial equality, not to mention "amalgamation." Despite claims to the contrary, many Quaker meetings segregated black worshipers into separate areas. Sarah Mapps Douglass, a black Philadelphian, recalled that her family was "squeezed into a little box under the stairs at Arch Street meeting."[22] Sheppard's interracial, transatlantic correspondence helped to assuage any anxieties he had about the inability of Quakers to embrace African Americans within the Society of Friends.

In 1836, Samuel Ford McGill finally arrived in Baltimore to begin his medical training. If had not already, he soon learned a lesson in American race relations when white students refused to associate with McGill and attempted to drive him from the medical school.[23] Eventually, Sheppard found a physician at the University of Vermont who was eager to take on McGill as a private student. Later he gained admission to the medical school at Dartmouth College, where he seems to have prospered. In November 1838, Samuel McGill departed from Baltimore for Liberia aboard the brig *Obregon*.[24]

McGill settled in to his new position as official physician for Maryland-in-Liberia and began what was to be a fairly regular correspondence with Sheppard. Though their exchanges often dwelt on more personal issues, frequently their letters turned to a discussion of the struggle against slavery. At times, especially in the early years of their correspondence, there seems to be a general agreement on the questions relating to American slavery. Over time, however, some crucial differences emerged, and McGill seems to have become more confident in asserting such differences.

Sheppard shared with his correspondent his frustration with free black resistance to colonization. He seems not to have understood why free African Americans should have been unwilling to submit to the plans of white colonizationists. "The people for whom I was devoting myself," he lamented, "refused to 'give me leave to toil' unless I did so under their dictation. I could not consent to make myself a slave to make others free."[25] At issue here is not simply the question of colonization, but also who is to be in control of any such plans.

He also wrote about other developments in the antislavery movement, often reflecting on the abolitionists who rejected African colonization. While in public many colonizationists denounced abolitionists, in his letters to McGill, Sheppard is more measured in his criticism. Though he continued to express his doubts as to the possibility that abolitionists might achieve their antislavery goals, he insisted that he did not want to stand in their way. He was convinced, however, that American prejudice was not so easily overcome, though Sheppard also admitted that he did not know if colonization could really accomplish the goal of complete emancipation.[26]

Sheppard maintained that the abolitionist movement was failing. "I have found few except Quakers and Methodists who will act for the blacks, and their interfering is fast declining, as the coloured people have nearly repudiated them." He places the blame for any declining support for antislavery squarely on the shoulders of African Americans.[27] Sheppard's letters seem to indicate that he was genuinely troubled by the resistance of free blacks to the colonization movement. Sharing these concerns with a black man who *had* embraced African colonization helped to assuage some of the guilt Sheppard seems to have felt about this. It also helped to reassure him that abolitionist criticisms of colonization were not legitimate.

Through his letters with McGill, Sheppard continued to create what he hoped would be a future of racial egalitarianism, made possible by distance. Again and again, Sheppard returned to this idea, the contrast between the fanciful abolitionist belief in the possibility of racial equality in the United States with the reality of the supposedly color blind relationship of the white colonizationist and the black Liberian. "My intercourse with you has been without reference to colour, complexion or cast," insisted Sheppard. "My opinion is abroad that complexion is not connected with mind, and I would willingly accelerate the period when arbitrary distinctions should be abolished."[28] Sheppard's correspondence with McGill, and to some extent with other Liberian emigrants, was a means of living out the racial arguments of a certain strand of colonization while refuting the claims of abolitionists that African colonization was merely a pretext for removing free blacks from the United States.

For his part, Samuel McGill also contributed to this depiction of colonization as a means of achieving racial equality. He contrasted his own prosperity and high social status with the limited possibilities faced by American free blacks. McGill also specifically contrasted himself with black abolitionists in the United States. Such men, McGill supposed, were easily deluded by the false promises of abolitionists, and "therefore led to seize on anything that presents itself . . . in order to keep his mind occupied or to render himself forgetful of his true social and political condition in the United States." He was optimistic that such delusions could not last however. "A few more years of oppression may be necessary and W will embark for Liberia—I cannot divest myself of this impression."[29] No doubt, Sheppard was encouraged by the fact that McGill echoed his belief that racial equality in the United States was an impossibility. This was evidence that the racial ideas of white colonizationists were not simply cover for bigotry.

If on the surface Sheppard's correspondence with McGill seems to demonstrate the possibility of racial equality, there was also an undercurrent that challenges this notion. Sheppard may have expressed a certain respect for McGill, and may have even treated him as an equal in certain circumstances, but it was also clear that Sheppard was McGill's patron. Even as Sheppard withdrew from some of his connections with colonizationists in the United States, he continued to devote his fortune to the support of Liberian settlers.[30] McGill's letters to Sheppard, then, must be seen in this context. Even as Sheppard sought accurate information about the conditions in Liberia, his correspondents would have been aware of their financial dependence on white supporters of colonization. To a certain extent, McGill's unflattering depiction of black opponents of colonization helps to reassure his patron, even as it assures McGill himself, that colonization was not an abandonment of the cause of the American slave.

Despite this imbalance of power, over time McGill seems to have become more comfortable making distinctions between his own views and those of many white colonizationists. In an 1849 letter to Moses Sheppard, McGill denied that he was any sort of moderate in regard to antislavery. "With the feelings I entertain on the subject of slavery," he boasted, "had I grown up in the States I should have been ten times more an object of distrust and suspicion than [black abolitionist, William] Watkins." He coupled this assertion, however, with an insistence that the abolitionists of the United States had exerted no influence in this area, and he dismissed them as hypocrites who "were unwilling to put into practice what they preach."[31] The context of this distinction is critical. His dismissal of the influence of abolitionists serves not primarily as a repudiation of abolition, but rather as an assertion of the natural opposition of African Americans to slavery. Contrary to the claims of many Southerners (and even many colonizationists), Sheppard asserts that resistance to slavery was not a product of the influence of white abolitionists. In McGill's hands, even the tropes of colonization become not a repudiation of antislavery radicalism, but a call for greater radicalism. Eventually, McGill's letters seem to be urging Sheppard in a more radical direction, even as they maintain their support for colonization as the best tool for such an effort.

Though Sheppard and McGill continued their correspondence, the differences that emerged between the two men over slavery challenge the notion that colonization, or at least the brand of colonization represented by Moses Sheppard, might have posed a realistic threat to the power of slaveholders. McGill seems to have had a mistaken notion of the attitudes of moderate whites toward slavery, assuming that they shared his disdain for the laws that rendered slavery legal, even as Sheppard insisted to his young protégé that the rights of slaveholders needed to be respected.[32]

Sheppard, on the other hand, seems to have grown increasingly frustrated with the agitation over slavery in the North. "The antislavery party," he wrote to a Pennsylvania Friend, "make more noise about one fugitive slave than the slaveholders of Maryland have made for all that have run away."[33] Despite his earlier defense of a man's refusal to participate in the return of a fugitive slave, Sheppard seems to have been more disturbed by the conflict promoted by Northern opponents of slavery than he was by the coercive aspects of the Fugitive Slave Law.

In this way, Sheppard reflected one of the central principles of the colonization movement: its insistence on consent. Sheppard's alienation from the colonization movement was in large part a result of his realization of the failure of this expected consent. It had become clear by the early 1850s that the resistance of American free blacks was not going to disappear. In private, Maryland colonizationists spoke of the need for some sort of "repulsion" in order to complement the "attraction" of Liberia, as a means of inducing free blacks to emigrate.[34] Publicly, they warned that those free blacks who did not emigrate consensually would someday be left with "no alternative but removal."[35]

Colonizationists also generally held that the enslaved should only be freed by the consensual actions of slaveholders. This posed an even greater barrier to the notion that colonization would ultimately lead to the end of slavery. Moses Sheppard and other Maryland colonizationists continued to hold out hope that a prosperous Liberian colony would liberate masters to emancipate their slaves, once they no longer feared that their actions would contribute to the growth of a free black population. If free blacks had demonstrated that they would not consent to colonization, slave owners had likewise indicated that consensual manumission might free some slaves, but it would hardly free them all.[36] Maryland colonizationists, however, remained wedded to the dream of consensual emancipation.

Samuel McGill's vision of antislavery differed significantly from the vision of white supporters of colonization. He denounced the Fugitive Slave Law, and he celebrated active resistance to it. He praised the fugitive slave for reclaiming his freedom. He hoped for reconciliation between the colonizationist and the abolitionist, but he recognized the futility of depending on the consent of slave owners as a means of fighting slavery. McGill saw in Harriet Beecher Stowe's novel, *Uncle Tom's Cabin*, a depiction of the sort of vigorous, active antislavery he supported. The novel ends with George Harris, one of its heroes, departing for Liberia: "The desire and yearning of my soul," he insists, "is for an African *nationality*."[37] Crucially, Harris had not been emancipated by a benevolent master, but he had won his own freedom by running away; later he even chased off a posse of slave-catchers with gunfire. McGill hoped that the novel might "make a powerful impression even on slaveholders themselves," but he surely recognized the significance of the character who became a Liberian not through the consent of a master, but through his own actions.[38] McGill, who at this point had become the governor of Maryland-in-Liberia, was so moved by the book, and its antislavery potential, that he sent its author a token of his appreciation. It was a massive gold ring with an accompanying message expressing "praise from one of the descendents of the race, whose wrongs and sufferings have engaged your attention and sympathy."[39]

McGill saw Liberia as the place where American free blacks were most likely to prosper, but he never gave up on his efforts to push for cooperation between the supporters of colonization and abolitionists. He thought that Stowe's book might be an important voice in this effort, but he despaired of his own ability to promote this end. "That my feeble advocacy cannot promote the anti-slavery cause in the United States I feel perfectly satisfied," he wrote to Sheppard in 1854, "In the U States the causes of Colonization and Abolition are made antagonistic; I do not view them in that light."[40]

Was McGill correct in seeing colonization and abolition as compatible? Did colonization pose a realistic threat to slavery in the border state of Maryland? An 1859 address delivered by Maryland colonizationist and president of the ACS, John H. B. Latrobe provides some insight. His presidential address that year was dedicated to expressing the principles and aims of African colonization. If he is to be counted as a reliable judge of the society of which he was the president, it seems that publicly the ACS had little to say about slavery. His address was published as a thirty-eight–page pamphlet, which made it clear that the removal of America's free black population was the goal of the organization. Tellingly, the only reference to slavery was to note that "the slave—protected, provided with food, shelter and raiment, treated in the vast majority of cases kindly, affectionately often—is without care as regards his physical wants, and with constitutional good humor passes happily, in the main, through life." There is not even a passing mention of the hope that the removal of free blacks would ultimately lead to the emancipation of slaves.[41] Certainly some Maryland colonizationists privately still hoped that this would be the case, but the need to avoid coercion of slaveholders led them to avoid making public even the mildest connection between colonization and emancipation.

Colonization coupled with the threat, even a distant threat, of government coercion posed a greater threat to border-state slavery. In Kentucky, Cassius Clay offered just such a proposal, suggesting a postnati emancipation law that would allow enough time, and incentive, for the potential free black population to be removed.[42] The words of Maryland colonizationists, however, both public and private, suggest that they had little stomach for such government intrusion into the property rights of slave owners. Latrobe, a frequent correspondent of Moses Sheppard, even went as far as to depict slaves as content.

Samuel McGill's vision of an antislavery colonization was a different story, but he seems to have had little success in convincing his patron. Moses Sheppard continued to cling to the notion that African colonization would lead to the ultimate end of slavery through the consensual, benevolent acts of masters. He continued to oppose slavery, but like many Quakers, he feared the violent conflicts that arose from the agitation of abolitionists, and he opposed the notion that the government should be used to coerce slaveholders. The historian Richard Newman has argued that the early 1830s transformation within the abolitionist movement was in part a shift from a deferential mode, in which respectable whites served as patrons of blacks to an immediatist one, in which blacks increasingly demanded equality.[43] Sheppard's relationship with McGill helped to bridge the gap between these two modes, enabling him to imagine that the older form of abolition could last, even in the face of the demands of American free blacks and the increasing militancy of the defenders of slavery.

By the 1850s, even Sheppard seemed to realize that his fantasy of a nonviolent, noncoercive end to slavery was unrealistic, and he despaired. His continued patronage of Liberian settlers seemed to have assuaged his guilt about this failure, but it also may have prevented him from embracing a course of action that had a more realistic chance of undermining slavery. It is impossible to know what Sheppard might have done in different circumstances, but it is clear that his brand of colonization posed little real threat to slaveholders. It was not absurd to think that the free black population of Maryland (or even the United States) might be removed to Africa, but it was absurd to believe that slavery could be ended peacefully and without government coercion.

NOTES

1. Moses Sheppard to Samuel Ford McGill, Feb. 16, 1849, ser. 2, box 2, Moses Sheppard Papers, Friends Historical Library (hereafter, Sheppard Papers).

2. McGill to Sheppard, Oct. 14, 1849, ser. 2, box 2, Sheppard Papers.

3. "The First Annual Report of the ACS," in *Annual Reports of the American Society for Colonizing the Free People of Colour of the United States* (New York: Negro Universities Press, 1969), 8–9.

4. Philip J. Staudenraus, *The African Colonization Movement, 1816–1865* (New York: Columbia University Press, 1961), 188–93; Benjamin Quarles, *Black Abolitionists* (New York: Oxford University Press, 1969), 5–8.

5. Staudenraus, vii; Quarles, 3–22.

6. See both William W. Freehling, "'Absurd' Issues and the Causes of the Civil War: Colonization as a Test Case," in *The Reintegration of American History: Slavery and the Civil War* (New York: Oxford University Press, 1994), 138–57; and *The Road to Disunion.* Vol. 2: *Secessionists Triumphant, 1854–1861* (New York: Oxford University Press, 2007).

7. Eric Burin, *Slavery and the Peculiar Solution: A History of the American Colonization Society* (Gainesville: University of Florida Press, 2005); Claude A. Clegg III. *The Price of Liberty: African Americans and the Making of Liberia.* (Chapel Hill: University of North Carolina Press, 2004); Marie Tyler-McGraw, *An African Republic: Black and White Virginians in the Making of Liberia* (Chapel Hill: University of North Carolina Press, 2007).

8. Ryan P. Jordan, *Slavery and the Meetinghouse: The Quakers and the Abolitionist Dilemma, 1820–1865* (Bloomington: Indiana University Press, 2007), 1–40; Thomas E. Drake, *Quakers and Slavery in America* (New Haven, Conn.: Yale University Press, 1950), 121–32.

9. "Colonization of Free Blacks," *Poulson's American Daily Advertiser*, Jan. 2, 1817.

10. For the public discourse of the ACS, see its newspaper, the *African Intelligencer*.

11. Jordan, 22, 35–36

12. Bliss Forbush, *Moses Sheppard: Quaker Philanthropist of Baltimore* (Philadelphia: J. B. Lippincott Company, 1968), 21–33, 130–32.

13. Paul Goodman, *Of One Blood: Abolitionism and the Origins of Racial Equality* (Berkley: University of California Press, 1998), 41–44; Richard S. Newman, *The Transformation of American Abolitionism: Fighting Slavery in the Early Republic* (Chapel Hill: University of North Carolina Press, 2002), 112–16.

14. Sheppard to Robert S. Finley, Apr. 27, 1833, ser. 2, box 2, Sheppard Papers. This Robert Finley was the son of the Reverend Robert Finley, who had been one of the guiding spirits of the founding of the ACS.

15. Historical Census Browser. University of Virginia, Geospatial and Statistical Data Center. Available at: http://fisher.lib.virginia.edu/collections/stats/histcensus/index.html (accessed Aug. 9, 2010); T. Stephen Whitman, *The Price of Freedom: Slavery and Manumission in Baltimore and Early National Maryland* (Lexington: University Press of Kentucky, 1997).

16. Forbush, 140–43, quote on 143.

17. Sheppard to Thomas Jackson, June 11, 1833, ser. 2, box 2, Sheppard Papers.

18. Forbush, 145–46.

19. Moses Sheppard to George McGill, Jan. 19, 1836, ser. 2, box 2, Sheppard Papers.

20. Moses Sheppard to George McGill, [n.d.], ser. 2, box 2, Sheppard Papers.

21. See, for example, *Address to the People of Maryland: With the Constitution* (Baltimore: Maryland State Colonization Society, 1831).

22. Donna McDaniel and Vanessa Julye, *Fit for Freedom, Not for Friendship: Quakers, African Americans and the Myth of Racial Justice* (Philadelphia: Quaker Press of Friends General Conference, 2009), 194–98, Douglass quoted on 195; Drake, 120–22.

23. Forbush, 146–47.

24. Ibid., 154–55.

25. Sheppard to McGill, Dec. 6, 1839, ser. 2, box 2, Sheppard Papers.

26. Ibid.; Sheppard to McGill, Nov. 20, 1842, ser. 2, box 2, Sheppard Papers.

27. Sheppard to McGill, Nov. 20, 1842, ser. 2, box 2, Sheppard Papers.

28. Sheppard to McGill, June 1, 1844, ser. 2, box 2, Sheppard Papers.

29. McGill to Sheppard, Mar. 11, 1845, ser. 2, box 2, Sheppard Papers.

30. Forbush, 159.

31. McGill to Sheppard, Apr. 25, 1849, ser. 2, box 2, Sheppard Papers.

32. McGill to Sheppard, Jan. 6, 1852, Sheppard to McGill, Mar. 25, 1852, ser. 2, box 2, Sheppard Papers.

33. Sheppard to Benjamin F. Taylor, Jan. 15, 1852, ser. 2, box 3, Sheppard Papers.

34. John H. B. Latrobe to Sheppard, Feb. 7, 1851, ser. 2, box 2, Sheppard Papers.

35. "Colonization Convention of Maryland," *Maryland Colonization Journal*, June 15, 1841, 15.

36. After dropping between 1830 and 1840, Maryland's slave population stabilized at around 90,000 between 1840 and 1860. Historical Census Browser. University of Virginia, Geospatial and Statistical Data Center. Available at: http://fisher.lib.virginia.edu/collections/stats/histcensus/index.html (accessed Aug. 9, 2010).

37. Harriet Beecher Stowe, *Uncle Tom's Cabin*, edited with an introduction and notes by Jean Fagin Yellin (New York: Oxford University Press, 1998), 440.

38. McGill to Sheppard, May 7, 1854, ser. 2, box 2, Sheppard Papers.

39. "Uncle Tom's Gold Ring," *Frederick Douglass's Paper*, June 3, 1853.

40. McGill to Sheppard, May 7, 1854, ser. 2, box 2, Sheppard Papers.

41. John H. B. Latrobe, *African Colonization—Its Principles and Aims: An Address* . . . (Baltimore: 1859), 9.

42. Freehling, *The Road to Disunion*, 227–29.

43. Newman, 1–15.

10 Friend on the American Frontier

Charles Pancoast's *A Quaker Forty-Niner* and the Problem of Slavery

JAMES EMMETT RYAN

Now, whatever idea we may form to ourselves of the typical American, or whether we think such a being exists at all, no one would ever imagine him to be a Quaker.
—Anonymous (1877)

AMERICAN QUAKER VIEWS CONCERNING slaveholding evolved over many decades until the nineteenth century, when opposition to slavery became firmly established among the Quaker faithful. This broad consensus, however, was fraught with disagreements over how Quakers should oppose slavery, whether politics was the appropriate avenue for Quaker resistance, and when, if ever, pacifist Quakers should themselves call for immediate emancipation when violence seemed the only possible consequence. Much of this debate was carried out in the public sphere or in meetinghouses, where leading Quakers articulated their views about race and slavery, but the opinions and attitudes of the average Friend during these public exchanges are still quite obscure to history. What can we surmise about how a moderately pious Quaker person would have understood issues such as slavery and race during a life devoted not to public activism or religious debate but instead to private activities such as business, travel, and courtship? Part of the answer to this question, I suggest, is in the private writings of Quakers who made no pretensions to civic leadership, and who made no special claims about their own piety.[1]

One example of private writing that sheds light on these issues is a memoir written by a young Quaker apothecary, Charles Edward Pancoast (1818–1906), who like many of his generation, journeyed west to seek adventure and fortune, leaving family and friends behind in Quaker New Jersey and in Philadelphia. As a younger son with no prospects for inheriting his father's farm, he was sent to Philadelphia for training as a druggist and, upon attaining adulthood, decided to seek his fortune on the Western frontier. Decades after he had returned to Philadelphia to resume a business career, he composed *A Quaker Forty-Niner:*

The Adventures of Charles Edward Pancoast on the American Frontier. This document, which had been kept in the Pancoast family as a cherished manuscript, first appeared posthumously in 1930, after the family submitted it for publication by the University of Pennsylvania Press. Although Pancoast's narrative has until now been neglected by scholars, the book is an important resource for literary and religious historians interested in the rich textures of everyday life on the antebellum frontier, especially those concerned with attitudes of Quakers toward the difficult issues of race and slavery.

Although he came of age at a time when Quaker activists such as Lucretia Mott and John Greenleaf Whittier were prominent abolitionists, Pancoast was neither an abolitionist nor a public figure. Nevertheless, ideas about race and slavery enter his memoir as aspects of a life devoted primarily to business and entrepreneurship, and his memoir serves as a useful index to the ways that ordinary Quakers of his generation perceived the national slave economy and the racial prejudices that formed its foundation. Most of Pancoast's account, though, details his own adventures and fortune-seeking in the Midwest and the Pacific Coast. Failing as a drugstore entrepreneur in Missouri, Pancoast spent time owning and operating a steamship on the Missouri River, and eventually found himself at work and seeking his fortune in business among the gold rush miners of California. In all, young Pancoast spent 14 years afoot in the hinterlands and byways of Western America, before returning home to settle in Philadelphia in 1854 at the age of thirty-six.

In the opening pages of his narrative, which he apparently wrote from memory or journal notes during his retirement years, Pancoast focuses first on the development of his own moral sensibilities and how they were shaped by his Quaker upbringing, with its peculiar speech, plain attire, twice-weekly meetings, and pious structures of daily life. Although he admits to some boyhood misdeeds, he also describes himself as being somewhat more upright in behavior than his peers. "When I come to review my conduct of those days," he writes, "I discover that there was some of the innate wickedness of the ordinary Boy in my character; but notwithstanding I was guilty of many boyish misdemeanors, I had an indwelling consciousness of right that made it impossible for me to do wrong without being strongly rebuked by a Spirit that confounded me in the act."[2]

We also learn from his narrative that, as a boy, Pancoast had become aware of slavery's insidious presence on the American scene, even in Quaker communities where abolitionism was relatively fervent and Friends had long urged their communities of the faithful not to own slaves. But the slave economy in New Jersey was in transition during his youth. As Pancoast was growing up, outright slavery was in rapid decline, but it would remain legal there until its permanent abolition in 1846. His memories of life in the New Jersey Quaker community illustrate the vexed relationships and tenuous allegiances between Quakers and slaves. For example, when he was only eight years of age, he recalls, "there was a settlement of Negroes not far from my Father's Farm, where a number of runaway slaves were harbored." One of these former slaves he describes as "an intelligent Young Fellow about seventeen years of age" employed by Pancoast's father. Hoping to assist the eager youth, Pancoast describes tutoring him: "my Brother and myself often devoted our evenings to teaching him." Months later, when a slave-catcher and the young man's former owner appeared at the Pancoast residence demanding the slave's return, the Pancoast family protected him from capture and allowed him to hide in the house and escape through the cornfield while his would-be captors were preoccupied. With some pride, Pancoast adds a filigree to his story by noting the young man's success in life: "The Boy [John S. Rock] . . . made his way to New York and from there to Boston, where some of the Abolitionists, discovering his Talents, sent him to London and educated him. He was admitted to the Bar in Boston, and afterwards to the Bar of the Supreme Court of the United States, the first Colored Person admitted to Supreme Court Practice." From this anecdote, we can presume that whatever the particulars of its views on racial equality, the Pancoast family was very much in step with Quaker teachings about the evils of slavery and was willing to endure considerable risk by sheltering at least one former slave from recapture.[3]

In 1839, the apothecary to whom Pancoast was apprenticed invited him to invest in a drug store partnership with one of his nephews in the fast-growing city of St. Louis. The description he provides of St. Louis in the summer of 1840 is vivid and throws into sharp relief the multiethnic, cosmopolitan life of an antebellum frontier city. Among the various groups he describes, the most prominent are those for whom commercial pursuits were foremost: swells and fortune hunters from New York City, Mormons on their way to the West, French fur traders and local landowners, "shiftless Squatters," and perhaps most notably "another class of Settlers, mostly Slave Holders, from the Southern States," who had come to speculate in frontier real estate. It is the slave-dealing Southerners for whom Pancoast reserves the sharpest criticism, for they constituted a scandalous and decadent "new class of Settlers [who] were Worshippers of the Institution of Slavery, with all its brutal tendencies, and of the Spirit of "Chivalry" prevalent in the Southern States; and although many Northern People were pouring into the City, when I arrived this Slave-holding class governed the City and Dominated all the Customs of Society."[4]

Pancoast had come of age during the 1830s, when the abolitionist movement was becoming radicalized and Friends in Quaker strongholds such as Philadelphia and the Delaware River Valley were embroiled in complex debates about slavery and its relationship to pacifism. Although Pancoast says nothing directly about the Philadelphia religious and political debates, he would have been aware of that city's violent events of 1838, when a proslavery mob burned down Pennsylvania Hall only three days after it was built. Pennsylvania Hall, which was designed to be an abolitionist meeting venue, had been commissioned by the Pennsylvania Anti-Slavery Society. The grand building hosted a number of abolitionist lecturers, including prominent Quakers, before it was destroyed. During the same year, a Quaker orphanage for African American children was attacked and damaged. Indeed, although Pancoast omits discussion of contemporary politics in Philadelphia, it is entirely possible that the tumultuous racial politics of Philadelphia may have played some part in his decision to turn toward the westward settlements of America to seek his fortune.

Excursions by Pancoast during the early 1840s led him from his new home base in St. Louis through parts of Kentucky, Missouri, and Illinois, and he describes encounters with frontier celebrities such as the famed evangelist Lyman Beecher; the frontiersman and Indian fighter Kit Carson; Democratic party leader Stephen A. Douglas; a young Abraham Lincoln, then a locally distinguished Republican politician in Springfield; and the Mormon leader Joseph Smith, whom Pancoast met on a riverboat in Illinois. As for Joseph Smith, Pancoast slyly describes him as having been drunk and "very mellow in consequence of his frequent potations." He reports further that when Stephen A. Douglas queried Smith about his drinking and asked "what his People would think of him if they should see him in this condition," Smith calmly and quickly replied that "he was compelled to do something occasionally to show his People that he was Human, otherwise they would constantly persist in worshipping him instead of the true God." The moral register in which such scenes are narrated by the young Friend prompted one reviewer of Pancoast's published memoir to observe how it embodied a tension between religious values and frontier reality, with the result that the memoir shows evidence not only of "the adaptability of 'Quaker' conduct to the exigencies of frontier life," but also "inward fidelity to the principles of that faith despite all the concessions extorted by untoward circumstances."[5] With flashes of humor and consistently well-wrought prose, Pancoast provides an account of his travels that registers a kind of Quaker everyman's perception of frontier life.[6]

By his own admission, the young Pancoast was above all concerned with seeking his fortune, first in the retail drug business and later in gold prospecting. But even as the allure of profit motivates his decisions, he takes time to document quotidian details of life on the frontier. Moreover, because he composed his memoir for publication after the upheavals of the Civil War and Reconstruction, he may have used the advantages of hindsight to emphasize certain aspects of his frontier adventures. For instance, it is evident from his comments in the memoir that he is opposed to slavery—an unsurprising position for a moderately devout Quaker of his generation—but he just as clearly is not yet the kind of egalitarian who would be able to promote full equality for the races. He thinks about African Americans in complex ways, although their distinctiveness as a "race" is never in doubt from his perspective. As for Native Americans, he is perhaps even more certain of his discrimination. Describing a journey across the Kansas territory, he recalls of the "half-civilized" Wyandotte and Delaware Indians in those parts that they were "generally squalid creatures, lamentably debauched and sunken in the scale of Humanity" and "that this condition was much the result of their association with White People, who furnished them with Whiskey and otherwise contaminated the morals of both their Women and their men." So it is that in a number of passages he writes of his certain opinion that while "Tribes of Wild Indians" remain admirably sober and chaste, native tribes who have been debauched and corrupted by white settlers on the frontier have been damaged to the point that they have become a repellent and barbaric culture mainly given over to warfare and immorality.[7]

Having said this, it is important to add that Pancoast's views about racial matters do not predominate in the memoir, which is not written as a treatise on slavery and includes commentary about American racial identities only in passing. In other words, Pancoast is alert to the intertwined problems of race and slavery, but for most of his account, they are not his central concern. Still, the inclusion of such details at the periphery of Pancoast's narrative provides valuable insight into the way that ordinary Quakers of this period might have considered the matter of slavery alongside other practical concerns. Indeed, his travel memoir has much in common with Mark Twain's *The Adventures of Huckleberry Finn* (1885), which, like Pancoast's memoir, was written in the aftermath of the Civil War and yet recounts the lives of ordinary American people caught up in attempts to sort their way through frontier lives in which slavery is just one of many pressing issues that aspiring middle-class citizens were forced to confront. Like Twain's work, slavery and its devastating consequences are included in Pancoast's memoir as part of the larger story of

American development; unlike Twain, however, Pancoast merely describes his memories of how race functioned in his travels through America. With no ambition to politicize or write polemically, Pancoast gives a fairly evenhanded and frank account that suggests in various ways how race and slavery framed the experiences of one moderately pious Friend. Reading the textures of his memoir, we begin to have a sense how an ordinary Quaker from Philadelphia would experience issues of race and slavery on the frontier, even as the Philadelphia of Pancoast's youth was itself embroiled in complex and sometimes violent debates over the fate of its African American population.[8]

Although his memoir for the most part avoids extensive discussion of politics or religion, the texture of cultural detail that he provides and his awareness of key public figures such as Abraham Lincoln and Joseph Smith suggest that the young Quaker was very much attuned to the social controversies of the day, even as his own faith was tested in various ways during his voyages into the West. It is also important to point out that although Pancoast was a Quaker, and that his perceptions were inevitably shaped by his religious beliefs and the antislavery community in which he was raised, he was nevertheless fairly moderate in his views about race, religion, and slavery. Moreover, as a birthright Quaker, he might have been expected at a minimum to embrace the plain life fully and without reservation, but instead it seems that part of Pancoast's motivation for travel was to enjoy some loosening of the Quaker discipline that had shaped his early youth. Raised to dress plainly and to behave with sobriety and rectitude, Pancoast nevertheless describes his own enjoyment of worldly pleasures during his sojourn across America, such as tavern life, drinking, gambling, dancing, and socializing with unattached young women.

During his westward sojourn, however, Pancoast was offended by a whole range of behaviors that settlers brought to Missouri, including the culture of dueling among Southerners, but even more so by their treatment of African Americans. While "the Spirit of Chivalry was fast being blotted out by the influx of Yankee enterprise," observed the young Philadelphian, "the Spirit of the Slave Holder was still dominant." Along with the spirit of the slaveholder came the gruesome practices of vigilantism and lynching that marked most publicly the power of white over black during the nineteenth century and even later. Ideologies and practical applications of white supremacy ruled the day, as in the following scene of lynching recounted by Pancoast:

> Soon after my arrival [in St. Louis], a Constable attempted to arrest a Negro Slave for some misdemeanor; the Negro resisted, and in the struggle killed the Constable with the blow of a Bludgeon. The Negro ran, but a

number of Citizens overtook him, and taking him to an open lot in the Suburbs, they chained him to a Stake and built up a fire around it. During the burning a leading Citizen of St. Louis, a high professor of Religion and a Deacon in the Church, imagined that the Lord (Instead of the Devil) had ordained him to throw more Combustibles on the Fire, and it was said that he threw powdered Sulphur on the poor Slave while he was burning and appealing for mercy to his God and the brutal People that surrounded him. I would make known the name of this Demon in Human shape, were it not that many of his Relatives and Descendants still occupy high places in St. Louis and the acts of this man would disgrace not him, but them, as he was deceased many years ago.[9]

Lynching and its violent rehearsal of white dominion over black bodies are fully exposed by this firsthand account by Pancoast, a Quaker who is ambivalent about race, opposed to slavery, and yet powerless to intervene. As this scene of racially motivated torture and execution shows, the experience of Missouri life for Pancoast was profoundly conditioned not just by the wealth of commercial opportunities that drew him to St. Louis, but also by the insidious logic of the slave economy and its disciplinary rituals.

The slave economy comes into even sharper focus with Pancoast's observations about a young African woman whom he encountered while making an excursion to the countryside surrounding Lexington, Missouri. After he leaves that riverfront community and crosses the "beautiful country settled by rich Slave Holders, with comfortable Dwellings and Outbuildings," Pancoast finds himself in a land of one-room cabins and poor squatters. Twenty-five miles from Lexington and its frontage on the Missouri River, he shelters for the night in the "miserable" town of Warrensburg, where he is startled to meet a newly enslaved young woman:

> Here there was a Log Hotel, where I procured a wretched Dinner served by a wild African Girl, six weeks in the country, who could not speak a word of any language but her own barbarous Jargon. She was tall, with a form as symmetrical as any Woman I ever set my eyes upon, but as black as a Raven. She did not deem it necessary to wear Clothes above her waist, but was adorned with a red Tunic below, and wore brass Bridle Rings in her ears for ornaments.

Shocked by slavery, Pancoast also disparages the rural Missouri women he labels as "Pioneer Wives" (transplanted poor whites from North Carolina) for their ill-kept homes, sickly children, crude manners, and lack of education by observing that "it was not surprising that they were so grossly ignorant of the World; nor that the Children became as wild as the Negroes of the African Jungle. (I have frequently seen the latter run like Deer at the approach of a Stranger and hide in the Bushes or under the Buildings.)"[10] Once more, Pancoast's attitudes about race show their complexity and this time emerge from his critique of the poor white squatters. Isolated from the more refined society available to the wealthy slaveholders living near the Missouri River, rural whites seem to live in ways that reduce them, in his opinion, close to an animal existence not unlike that of the African. Slavery and its brutalities are thus anathema to Friend Pancoast, but the wildness and animal qualities that he associates with dark-skinned persons of African descent he perceives as similarly repulsive. His alarm at the poor white squatters, as evidenced by his description of them as living like natives of the jungle, therefore serves as a way for him to register his racist way of perceiving the African slave but at the same time to allow for the possibility that whites, too, could become similarly debased under frontier conditions.

Although he opposes slavery, Pancoast associates African Americans with barbarism and subhuman qualities, and they are consistently described as a social force rather than as individual persons. Few of the black characters described in A Quaker Forty-Niner are given a specific name or described as having any depth of character or personality, and one is simply given the name "the Colored Man." While Pancoast had indeed provided a recollection from his youth in New Jersey of having come to the aid of an escaping slave, his representations of slaves on the frontier are notably less sympathetic. Much of his description of Missouri life focuses on the violent and criminal dimensions of the frontier, and he recounts not only the high life and alcohol-fueled merriment of the steamboats and port cities, but also numerous scenes of rowdy criminality, reckless gunplay, and vigilante justice. The inflection of vigilantism with aspects of slavery is especially prominent in a scene featuring the sleepy outpost of Warsaw, Missouri, where the town had recently been thrown into turmoil because "a worthless Fellow had brought a Harlot into Town and rented a House, which a number of men were in the habit of visiting." Shocked into action by the brothel's success in what Pancoast with some irony calls, "this Virtuous Community," a band of vigilantes takes to the streets. The chaotic scene gives some indication of Pancoast's complex moral and racial sensibilities:

Wilson's Band organized and caught the Woman's Pal in the Street, took his Knife and Pistol away, and tying his feet together, rode him on a sharp

Rail through the Streets to the Musick of Fife and Drum. After exposing him to the whole Town, they marched him to the River with the intention of ducking him. . . . [He was told] he could leave immediately, but if ever caught there again he would be roughly handled; and he departed on double quick time amid the hoots and jeers of the Party. . . . The Woman was notified to move away within two days, and hired one of McGowan's Teams to take her Goods to Jefferson City. . . . Before she was loaded up about one hundred Negro Wenches appeared on the ground, armed with Tin Pans, Bells, and a number of other horrifying Musical Instruments. . . . The Negroes followed the Team for about a half a mile, dancing, singing, hooting, and beating their various horrid-sounding Implements.[11]

As with Pancoast's previous description of a half-nude black serving girl and a black man's suffering in the Missouri lynching scene, once again African Americans are presented in a kind of narrative vacuum: without name, depth of personality, or distinctive character. Pancoast's precise attitudes toward persons of color are not easy to measure, although the "Negroes" whom he presents function as indices to a broader lack of civility on the frontier. The racialized scenes in his memoir signify in various ways, but each of these scenes marks out an aspect of the slave economy from the scandalized perspective of Quaker religious values: a black man lynched and tortured signify both racial supremacy and lawlessness; the young black woman enslaved and made to serve whites in a rural hotel brings home slavery's violent displacement of the innocent; and the flash mob of "Negro Wenches" who noisily run the prostitute out of Warsaw figure as brute vigilantes but also as agents of the kind of Bedlam and disorder that most offended Pancoast's sensibilities. Indeed, Pancoast is concerned enough about the lawlessness and danger signified by this scene that soon after he symbolically abandons his Quaker pacifism by electing to carry a concealed pistol.

Pancoast eventually sheds light on a new dimension of his thinking about race and slavery, and in so doing shows the evolving relationship between his ideas about slavery and his business principles. He soon realized that he was one of the few Missourians of his community who strongly disapproved of the slave trade, yet he became simultaneously aware that his success in business could be harmed if it were to become widely known that, as he plainly admitted, "my Quaker education had given me a strong natural aversion to the Institution of Slavery." He was not so fervent an abolitionist as to publicize his morality when it might reduce his profits. As he acknowledges, "my natural caution admonished me to avoid the subject as far as possible in this

Slave-Holding Community." Nevertheless, his restraint is unsettled after he befriends an attractive young woman, lodged at his hotel, who held strong antislavery opinions. She was "a Lady School Teacher, a Native of Massachusetts and the Daughter of a Methodist Preacher, then living in Illinois." Soon enough, the young Quaker began spending his leisure hours in conversation with her.[12]

"Like most Massachusetts Women," Pancoast recalled, "she had a great antipathy to the Institution of Slavery, and could not help expressing her sympathy with the poor Slaves." The "Christian Sentiments" expressed by Pancoast's new lady friend were welcomed by the young Quaker druggist, one of the few sympathetic acquaintances she had made, although he warned her not to broadcast her abolitionist views to their overwhelmingly proslavery neighbors. Soon enough, though, her antislavery sympathies were discovered and the proslavery town fathers forced her to abandon her school and leave town within twenty days. Just as the Missouri charivari mob had banished the pimp and prostitute with a clangorous and deafening performance, so too did they provide the young schoolteacher with a cruel and noisy banishment. When the schoolteacher's father, a noted preacher, arrived in Warsaw to retrieve his daughter, Pancoast observes that the community—including its most ostentatiously religious and devout citizens—treated him with contempt as well: "He was not asked by the Church People there to deliver a Sermon; so great was the terrorism of the System of Slavery that these Christian People, if they desired it, dared not give the poor Girl or her Father a word of sympathy; and I myself kept as much aloof from the affair as possible." Worse treatment yet was in store as the schoolteacher and her father rode out of town for the last time. Hearing "a great noise in the Street" outside his place of business, Pancoast suddenly realizes that yet another charivari mob had formed, and once again he provides a dramatic recounting of slavery's hegemony among the frontier settlers:

> Looking out, I saw a crowd of Women with horrid noisy Instruments such as I had listened to a few months before, when the Harlot was drummed out of Town; only now I observed that this motley crowd was headed by several of the leading White Women of the Town, who called themselves Ladies. In the midst of this assemblage of "Ladies" (white and black) could be seen the Reverend Old Father and his Daughter in their Gig, the Old Man driving his Horse on a walk, calmly turning his eyes from side to side, as if taking notes of this (to him) unprecedented exhibition of the degradation of Slavery. The half-civilised Wenches and their Demon Mistresses howled,

clattered their noisy devices, and abused the Old Man and his Daughter with opprobrious and insulting epithets . . . and gave them a set-off that would have done credit to the inhabitants of a Jungle.[13]

Pancoast barely escapes this violence and is forced to draw his handgun when confronted by one of the proslavery men who suspected that he might be an agitator against slavery. It is only by menacing the attacker with his pistol that Pancoast avoids serious harm.

The Missouri portion of Pancoast's adventures lasts until 1849, when he and his friends got news of the California gold rush. Having failed to achieve the business success that had been his ambition—the drug store failed to turn a significant profit, and his short-lived career as a steamboat pilot came to naught—Pancoast turned toward California to try his hand again at making a fortune. The second half of Pancoast's memoir details his travels as he makes the journey toward California, trading a druggist's business in the slave state of Missouri for new prospects. Most of those adventures between the years 1849 and his final return to the East in April 1854 distract him from the intense moral ambivalence that he experienced in response to Missouri's brazen and violent version of slavery. His commentary on race thus is more subdued in the latter part of *A Quaker Forty-Niner*, which is filled with vivid scenes of frontier life, including numerous encounters (some of them violent) with Native American tribes.

On the basis of the recollections included in his memoir, Pancoast could be fairly described as a rather ordinary, yet ambitious, American man with moderately strong Quaker religious values. The opportunity for narrating a retrospective account gives him an opportunity to describe himself as having held antislavery positions, but he is also honest enough to admit that his own ambitions for attaining financial security motivated him much more than Quaker religious principles did. When a choice had to be made between resisting slavery and enlarging his business profits, he consistently and unapologetically chose profits over any moral principle related to his stated belief that slavery was sinful. When his business failed in 1849 and the golden vistas of California beckoned him westward, Pancoast remembers, his thoughts were tied to ambitions for his own freedom and independence, not the freedom of others who happened to be enslaved. His great fear, he insists, was not poverty but the idea of his own subservience, and he states baldly, "I could cheerfully bear Poverty and Hardship, but could not brook the idea of being a commonplace Young Man serving a Master who exacted of me routine service for a small remuneration." Having himself once been a lowly apprentice, the last thing Pancoast was prepared to consider was the possibility of working for anyone but himself. It also seems reasonable to suppose that this independent streak, tied to his own work history and humble beginnings, may have shaped his views of slavery in significant ways. His concept of commercial and personal independence finds its way into descriptions of the work that he performs, as when a shortage of money forces him to labor as a clerk for a sharp-dealing and hard-drinking Sacramento druggist, "a bristling Jew who had learned his business in New York, but had been a Slave Driver in South Carolina." Pancoast can tolerate the work for only a few weeks, for his employer "pushed me all day in his Nigger-driving style, and I was ready to drop when bedtime came."[14] Pancoast in settings such as this is able to accept the reality of servitude even as he disapproves of it morally, and he strives to position himself as a person for whom slavery is yet another version of human subordination among many varieties that he detests.

That actual slavery is associated with African Americans appears to be a less important fact to him than the harsh recognition that tyranny and exploitation are a part of the human condition and rife in frontier America. As an educated Quaker, Pancoast would certainly have internalized the principle that human beings are entitled to respect and opportunity because of their equality in the eyes of God and the availability of the Inner Light to all persons. However, his memoir reveals him to be no abolitionist and no egalitarian for the races. Instead, he is at crucial junctures silent as others are oppressed, associates African Americans and some Native Americans with barbarism, and expresses a dread of interracial activities. Still, Pancoast's moral compass has a true aim when it comes to respect and honorable behavior, and race is only one factor in shaping his perspectives in these areas. For instance, in the closing pages of *A Quaker Forty-Niner*, we follow Pancoast in the fourteenth year of his travels, during which he is following an itinerary that will lead him down the Western Coast of Mexico, across Nicaragua by steamship, and then northward by sail and eventually home to Philadelphia.

It is fitting that one last anecdote should conclude this discussion of a quite ordinary, upwardly striving, and moderately devout Quaker entrepreneur. The final leg of Pancoast's journey included a slog across mosquito-infested Nicaragua, and specifically a steamship ride across the shallow and swampy Lake of Nicaragua. It is here that Pancoast and his fellow passengers find themselves at the mercy of a ship's captain who behaves with little regard for their safety: "Our Captain was black as a Colored Man, and I took him for a Native or a St. Domingo Negro; but I ascertained that he was a Native of New Orleans. He was a veritable Tyrant, and devoid of all Human Sympathy."[15] Pancoast describes being ordered with a hundred other passengers to go overboard and push the steamer over a sandbar, but then being nearly abandoned when, after the vessel was freed, the martinet captain steamed ahead without regard to their rescue or safety. Later in the steamship voyage, the captain withheld food and water from his passengers, so that they were literally starving when they finally arrived at their destination. For Pancoast, the critical point in this miserable journey is not the captain's precise racial identity—which is rather ambiguous—but instead his tyrannical and merciless treatment of others. By the conclusion of his many years sojourning in the West, Pancoast had nothing like a vision of freedom or civil rights for all persons, without regard to race, but he had certainly made decisions about unjustly applied power and the kind of tyrannical behavior that makes impossible a genuinely civilized life.

As Pancoast would have admitted, his own personal qualities were rather unexceptional and much like those of other Americans and many Quakers of his generation who experienced the social upheavals and the rise and fall of the slave economy during their own lifetimes. Although he was an articulate man of sensibility and moderate habits, he was not the kind of man for whom moral bravery came easily. His retiring ways and commercial ambitions disqualified him for the life of an activist while making him content to observe injustices without feeling obliged to act vigorously on behalf of the oppressed. Concluding his memoir in 1890, an aging Pancoast admits that his striving for a high station in life had not been entirely realized, even though his mature years brought him a moderate prosperity as a real estate agent. Allowing that he is mainly content with the experiences of his long life, he reflects, "I have now no feeling of Remorse in consequence of any act in my life, but rather deem it Regret that I have not done all the Good to my Fellow Creatures that I might have done. . . . But with all my shortcomings and imperfections I have the satisfaction of believing that I have never knowingly or maliciously wronged either Man or Woman." Believing himself to have lived a life in sympathy with civilized behavior, social progress, and racial justice, and yet aware of his inevitable missed opportunities for righteous action, Pancoast closely resembled many Quakers and other well-meaning citizens of his generation. High-minded and religiously educated and yet restless and eager for prosperity on the new American frontiers, he shows himself to have been an ambitious, thoughtful, but limited person sorting through vexed notions of racial identity while cautiously witnessing the decline of slavery.[16]

Anonymous, "John Greenleaf Whittier," *Catholic World* 24 (Jan. 1877), 437.

1. Ryan P. Jordan in *Slavery and the Meetinghouse: The Quakers and the Abolitionist Dilemma, 1820–1865* (Bloomington: Indiana University Press, 2007) documents "the growing gulf between abolitionist Friends and their clerical leadership" (45) during the 1830s and 1840s (41–66). See also Jordan P. Ryan, "The Dilemma of Quaker Pacifism in a Slaveholding Republic, 1833–1865," *Civil War History* 53, no. 1 (2007): 5–28.

2. Charles Edward Pancoast, *A Quaker Forty-Niner: The Adventures of Charles Edward Pancoast on the American Frontier*, ed. Anna Paschall Hannum (Philadelphia: University of Pennsylvania Press), 3.

3. Ibid., 5.

4. Ibid., 39.

5. Homer C. Hockett, "Review of *Charles Edward Pancoast: A Quaker Forty-Niner,*" *Mississippi Valley Historical Review* 17, no. 4 (1931): 620–21

6. Pancoast, 42–43. Quotations from Pancoast's memoir are cited with his frequent nonstandard capitalization and with his occasional variant spellings.

7. Ibid., 178. After his return from the frontier, Pancoast was a member of the Philadelphia-based Indian Rights Association, an influential advocacy group co-founded in 1884 by Henry Spackman Pancoast (1858–1928) and Herbert Welsh.

8. Ibid., 43–44. On racial politics and its associated violence in antebellum Philadelphia, see Samuel Otter, *Philadelphia Stories: America's Literature of Race and Freedom* (New York: Oxford University Press, 2010).

9. Pancoast, 39.

10. Ibid., 86, 87, 91.

11. Ibid., 109–10.

12. Ibid., 111–12. On Protestant evangelical views of frontier slavery, see Laurie F. Maffly-Kipp, *Religion and Society in Frontier California* (New Haven, Conn.: Yale University Press, 1994).

13. Pancoast, 112–13. On charivari, see E. P. Thompson's 1972 essay, "Rough Music," in *Customs in Common* (New York: New Press, 1991), 467–531. For a discussion of American charivari, see Dale S. Cockrell, *Demons of Disorder: Early Blackface Minstrels and Their World* (Cambridge: Cambridge University Press, 1997).

14. Pancoast, 364.

15. Ibid., 384.

16. Ibid., 392.

PART III   *Did the Rest of the World Notice?*
The Quakers' Reputation

11   The Slave Trade, Quakers, and the Early Days of British Abolition

JAMES WALVIN

THE RISE OF BRITISH POPULAR SUPPORT for abolition of the Atlantic slave trade after 1787 was rapid and totally unexpected. In its origins and during its early days, Quakers were pivotal. They were the pioneers of demands for ending the slave trade, and their influence and assistance proved vital in the transformation of abolition from a marginal, minority topic into a popular political concern. But even the founding band of abolitionist Quakers were taken by surprise by the way British abolition blossomed after 1787. The intellectual roots of abolition can be traced back much earlier and, though abolitionist sentiment, on both sides of the Atlantic, germinated over a long period of time, *the* most striking feature of abolition in its early years was the flowering of widespread *public* support for the cause.

Indeed, the recent awareness among historians of the importance of abolition as a popular phenomenon has, to a marked degree, transformed our understanding both of the nature, and of the success, of abolition itself. Only a generation ago, abolition tended, by and large, to be discussed as an aspect of parliamentary affairs, or as a feature of evangelical politics. But they too have tended to be marginalized. When historians discussed the progress of abolition, it tended to be the story of abolition *within* Parliament. It remains true that parliamentary politics and the course of evangelicalism remain central to any understanding of how the British slave trade was ended. (After all, it was an act of Parliament that ended the trade, and it was a powerful group of evangelicals who became the main driving force behind parliamentary abolition.) But historians have come to recognize that it was the surge of public support that lodged the issue into the political arena. There was, after 1787, a rising popular distaste about the slave trade among the British public at large that ran ahead of conventional political opinion. Indeed, parliamentarians themselves recognized that the public was in advance of Parliament on the subject of the slave trade. It was the growing strength and ubiquity of public abolition that forced Parliament first to recognize the problem of the slave trade and finally to do something about it. In all this, Quakers were an essential catalyst. But they too have tended to be marginalized. Yet they were both the inspiration and the organizational platform without which popular abolition could not have thrived.

The man who pioneered the abolitionists' research into the slave trade and the slave ships was Thomas Clarkson. It was his empirical investigations among slave captains, sailors, and slave ship rosters that teased out the hard facts and figures about life—and more important, of death—on board the slave ships. It was Clarkson's social scrutiny of evidence (about tonnage, manning levels, mortality rates, and of commodities imported and exported) that shifted the entire discussion about the slave trade. In the wake of Clarkson's pioneering investigations, discussion about the slave trade switched to a detailed analysis of the data. Thomas Clarkson and subsequent abolitionists ensured that the debate about abolition was not merely a recitation of moral outrage or religious disapproval (though there was plenty of both) but more about the *facts*. And once those facts were rehearsed in public (in cheap or free literature and in packed lecture halls), they proved irresistible. It was the hard evidence, culled from the belly of the slave ships, that both shocked and persuaded. Faced by a presentation and tabulation of statistical data from the slave ships, British audiences and readers were swiftly won over to the side of abolition. Moreover, it was evidence that the slave lobby could not counter or refute.

Thomas Clarkson is recognized as the remarkable foot soldier of the abolition cause. He embarked on a national one-man crusade against the slave trade, speaking across the country and traveling many thousands of miles to take the abolitionist cause to all corners of the kingdom. But he also *researched* the topic as he traveled. In time, he also harnessed the goods and products of Africa, which he trundled around the country in his famous chest of drawers, which he displayed to crowded audiences—in order to illustrate that Africa offered a cornucopia for normal trade.[1] Here was a continent brimming with produce and commodities, and filled with potential consumers of British-made goods, that beckoned the ambitious British trader. In essence, Clarkson offered an economic argument that there was huge economic potential for *normal* trade between Britain and Africa—if only the British could free themselves from their traditional addiction to trading for African humanity. What is not fully recognized is that Clarkson's approach to the slave trade formed a new methodology that originated among his Quaker contacts.

What inspiration lay behind Clarkson's abolitionist tactics? How did he devise his methodology? He was, after all, a very young man—in his early twenties—when he embarked on his first abolitionist activity in 1787. He was a recent Cambridge graduate, his early ambition to be a clergyman stalled then supplanted by his resolve to persuade people about the iniquities of the Atlantic slave trade. Clarkson's early success and inspiration owed much to his Quaker friends, contacts, and literature. As he toured the country promoting his case, he acquired ever more information, and he was often dependent on Quaker contacts, first in London and, in time, across the country, noting that "their houses were of course open to me in all parts of the Kingdom."[2] But even *before* he set out along these Quaker networks, he had been edged toward his research by one critical Quaker publication.

Thomas Clarkson was a brilliant Cambridge undergraduate, armed with a bachelor's degree in mathematics in 1783 and a prize for the best Latin essay in 1784. When the vice-chancellor, Dr. Peter Peckard, announced an essay prize on slavery, Clarkson rose to the challenge. Although the essay was framed in very general terms, Clarkson, remembering what Peckard had said in a recent Cambridge sermon, decided to concentrate on the African slave trade. He felt under considerable intellectual and social pressure to perform well in the competition and, to add to his anxiety, he knew nothing about the African slave trade. "But alas!," he wrote, "I was wholly ignorant of this subject; and, what was unfortunate, a few weeks only were allowed for the competition. I was determined, however, to make the best use of my time." Clarkson needed to find as much evidence as possible—and quickly. Fortunately, he "got access to the manuscript papers of a deceased friend, who had been in the trade." In addition, he collected information from "several officers who had been in the West Indies." His lucky break, however, came when he made a special trip to London to buy a copy of Anthony Benezet's *Historical Account of Guinea*, a pioneering abolitionist tract written by one of North America's most prominent Quakers that was published by London Quakers only months before. Clarkson found it a revelation. "In this precious book I found almost all I wanted."[3]

Studying Benezet's *Historical Account* proved a critical turning point. It was based on detailed research and sought to cast aside the deeply entrenched racial prejudices about Africa and Africans, illustrating instead not merely the equality of Africans, but doing so by the careful use of primary, empirical data. It was, at once, both a pioneering (almost anthropological) study and a bold (and very exceptional) assertion of African equality.[4] Benezet also incorporated the available evidence about the slave ships, scrutinizing published data in order to calculate the true size of the slave trade.[5] His findings—more important perhaps, his method—were to enter the abolitionist campaign largely via Thomas Clarkson.

When he began research for his essay, Clarkson was unaware of the earlier literature on the slave trade, and Benezet's book was able to steer him toward the available literature. More important still perhaps, Benezet provided a methodological blueprint for research. Benezet's book was informed and shaped by hard, empirical data: by looking at Africa and Africans through the eyes of men who had been *personally* involved, men who had been to Africa, who had lived and worked there, and who had worked on the slave ships. It provided a template that Clarkson was to make his own. By chance, Clarkson hit upon a critical and revealing approach: a means of discussing the slave trade via primary evidence. He now set out to find and arrange hard data from the ships and to collect verbatim accounts from men who sailed the slave ships. Clarkson quickly learned how to acquire and process such primary data from a firsthand source.

Other Quakers urged Clarkson to look closely at the slave ships. William Rathbone, a prominent Liverpool Quaker merchant familiar with local slave ships, encouraged Clarkson to study the muster rolls of those ships to unearth the factual evidence of life and death on the slave ships.[6] More broadly, Clarkson was deeply impressed by the attention that Quakers paid to the paperwork both in the Society's meetings and their commercial businesses. This "looking over the papers," the beady-eyed bookkeeping that was vital to Quaker commercial success, also generated a culture of arithmetical and statistical scrutiny that was to be a feature of the subsequent scrutiny of slave trade data. Regular and meticulous accountancy—and outside supervision of that data—was basic to Quaker life (both at work and in the meetinghouse).[7] It impressed Clarkson and encouraged him to adopt a similar attention to the data in the paperwork spawned by the slave trade.[8] Quite unconsciously, Thomas Clarkson had alighted upon a new methodology that he was to perfect and develop with great success over the next few years. It soon yielded rich returns, providing statistical, firsthand data that was incontrovertible and that became the shank of abolition activity thereafter—and well into the nineteenth century.

Clarkson realized that earlier authors on the slave trade were writing at a time when the slave trade was *not* a contentious issue. The authors—surgeons, captains, traders—had been able to write freely and openly about their experiences of the slave ships, without fear of incriminating themselves or worrying about how their accounts might be interpreted. Theirs were honest accounts, unadorned by the sorts of qualifications and reservations that inevitably crept into the literature after 1787, when the slave trade became a contentious political issue. There was an authenticity to this voice that Clarkson wished to capture.

Thomas Clarkson's immediate task—writing his Cambridge essay—was daunting. He recalled that "no person can tell the severe trial, which the writing of it proved to me." He even kept a lighted candle at his bedside in case a nighttime idea might strike, and he needed to jot it down. Although he had looked forward to the intellectual challenge of writing the essay, he now found himself deeply troubled by a frank reality he had not anticipated: not the demanding discipline of research and writing, but the brutal horrors of the slave trade. "It was but one gloomy subject from morning to night. . . . I sometimes never closed my eye-lids for grief." As he toiled with the task, Clarkson's essay was transformed from "a trial for academical reputation" into a work "which might be useful to injured Africa." Like others before him, Clarkson was first shocked, then galvanized, by what he learned.[9]

Clarkson's essay duly won the vice-chancellor's prize, and he read the essay in the Cambridge Senate House to approving applause. What followed has entered the folklore of the history of abolition. After delivering the lecture, and on his way back to London, lost in thought about the significance of the essay, Thomas Clarkson dismounted from his horse at Wades Mill in Hertfordshire. He realized "if the contents of the Essay were true, it was time some person should see these calamities to their end. Agitated in this manner I reached home." That summer, Clarkson lived in a state of some anxiety, plagued by the same recurring thought. "Are these things true?" In his heart, he knew that they were, but he felt that he alone realized this.[10] He yearned to know of other people—politicians, clergymen—who might also take up the cause of the slave trade. But Clarkson felt powerless: what could an unknown twenty-five-year-old achieve on his own? Still, he slowly came to appreciate that he *could* do something practical: he could translate his essay (from Latin), revise, extend, and finally publish it—and hope for a public response. Thus, in mid-November 1785, Thomas Clarkson began the work, at home in Wisbech, that would transform his life and have an incalculable influence on the history of the British slave trade.

With the essay translated, in the new year 1786, Clarkson headed to London to find a publisher. An old Quaker family friend from Wisbech took him to meet James Phillips, the Quaker publisher and bookseller, who in his turn, introduced Clarkson to a circle of prominent London Quakers.[11] As his network of London contacts expanded, Clarkson became aware of that coterie of Quakers and associates, including Granville Sharp, who had been active, for some years past, both for black legal rights in England and against the slave trade. This devout young man was now convinced that "the finger of Providence was beginning to be discernible; that the day-star of African liberty was rising, and that I probably might be permitted to become a humble instrument in promoting it."[12]

As Clarkson worked with James Phillips on the publication of his essay, his new metropolitan friends strengthened and reassured the young author through his periodic moments of doubt and uncertainty. Finally, in June 1786, one year after he had read his Latin essay in Cambridge, Clarkson published his book under the title *Essay on the Slavery and Commerce of the Human Species, Particularly the African.* By then, he had been integrated into a group of like-minded people, who were to form the core of the later Clapham Sect and who met at Barham Court in Teston, Kent. Teston was to be the location and heart of the early evangelical attack on the slave trade, and the people around Clarkson at Teston were all eminent and influential figures. They were, however, busy people, preoccupied with their own political, personal, or commercial interests, and none was able to concentrate *solely* on the slave trade. Only the young Clarkson seemed in a position to devote himself uniquely to the cause.[13] Knowing that he would have to abandon his clerical ambitions (to his family's inevitable disappointment), Thomas Clarkson nonetheless publicly pledged in 1786, "that I would devote myself to the cause of the oppressed Africans."[14]

Clarkson had initially assumed that his was a lonely crusade and had been astonished to learn that so many others were *already* arguing and writing about the slave trade. By the summer of 1786, however, he was firmly embedded in a network of abolitionist sympathizers and had become one of an expanding circle outraged by what they knew of the slave trade and who were determined to end it. Even so, their numbers were small and they were confronted by a massive, entrenched, and prospering industry. We now know that, after the peace of 1783, the British slave trade boomed. In the last half of the 1780s, for example, more than half a million Africans were shipped to the Americas.[15] The slave trade lobby, merchants, financiers, shippers (in Liverpool, William Gregson and his local associates, for example, had ten ships at sea or preparing to transport Africans to the slave colonies in the years 1785–1788)[16] could never have imagined that this small coterie of critics, however articulate, influential, and dedicated, would become such powerful political adversaries. Still less could they have dreamed that this small band of critics would, within a generation, bring Britain's mighty slave trade to its knees.

The process effectively began in 1783 when London Quakers established a twenty-three-person–strong committee to study the slave trade.[17] At much the same time, informal groups of Quakers—some of them with experience with North American slavery via their commercial or preaching tours in the colonies—began to meet informally to see how best they might promote abolition. Such informal gatherings were a means of circumventing the tight Quaker discipline that characterized formal proceedings within the Society of Friends and might prove quicker and more effective than the slightly bureaucratic methods of the Society itself. One such group, of six Quakers, decided, in the summer of 1783, to sponsor abolitionist essays, letters, and articles in the press. Thus, over the next five months, abolitionist pieces began to appear in newspapers in London and major provincial centers: in Norwich, Bath, York, Liverpool, and Bristol—and in newspapers as far afield as Newcastle and Dublin. At the same time, men in London, led by the publisher James Phillips, were active in persuading the twenty-three-person–strong committee of the Society of Friends to declare publically against the slave trade. In October 1783, two thousand copies of a fifteen-page tract, *The Case of Our Fellow Creatures, the Oppressed Africans. . . .* were published. In the following year, copies were distributed to all new members of Parliament (MPs), major cabinet members, and to the royal family.[18]

Such Quaker literature began to seep across the country and addressed not merely the morality (and theological) outrages of the slave trade, but also confronted directly the economics of Britain's involvement in slaving. The literature represented a determination to establish not only a broadly based humanitarianism, but also formed an appeal to British consumers to abandon slave-grown produce and to base their consumption on moral grounds. In the process of distributing such tracts, through sympathetic associates from other churches and religious organizations on both sides of the Atlantic, Quakers not only tapped into a broad sense of unease about the slave trade, but also established the organizational contacts, notably with the Church of England, which were to prove important in the subsequent abolitionist campaign.

When the Society for Effecting the Abolition of the Slave Trade was founded in May 1787, it set itself the task of "procuring such Information and Evidence, and for Distributing Clarkson's Essay and such other Publications, as may tend to the Abolition of the Slave Trade." They also set out to raise funds to make this possible.[19] It was, essentially, a Quaker organization, as Granville Sharp told his brother John that July: "A Society has lately been formed here for the purpose of opposing the Slave Trade: though the Members are chiefly Quakers, I thought it was my duty, when invited, to join them in so just a measure."[20] This founding band of abolitionists realized that Thomas Clarkson's initial essay was too big, too densely argued, for popular consumption. They wanted a short, snappy tract for a more popular market and, therefore, commissioned Clarkson to produce an eight-to-ten-page *Summary View of the Slave Trade.* This was quickly followed by another sponsored tract, *An Essay on the Impolicy of the African Slave Trade.* First read to the Abolition Committee, the essay was suitably corrected, and two thousand copies published and distributed "to various parts of the kingdom." Thus began the drive to win over the public by carefully crafted propaganda, all grounded in firsthand, eyewitness experience of the slave trade, and made available in accessible, cheap or free pamphlets. It was an appeal to the literate: to men and women who would heed published arguments if presented to them in an easily available and manageable format.[21]

At the same time, abolition took root in Parliament. In the course of 1787, William Wilberforce MP had come into contact with Thomas Clarkson and a group of anti–slave-trade activists who persuaded Wilberforce to speak for abolition in Parliament.[22] Thereafter, the story of the progress of abolition through Parliament is closely associated with the work of William Wilberforce himself. But the most remarkable and innovative aspect of the new campaign against the slave trade was not so much in Parliament, but among the public at large. This public agitation was led by Thomas Clarkson, who set out to inform the nation about the slave trade via a series of punishing lectures tours. By 1794, he had covered an astonishing 35,000 miles, speaking, organizing new committees, and gathering new evidence about the slave ships from ports across Britain, and incorporating that data into his lectures and writings.[23] Demands for abolition of the slave trade, picked up by small local groups of like-minded people (often initiated by local Quakers) swiftly gathered strength and voice across Britain. In the process, the demand to end the slave trade was transmuted from a minority issue—the preserve of small handfuls of people—into a national clamor. Within months of the founding of the Abolition Society, that is, by the end of 1787, the abolition campaign had become genuinely popular nationwide and was cutting across the boundaries of class, region, and gender. But how had that happened, and all in a matter of months?

Quite simply, abolitionist literature regaled the reading public with the stark realities—the truth—from the slave ships. The brutal and sometimes unspeakable details about the fate of *all* Africans transported across the Atlantic were exposed in graphic and irrefutable detail. The slave ships formed the heart of the abolitionist message and were portrayed in their full horror via images, data, and firsthand testimony. First of all, those realities shocked, then angered the British people. Once angered by what they learned, they resolved to demand that Parliament, which was vital to the emergence and development (indeed to the very survival) of the British slave trade, should bring it to an end.[24]

The pioneering abolitionists whipped up popular antipathy to the trade and lodged that feeling in Parliament, via hundreds of petitions, that were signed by thousands of people. All this was paralleled by a barrage of published information and argument hostile to the slave trade. In the process, abolitionists established a pattern that was to characterize their politics right through to 1807. It seems clear that public feeling about the slave trade moved ahead of Parliament. Indeed, the *speed* with which antagonism to the slave trade sprang up across Britain surprised the abolitionists themselves, even though it was prompted by their own efforts.

After May 1787, abolitionists generated an extraordinary volume of printed material aimed at the British public. Clarkson calculated that, in the first year alone, the Abolition Committee had issued "not at random, but judiciously and through respectable channels" 51,432 pamphlets and books and 26,525 reports and papers. In addition, scarcely a daily newspaper or monthly magazine failed to carry items about abolition.[25] All this was orchestrated by an abolitionist organization that, though originating in London, quickly sprouted *local* roots. Quakers (with their excellent organizational facilities) were often the initial activists, but they quickly attracted a wide range of committed provincial followers. Within months, the pioneering abolitionists found that they had been midwife to a genuinely *national* organization that, in its turn, spat out and distributed an ever-growing volume of publications, sponsored both by London and by local abolition committees.

To parallel the printed word, the abolitionist message reached large crowds of interested people at lectures across the nation. Abolitionist speakers, led by the indefatigable Clarkson, were always guaranteed a full house and a good reception wherever they spoke. When Clarkson spoke in a Manchester church, he found it "was so full that I could scarcely get to my place."[26] The aim of all this effort was to generate public anger, and to direct it toward Parliament, in the hope that the legislature would recognize the iniquities of the slave trade—and abolish it. In 1787, the most effective way of generating and directing public feeling was to organize petitions. In that first wave of agitation, an estimated 103 abolition petitions, signed by tens of thousands of people, descended on Parliament.[27]

By the end of May 1788, only one year after the launch of the Abolition Society, Parliament had been inundated by abolition petitions. The table of the House of Commons "was loaded with petitions from every part of the kingdom." In the words of Prime Minister William Pitt, no one doubted that the slave trade "had engaged the public attention to a very considerable degree."[28] Unparalleled numbers of ordinary people turned to the abolition cause and scratched their names in their tens of thousands onto abolition petitions. By the summer of 1788, the slave lobby recognized "the stream of popularity [which] runs against us."[29] In the House of Lords, Lord Carlisle said, "It was a matter of public notoriety, that the question of the Slave Trade had engrossed the attention of every part of the kingdom for above these twelve months."[30] The impact of abolition petitioning went far beyond the history of the slave trade. It showed how the public mood could be captured and channeled toward Parliament. Here was a method for expressing public opinion that was to influence reforming politics for the next half century, right down to the Chartist movement.[31]

Both Lords and Commons recognized the national popularity of abolition and the *unpopularity* of the slave lobby (however much economic benefit flowed from their activities). The once-unchallenged political sway of the West India lobby had been seriously damaged. By 1788, it was clear that abolition had undermined the political influence of the slave lobby. Spokesmen for the slave trade were roundly condemned and out-argued. Abolition had gained the political and moral high ground and was never again to relinquish it to the slave lobby.

These first abolition petitions were intended to coincide with a parliamentary scrutiny of the slave trade that had been initiated by Prime Minister William Pitt, who, in his turn, had been influenced by his old friend Wilberforce. Pitt also met Thomas Clarkson, grilling him for two hours about the data Clarkson had assembled about the slave trade. The prime minister thereafter initiated an enquiry by a committee of the Privy Council. For a year between 1787 and 1788, that committee listened to and gathered information about the slave trade. It was, once again, a reprise of Clarkson's method of accumulating firsthand information from men with personal experience of the slave ships. Clarkson was, once more, central; he choreographed key witnesses from the ranks of ex-slavers, clerical abolitionists, and others well-versed in the details of the trade. The abolitionist arguments presented to the Privy Council were fiercely contested by spokesmen from the slave lobby, but their main difficulty—an insurmountable obstacle, really—was that the bleakest of evidence about the slave trade now paraded before the Privy Council and in Parliament was simply irrefutable. When abolitionists lobbied MPs, they realized that they had strong support in the Commons (although the Lords was to remain resistant to abolition throughout.) Indeed, Edmund Burke scolded the House of Commons for not heeding the popular voice on the slave trade earlier.[32] Nonetheless, by May 1788, it was clear that the question of abolishing the slave trade had taken root in Parliament. Within the space of a mere twelve months, abolition had secured a parliamentary foothold and had tens of thousands of supporters throughout Britain.

Thomas Clarkson's influence in all this was evident. Parliamentary investigations into the slave trade (within the Privy Council, and research by individual MPs) effectively copied the method he had devised for writing his Cambridge essay. By tapping into the experience and memories of sailors and traders, by scrutinizing the available maritime and commercial data, Clarkson had established a highly effective methodology, and in the process had created an influential political tool for attacking the slave trade. Moreover, the voices of slave captains and surgeons, aligned with raw data from the slave ships (the levels of sickness, suffering, and death among Africans—and sailors) proved both astonishing and unassailable. This scrutiny yielded some surprises, notably the evidence of high mortality rates among the crews of the slave ships. (William Pitt was personally moved by evidence about sailors' deaths that Clarkson presented to him from ship's rosters.) All this potent evidence, long hidden in the belly of the slave ships, was now freely and widely available in print. It reached and persuaded legions of people previously ignorant about the slave trade. The slave trade could be *proved* to be a dangerous business. An irresistible feeling began to emerge, from within the Privy Council hearings, and at crowded public meetings across Britain, that the slave trade was a moral, dangerous, and often fatal abomination.

Only four years had passed between the first Quaker petition to Parliament against the slave trade, and Parliament's first serious scrutiny of the slave trade in May 1788, but, in that time, huge numbers of British people had begun to learn about the slave trade in very great detail. The revelations about the slave ships possessed an *immediacy* that was lacking in earlier ethical and religious condemnations of the slave trade. What had emerged was a new critique: one shaped by eyewitness accounts and statistical analysis—and all aimed at unprecedented numbers of British people. The thousands of abolition tracts, pamphlets, essays and articles, public lectures, and, eventually, parliamentary scrutiny, fed into and enlarged the dramatic upsurge of popular abolition sentiment.

Thomas Clarkson's method of unearthing and publicizing primary evidence also had a remarkably energizing effect across the country and was largely responsible for encouraging a vogue for local empirical analyses of slave trade data. Critics and intellectuals everywhere turned their attention to the data from the slave ships, analyzing, disputing, and republishing their findings across Britain. It is true that in large part the timing was fortuitous, for Clarkson's calculations paralleled the new vogue for statistical analysis among groups of educated people dotted around provincial Britain, many of whom were drawn to the scientific and mathematical societies that proliferated (often in unlikely places) in the late eighteenth century.[33]

To take one example, a Mr. Clarke of Salford ("universally known to rank among the first mathematicians of this kingdom") responded to the mathematical challenge posed by Clarkson's data. He illustrated, statistically, the fatal and harmful consequences of the trade and incorporated his own findings into an abolitionist pamphlet published in Warrington.[34] Here was one simple, local example, from the northwest of England, of a national pattern of provincial society responding to the abolitionist prompting from London. But it also illustrates the widespread appetite for the application of mathematical and statistical analysis to pressing social and political problems. Statistics were to become a dominant social and political tool in nineteenth-century Britain, and they ranged from counting the population (first done in the 1801 *Census*) to analyzing poverty and illness. Statistics provided the means toward a greater understanding of an increasingly complex world at large. The debate about the slave trade after 1787 provided an early and effective example of how that might be done. Within a year, sixty thousand people petitioned Parliament for an end to the slave trade.[35] Twenty years later, Parliament declared the slave trade to be illegal.

Although abolitionists had to wait two decades after the foundation of the Abolition Society for success, the wonder is that abolition passed through Parliament at all, because those twenty years were characterized by political turmoil, revolution, warfare, and slave revolts. The early optimism and support for abolition after 1787 was simply ground down by the mid-1790s by a rising tide of reactionary alarm about the mounting unrest and dangers in Britain, Europe, and the slave colonies. Popular politics, of all kinds, withered. The most daunting threat flowed from the volcanic slave revolt in Saint-Domingue, which, after 1791, sent waves of discontent (and ideas about liberty) rippling through the slave quarters of the Americas. In November 1791, the Colonial Office received word from Jamaica that "the ideas of liberty have sunk so deep in the minds of all Negroes, that wherever the greatest precaution[s] are not taken they will rise."[36] Slaveholders everywhere had good reason to feel threatened. The contagion of liberty, unleashed first by France, then by Saint-Domingue, made it obviously dangerous to tamper with the slave trade and slavery. Abolition supporters (including the normally irrepressible Wilberforce) languished, both in Parliament and in the country at large. One of the founders of the Abolition Society, the Quaker Joseph Woods, said in 1796, "I keep myself as quiet as I can in my own habitation."[37]

All this quickly changed in the early years of the new century when a transformed political climate brought to power new ministers and new governments sympathetic to ending the slave trade. Parliament finally passed the necessary legislation, first in 1806 (in the form of the Foreign Slave Trade Act) and finally, in 1807, the Act for Total British Abolition. On March 1, 1807, the Commons passed the abolition of the slave trade by 17 votes to 175 before it passed through the once-reluctant Lords.[38] Finally, on March 25, 1807, the House of Commons rose to give a standing ovation (so rare that no one could remember the last time it had happened) for William Wilberforce, who quietly sat in his place, tears streaming down his face.[39] However much historians have argued about how the Abolition Act came into being, those most closely involved, in Parliament—the MPs who actually voted for abolition—were in no doubt that Wilberforce had been indispensable. A year later, the United States passed their own abolition legislation (although by then the slave trade to North America was relatively small and unimportant because the North American enslaved population was growing rapidly of its own accord).

Looking back, the twenty years after 1787 seems a short period for the conception, growth, and ultimate success of abolition—all in the teeth of hostile political circumstances, to say nothing of the dogged resistance of the powerful slave lobby. Clearly, the roots of abolition were complex and deep, and they stretched back far beyond 1787. But in the critical, early days, the Quakers were vital. Theirs had already been a pioneering and lonely voice in the wilderness, given transatlantic focus by Anthony Benezet. Inspired by Benezet, and influenced by the social and cultural company of the Society of Friends, Thomas Clarkson developed that remarkable methodology that was crucial in transforming abolition into a popular political force. The result, by the end of 1787, was that abolition was a popular force in the land. In the process, evidence from the slave ships coalesced into an unanswerable argument for abolition. Through all this, as in so many other areas of contemporary life, the Quakers had exercised a profound influence out of all proportion to their numbers.

NOTES

1. Thomas Clarkson's African box, item 22, in *The British Slave Trade: Abolition, Parliament and People*, ed. Stephen Farrell, Melanie Unwin, and James Walvin (Edinburgh: Edinburgh University Press, for the Parliamentary History Yearbook Trust, 2007), 308–13.

2. Thomas Clarkson, *A Portraiture of Quakerism, As Taken from a View of the Moral Education, Discipline, Peculiar Customs, Religious Principles, Political and*

Civil Economy, and Character of the Society of Friends, 3 vols. (London: Longman, Hurst, Rees, and Orme, 1806), 1: i.

3. Thomas Clarkson, *The History of the Rise, Progress, and Accomplishment of the Abolition of the African Slave-Trade by the British Parliament*, 2 vols. (London: Longman, Hurst, Rees, and Orme, 1808), 1: 207, 403.

4. Maurice Jackson, *Let This Voice Be Heard: Anthony Benezet, Father of Atlantic Abolitionism* (Philadelphia: University of Pennsylvania Press, 2009), chap. 4.

5. Jackson, 160.

6. Clarkson, *History*, 1: 371.

7. James Walvin, *The Quakers, Money and Morals* (London: John Murray, 1997).

8. Clarkson, *Portraiture*, 1: i; 2: 51.

9. Clarkson, *History*, 1: 208–9.

10. Ibid.

11. Ibid., 1: 216–17; Judith Jennings, *The Business of Abolishing the British Slave Trade, 1783–1807* (London: Frank Cass, 1997), chap. 3.

12. Clarkson, *History*, 1: 214–16.

13. For the importance of Teston, see Christopher Leslie Brown, *Moral Capital: Foundations of British Abolitionism* (Chapel Hill: University of North Carolina Press, 2006), 341–53.

14. Clarkson, *History*, 1: 225.

15. For the slave trade data, see "Estimates, Five Year spans," *Trans Atlantic Slave Trade Database*, available at: http://www.slavevoyages.org/ [Accessed August 17, 2012].

16. "William Gregson, Voyages, 1785–1790," *Trans Atlantic Slave Trade Database*.

17. Clarkson, *History*, 1: 118–20.

18. Jennings, 24–25.

19. Minutes of the London Abolition Committee, 3 vols., Add Ms 21, 254–21,256, I, May 22 1787 [British Library]; Clarkson, *History*, 1: 277–78.

20. July 19, 1787, Granville Sharp to John Sharp, Granville Sharp Papers, Gloucester Record Office.

21. For the story of popular literacy, see David Vincent, *Literacy and Popular Culture, England, 1750–1914* (Cambridge: Cambridge University Press, 1993).

22. William Hague, *William Wilberforce: The Life of the Great Anti-Slave Trade Campaigner*, (London: HarperPress, 2007).

23. James Walvin, "The Propaganda of Anti-Slavery," in James Walvin, ed., *Slavery and British Society, 1776–1846* (London: Macmillan, 1982), 52.

24. The popularity of abolition is explored in Seymour Drescher, *Capitalism and Antislavery: British Popular Mobilization in Comparative Perspective* (New York: Oxford University Press, 1987).

25. Ellen Wilson, *Thomas Clarkson: A Biography* (York: William Sessions, Ltd., 1989), 42.

26. Clarkson, *History*, 1: 418.

27. William Cobbett ed., *The Parliamentary History of England from the Earliest Times to the Year 1803, 36 vols. (London: Longman, 1815)*, Vol. 27 (1788–1789), cols.

396, 498, 501, 644. See also *Gentleman's Magazine*, 58: II (July–December 1788), 610–13, 794–800.

28. *Parliamentary History*, 1066–1918, 27: cols. 495–501.

29. Quoted in Seymour Drescher, "Public Opinion and Parliament in the Abolition of the British Slave Trade," in Farrell et al., 51.

30. *Parliamentary History*, 27: 644.

31. Betty Fladeland, "'Our Case Being One and the Same,' Abolitionists and Chartism," in Walvin, ed., *Slavery and British Society, 1776–1848*, chap. 3; James Walvin, "William Wilberforce, Yorkshire and the Anti-Slavery Movement, 1787–1838," in John Hargreaves and Hilary Haigh, eds., *Slavery in Yorkshire: Richard Oastler and the Campaign against Child Labour in the Industrial Revolution* (Huddersfield, U.K.: University of Huddersfield Press, 2012).

32. Wilson, 43–44.

33. See for example Jenny Uglow, *The Lunar Men: The Friends Who Made the Future, 1730–1810*, (London: Faber, 2002).

34. Thomas Cooper, *Supplement to Mr Cooper's Letters on the Slave Trade* (Warrington: W. Eyres, 1788), 37.

35. Seymour Drescher, *Abolition: A History of Slavery and Antislavery* (Cambridge: Cambridge University Press, 2009), 215.

36. Anonymous Letter, November 18, 1791, in C.O. 137/89. The National Archives, Kew.

37. Quoted in Jennings, 89.

38. For full details of the parliamentary campaign, see Roger Anstey, *The Atlantic Slave Trade and British Abolition, 1760–1810* (London: Macmillan, 1975).

39. Robin Furneaux, *William Wilberforce* (London: Hamilton, 1974), 253; Hague, 354.

12 The Quaker Antislavery Commitment and How It Revolutionized French Antislavery through the Crèvecoeur–Brissot Friendship, 1782–1789

MARIE-JEANNE ROSSIGNOL

SLAVERY AND ANTISLAVERY AT THE HEART OF THE *LETTERS*

J. Hector St. John de Crèvecoeur's *Letters from an American Farmer* was long seen as the first expression of American literary consciousness.[1] Ending with a letter titled "What Is the American, This New Man?," the first three letters in a book that contains twelve could understandably be seen as praising the new American nation at the time the book was published, and later at the heyday of American studies in the United States. But contemporary critics are now challenging this view, placing the book in its proper historical perspective and assessing Crèvecoeur's personality in a more nuanced way.[2] My own point in this chapter is that an essential key to interpreting *Letters* is to read it from an antislavery angle. Crèvecoeur's admiration for Quakers and their commitment is obvious throughout the book. It is all the better understood when one knows of his antislavery activities in the United States and France between 1785 and 1787, and how Jacques-Pierre Brissot, later to found the first French antislavery society, was deeply influenced by the older man.

The historical record does not sustain an interpretation of *Letters* as favorable to the new American nation: Crèvecoeur left a war-ridden United States under suspicion of loyalism in 1781.[3] *Letters*, as they were first published in 1782, praise the British colonies in North America, and Britain itself as a benevolent power.[4] The "frontier" is described as a haven for disreputable characters, while Indians (against whom the patriots warred in the West) are depicted in preromantic hues. As a former soldier in the French army, which eventually lost Canada to the British in 1760, Crèvecoeur may have been skeptical of the unnatural wartime alliance between George Washington, a former officer in the British militia, and his Seven Years' War enemies, the French.[5] Only later, in the 1784 French edition of the *Letters*, did Crèvecoeur position himself as a pro-American author, dedicating the revised version of the *Letters* to Lafayette.[6] This was a time when he was trying to reinvent himself as an expert on North America, hoping to gain employment through his aristocratic contacts in the French civil service. Indeed, after a brief stay in France between 1781 and 1783 during which he renewed his long-severed family relations and developed connections with the enlightened liberal nobility, Crèvecoeur returned to New York as the French consul in the United States capital, eventually dying in France after his final return in 1790.

While Crèvecoeur's national and political allegiances do not require much further research, a fresh look at his writings is nevertheless still necessary. Indeed, his focus on Quakers and slavery has not been the source of much interest on the part of literary critics and biographers, even the most recent ones.[7] Although they usually highlight the letter explicitly devoted to slavery (Letter IX "Description of Charles Town; Thoughts on Slavery; On Physical Evil; A Melancholy Scene"), and note the positive references to Quakers (Letters IV to VIII), they have not examined these two subjects in conjunction, as I believe they should be. Howard Crosby Rice analyzed the many references to the Quaker sect and community as a mere attempt to conform to a French fashion in "philosophical circles," which according to him explained why Quakers were given even more prominence in the 1784 French-language edition. However, the English-language edition was not meant for the French public and already contained vast sections focusing on Quakers and slavery. Bernard Chevignard also underlined Crèvecoeur's interest in Quakers. He connected it neither to any kind of antislavery activity on the part of the former French exile, however, nor to the many references to slavery in the book. According to him, Crèvecoeur was merely mythologizing North American Quakers. Most recently, Dennis D. Moore has underlined the positive references to Quakers, tracing the origin of such mentions to Voltaire's *Lettres philosophiques* (1732), as is often done. He has not connected these references to Crèvecoeur's potential antislavery convictions. The Abbé Raynal is mentionned neither in his bibliography nor in the index to the book.[8]

Yet the dedication of the English publication to the Abbé Raynal, who popularized the criticism of colonialism and slavery in the 1770s, followed in the 1784 Paris edition of the *Letters* by a long introductory letter praising the abolitionist Quaker Warner Mifflin, should have called attention to the centrality of this preoccupation.[9] Indeed, the question of North American slavery, and of its necessary eradication in Quaker fashion, pervades *Letters*. First, the dedication to Raynal requires examination. Because Raynal's book described and denounced the African slave trade, *Letters* is thus placed under the moral tutelage of the most popular antislavery thinker in the second half of the eighteenth century. Indeed, Crèvecoeur addresses Raynal directly: "A few years since, I met accidentally with your *Political and Philosophical History* and perused it with infinite pleasure. . . . As an eloquent and powerful advocate, you have pleaded the cause of humanity in espousing that of the poor Africans."[10]

Studded with references to colonial slavery, the *Histoire* has become famous for its prescient warning that slave rebellion would erupt if colonial metropolises did not act quickly to eradicate slavery.[11] But the Abbé Raynal was also very pragmatically aware of the current emancipation of slaves by the Quaker community in North America, considering that it was a concrete example and a sign of hope.[12] In "Indentured Servants, Blacks and Quakers" (book 18, chapter 32), he wrote, "however the Quakers have recently given an example that must prove epochal in the history of religion and humanity," a passage that seems to have been overlooked by recent French critics.[13]

Crèvecoeur's *Letters* is to a large extent an elaboration on this particular passage. Drafted by a British colonist, it was meant to proffer the testimony of one North American on the advancement of the "revolution" of antislavery led by Quakers in North America, and it was recognized as such by contemporaries, primarily by Brissot.[14] In order to make his point, Crèvecoeur chose to suffuse his book with references to Quakers and slavery and, most tellingly, to devote long central chapters to out-of-the-way Quaker settlements, most particularly Nantucket.

Nonetheless, as has been observed by literary critics, it is often hard to establish whose point of view is expressed in *Letters*: that of James, a fictional narrator, or that of Crèvecoeur, the author (if not that of others), making it difficult for the reader to grasp a consistent position on antislavery and slavery in what remains a work of fiction.[15] Yet such a view does emerge progressively. At first, in the letters where he describes his North American paradise, farmer James is no abolitionist. In Letter I, he even compares favorably the fate of his "Negroes" to that of Russian "boors," thus testifying to a paternalism that was to become typical later on in the United States. On the part of Crèvecoeur, this may also have reflected a nonracial apprehension of slavery as one form of unequal, exploitative, and eventually expensive labor, a view that was characteristic of the French physiocrats.[16] James takes it for granted that "Negroes" are part of the colonial landscape. His early references to Quakers in the volume insist on their peacefulness, not their antislavery activism.[17] Yet Crèvecoeur's specific positive interest in the Quaker sect surfaces as early as Letter III ("What Is the American, This New Man?"). Although one of Crèvecoeur's aims as part of his overall argument in this letter is to show that all sects can cohabit peacefully in the new North American territories, he also praises the Quakers living on the frontier as resisting the general degradation of education and culture there.[18]

Following Letter III, Crèvecoeur's indirect praise of the Quaker sect is brought to the fore through his description of the exemplary island of Nantucket, where Quakers make up a large part of the population (Letter IV).[19] The island is characterized by such a remarkably peaceful history that "the inhabitants have no annals."[20] Praise for the Quakers and their many virtues is expressed in Letter V, which is still focused on the Nantucket population. A brief positive reference to the Quakers is to be found in Letter VI, a description of Martha's Vineyard, where Quakers thrive as owners of fisheries, while the description of Nantucket Island is continued in Letter VII, together with that of another famous Quaker settlement, New Garden in North Carolina. Beyond providing the author with an opportunity to insist on the peacefulness of the Quakers, Letter VII is the first instance where he mentions their commitment to antislavery, unique at the time in the colonies, writing, "there is not a slave I believe on the whole island, at least among the Friends; whilst slavery prevails all around them, this society alone, lamenting that shocking insult offered to humanity, have given the world a singular example of moderation, disinterestedness, and Christian charity in emancipating their Negroes."[21]

Letter VIII carries on the description of the "customs" of the admirable Nantucket Quakers, shown as simple, hard working, and loving. Next, Letter IX, famous for its somber description of a tortured slave right after an evocation of the wealth and luxury encountered in Charleston, vividly contrasts with the egalitarian scenes prevailing in Nantucket. The narrator emotionally denounces the slave trade and the abuses connected with slavery, eventually expressing his belief in the equality of all men in vibrant preromantic tones: "Oh, Nature, where art thou? Are not these blacks thy children as well as we?" Taking up themes specific to abolitionist literature (explicit references to Benezet were to be found in the 1784 edition), he denounces the crimes committed against Africa by the exploitation of its people: "were I to be possessed of a plantation, and my slaves treated as in general they are here, never could I rest in peace; my sleep would be perpetually disturbed by a retrospect of the frauds committed in Africa." Yet, echoing Raynal, he exonerates himself and the Northern colonies from most of the blame: "We have slaves likewise in our northern provinces; I hope the time draws near when they will be all emancipated, but how different their lot!"[22] Whereas slavery in the

South comes very close to the Caribbean model, Northern slavery is looked upon as a benign system moving toward total eradication. This distinction between Northern slavery and Southern/Caribbean slavery was reinforced in the 1784 French edition, in which one letter dealt with a trip taken by the narrator to Caribbean islands.[23] Thus did Crèvecoeur's testimony comfirm the ideas Raynal had developed: slavery was to be dissolved through gradual emancipation; Caribbean colonists had to embrace reform and should follow the example of the British North American colonies as inspired by Quakers.[24]

Antislavery may also connect Letter IX, culminating in the slave's persecution, with the briefer letter that follows in which the narrator describes the fight between a black snake and a water snake, ending with the victory of the black snake.[25] That shorter, perhaps metaphorical, reflection on the final conflict between white colonists and their black bondmen was, however, not retained in the French edition of 1784 and definitely stands apart from the rest in the English edition. The scene may also have been included by Crèvecoeur to illustrate his interest in natural observation, at a time when such activities were prized as sure signs of enlightenment. There are other such descriptions in the volume. Indeed, Letter XI, narrated by a Russian gentleman, reports a visit to botanist John Bartram, whom Crèvecoeur did know. His interest in natural history qualified him for membership in the French Academy of Science on his return to his home country.[26] The visit to Bartram proves to be the final opportunity to praise both Quakers and their antislavery convictions. Bartram's household includes "Negroes" who sit at the end of the dinner table and appear to be his slaves. Yet after a long conversation, during which Bartram echoes farmer James's overall belief that North America is meant to welcome Europeans fleeing poverty and tyranny, the Russian is told that these are no slaves. Obeying the Quaker community's mandate no longer to keep slaves, and inspired by authors such as Benezet, Bartram has emancipated his bondmen, proclaiming "yet of late, in consequence of the remonstrances of several Friends and of the good books they have published on that subject, our society treats them very differently. With us they are now free."[27] Letter XI ends with more praise of the Quaker community in Pennsylvania, whose generous views induce the Russian to spend two entire months with them. The book concludes with the narrator's despair at the coming civil war.

Thus, out of twelve letters that are to be found in the final 1783 English edition, Letters IV, V, VII, VIII, IX, and XI all deal with Quakers, slavery, or both. In addition, Quakers are also briefly mentioned in Letter VI, while Letter X can also be considered as an allegorical commentary on the eventual eradication of the slave owner by the slave. As a result, *Letters,* as it was published in London, could but be read as pro-Quaker *and* antislavery propaganda.[28] Its overall purpose was to praise the British North American colonies, as they offered an asylum for Europeans against religious intolerance or political tyranny, but the Quakers' lifestyle and beliefs, their simplicity of manners and courageous emancipation of enslaved blacks, best exemplified the hope of the New World. By contrast, the Southern colonies offered a cruel imitation of West Indian colonial conditions from which Crèvecoeur tried hard to distinguish the Northern colonies, most particularly Pennsylvania.[29] As we saw, the 1784 French edition was by no means a mere translation by Crèvecoeur of his English-language work. It started with a long introduction on Warner Mifflin's career as an emancipationist, including references to Anthony Benezet. Like the dedication to Raynal (now replaced by a dedication to Lafayette), such an introduction could not but instill in readers the conviction that this was a piece of antislavery literature.[30] Also included were a history of the Quaker sect and other Mifflin anecdotes.[31]

BRISSOT AND CRÈVECOEUR: FROM *LETTERS* TO *EXAMEN CRITIQUE*/*A CRITICAL EXAMINATION*

Letters from an American Farmer proved to be a best seller when it came out in England in 1782. London was then one of the major places where the French "literary underground" could publish magazines and books free of government censorship. A number of French journalists thus resided in London and contributed to various publications. One of them was Jacques-Pierre Brissot de Warville. Fluent in English and an Anglophile, the future leader of the French Revolution could hardly ignore the buzz that followed the publication of *Letters,* all the more so as he was employed as a journalist for the London-based *Courier de l'Europe,* a popular French-language magazine founded by Serres de la Tour in 1776 to cover international affairs freely, among which was the American Revolution. Brissot was trying to launch his own magazine, the *Journal du lycée de Londres,* between 1782 and 1784, and working for the *Courier* helped defray his other expenses. As the fame of *Letters* spread, it drew comments in the *Courier de l'Europe* because this magazine regularly published reviews on the London literary and theater scene in addition to articles on international events. Brissot was in charge of reviews, so he may well have penned the unsigned reviews bearing on *Letters.*[32] On March 14, 1783, an article praised the author of *Letters,* J. Hector St. John (Crèvecoeur's name as a farmer in the British colonies and as author of *Letters*) for his "wise and judicious reflections on the slavery of Negroes." This was followed on April 18 by a long unsigned letter to the editor titled "On the Slavery of Negroes/Sur l'esclavage des Nègres," which started with a reference to the "excellent chapter On Negro Slavery" in *Letters from an American Farmer*, then praised Raynal for his own attack on slavery, but moved on to say that "the Quakers of Pennsylvania have done more [than Raynal]; they have put into practice the human principles that guided the historian's pen: they freed their Negroes." Adding that "neither this striking example nor the thousand philosophical reasons used to abolish slavery have yet managed to make the Sugar Islands settlers change their mind and their behavior," the author denounced the ill-treatment blacks received on the Caribbean Islands. Finally the author sharply responded to an attack on Quakers he had recently read in *Le Mercure de France*: "the anonymous writer makes fun of the Quakers, their doctrine, their humanity [. . .] As for me, I prefer a Quaker without buttons and ceremony, who says thee to me, and makes as many happy people as he has children and slaves."[33] By the spring of 1783, thanks to Crèvecoeur's publicizing of the Quakers' antislavery convictions, as well as his portraying of them as archetypal simple, happy, and free Americans, the sect had paradoxically come to embody antislavery and revolution. Obviously, not all readers adhered to the laudatory description of Quakers in *Letters*, as the derogatory comments in *Le Mercure de France* evidence. Interestingly, the sensitivity of the author to any ridicule poured on the Quakers points to the enthusiastic Brissot, who later drafted a vibrant defense of North American Quakers in a 1786 pamphlet.

Brissot had been exposed to the Quaker community during his eighteen-month London stay (November 1782–May 1784), at a time when British Quakers were moving toward greater activism on behalf of antislavery under the impulse of North American Quakers.[34] As he came back to France in the spring of 1784, he remained in contact with Quaker bookseller James Phillips. Only after he read *Letters* did Brissot seize on antislavery as a central preoccupation. Although he may have met Crèvecoeur in 1781–1782 through Benjamin Franklin, *Letters* had not yet been released and, in his published correspondence, Brissot does not at that point mention meeting Crèvecoeur.[35] Considering Brissot's inflamed support for the book in the *Courier de l'Europe* in 1783, we must then come to the conclusion that reading *Letters* formed a turning point in his career as an activist, prompting him to seek an acquaintance with Crèvecoeur. Indeed, Crèvecoeur's son dates the connection between Brissot and his father only from the post-1782 period: 1785 in Paris, when Crèvecoeur was back from New York on sick leave. By then, Brissot had also been able to read the French-language edition of *Letters*, including the long introductory chapter on Warner Mifflin.[36] One reason Crèvecoeur may not have discouraged Brissot's friendship in 1785 was his own antislavery commitment beyond the drafting of *Letters*. Indeed, in August 1785, Crèvecoeur had been accepted as a member of the fledgling New York Manumission Society, the only foreigner to be so invited.[37] He may have joined to cement his own connections with important New York members such as John Jay and Alexander Hamilton, but, given the antislavery slant of *Letters,* this move probably resulted from his own convictions—and he proved willing to share them and to act on them on his return to France.

Unless one is aware of the connection between Brissot and Crèvecoeur between 1785 and 1787, one can hardly understand Brissot's passionate defense of Quakers in the 1786 pamphlet that attacked academician François-Jean de Chastellux's supposed aspersions on them. Brissot's 1786 attack on Chastellux was definitely "disproportionate," as the condemned passages in Chastellux's 1785 *Voyages* certainly did not represent the philosopher's main argument.[38] Indeed the liberal academician's narrative of his travels in the United States during the War of Independence was mainly favorable. Brissot's reasons for writing a whole pamphlet to denounce portions of the academician's book were twofold: First, those excerpts had been reprinted in the press as representative of the whole, and needed countering. Second, they incriminated the very dimensions of the American revolutionary experience, which portended positive changes for the rest of the world, including the universal emancipation of slaves. Such is Brissot's opening salvo against Chastellux and his rationale for writing the book:

> Poison! You will be surprised at the word; but it characterizes with acute precision what you put forth about Quakers, Negroes, and the People [. . .] By decrying the former, you hurt the good their holy example produces; by refusing the title of men to the latter, you make it possible, if not to pour their blood, at least to treat them as beasts of burden; you put a stop to the philosophical commotion which is likely to cause their universal emancipation. By bringing the people down, you suggest his chains should be tightened wherever he wears them.[39]

Then Brissot moved to defend the Quaker "example" by openly relying on the well-known *Lettres* and praising Crèvecoeur, presented as a personal friend and an expert on North American Quaker manners. After defending the moral record of Quakers in economic dealings, and narrating their religious history, Brissot concluded by focusing on the "Political Principles of Quakers," which included "the universal emancipation of Negroes." He waxed lyrical about this most "sublime gesture of love for the public good," as a result of which "millions of miserable beings are returned to Society, life, virtue," thus thwarting Chastellux's arguments that described the Quaker sect as too commercially minded and little concerned with public affairs.[40] The pamphlet also included the portraits of two major Quaker figures, Thomas Fothergill and Anthony Benezet. As for Benezet, it insisted on his educational efforts on behalf of blacks, but also mentioned the Pennsylvania Emancipation Law of 1780, as well as Benezet's role in the founding of the first abolition society. Thus, this (long) part of the pamphlet reflects Brissot's information on Quakers, and their role in the emancipation of their slaves in North America, which he believed would serve as an inspiration to the rest of the world.[41]

THE QUAKER ARGUMENT IN THE BIRTH OF ORGANIZED FRENCH ANTISLAVERY

Later in his life, Crèvecoeur openly disowned Brissot as a friend when he did not welcome him in New York as the younger man was starting his tour of the New World in the summer of 1788. But their friendship was certainly not at an end in the immediate wake of the 1786 *Examen Critique*, although an attack on the famous Chastellux may have caused the well-connected Crèvecoeur some embarrassment.[42] Indeed the two continued their relationship over the next two years, advancing Franco-American relations in ways that were to lead directly to the creation of the first French antislavery society, the Society of the Friends of the Blacks, in Paris in February 1788. First, Brissot, his friend Clavière, and Crèvecoeur worked together between 1785 and 1787 toward an increase in Franco-American trade. Beyond cementing the alliance between the two countries, the three men considered that Atlantic commerce had a higher purpose and would also bring about international peace. Their joint interest in this cause led them to create the Gallo-American Society (GAS) in the spring of 1787. Part of the agenda of the GAS was to bring about the abolition of slavery, one year before the creation of the British Society for Effecting the Abolition of the Slave Trade.[43] After Crèvecoeur left for the United States in the spring of 1787, the GAS was no longer active, but Brissot and Clavière started focusing all their efforts on antislavery. What had been only one of the goals of the GAS, the antislavery struggle, thus blossomed in 1788 into a self-contained association, the Society of the Friends of the Blacks, whose avowed aim was to use the North American example in order to promote the eradication of the slave trade and slavery in the French colonies.[44]

In the founding speech he delivered to the Friends of the Blacks on January 19, 1788, Brissot once again praised the North American Quaker efforts, which he considered as having triggered the "revolution" of antislavery, the very term that Raynal, and later Condorcet, had used to describe the antislavery struggle.[45] It is usually believed that Brissot and Clavière created the Friends of the Blacks at the "urging" of the founding members of the British society, as the subtitle to the speech says, but the speech started by looking back at the North American example, in its North/South complexity. The authors of North American antislavery pamphlets, Benezet and John Woolman, were both mentioned. Before the French antislavery activists really had time to work together with the British, the French Revolution broke out, raising the question of race and slavery in the French colonies in ways Brissot had not expected (he hoped for gradual emancipation and reasonable conduct on the part of the colonists as a result of American emancipation, not for class and race war as in Saint-Domingue). Brissot himself was to die under the guillotine on October 31, 1793, a victim of the Terror, having mainly devoted his energy to France's wars and political situation. Before all that was to happen, the future revolutionary leader did visit the United States in the summer and early fall of 1788, meeting in New York and Philadelphia with Quaker leaders he had come to idealize after reading Crèvecoeur, such as Warner Mifflin. Although the author of *Letters* did not welcome the recent founder of the Friends of the Blacks in America, and apparently no longer busied himself with antislavery activism after the start of the French Revolution, dying only in 1813, he was nevertheless later enshrined in the history of French antislavery.

CONCLUSION

In 1808, Henri Grégoire, an active member of the first French antislavery society (1788–1791), and the main engineer of its renaissance in 1796, wrote a book titled *Enquiry concerning the Intellectual and Moral Faculties and Literature of Negroes*.[46] It was meant to oppose theories of racial inferiority, to denounce slavery, and to demonstrate the essential equality between human beings. It was preceded by a dedication to "all the brave men who have pleaded the cause of the unhappy Blacks and Mixed-Blood, either through their writings, or through their speeches in political assemblies, in societies established for the abolition of the slave trade, the relief and the freedom of slaves." An alphabetical list of these brave men followed, listed by nationality.

First came the French, including such names as "Antoine Benezet" (Anthony Benezet, now seen as the French Huguenot emigrant he indeed was), "Brissot" and "Clavière," the first two presidents of the French Society for the Friends of the Blacks, "Condorcet," their successor, and many others, either members of the Society such as "Lafayette" or earlier supporters of the antislavery cause such as Montesquieu. The list included "Saint-John-Crevecoeur."

A long list of English supporters then followed, incorporating all the figures active in the campaign leading to the abolition of the trade in 1807, Quakers, Anglican preachers, and Tory ministers—including also one Hector Saint-John: intriguingly, Grégoire seems to have thought that Hector Saint-John, the author of *Letters* in English, and Saint-John de Crèvecoeur, the author of the French version, were not one and the same person. Thus was Crèvecoeur praised twice for his commitment. The American list that came next was much shorter and featured such revolutionary figures as Thomas Jefferson, Benjamin Rush, and Joel Barlow. Jefferson's presence on the list proved to be somewhat awkward as in later correspondence he refused Grégoire's position that blacks' intellectual accomplishments could compare with those of whites.[47] Grégoire's list also included black and "mulatto" authors, German, Danish, Swedish, Italian, and Spanish antislavery activists, as well as supporters from the Netherlands.[48] But as we have seen, Crèvecoeur and his Quakers were not forgotten in the pantheon of antislavery heroes. Indeed, they had inspired the French movement to a large extent, pragmatically showing that emancipation could be a reality.

NOTES

1. As is evidenced in the popular edition by Albert E. Stone of *Letters from an American Farmer and Sketches of Eighteenth-Century America* by J. Hector St. John de Crèvecoeur (Harmondsworth: Penguin Books, 1981), 7; Dennis D. Moore, ed., *More Letters from an American Farmer: An Edition of the Essays in English Left Unpublished by Crèvecoeur* (Athens: University of Georgia Press, 1995) confirms this is the traditional view, but he distances himself from it, xxxvii; Bernard Chevignard, *Michel Saint John de Crévecoeur* (Paris: Belin, 2004), 57.

2. Bernard Chevignard, "St. John de Crévecoeur in the Looking Glass: Letters from an American Farmer and the Making of a Man of Letters," *Early American Literature* 19, no. 2 (Fall 1984), 176; Doreen Alavarez Saar, "'Crèvecoeur's Thoughts on Slavery': Letters from an American Farmer and Whig Rhetoric," *Early American Literature* 22, no. 2 (Fall 1987): 193–203; Christopher Iannini, "'The Itinerant Man': Crèvecoeur's Caribbean, Raynal's Revolution, and the Fate of Atlantic Cosmopolitanism," *William and Mary Quarterly*, 3rd ser., 41, no. 2 (April 2004): 201–34.

3. Moore, xlvii; Howard Crosby Rice, *Le cultivateur américain, étude sur l'œuvre de Saint John de Crèvecoeur* (Paris: Honoré Champion, 1933), 20. See Edward Larkin, "The Cosmopolitan Revolution: Loyalism and the Fiction of an American Nation," *NOVEL: A Forum on Fiction* 40, nos. 1/2 (Fall 2006–Spring 2007), 52–76, for an analysis of Crèvecoeur's loyalism.

4. *Letters from an American Farmer* was first published in English in 1782; a second English-language edition came out in 1783. These two editions being radically different from the 1784 edition in French, I will refer to the final 1783 edition.

5. "Snow Storm," in Moore, 152.

6. Michel Guillaume Jean, dit Saint Jean de Crèvecoeur, *Lettres d'un cultivateur américain, écrites à W.S, Ecuyer, Depuis l'année 1770, jusqu'à 1781, Traduites de l'Anglois par ****, vol. 1 (Paris: Cuchet, 1784), iii–v. Available at: http://gallica.bnf/ (accessed June 21, 2012). Rice, 83.

7. Robert Sayre, *La modernité et son autre. Récits de la rencontre avec l'Indien en Amérique du Nord au XVIIIè siècle* (Bécherel: Les Perséides, 2008), 33–62.

8. Rice, 83; Moore, xxxiii; Bernard Chevignard, "Une Apocalypse sécularisée: le quakerisme selon Brissot de Warville et St John de Crèvecoeur," in *Le facteur religieux en Amérique du nord*, ed. Jean Béranger (Bordeaux: Institut d'études politiques de Bordeaux, 1981), 49–69.

9. "To the Abbé Raynal, F.R.S." Raynal published in 1770 his *Histoire philosophique et politique des établissements et du commerce des Européens dans les deux Indes*, which instantly became an international bestseller of anticolonial literature. Volume 6, book 11 specifically targets slavery. Parts of book 11 were later found to have been written by Diderot: see Jean Ehrard, *Lumières et esclavage: L'esclavage colonial et l'opinion publique en France au XVIIIè siècle* (Bruxelles: André Versaille, 2008), 200; Crèvecoeur, *Lettres*, x–xxii.

10. Crèvecoeur, *Lettres*, 37–38.

11. Abbé G. Th. Raynal, *Histoire philosophique et politique des deux Indes: Avertissement et choix de textes par Yves Bénot* (Paris: La découverte, 2001), 202.

12. By 1770, North American Quakers had gradually challenged slavery in their own community, first condemning slave-trading, then slave-owning. This was known in Europe. In 1780, when the last revised edition of the *Histoire* was published, gradual emancipation had been voted into law in Pennsylvania.

13. Raynal, 312–14; Ehrard, 206.

14. Raynal, 201: emancipation is a "revolution."

15. Larkin, 54.

16. Ehrard, 121–32.

17. Crèvecoeur, *Lettres*, 52–53, 95, 63.

18. Ibid., 75–76.

19. Quakers settled on Nantucket Island and prospered there, dominating its religious and economic life until the early nineteenth century, see Robert E. Leach and Peter Gow, *Quaker Nantucket: The Religious Community behind the Whaling Empire* (Nantucket: The Mill Hill Press, 1999).

20. Crèvecoeur, *Letters*, 111.

21. Ibid., 153.

22. Ibid., *Letters*, 169–71.

23. Moore, 106–13. Crèvecoeur, *Lettres*, 219–41.

24. Ehrard, 190–91, 201–3.

25. Agnès Derail, "Le serpent dans le jardin: nature et servitude dans *Letters of an American Farmer*, de Michel Saint-John de Crèvecoeur," paper given at the French Association of American Studies Conference, May 27, 2010; Crèvecoeur, *Letters*, 186.

26. He became a corresponding member in 1783.

27. Crèvecoeur, *Letters*, 188, 196.

28. The letter on slavery was reproduced in various British magazines: Gay Wilson Allen and Roger Asselineau, *St. John de Crèvecoeur: The Life of An American Farmer* (New York: Viking, 1987), 72.

29. Rice admits *Letters* includes antislavery passages, but he does not believe that antislavery gives coherence to the book: *Le cultivateur*, 114.

30. Crèvecoeur, *Lettres*, x–xxii. Reference to Benezet: xiii.

31. Ibid., 172–99.

32. Robert Darnton, *The Literary Underground of the Old Regime* (Cambridge: Harvard University Press, 1982). Simon Burrows, *Blackmail, Scandal, and Revolution: London's French Libellists, 1758–92* (Manchester: Manchester University Press, 2006), 48–68. Perroud in his "Notice" explains Brissot was in charge of the "Variétés" between February and November 1783. But there is no "Variétés" section in the *Courier de l'Europe*, just the "Mélanges": We have to assume Brissot was the author of these two texts playing up Crèvecoeur's antislavery message. See Claude Perroud, "Notice sur la vie de Brissot," in Jacques-Pierre Brissot de Warville, *Correspondance et papiers, précédés d'un avertissement et d'une notice sur sa vie*, ed. Claude Perroud (Paris: Librairie Alphonse Picard, 1912), xxv–xxx.

33. *Le Courrier de l'Europe*, March 14, 21, and April 18, 1783.

34. Christopher Leslie Brown, *Moral Capital: Foundations of British Abolitionism* (Chapel Hill: University of North Carolina Press, 2006).

35. On the Franklin–Crèvecoeur connection, see Claude-Anne Lopez, *Mon Cher Papa: Franklin and the Ladies of Paris* (New Haven, Conn.: Yale University Press, 1990). On Brissot and Franklin, see Frederick A. de Luna, "The Dean Street Style of Revolution: J. P Brissot, Jeune Philosophe," *French Historical Studies* 17, no. 1 (Spring 1991), 165.

36. Robert de Crèvecoeur, *Saint-John de Crèvecoeur, sa vie et ses ouvrages 1735–1813* (Paris: Librairie des bibliophiles de Paris, 1833). Available at: http://gallica.bnf.fr/ (accessed August 23, 2010), 120–21.

37. New York Manumission Society papers, reel 1, August 11, 1785.

38. Bernard Chevignard, "Une Apocalypse sécularisée," 55. François-Jean de Chastellux, *Voyage de M. le chevalier de Chastellux en Amérique* (n.p., 1785).

39. Jacques-Pierre Brissot de Warville, *Examen critique des voyages dans l'Amérique septentrionale de M. le marquis de Chastellux, ou Lettre à M. le marquis*

de Chastellux, Dans laquelle on réfute principalement ses opinions sur les Quakers, sur les Nègres, sur le Peuple, et sur l'Homme (London, 1786), 2.

40. Ibid., 17–19, 26, 27, 31, 67.

41. Ibid., 79, 81–82.

42. Robert de Crèvecoeur, *Saint-John de Crèvecoeur*, 131.

43. On Crèvecoeur's leaving to return to his posting in New York, Brissot summarized the goals of the Gallo-American Society, among which was the destruction of "slavery for Negroes, or help the Quakers carry out that destruction," in Brissot, "Procès-verbaux de la Société Gallo-Américaine, Séance du 3 avril 1787," in *Correspondance et papiers,* 134–35.

44. The best introduction to the Society of the Friends of the Blacks is Marcel Dorigny and Bernard Gainot, eds., *La Société des Amis des noirs 1788–1799: Contribution à l'histoire de l'abolition de l'esclavage* (Paris: Editions de l'Unesco, Edicef, 1998). Faced with intense planter opposition, the Friends of the Blacks stopped their activities in 1791. The French abolition of slavery in 1794 was mainly due to events during the Saint-Domingue insurrection.

45. "A Speech on the Necessity to Establish in Paris a Society That Would Concur with That of London, To Abolish the Slave Trade and the Slavery of Negroes. Pronounced on February 19, 1788, at a Meeting of a Few Friends, Gathered at the Urging of the London Committee" in *La Révolution française et l'abolition de l'esclavage,* Vol. 6: *La Société des Amis des Noirs* (Paris: EDHIS, 1968), 12.

46. Abbé Grégoire, *De la littérature des Nègres, ou Recherches sur leurs Facultés Intellectuelles, leurs Qualités morales et leur Littérature* (Paris: Maradan, 1808).

47. Grégoire dealt with Jefferson's ambiguous position as early as chapter 2, in which he complained that the American leader followed Hume and "Chatelux" in denying blacks the ability to display intellectual achievements similar to those of whites, cf. 36. Obviously, Brissot's attack on Chastellux was still taken at face value by this veteran of the antislavery wars.

48. Grégoire, *De la littérature des Nègres*, v–x. Available at: http://gallica.bnf.fr/ (accessed August 23, 2010).

13 Thomas Clarkson's Quaker Trilogy
Abolitionist Narrative as Transformative History

DEE E. ANDREWS AND
EMMA JONES LAPSANSKY-WERNER

WHO WAS THOMAS CLARKSON? In his lifetime, he was the abolitionist par excellence, an advocate of social justice in a cause whose founders—the Committee for Effecting the Abolition of the African Slave Trade—fit inside one small printing-house office. By the end of his life, abolitionists' regard led to Clarkson's election as presiding officer of the first international gathering of many dozens of antislavery's leading lights. Clarkson's visage graced the commemorative medal cast for the occasion, and his presence, surrounded by an admiring younger generation, was immortalized in B. R. Haydon's massive group portrait.[1]

Although his renown faded after his death, recent scholarship and popular culture has rekindled interest in Clarkson as a powerful player in the history of Britain's decision to outlaw the African slave trade, most especially through the work of scholars Adam Hochschild, David Brion Davis, Christopher Brown, and Brycchan Carey.[2] Yet Clarkson's story remains elusive, the nature and caliber of his significance as often assumed as understood. At the core of his importance were two intertwined aspects of his lifework rarely explored by his biographers and admirers: his connections with the Religious Society of Friends (Quakers) and his profession as an author.

Clarkson's fascination with Quakers began early, with his involvement in the London committee and his award-winning Cambridge University thesis, published as *An Essay on the Slavery and Commerce of the Human Species* by Quaker printer James Phillips in 1786. Thereafter, he became immersed in Quaker antislavery networks and friendships, forming an especially close alliance with Quaker pharmacist and reformer William Allen, as well as making connections with Friends' monthly and quarterly meetings throughout the British Isles. Although Clarkson never joined the Society of Friends, and although not all Quakers were abolitionists, these networks were critical to his development as an activist in the mass mobilization against the slave trade.

The Quakers were also essential to his development as a writer. From his pioneering activism in the 1780s, through his temporary retreat to the safe haven of the Lake District at the height of the French Revolution, to his reemergence in the first decade of the nineteenth century, Clarkson's empirical and moral approaches to writing about social reform and virtue were often based on a romantic narrative of Quaker culture and history. In the spirit of what literary historian Richard Holmes has called "the age of wonder," Clarkson blended the moral system of Quakerism with history-as-scientific-fact and his personal memoir as abolitionist-hero to become the antislavery movement's first authoritative chronicler.[3]

What we will call Clarkson's "Quaker trilogy"—comprising *A Portraiture of Quakerism, The History of the Rise, Progress, and Accomplishment of the Abolition of the African Slave-Trade,* and *The Memoirs of the Private and Public Life of William Penn*—appearing between 1806 and 1813, embodied the author's efforts in the wake of the French Revolution to reestablish abolition of the slave trade as a respectable and still international cause.[4] In the *Portraiture* and the *Memoirs,* Quakers were unsurprisingly center stage. But in the *History,* they are central as well, though with little attention given to Quaker abolitionists' on-going struggle to raise the Friends' own consciousness about the dangers of slaveholding, or Quaker activists' sometimes "strategic deceptions" for achieving abolition.[5] In the process, Clarkson not only slanted the Friends as the unambivalent agents of antislavery and himself as the premier chronicler of this great moment in British and American social activism, but he also designed a new kind of history: one that sought to combine the empirical drive of social science with the passion of social reform.

THE BURDEN OF RADICAL FAME

Thomas Clarkson was on the cutting edge of his time. His 1786 *Essay* catapulted him into international fame. By May 1787, when the London Committee for the Abolition of the Slave Trade was formally organized, Clarkson, already aspiring for authorship, embarked upon an ambitious writing program. While sustaining a grueling investigative agenda for the committee, by 1791 he had composed five antislavery titles that were published by London Quaker printer and book seller James Phillips, a founder of the committee and Clarkson's chief early patron. Among these, the *Essay* and *An Essay on the Impolicy of the African Slave Trade* were rapidly reissued by American Quaker printers. The young author was Phillips's most important antislavery spokesman.[6]

Clarkson's subsequent withdrawal from activism was the consequence both of his exhausting efforts and a number of startling national and international changes in the 1790s: the outbreak of the French Revolution and war between Britain and France, the execution of French antislavery allies—including Brissot de Warville, the "Clarkson of France"—the prosecutions of radical Constitutionalists in Britain, and the revolution in Haiti. Clarkson's political and social-justice work made him a certain subject for governmental scrutiny and possible prosecution for treason. In the summer of 1793, he retreated to the Lake District, where he befriended the leaders of the Romantic revolution in letters—William and Dorothy Wordsworth, Samuel Taylor Coleridge, and Robert Southey—and ultimately married Catherine Buck, free-thinking daughter of an East Anglian squire.[7] Throughout this period of retrenchment, Clarkson maintained his ties to the Friends, who shared his faith in the efficacy and moral certainty of nonviolent war with words. In the Quaker community, he found his chief moral argument—that the slave trade was not a political cause so much as a moral one, emanating from a religious society dedicated to a higher moral law—and his new calling as a sociological and historical author.

MORAL REHABILITATION:
A PORTRAITURE OF QUAKERISM

When Clarkson returned to publishing in 1806, after a hiatus of thirteen years, James Phillips had died and the three volumes of the Quaker trilogy were produced by Presbyterian printer Richard Taylor and the house of Longman, Hurst, Rees, and Orme, the pioneering publishers of Wordsworth and Coleridge's Lyrical Ballads. Nevertheless, the success of Clarkson's books continued to depend on a wide network of Quakers. Chief among these were the chemist and pharmacist William Allen, at whose London home in a cramped but private room above the kitchen Clarkson wrote much of his work, and William Dillwyn, a transplanted American, who served as his link to American Friends.[8]

In A Portraiture of Quakerism, Clarkson developed his premise that the morals and theology of the Religious Society of Friends were crucial to the early development of abolitionism, a claim that has remained a central tenet of both Quaker and abolitionist history. Although antislavery formed a very small part of the work, the Portraiture set the moral and social context for nearly all of Clarkson's future writing. The prospectus for the Portraiture emphasized that the larger purpose of the study was "to make the World better acquainted with the Principles of the Friends, and with the Effects of these upon moral Conduct and Happiness," as well as "to give the Legislature as well as the Magistrates of the Land a copious Insight into the Reasons which the Friends have for some of their Scruples, which are often an occasion to them of severe Suffering." The three-volume work opens with a tribute to Quaker support for abolition and continues with an encomium to Quaker values: "Those who profess [Quakerism] consider themselves bound to regulate their opinions, words, actions, and even outward demeanour, by Christianity, and by Christianity alone."[9] Clarkson lauded what today would be called the "lifestyle" of the Friends: their education, "peculiar customs," social mission, such ceremonies as they had, and only secondarily their distinctive Christian governance. He especially admired Quaker family life: its community support, its closeness, and its embrace of the idea that personal and corporate philanthropy is a prerequisite to social salvation—for both individuals and the community. He described Quakers' "moral education" in glowing terms.[10]

Clarkson wrote the *Portraiture* as a naïve observer, a posture evident in passages regarding Quakers' behavioral restrictions. Quaker prohibitions against gambling, dancing, singing, novel-reading, and other entertainments were also highlighted, the more to emphasize the sober state in which Quakers receive the Holy Spirit in their services, an openness that Clarkson believed made Friends tolerant of other faiths. He described Quakers' character as marked by benevolence, calm, reasonableness, and courage, although he believed that their approach to Christianity was occasionally marred by lack of learning and an excess of mysticism. Clarkson, in other words, like a number of enlightened reformers and the Romantics, harbored an idealized admiration for Friends.[11]

The *Portraiture* was published in London in May 1806. The initial run of 2,500 copies—distributed by informal Quaker book "agents" throughout the kingdom—sold fast, resulting in rapidly released second and third editions. Clarkson provided a special subscription rate for Friends, and by June 1806, he was already making arrangements for an American edition. New York Quaker publisher Samuel Stansbury was in such haste to issue the *Portraiture* that he employed three different printers, one for each volume. By summer 1807, a second American edition was in the works by Philadelphia Quaker publisher James Pemberton Parke, grandson of the president of the Pennsylvania Abolition Society.[12] Clarkson had reestablished himself, this time as a talented scholar. Although the success of his works depended heavily on distribution through Quaker networks on both sides of the Atlantic, the engagement of a *non*-Quaker printer and publisher—the latter among the most important in Romantic circles—burnished his literary reputation.

Despite its length and price, Clarkson's *Portraiture* was his most enduring work: partly because of purchase by many Friends, Quaker meetings, and Quaker libraries, but also because it was one of the few in-depth studies of the Quakers by a non-Quaker. Here, as in so many areas of his work, Clarkson was a genuine innovator, introducing a form that would today be classed as sociology of religion, remarkably free of cant and gratuitous piety, sometimes overtly sympathetic, but always methodologically "modern."

THE ROMANTIC HERO AS HISTORIAN: *THE HISTORY OF THE ABOLITION OF THE AFRICAN SLAVE-TRADE*

Literary and historical circumstances accounted for the timing of the second installment in Clarkson's Quaker trilogy: *The History of the Rise, Progress, and Accomplishment of the Abolition of the African Slave-Trade.*

The first was not fortuitous. In 1805, Robert Bisset, conservative historian and biographer of Edmund Burke, issued a blistering attack on the antislavery vanguard in general and on Clarkson in particular in a take-no-prisoners epic, *The History of the Negro Slave Trade, in Its Connection with the Commerce and Prosperity of the West Indies, and the Wealth and Power of the British Empire.* Bisset set the Religious Society of Friends apart for special condescension. "Statesmen, lawgivers, and patriots in the freest country of the world," he asserted, "all admitted a master's right to a Slave to be founded as strongly as any other right or property," all except Quakers. The idea that purchasing slaves was in any way criminal "never occurred to a single person, except those laughable but innocent fanatics, the Quakers." Their great champion, Thomas Clarkson, furthermore, was a "candidate for literary glory," who chose the slave trade as the subject of his inaugural *Essay* for the opportunities it provided for pathos. Clarkson's case against the trade, he argued, "was not a question of fact and deduction, but a theme of representation. It did not require the talents of the historian or philosopher, but the talents of a dramatist." Furthermore, Clarkson was "not very nice in his selection of company. Many of those advocates for the Negroes were to be found preaching humanity in the ale-houses and brothels of Liverpool."[13] Bisset set out to destroy abolition through a deductive historical method, a seductive writing style, and acid character assassination. In short, he dismissed the abolitionists' arguments as the chimera of deluded religious fanatics and literary opportunists.

Bisset's *History* was unexpectedly ill-timed, however, appearing in print as waves of renewed public revulsion against human trafficking, combined with Parliamentary expedience, pushed abolition back onto the public stage and provided the second opening for Clarkson's *History*. These conditions, and Bisset's premature death, left Clarkson well positioned to defend the Quakers' honor and to present a history based on a method now recognizably social-scientific: an *inductive* method, in which the author drew his facts from wherever he might, even if it meant exploring aspects of society rarely featured in historical texts.[14]

As James Walvin also explores in chapter 11 of this volume, the *History* was to be an *empirical* treatment of abolition, based on data that Clarkson had carefully assembled and analyzed since his earliest work in the movement, combined with a deeply personal testament against the trade. Clarkson began to collect material sometime in 1806, expecting, as he told William Dillwyn, that abolition was near at hand. His job now was no longer to make abolition respectable—that was accomplished by William Wilberforce and other activists now in the field—but to make it a completed fact, and one in which his conversion to antislavery through the work of the Friends would play a central role. Clarkson wrote the book quickly, with the 323-page volume 1 already at the press by September 1807, and the 316-page volume 2 ready for printing around mid-January 1808. In the initial version of the prospectus, he emphasized two major topics: the four "classes" of abolitionist "forerunners"—two composed of Quakers—and his own sufferings for the cause. A second version of the prospectus downplayed Friends' involvement, as urged by one of his Quaker supporters to avoid offending readers of other faiths: as always, strategy was important.[15]

We know these details regarding the production of the *History* from the original two-volume manuscript, housed at Haverford College Library, along with numerous extant sources relating to the planning, writing, printing, and distribution of Clarkson's works.[16] The manuscript—likely a penultimate draft prepared for his friends, including the Wordsworths, to review—represents a rare and important record of the author's writing habits and his larger intentions for his study. Writing in his own hand, and employing carbonized paper for volume 2 (another example of Clarkson's eagerness to innovate, carbon-copying having been patented by Ralph Wedgwood just a year earlier),[17] Clarkson made numerous revisions throughout both volumes. He appears to have been a fluid composer, for whom the many events of his life's work were well stored in his memory, though he certainly relied on a library of sources—his own, or more likely, his Quaker friend William Allen's—that included a wide array of poetry, correspondence, and Parliamentary records. These he quoted at length and in detail. In only one instance at this stage of production was an external document "wafered" into the text: a copy of Anthony Benezet's 1783 letter to Queen Charlotte.

The impact of the Society of Friends on Clarkson's thinking is apparent in the numerous passages in the manuscript "History" that implicitly or explicitly credit Quakers with a major role in the abolition of the slave trade. This is evident at the start of the first volume and at the close of the second, including in the modest changes Clarkson made for the final printed edition. Most notably, despite focusing so intensely on the British Parliament, the final version of the manuscript highlights the work of Quaker-style voluntary associations. The word national appears just once in the first twenty-five pages that open volume 1 and the seventeen pages that conclude volume 2. Conversely, repeated references to "the Almighty," "the Divine," and the problem of evil appear throughout. Likewise, Clarkson stresses the necessity of acting in accordance with Christian morals, an emphasis in sympathy with the Quaker belief that major social changes emanate not from "the world's" people but from divine intervention. Quaker inspiration manifested itself in other ways, including in Clarkson's efforts not to overdo it. While he assigns prominent roles to Friends in his narrative, his many revisions hint at a certain discomfort with overemphasizing human agency. And while most of his changes aim at making his expression more precise or his facts more accurate, a number of excised sections rein in his unbridled euphoria about Quaker beliefs and people. Most notably, he trimmed back one lengthy laudatory passage about New Jersey abolitionist John Woolman.[18]

In his first draft of volume 2, Clarkson's homage to "worldly" aspects of abolition consists of virtually verbatim transcripts of Parliamentary debates. Clarkson's revisions follow a different political tack from volume 1, as he seems to have removed passages that might offend other constituencies in Britain—various members of Parliament, or inhabitants of the soon-to-be former slave-trading cities—or that might offend patriotic loyalties. References to the "national disgrace" of the slave trade and to national guilt are excised. Conversely, arguments against abolition—that it would break a compact between the mother country and West Indian planters, and that the Maroons of Jamaica were unwilling to work—are likewise eliminated.[19]

Nevertheless, the focus on the role of the individual following God's will in the abolition of the trade—rather than on the nation redeeming itself—remains strong in both the manuscript and print versions. Thus, of the critical moment in February 1807 when Parliament moved to draw up the bill for abolition, the *manuscript* version reads: "all young Men, who were members [of Parliament], seemed especially to participate, thus giving the best hope to their Country of a career of true Usefulness, I mean by espousing the side of Virtue." Clarkson continues: "There was also a sort of religious feeling in the House, such as the oldest Member had never witnessed, and this proceeded so far, that even a Conversion of the Heart seemed to take place under it." In the *printed* edition, Clarkson struck all but the last sentence and reshaped the passage to fit his overarching theme of the primacy of moral consciousness: the enthusiasm "which was of a moral nature, was so powerful, that it seemed even to extend to a conversion of the heart."[20] In the famous passage that recounts his own conversion to antislavery—as he rested on a Hertfordshire roadside after winning the thesis prize at Cambridge ("I was more than two hours in solitude under this painful conflict. At length I yielded . . . in obedience, I believe, to a higher Power.")—few changes mark the text, as if this episode is burned into the author's memory. It is striking how closely Clarkson's epiphany resembles the "opening" (i.e., insight) and "convincement" recorded by Quaker founder George Fox in his spiritual autobiography ("I wondered why these things should come to me. I looked upon myself, and said, 'Was I ever so before?'"). Clarkson seamlessly introduces himself as an active "coadjutor," but in short order, insecurity seems to set in as he works to avoid charges of egotism. The ease and fluidity of his description of the conversion moment gives way to writing marked by multiple strikeouts and adjustments.[21]

The *History*, amounting to more than 1,150 pages in print and published on May 30, 1808—almost precisely one year after Parliament's enactment of abolition—was a big gamble for its author. The large run—five thousand copies in the first edition, twice as large as the *Portraiture*—reveals his publisher's estimation of Clarkson as a writer. In addition, the *History* included several expensive engravings, one of them a reproduction of the well-known cross-section of the slave ship *The Brookes*.[22]

As early as June 1807, having achieved significant success in the American market with the *Portraiture,* Clarkson was arranging for a Philadelphia edition of the *History*. In May 1808, James P. Parke proudly advertised that he had received the manuscript (directly from the author, as a form of international copyright, and hence its ultimate destination at an American library), and that the book would appear "as soon as the number of subscriptions would warrant its publication." The Philadelphia edition, ready for subscribers by November 18, 1808, was virtually identical to the London edition and embellished with careful reproductions of the illustrations by noted engraver William Kneass.[23] The work was in many Americans' hands by January 1, 1809: eight months after the Parliamentary ban on the slave trade and one year after the implementation of abolition by the United States Congress.

Despite these hopes, the *History* did not achieve as great a momentum as had the *Portraiture.*[24] A weighty and expensive book—priced at 1 guinea for subscribers and £1.4.0 for nonsubscribers in Britain, and $3.00 for American subscribers—the *History* assumed a readership as passionate as its author about a now-twenty-year-old cause, and as fascinated by Quaker activism. But it was published just as the natural allies against the trade—Great Britain and the United States—were divided by embargoes and impending war. Potential readers' attentions were apparently elsewhere, and Clarkson would not undertake such an ambitious project regarding antislavery again.

QUAKER CODA: *THE MEMOIRS OF WILLIAM PENN*

The *History* was, however, not Clarkson's last tribute to, or use of, the Friends. The third volume in his Quaker trilogy, *The Memoirs of the Private and Public Life of William Penn,* was conceived toward the end of 1808, when its author began to collect materials on the Pennsylvania founder's life. The two-volume work was released in 1813, in a print run the same as the *Portraiture*: 2,500 copies—half the size of the *History.* These more modest numbers sold quickly, many once again through Quaker subscriptions.[25] A new edition was released the following year, illustrated with a frontispiece portrait of Penn, together with the two sides of a medal commemorating Penn's Treaty with the Indians. Likewise, in the United States, Bradford and Inskeep issued simultaneous editions in Philadelphia and New York in 1813, and two competing editions appeared in Philadelphia in 1814. The biography was reissued numerous times thereafter, as the standard life of Penn: Clarkson had once again earned his reputation as an author-scholar of note through specific work on the Friends. As one flattering Philadelphia correspondent later claimed, the *Memoirs* was "in the hands of all the inhabitants of this City," or at least among the Quaker inhabitants.[26]

With the publication of the *Memoirs,* Clarkson had surely come to see himself as a professional historian and man of letters. Like his previous works, the Penn volume aimed to present a fully documented history. Clarkson consulted widely in public and private sources, some, including *Votes and Proceedings of the House of Representatives of Pennsylvania,* Robert Proud's *History of Pennsylvania,* and Mathew Carey's *American Museum,* shipped to him by his American Quaker contacts. Throughout the two volumes, he refers repeatedly to the authority of his sources or indicates when little is known. His voice occasionally intervenes in the narrative, noting when a particular correspondence or event moved him. Drawing on his now-easy familiarity with Quaker spirituality, he translated various passages in Penn's writings for the non-Quaker reader. He included anecdotes to underscore his positive depiction of the Quaker leader's benevolence even in small things, such as Penn's kindness to a Quaker girl as she walked barefoot along Pennsylvania's Darby Road to attend a meeting for worship at Haverford.[27]

The shift in the political and religious climate by 1812–1813 was reflected also in Clarkson's unusual use of biblical metaphors at the very end of the memoir, encouraging good "Governors" to be as "the greatest benefactors of the human race," who "by discharging their great and extensive Stewardships faithfully" also "exchange their earthly for incorruptible crowns of glory at the Resurrection of the Just." As he would tell the emperor of Russia in an unusual interview in Paris in 1818, Clarkson hoped the czar would run the Holy Alliance the way that William Penn had run Pennsylvania, according to the "Principles of the Gospel." At this juncture, he carefully supplied the czar with all three volumes of his trilogy—the *Portraiture*, the *History*, and *William Penn*—bound in purple morocco.[28]

The *Memoirs* is a reminder of the extent to which Clarkson's use of the Quakers to legitimize radical—and internationally relevant—reform had not changed, despite the recent capture of Napoleon and British patriotism being at fever pitch. Indeed, the last chapters of this thousand-page Penn biography focus on Clarkson's main preoccupations—justice to the outcast, displaced foreigners, Indians, and Africans foremost among them—and the historical significance of the Quaker testimony against war. The fact that Penn had bought and sold slaves was omitted from the story.[29]

CONCLUSION: THE NATURE OF TRANSFORMATIVE HISTORY

Thomas Clarkson's Quaker trilogy, as we have chosen to call it—the *Portraiture*, the *History*, and the *Memoirs of William Penn* taken together—was no mean accomplishment. Amounting to a production of more than 3,400 octavo pages in less than ten years, reprinted almost immediately in the United States and cited for decades afterward as the authoritative treatments on contemporary Quakerism, the end of the British slave trade, and the founder of Pennsylvania, the three works represented the kind of combined Enlightenment and Romantic project in which participants in the "age of wonder" reveled: based on thorough, even tediously repetitive fact-gathering and documentation, while at the same time rich in sensibility—with sentiments freely expressed—and nobly internationalist in aspiration. Clarkson hoped through these methods to use historical narrative as a transforming force: where through diligence and good evidence, the true fact-based story of human injustice might emerge and the "just" might be vindicated, with injustice never forgotten and never repeated; the truth will out.

That, however, was not entirely what happened to Clarkson's trilogy. Almost immediately, his work was interpreted in ways that removed it from its Quaker internationalist impulse. On the day of the *History*'s publication, May 30, 1808, William Hayley sent Clarkson a celebratory sonnet personifying the author as the nation's delivering hero, rather than moral Christianity's spokesman:

Thou just Historian of those Toils complete,
That terminate a nation's Guilt, and shame,
In Virtue's Blaze of philanthropic Fame!
Hail! generous Clarkson![30]

Romantic fellow travelers, Robert Southey and Samuel Taylor Coleridge, in their simultaneous reviews of the *History*, characterized the book's main point as a salvation and vindication of the British nation and Africa alike, written by not just any man but one who had suffered emotional devastation for the nation's betterment. "To Mr. Wilberforce as a public man," Southey wrote, "to the Quakers as a collective body, and to Thomas Clarkson as the prime mover, England and Africa are indebted for this deliverance from this enormous evil." The slave trade, Coleridge wrote in a paradoxical vein, "is a war in which the victors fall lower than the vanquished; in which the oppressors are more truly objects of pity than the oppressed."[31] Several years later, James Montgomery's *The Abolition of the Slave Trade: A Poem,* illustrated with cameo portraits of Clarkson, Wilberforce, and Granville Sharp as Roman senators, delivered a panegyric to Clarkson ("He rose o'er Afric like the sun in smiles, / He rests in glory on the western isles") and recommended the *History* to the poem's readers.[32]

In time, conversely, a reaction would set in. In the 1830s, shortly after Wilberforce's death, his conservative sons accused Clarkson of self-aggrandizement at the expense of the reputation of their father in the *History*'s account of the origins of the movement. In 1849, in a thinly veiled assault on Clarkson's biography of William Penn, Thomas Babington Macaulay in his *History of England* depicted the Quaker leader as the "political pimp" of James II: or so future Liberal MP William Edward Forster put it in a lengthy introduction to a new edition of the *Memoirs*. Forster called Macaulay's work a "historical romance"—a now much reduced use of the phrase to mean a history deficient in facts.[33]

Readers today may also ask why Clarkson, the ultimate "Quaker-phile," who was known to describe his values as virtually identical with the sect, never joined the Religious Society of Friends.[34] Clarkson left us few clues about this question, but the Quakers, for all their admirable family life and commitment to reform, may have been too theologically reticent to compete with the evangelical fervor of many of Clarkson's other allies. Or the abolitionist's political compass may have steered him more toward the well-connected Anglicans than toward the politically powerless Quakers.

Clarkson's trilogy, finally, and, most importantly his *History*, raise the issue as to whether the author's twin emphases on the moral superiority of the Friends and the centrality of Quakers to abolition have led to two widely held misconceptions by both scholars and the general public. The first is that the Friends "as a collective body," to use Robert Southey's phrase, had always opposed slavery and the slave trade, and that Quakers, British and American, were synonymous with abolition.

The other misconception is that the original abolition movement was a thoroughly white story. The absence of African activists in Clarkson's Quaker trilogy is puzzling, given the author's own close connections to Africa and the African Atlantic—through his brother John Clarkson, first governor of Sierra Leone—his familiarity with Olaudah Equiano's best-selling slave narrative, published in 1789, and his friendship with the Christophe family of Haiti.[35] Although he espoused a love of Africa, he omitted black voices from his chronicles, and black *people*, as opposed to black *victimhood*, are scarcely visible. Though he may have risen "o'er Afric' like the sun in smiles" in the eyes of many of his fellow white Britons, how was Clarkson seen by—and to what extent did he really see—the lives and perspective of the many Africans who now lived in the eighteenth-century "western iles" with him? Could it be that Clarkson feared that making abolition palatable to a larger British book-buying public required placing men such as Ignatius Sancho, Olaudah Equiano, and Quobna Ottobah Cugoano on the sidelines?

Clarkson's narratives, both his trilogy and his own biography, reveal much about the complex web of enlightened, romantic, and religious discourses that writers in the early years of antislavery activism merged so effectively and distributed so widely—not least of all through the agency of Quaker printers, literary publishers, and their many customers on both sides of the Atlantic. Clarkson's close identification with the Friends was essential to his invention of himself as an empirical, scholarly, and professional author. In the Quakers, Clarkson found a small core of kindred spirits and moral justification for his own radicalism and for his lifelong abhorrence of slavery, however far removed it was from his daily life. His glorification of Quaker life and antislavery leadership permitted him to produce an abolitionist history acceptable to both British and American readers, even if, or perhaps because, it excluded the black presence. Future Friends would nonetheless take particular inspiration from Clarkson's interpretation of the Quakers' long-standing commitment to abolition. They and their many non-Quaker allies, black and white, would *need* inspiration and stamina in the long struggle ahead to end the unparalleled evils of slavery.

NOTES

1. Ellen Gibson Wilson, *Thomas Clarkson: A Biography* (York: William Sessions, Ltd., 1989); medal in Quaker Collection, Haverford College Library, Haverford, Pa.; *Description of Haydon's Picture of the Great Meeting of Delegates* (London: Charles Reynell, 1841).

2. Adam Hochschild, *Bury the Chains: Prophets and Rebels in the Fight to Free an Empire's Slaves* (Boston: Houghton Mifflin Co., 2005), chap. 6; David Brion Davis, *Inhuman Bondage: The Rise and Fall of Slavery in the New World* (Oxford: Oxford University Press, 2006), 189–90; Christopher Leslie Brown, *Moral Capital: Foundations of British Abolitionism* (Chapel Hill: University of North Carolina Press: 2006), 433–50; Brycchan Carey, *British Abolitionism and the Rhetoric of Sensibility: Writing, Sentiment, and Slavery, 1760–1807* (Basingstoke, U.K.: Palgrave Macmillan, 2005), 130–37.

3. Richard Holmes, *The Age of Wonder: How the Romantic Generation Discovered the Beauty and Terror of Science* (New York: Pantheon Books, 2008). See also James Walvin's essay, chapter 11, in this volume.

4. Thomas Clarkson, *A Portraiture of Quakerism, as Taken from a View of the Moral Education, Discipline, Peculiar Customs, Religious Principles, Political and Civil Economy, and Character of the Society of Friends*, 3 vols. (London: Longman, Hurst, Rees, and Orme, 1806); *The History of the Rise, Progress, and Accomplishment of the Abolition of the African Slave-Trade by the British Parliament*, 2 vols. (London: Longman, Hurst, Rees, and Orme,1808); and *Memoirs of the Private and Public Life of William Penn*, 2 vols. (London: Longman, Hurst, Rees, Orme, and Brown, 1813).

5. See Jean R. Soderlund, *Quakers and Slavery: A Divided Spirit* (Princeton: Princeton University Press, 1988), and recent studies by Brycchan Carey, Ryan Jordan, Maurice Jackson, and Geoffrey G. Plank. On Quaker strategizing, see Kirsten Sword, "Remembering Dinah Nevil: Strategic Deceptions in Eighteenth-Century Antislavery," *Journal of American History* 97 (September 2010): 315–43.

6. "Minute-book of the Committee for the Abolition of the Slave Trade," vol. 1, opening pages, Add MSS 21254, Manuscripts Collection, British Library, London; Thomas Clarkson, *An Essay on the Slavery and Commerce of the Human Species, Particularly the African, translated from a Latin Dissertation, which was honoured*

with the First Prize in the University of Cambridge, for the Year 1785 (London: James Phillips, 1786); *An Essay on the Slavery and Commerce of the Human Species . . .* (Philadelphia: Joseph Crukshank, 1786); *An Essay on the Impolicy of the African Slave Trade* (London: James Phillips, 1788); *An Essay on the Impolicy of the African Slave Trade* (Philadelphia: Francis Bailey, 1788); Hochschild, 90–96, Brown, chap. 7.

7. Wilson, chaps, 6 and 7; Hochschild, 246–48.

8. Wilson, 120–21. See also Dillwyn correspondence cited in subsequent notes.

9. Prospectus, Thomas Clarkson Correspondence, Anti-Slavery Collection, C107/148, Rhodes House Library, Oxford; Clarkson, *Portraiture*, 1: i, 4.

10. Clarkson, *Portraiture*, 1: 81, 130–75.

11. Ibid., 2: 4–39; 89–101; 3: 150–296.

12. William Dillwyn to James Pemberton, 5th month 20, 1806 and 6th month 4, 1806, Correspondence, vol. 56, box 2, Pemberton Papers, MSS #484A, Historical Society of Pennsylvania, Philadelphia; Clarkson, *Portraiture*, New York edition, 1806; Advertisement, Poulson's *American Daily Advertiser* (Philadelphia), August 24, 1807.

13. Robert Bisset, *The History of the Negro Slave Trade, in Its Connection with the Commerce and Prosperity of the West Indies, and the Wealth and Power of the British Empire*, 2 vols. (London: S. Highley, et al., 1805): 1: 51, 58, 160, 166.

14. See insights regarding inductive method in Carey, 26; and commentary on the "problematic" character of the *History*, part chronicle, part memoir, in Brown, 433–44.

15. Entries for September 24, 1807, and January 23, 1808, in Cash Book, 1803–1809, Richard Taylor and Co. Papers, St. Bride's Library, London; Thomas Clarkson to Thomas Thompson, September 21, 1807, MSS 325, Quaker Collection, Haverford College Library; Prospectus, dated 11th month 7, 1807 by William Dillwyn, Correspondence, vol. 56, box 2, Pemberton Papers.

16. "History of the Rise, Progress, and Accomplishment of the Abolition of the Slave Trade," 2 vols., MSS #975A, Quaker Collection, Haverford College Library.

17. Barbara Rhodes and William Wells Streeter, *Before Photocopying: The Art and History of Mechanical Copying, 1780–1938* (Newcastle, Del.: Oak Knoll Press, 1999), chap. 1.

18. "History," opening pages of vol. 1 and closing pages of vol. 2; vol. 1, chap. 5, esp. 91–102.

19. Ibid., vol. 2, chaps. 4 and 9.

20. Ibid., vol. 2, 455; *History*, 2: 575.

21. "History," vol. 1, chap. 8; Clarkson, *History*, 1: 229–30; George Fox, *A Journal or Historical Account of the Life, Travels, Sufferings, Christian Experience, and Labour of Love*, 3rd ed., corr. (London: Luke Hinde, 1765), 3; "History," vol. 1, 157–59.

22. Check Book [ca. 1808], Richard Taylor and Co. Papers; "History," vol. 2, 90–91.

23. Poulson's *American Daily Advertiser* (Philadelphia), Advertisements, May 4, 1808 and November 18, 1808; Clarkson, *History* (Philadelphia: James Parke, 1808).

24. Total sales are unknown but, unlike the *Portraiture* and *William Penn*, the *History* did not go into multiple editions in either Britain or the United States.

25. December 1, 1812, Letter Books, in vol. 2, books 97 and 98, MS 1383, Longman's Archives, Special Collections, University of Reading.

26. See Philadelphia and New York editions, Friends Collection, Earlham College, Richmond, Ind.; J. Francis Fisher to Thomas Clarkson, April 29, 1834, Thomas Clarkson Papers, CN 96, Huntington Library, San Marino, Ca.

27. Clarkson, *Memoirs*, 1: ix–xii; 2: 229–30.

28. Ibid., 2: 488; Interview with the emperor of Russia, October 9, 1818, Thomas Clarkson Papers, CN 60, Huntington Library.

29. Harry Emerson Wildes, *William Penn* (New York: Macmillan, 1974), 323–24.

30. [William] Hayley, "Sonnet to Mr. Clarkson on his History of the Abolition of the African Slave Trade, May 23, 1808," Add. MSS 41267A, Manuscripts Collection, British Library.

31. *Annual Review, and History of Literature, for 1808*, vol. 7 (1809): 148; *Edinburgh Review, or Critical Journal, for April . . . July 1808*, vol. 12 (1808): 356.

32. *The Abolition of the Slave Trade: A Poem, in Four Parts* (London: R. Bowyer, 1814), pt. 4, l. 129.

33. Robert Isaac Wilberforce and Samuel Wilberforce, *The Life of William Wilberforce*, 5 vols. (London: John Murray, 1838); W. E. Forster, Preface, *Memoirs of the Public and Private Life of William Penn* (London: C. Gilpin, 1849), xxvii, xvi.

34. Clarkson's pacifism lends further credence to this view: see Wilson, 132–34; 145.

35. Ibid., chap. 12; James Green, "The Publishing History of Olaudah Equiano's *Interesting Narrative,*" *Slavery and Abolition* 16 (1995): 362–75.

14 The Hidden Story of Quakers and Slavery

GARY B. NASH

THE STORY OF QUAKER LEADERSHIP in the abolition movement has been known and proudly recounted by Friends and friends of Friends for two centuries. Though only a miniscule fraction of religionists in America, Quakers were indisputably in the forefront of the crusade to end slavery, just as they were on the front lines of other reform movements for penal reform, public education, women's suffrage, Native American rights, civil rights, and the end of war. Yet the Quakers' role in ending the Atlantic slave trade and chattel bondage has been obscured for generations, and it is nearly as obscured today as it was a century ago so far as the general public is concerned. To be sure, the scholarly literature on the Quaker involvement in abolishing slavery has mushroomed; yet public consciousness remains largely as it was in the days of our grandparents.

One way of measuring this historical amnesia is to consult the schoolbooks read by American youth. For the period before World War I, when only about 2 percent of all Americans went to college, it is reasonable to assume, as Ruth Miller Elson argues, that ideas and attitudes held by ordinary persons were largely shaped by what they found in their schoolbooks.[1] With that in mind, it is instructive to observe that young Americans before World War I learned almost nothing about the Society of Friends and the Quakers' foundational principles and even less on Quaker attitudes toward slavery and their role in its abolition. Most of the books were written by Protestant New Englanders, whose own ideological leanings were not friendly to much of what Quakers held most dear. For example, the ideal woman had "no interests or ambitions of her own," spending "her life in happy submission to the will of others and taught that public speaking was 'highly improper.'"[2] The activist role was universally proscribed and thus a woman such as Lucretia Mott was hardly to be held up as a model American woman.

Quaker pacifism raised a second problem about the appropriateness of American youth studying Quakers at all. Elson has a thoughtful discussion of the yearning for peace presented to youthful readers in some books, but shows that it was greatly outweighed by the emphasis on militant national-ism. "Nationalism and pacifist sentiments are often mutually exclusive," she writes, "and, with [a] few exceptions . . . nationalism always conquers." For more than a century, the schoolbooks portrayed "the most illustrious activity in which one can engage" as fighting and dying for one's country.[3]

Another reason to steer clear of Quakers and their abolitionist activism was the schoolbook authors' unquestioned certitude that Africans and their descendants were the most degraded of the so-called races "defined by inher-ent physical, intellectual, and spiritual qualities."[4] Even after the Civil War, when the books began to accept the rightness of emancipation, they typically noted the inherent, unpromising qualities of the enslaved African, and once free, black Americans "disappear from the schoolbooks."[5] If it is true that the golden age of children's literature was from about 1870 to 1920, it was certainly not the golden age of children's history. As Elson has shown, the schoolbooks were designed to nurture moral values and unconditional patriotism, while bringing into the master national narrative only a narrow slice of people who created the past.[6]

For schoolbooks read after World War I, we can focus on the ones written by David Saville Muzzey, a patrician New Englander descended from a long line of preachers and teachers extending back to the Puritans. Probably half of all youthful readers between World War I and the Cold War, some fifty million, imbibed their American history from his pages. Muzzey was mildly liberal on some issues such as the neglect of the nation's poor and Progressive era political reform, but he was offended by radical laborites, appalled by radical Reconstruction, and dismissive of Americans with dark skin.[7] Muzzey com-mended the "peace-loving Friends, or Quakers" for fair dealing with Indians (though Indians displayed "a stolid stupidity that no white man could match"); for scaling back capital offenses; and for becoming the first province "to raise its voice against slavery."[8] However, Muzzey never explained the Friends' peace testimony or later their passive resistance, and this avoidance of what it meant to be "peace-loving" or "peaceful" was followed by all subsequent textbook writers who, it seems, knew that they and their publishers could not afford to introduce students to the Quaker commitment to nonviolence. After the American entry into World War I, many historians, in Peter Novick's account, felt remorse "for having insufficiently promoted American patriotism [and] for having left American youth morally unprepared for their military duties. That was certainly the position of Frederick Jackson Turner, who believed that historians "will feel a sense of treason to their cause if they are silent while pacifists set forth the meaning of American history."[9]

Nor was Muzzey willing to address the origins of racial slavery, its growth, or how enslaved Africans responded to it. Students learned of slavery only when it became a political problem over which white legislators debated fiercely and reached compromises—at the Constitutional Convention, during the crisis over Missouri's entrance to the Union, and finally during the run-up to the Civil War. African Americans themselves are ciphers, voiceless and mindless, appearing only on occasion as "grateful if uncomprehending recipients of racial and social uplift."[10] Even as freedmen they were hardly worthy of notice. Not even the Fourteenth and Fifteenth amendments were a credit to the nation as the suffrage given to the freedmen, in Muzzey's words, "set the ignorant, superstitious, gullible slave in power over his former master."[11]

As for abolitionist sentiment before the 1830s, Muzzey displayed an inexplicable tilt toward Southerners. In his schoolbooks, not Quakers but Washington, Jefferson, Madison, and John Randolph are those who first expressed "antislavery feeling," and it is in the South, not in Philadelphia, where "the first antislavery societies were formed."[12] After 1830, Garrison, and Garrison alone, nails the antislavery colors to the mast. Quakers, along with black abolitionists, were entirely missing in action.

One of Muzzey's colleagues at Columbia, until he resigned in 1917 in protest to the firing of three colleagues who opposed conscription, let slip what may be the first indication of the extent of enslaved Africans in North America presented in a high school textbook. This was Charles A. Beard, who, writing with his wife Mary Beard, included two pages on Africans as part of a discussion of free immigrants, indentured servants, and deported criminals who populated British colonial America. Though Quakers warranted only a slight mention—two sentences on Penn and nothing on the growth of the antislavery prerevolutionary commitment of Quakers—the Beards provided the only account I have seen in textbooks of this era of the rapid growth of slavery after the Revolution, the only reference to the Pennsylvania gradual abolition act of 1780 and similar acts in other Northern states, and the only reference to colonization schemes to return free blacks to Africa.[13] Theirs is also the most stirring account of the early-nineteenth-century abolitionists, and it is in this book that Harriet Tubman was first introduced to high school students, so far as I have been able to ascertain.[14]

One can examine dozens of other middle and high school history books between the wars, but my sampling indicates that the greatly envied Muzzey set the pace. However, two authors who were churning out textbooks might have made a difference given their unusually enlightened view of Native Americans and their professed desire to help young learners see multiple points of view and empathize with the nation's many peoples. The first was Harold Rugg, a ninth-generation New Englander who worked as a weaver in a Massachusetts textile mill in order to understand industrial labor and the quality of life at the bottom of the social hierarchy. Teaching at the Columbia Teachers College's experimental Lincoln School, he drew ideas and strategies from Progressivism that strove to nourish creative abilities of young boys and girls. "Pupils must learn to think critically about modern problems" and teachers must instill in their pupils "tolerant understanding," Rugg insisted. Ask students, he advised, "Why do you think so?" "Are you open-minded about the matter?" "What is your authority?" "Have you considered all sides of the case?"[15]

Rugg held true to this standard in treating Native Americans. In his *History of American Civilization*, the opening chapter, thirty pages long with sympathetic images of native people and a map of the major tribes in North America, leads students on a tour of how the Indian people were divided into many tribes and lived in many different ways. Not a word appears about savagery, paganism, cannibalism, scalping, or torture. After a sympathetic portrait of a Creek village in the Southeast, Rugg asks the student: "Do you think that people who were able to live as the Creeks lived were uncivilized?" and "Was it right for the more numerous Europeans to drive back the scattered tribes of Indians?"[16]

Writing at the same time, Yale's Ralph Gabriel, writing with Mabel B. Casner, a West Haven, Connecticut, elementary school teacher, had a chapter as sympathetic to native people as Rugg's was. Class discussion topics that open each chapter are revealing: "Do you know persons who are Indian or persons who have had Indian ancestors?" "What facts can you tell about these famous Indian men and women: Pocahontas, Massasoit, King Philip, Pontiac, Tecumseh, Dr. Eastman, Red Cloud, Geronimo, Sitting Bull?"[17] Nonetheless, this remarkable departure from the savagery versus civilization template of presenting Indian–European contact did not extend to racial slavery and its Quaker opponents. Casner and Gabriel, following Muzzey, devoted a total of four sentences to how slaves lived and left young readers with the feeling that slave labor was not so bad. Of all the schoolbook writers, Rugg probably went the furthest. Though silent on early Quaker abolitionist efforts, he at least gave a few pages on slavery in the South in the antebellum period, where the enslaved are seen to have led a sparse life of unending toil; and he added four pages on "the Crusade against Slavery" in the 1830s, where students learned that the Quakers "played a very important part."[18] This was as far as any textbook writer would go, and Rugg would soon pay a steep penalty for it.

What explains the erasure of Quakers and slavery over a period of two centuries of textbook writing? One answer might be that the documentary record had not been sufficiently revealed or that monographic histories based on the recovery of primary sources had not yet been published so that textbook writers could consider and utilize them. While this might explain nineteenth-century schoolbooks, it cannot justify the books put before young learners after about 1920. The problem was not with the available scholarship on Quakers and slavery; the problem was what to do with it. This raises the difficulty that all schoolbook authors faced: accommodating public pressure and sparring with publishers, who were usually determined not to risk school adoptions, often influenced by powerful patriotic white citizen groups, where militant nationalism reigned and dying for one's country was considered the supreme good. By 1928, Muzzey was running for cover, dodging charges of writing "treason texts" that discussed Loyalism during the American Revolution and presented students with other purportedly pro-British propaganda. Even though he said almost nothing about Quaker pacifism, Muzzey's attackers charged that they had uncovered "interlocking directorates between [a] textbook publishing firm and seven alien agencies." The publishing house was in fact Ginn & Company, Muzzey's publisher and the largest producer of schoolbooks in the United States at the time. The seven conspiring agencies were the World Court League, the League of Nations Union, the League of Nations Non-Partisan Association, the World Peace Foundation, the World Alliance for Promoting International Friendship through the Churches, the New York Peace Society, and the New York Union for International Justice. Ginn's offices in Boston, Muzzey's detractors charged, were "the largest breeding-nest and roosting-place in America of Anglo-American and pacifist organizations."[19]

In the South, "lost cause" deep-dyed Confederates hated textbooks written by Northerners and were highly successful from the 1920s to 1940s in getting the publishing houses to produce blatantly pro-Southern textbooks for the segregated white public schools. It goes without saying that these books cleansed the historical record of Quakers and their abolitionist campaigns while treating slavery itself as the best thing that happened to Africans in human history.[20]

From the other end of the spectrum came an insistent campaign in the interwar period, spearheaded by the National Association for the Advancement of Colored People, to provide schoolbooks for black youngsters in the segregated South to end what the NAACP called "a conception of the character, capacity, history, and achievements of the Negro utterly at variance with the facts, and calculated to arouse against him feelings of aversion and contempt."[21] Carter G. Woodson, founder of the Association for the Study of Negro Life and History and inaugurator of Negro History Week (first observed in 1926), led the way with textbooks written for black students from elementary grades to college that were widely read in black Southern schools.[22] Ironically, black students, reading about slavery, Quakers, and the abolitionist movement in alternative textbooks, were far ahead of white students who were working from textbooks written by the white titans of the historical profession. Woodson brought the Germantown 1688 protestors, Ralph Sandiford, Benjamin Lay, John Woolman, and Anthony Benezet into the narrative of prerevolutionary history, whereas white-generated textbooks ignored them. Consigned to wretched school facilities and taught by underpaid teachers, black students from the 1920s to 1960s were reading much more about Quakers and slavery than relatively privileged white students were, whether in elementary, middle, or high schools, or at universities and colleges.

If students coming to college after World War I were barely cognizant of the Society of Friends or slavery in the colonial period, they were likely to leave college knowing little more. College textbook writers, then as now, were less subject to public and political pressure in recapturing the American past. Yet while freer to step where authors of precollege textbooks might fear to go, they were part of the historians' guild, where racialist thinking was widely shared. There were exceptions—white historians such as Herbert Aptheker and Philip Foner and black historians such as Carter Woodson and W. E. B. DuBois. But these were precisely the dissident historians that mainstream publishers would not touch, knowing not only that the market for their books was almost nonexistent but that publishing such counternarratives could jeopardize the entire future of a publishing house.

The most widely read college-level survey of American history used in the 1930s through the 1950s was *The Growth of the American Republic* by Samuel Eliot Morison and Henry Steele Commager. Weighing in at nearly 1,400 pages, it told students almost nothing about Quakers except that Philadelphia and Pennsylvania were dominated by "the Quaker aristocracy" throughout the colonial period, and, in the early nineteenth century, "the Quakers kept up a mild and ineffectual protest" against slavery. Students learned nothing about Quaker pacifism or the role of women in the Society of Friends, nothing of men such as Benezet and Woolman, nothing about the Pennsylvania Abolition Society, and nothing about the likes of Mott or for that matter any abolitionist except Garrison, who "employed language that made impossible the peaceful attainment of his ends."[23]

As for the slaves themselves, they could be summed up simply as "Sambo, whose wrongs moved the abolitionists to wrath and tears . . . [but] suffered less than any other class in the South from its 'peculiar institution.' The majority of slaves were adequately fed, well cared for, and apparently happy. Although brought to America by force, the incurably optimistic negro soon became attached to the country, and devoted to his 'white folks.' Slave insurrections were planned—usually by the free negroes—but invariably betrayed by some faithful darky; and trained obedience kept the slaves faithful throughout the Civil War." The "average" slave was "childlike, improvident, humorous, prevaricating, and superstitious," and "there was much to be said for slavery as a transitional status between barbarism and civilization. The negro learned his master's language and accepted in some degree his moral and religious standards. In return he contributed much besides his labor—music and humor for instance—to American civilization." In three pages, the history of African Americans before the Civil War is complete.[24] It is no wonder that W. E B. DuBois would write five years later that "I stand . . . literally aghast at what American historians have done to this field . . . [It is] one of the most stupendous efforts the world ever saw to discredit human beings, an effort involving universities, history, science, social life, and religion."[25] Though sharply criticized for the demeaning Sambo passage, Morison would not jettison it until the fifth edition in 1962.[26]

Far away from the Northeast bastions of textbook writing, Max Savelle, at Stanford, published a college textbook in 1942 on the colonial period that took infant steps toward addressing the connection between Quakers and slavery. In his *Foundations of American Civilization,* there are slaves suffering in the Middle Passage, but no slave experience. Lord Dunmore flees a British ship in Chesapeake Bay but issues no proclamation; no blacks, accordingly, are involved in the Revolution. However, Savelle was unusual in devoting a page to the saintly John Woolman with a long quote from his journal and a nod to his pivotal role "in the growing movement against slavery."[27]

After World War II, most textbook writers hurried to the political center and rightward as anti-Communist fervor took hold. If the ultrapatriotic attacks on textbook writers in the 1920s and 1930s drove schoolbook writers away from any inclinations they had to deal with Quaker pacifism, the horrors of slavery, or Quaker leadership in abolitionist movements, the consensus period, ushered in by the Cold War, perpetuated if not increased neglect on these matters. Thomas A. Bailey's *American Pageant,* a college favorite first published in 1956 and the reigning textbook in the Advanced Placement U.S. History exams that the College Board initiated in 1970s, provides a good example of consensus history uncongenial to either Quakers or the enslaved. Bailey painted a sympathetic portrait of William Penn and the "humane Quakers [who] early developed a strong dislike of Negro slavery." But the Quakers never reappear until Lucretia Mott strides forth in the 1830s as part of a "belligerent bevy of female agitators." Blacks themselves appear only as a white problem to be solved in the nineteenth century, and they are voiceless after the "hothead" Garrison, representing "the lunatic fringe," stirs up big trouble.[28]

At the high school level, McCarthyism brought loyalty oaths required of teachers in more than half the states, removal of books from school libraries as red-tainted, and attacks on textbooks that failed to label Social Security and other New Deal programs as "evil."[29] Quakers and their antislavery efforts remained largely absent from textbooks at any level.

If there was one exception to textbooks that scanted Quakers and their role in abolitionism, it was also the book that mocked the Friends and propped them up as examples of how to fail as reformers. In the first of his three-volume history of the United States, published in 1958 as *The Americans: The Colonial Experience*, Daniel Boorstin gave more pages to the Quakers than I have seen in any book written for college students and the general public. But any uncritical reader would have put the book down with a thorough disgust with Quakers. Boorstin recounted the Quaker thirst for martyrdom in their early years in North America and then moved on to relate "one of the greatest lost opportunities in all American history" as Quakerism "built a wall around itself," "not by being false to their teachings, but by being too true to them." Of all their excesses of "uncompromising obstinacy," "self-deception," "overweening purity," and "arrogant and purposeless insistence on hat-honor," their peace testimony was their crowning mistake. Writing as if determined to bury any place for the Quakers in American history books, he told readers how the Friends misjudged the "scalp-hungry" Indian, who "was omnipresent" and "struck without warning and was a nightly terror in the remote silence of backwoods cabins," and how the Quakers, obsessively holding to their pacifist principles, finally withdrew from government in 1756.[30] The Quakers suffered from "the curse of perfectionism," marginalized themselves, and made their values irrelevant to pragmatic fellow Americans.[31]

How did Boorstin's vendetta against Quakers relate to their antislavery commitment? It is a subject untouched because slavery itself warrants only three sentences on how slaves began replacing indentured servants in late-seventeenth-century Virginia and two references to the Georgia Trustees in London, indicted by Boorstin for prohibiting slavery and hence hobbling enterprising colonists. There is no African American experience under slavery; there is no Quaker movement to withdraw from the slave trade and then disavow slave-keeping as the revolutionary storm clouds gathered; there is no rise of abolitionist sentiment as part of the natural rights argument underlying the Declaration of Independence. The book won the Bancroft Prize in 1959.

Given Boorstin's disdain of Quakers, what might one expect in *The National Experience,* the second volume of his trilogy? Boorstin treated slavery only as a problem roiling North–South politics and never addressed abolitionism as a movement. That being the case, there was no need to include Quaker or black abolitionists as part of the "national experience." In 517 pages, even Harriet Beecher Stowe and Frederick Douglass escape notice.

Happily, I have found no textbook writers who followed Boorstin's disparagement of the Quakers. By the 1960s, many were distancing themselves from consensus versions of American history, and beginning, if only faintly, to follow the scholarship of such antiracist historians as Kenneth Stampp, John Hope Franklin, Benjamin Quarles, Herbert Aptheker, Howard Beale, and C. Vann Woodward, who were turning on its head the treatment of slavery and the character of Reconstruction. Here was the beginning of a more inclusive American history and the end of patently racist depictions of people of African descent, Native Americans, and other minority groups. When that happened, Quakers had a better chance of slipping onto the stage.

This happened in one breakthrough book for middle school youngsters written after the California Board of Education called for a multicultural approach to American history a few years after Boorstin's *Colonial Experience* appeared. Written by John Caughey at University of California, Los Angeles, John Hope Franklin at the University of Chicago, and Ernest May at Harvard, the book was titled *Land of the Free: A History of the United States* and reached thousands of schools after its publication in 1966. Dealing with the land of the unfree as well as the free, it introduced teenagers to the Quakers' pacifism and relative gender equality, and—in perhaps the first time mentioned in a schoolbook—the Germantown 1688 Quaker protest against slavery.[32] Though students would not encounter Quaker abolitionists until an account of antislavery activism mentioned Lucretia Mott and Levi Coffin, they did encounter slaves responding to Dunmore's Proclamation of 1775 in search of the freedom promised by the British. The authors did not dwell on the irony that enslaved Africans fought on the British side for the same principles that animated the "men of '76," but at least the teacher had the opportunity to broach this paradox.[33]

Such inconvenient truths might have slipped by ultraconservative California politicians, but devoting an entire chapter to slavery and abolitionism in the antebellum period did not. A feature page told Harriet Tubman's story—"The Stand for Freedom"—followed by several pages on abolitionists never before or barely mentioned such as William Wells Brown, the Tappan brothers, Wendell Phillips, Lucretia Mott, and Frederick Douglass.[34] The book horrified conservatives. California's Superintendent of Public Instruction Max Rafferty scorched the book. Traveling the state with bullhorn and microphone, he yowled that "*Land of the Free* is not pornographic, it is worse than pornographic."[35] However, the book remained standard reading in the schools for years.

By the 1970s, college textbooks were beginning to take Quakers seriously and show, even if sparsely, their importance in the abolitionist movement. Modestly revised every four years, the books received major overhauls in the early 1990s when rising young historians infused them with social history scholarship that was more amenable to reform movements and minority groups, as well as readier to portray ambiguities and paradoxes in American history. John Woolman, but rarely Anthony Benezet, began to appear as a herald of antislavery before the American Revolution. Enslaved Africans became essential in building the colonial economy, while resisting and rebelling against slavery and then playing an important role in the American Revolution, predominantly by fleeing to the British to gain freedom. And Quakers made at least cameo appearances in the antebellum period as antislavery stalwarts.

While new college textbooks written in the last two decades have expanded the coverage of Quakers and slavery, the books that cater to the millions of mostly white students in the proliferating Christian academies have moved backward. The favored book is titled simply *United States History for Christian Schools*, published by Bob Jones University Press. Of the scores of textbooks published in the last half-century that I have scrutinized, this has the slightest coverage of Quakers, abolitionism, and slavery. Here is a replica of the so-called mint julep, all-white textbooks published for the Southern market years ago. What students do learn a great deal about is providential history—how God's hand can always be seen in a nation's development and that those who are spiritually dead—the Mormons are indexed as a cult—cannot improve society, whatever their good intentions.[36]

For those not explicitly subscribing to a providential history, William Bennett's *America: The Last Great Hope* (2006) provides an alternative Christian view that takes us back more than a century to find its equal. Bennett takes notice of the Quakers as Pennsylvania's founders, and he is forthright in stating their refusal to conduct war. Then they disappear into thin air, only to reappear as supporters of the Underground Railroad a century and a half later. Students learn that Bennett does not like slavery very much but dislikes abolitionists such as Garrison even more. Garrison, he writes, "hated the Constitution. He hated the Union. At times, he seemed to hate America and his fellow Americans, too. This utterly humorless man would have been even more dangerous if he had commanded a large political following—as Calhoun did. But Garrison damned any of his followers who took any part in politics. Thus, he condemned his Anti-Slavery Society to the fringes of American politics."[37]

As for the slaves, they cannot be the subject of Quaker abolitionist efforts in the second half of the eighteenth century because, in fact, they do not appear in the book until the narrative reaches the 1830s. Slavery as an institution is first mentioned in connection with the Northwest Ordinance and the debates over the Constitution (where Bennett argues that the Three-Fifths Compromise "provided an *incentive* for states to continue the emancipation process").[38] Enslaved Africans and their descendants appear only as appendages to the political struggle of white Americans over the slavery issue.

Some progress has been made in reaching young learners, college students, and the public about the role of the Quakers' involvement in slavery, their withdrawal from it, and the critical roles they played in the abolitionist crusade. Much remains to be done. It is encouraging that the much-admired PBS series *Africans in America,* in its segment "City of Brotherly Love," brings Anthony Benezet and the Pennsylvania Abolition Society to life and revisits the creation of black independent churches under Richard Allen and Absalom Jones; however, the importance of Benezet is underplayed as is that of African Americans in the Revolution.

The bicentennial of the abolition of the slave trade in Great Britain and the United States in 2007 provided a rare opportunity to raise the consciousness of the Friends' role. England fairly vibrated with discussions, commemorations, and exhibits in 2007—everything from a Parliamentary debate about abolishing the slave trade, BBC websites, an exhibition in Westminster Hall attracting a hundred thousand visitors, others at the National Portrait Gallery, the British Museum, and in municipal exhibitions from one end of the country to the other, including an Equiano exhibition in Birmingham. Everywhere bookstore windows were filled with new books on slavery, the slave trade, and abolition; banners hung from city halls, people jingled two-pound coins commemorating the slave trade abolition, and local churches, libraries, and museums promoted their own programs for civic engagement. "It was almost impossible to avoid the public discussion about the abolition of the slave trade," writes James Walvin, a prolific writer on the topic; "it is hard to think of a comparable historical anniversary attracting such ubiquitous, wide-ranging cultural and social attention."[39]

On the western side of the Atlantic, aside from a handful of academic conferences and symposia, the television-watching and museum-going public learned nothing of Woolman, Benezet, and the Quaker flag bearers of abolitionism. As for the bicentenary of the abolition of the slave trade, the Rhode Island Historical Society was one of the few institutions to mount an exhibit. But in the United States, in stark contrast to England, the two-hundred-year anniversary of the end of the legal American slave trade on January 1, 1808, fell like a wounded bird.[40]

How might the story of Quakers, slavery, and abolitionism gain recognition in the schools and in the public's awareness? Two remedies to historical amnesia administered at ground level are commemorative sculpture and urban murals. Sculpture is perhaps the nation's first mass-appeal art form, contributing to the national identity and helping to define the national character by paying tribute to individuals who have made a difference. One estimate puts the number of outdoor sculptures at over fifteen thousand—a three-dimensional honor roll of important Americans. But just as Quakers have been elided from the textbooks until recent years, public sculptures of the Quaker vanguard heroes against slavery are poorly represented in public places. The one exception to a national landscape barren of historic sites where the visitor can do more than glance at a wayside marker is the Levi Coffin House State Historic Site in Fountain City, Indiana. However, the statue erected last year on Wilmington College's campus in Ohio, titled "Who Sends Thee," may inspire other sculptural remembrances of the Quaker campaign against slavery. In gazing at the 750 pounds of sculpted bronze, viewers can learn of Isaac and Sarah Harvey, inconspicuous Quakers, making their way to Washington in 1862 to speak with President Lincoln about emancipating the slaves.

Outdoor urban murals, which have flourished in Philadelphia and other cities, may be even more important than public sculptures because they arrest the eyes and engage the minds of huge numbers of pedestrians hurrying to and fro. Telling stories in image and word on the sides of buildings often two or three stories high, they help define a city's values by providing an outlet for community expression concerning social and political issues. In multiethnic cities, they have become a key means for minority groups to present their own understandings of their history.

One example in Philadelphia is the mural executed at Chestnut and Ninth streets, unveiled in July 2000. Recalling the city's Underground Railroad of the 1850s, the mural presented radical abolitionists in dramatic poses. Standing tall in vivid colors is life-sized Harriet Tubman, the "station master," who aided thousands of "passengers" in casting off their chains and making their way north to the Quaker city. Flanking Tubman stand "conductors" William Still and Lucretia Mott, both well known at the time but forgotten by the twentieth-century citizenry because textbooks and the media had given them paltry, if any, notice. Even more lost to the public's memory were others whose names were inscribed on the mural's honor roll—Passmore Williamson, Robert Purvis, Richard Allen, Charles and Joseph Bustill, Isaac Hopper, Henrietta Bowers Duterte, and Samuel Johnson and family. Schoolchildren recruited to help paint the mural were learning for the first time that an intrepid band of Philadelphians, many decades ago, helped thousands of people escape slavery's clutches and follow the North Star to William Penn's city. The thousands who attended the unveiling looked up at the mural's message: "Philadelphians, men and women, young and old, from all races, religions, and walks of life, kept the freedom train rolling." Unfortunately, the mural was destroyed several years later when a high-rise building was erected on the empty lot that permitted sight lines along Chestnut Street to the mural. Other murals in Philadelphia, however, relate chapters of the city's history of slavery, abolition, and the Quaker heritage.[41]

In time, the Society of Friends may get its due, but Quakers have never been self-promoters, so the story will have to be told largely by others—in word, on film, in sculpture, and through other visual arts. The three-hundredth anniversary of Anthony Benezet's birth in 2013 was one of many commemorative opportunities to bring forward a forgotten hero of abolitionism. Recent scholars have added greatly to our understanding of the humble teacher, author, and quiet reformer, but the larger task remains to reach the public consciousness, on particular figures to be sure but also on the mass of people, white and black, free and enslaved, male and female, who endured slavery, fought against slavery, and in the end prevailed.[42]

NOTES

1. Ruth Miller Elson, *Guardians of Virtue: American Schoolbooks of the Nineteenth Century* (Lincoln: University of Nebraska Press, 1964), vii. But see also Terrie Epstein, "Adolescent Perspective on Racial Diversity in U.S. History: Case Studies from an Urban Classroom, *American Educational Research Journal* 37 (2000), 185–214.

2. Elson, *Guardians of Virtue*, 303–4.

3. Ibid., 326.

4. Ibid., 66, 87.

5. Ibid., 93, 96. At least one black historian, Edward Austin Johnson tried to restore African Americans to their pivotal place in the development of the country. See *A School History of the Negro Race in America* (1891). If there was one advantage to segregated schools, it at least allowed black students to learn about *their* history.

6. Though most young Americans read the fairly uniform textbooks written by Protestant New Englanders, some Catholic- and Confederate-flavored books competed for niche markets. See Joseph Moreau, *Schoolbook Nation: Conflicts over American History Textbooks from the Civil War to the Present* (Ann Arbor: University of Michigan Press, 2004), chaps. 2–3.

7. For a consideration of Muzzey's textbooks, see Frances Fitzgerald, *America Revised History Schoolbooks in the Twentieth Century* (Boston: Little, Brown, 1979), 59–70.

8. David Muzzey, *History of the American People* (New York: Ginn and Co., 1927), 65. Muzzey's books would be reprinted with revisions into the 1960s with his last edition published in 1961; after his death in 1965, Arthur Link did a final revision.

9. Peter Novick, *That Noble Dream: The "Objectivity Question" and the American Historical Profession* (Cambridge: Cambridge University Press, 1988), 117–18.

10. Moreau, *Schoolbook Nation*, 139.

11. David Saville Muzzey, *An American History* (Boston: Ginn and Co., 1911), quoted in Moreau, *Schoolbook Nation*, 89.

12. David Saville Muzzey, *History of Our Country* (Boston: Ginn and Co., 1937), 272–75.

13. Charles and Mary Beard, *History of the United States* (New York: MacMillan, 1927), 16–17, 316–24.

14. Ibid, 331.

15. Quoted in George H. Sabine, Arthur N. Holcombe, Arthur W. Macmahon, Carl Wittke, and Robert S. Lynd, *The Textbooks of Harold* Rugg (New York: American Committee for Democracy and Intellectual Freedom, 1942), 25.

16. Harold Rugg, *History of American Civilization, Economic and Social* (Boston: Ginn and Co., 1930), 11, 198.

17. Ralph Gabriel and Mabel B. Casner, *Exploring American History* (New York: Harcourt, Brace, and Co., 1935), 51, 71–72.

18. Rugg, *A History of American Government and Culture: America's March toward Democracy* (Boston: Ginn and Co., 1931), 276–78, 301–4.

19. Gary B. Nash, Charlotte Crabtree, and Ross Dunn, *History on Trial: Culture Wars and the Teaching of the Past* (New York: Alfred K. Knopf, 1997), 30–31; Moreau, *Schoolbook Nation*, 196–207.

20. Jonathan Zimmerman, *Whose America? Culture Wars in the Public Schools* (Cambridge: Harvard University Press, 2002), 35–42.

21. Quoted in Zimmerman, *Whose America?*, 32 from the papers of the NAACP.

22. Woodson's textbooks included *The Story of the Negro Retold* (Washington, D.C.: Associated Publishers, 1935); *Negro Makers of History* (Washington, D.C.:

Associated Publishers, 1928); and *The Negro in Our History* (Washington, D.C.: Associated Publishers, 1922). See Zimmerman, *Whose America?*, 42–54; and Wilson J. Moses, *Afroutopia: Roots of African American Popular History* (Cambridge: Harvard University Press, 1998).

23. Samuel Eliot Morison and Henry Steele Commager, *Growth of the American Republic,* 2nd ed. (2 vols.; New York: Oxford University Press, 1937), 1: 423.

24. Ibid., 1: 423. Morison expressed his disdain for what he saw as the pacifism of interwar historians by claiming that they "rendered the generation of youth which came to maturity around 1940 spiritually unprepared for the war they had to fight." (*Faith of a Historian,* quoted in Novick, *Noble Dream,* 316.) After many editions, William Leuchtenberg was added to revamp the narrative so as to reflect the scholarship in the 1960s and 1970s on slavery and African Americans. Quakers get fuller treatment than in earlier editions, but they play no role in early abolitionism.

25. Quoted in *History on Trial,* 61, from *Black Reconstruction* (1935), 725, 727.

26. *Whose America?*, 111.

27. Max Savelle, *Foundations of American Civilization: A History of Colonial America* (New York: Henry Holt, 1942), 552–53.

28. Thomas A. Bailey, *American Pageant: A History of the Republic, 2nd ed.* (Boston: D. C. Heath, 1961).

29. Moreau, *Schoolbook Nation,* 253–63; *History on Trial,* 67–70; Jack Nelson and Gene Roberts, Jr., *The Censors and the Schools* (Boston: Little, Brown, 1963); Zimmerman, *Whose America,* chap. 4.

30. Daniel Boorstin, *The Americans: The Colonial Experience* (New York: Random House, 1958), 34, 41, 49, 348.

31. Ibid., 54–55, 64, 69.

32. John Caughey, John Hope Franklin, and Earnest May, *Land of the Free: A History of the United States* (New York: Benzinger Brothers, 1966), 78–80, 113. See Moreau, *Schoolbook Nation,* 266, 283–305.

33. *Land of the Free,* 307–10, 141, 143, 147.

34. Ibid., 303–10.

35. Related to me by John Hope Franklin at Duke University conference in 1996.

36. To take a single example, the section on Progressivism concludes with the stricture that "progressives proposed false solutions to man's problems. They believed that through education, improving living conditions, and providing more equal political and economic opportunities, they could solve man's difficulties. Such a position ignores the Biblical teaching that man's basic problem is not his ignorance or his environment; it is his sin—a problem which can be remedied only through forgiveness and cleansing by God through the death and resurrection of Christ" (442). An end of chapter "content question" asks: "In what way was the progressive view of the nature of man faulty?" (443).

37. William Bennett, *America: The Last Best Hope,* 2 vols. (Nashville, Tenn.: Thomas Nelson, 2006), 1: 285.

38. Ibid, 1: 125.

39. James Walvin, "The Slave Trade, Abolition, and Public Memory," *Transactions of the Royal Historical Society* 6th ser., 19 (2009), 139–49.

40. See Scott Horton, "The Forgotten Bicentennial," *Harper's Magazine*, December 31, 2007.

41. For more on this mural see my *First City: Philadelphia and the Forging of Historical Memory* (Philadelphia: University of Pennsylvania Press, 2002), 325–27.

42. Among a number of recent scholarly contributions, the most comprehensive are Maurice Jackson, *Let This Voice Be Heard: Anthony Benezet, Father of Atlantic Abolitionism* (Philadelphia: University of Pennsylvania Press, 2009) and Brycchan Carey, *From Peace to Freedom: Quaker Rhetoric and the Birth of American Antislavery, 1657–1761* (New Haven: Yale University Press, 2012). Carey's insistence that early Quaker abolitionists such as Benjamin Lay, seen previously as a crazed disturber of the peace, were vital parts of a continuing discourse over the evils of slavery may even bring such forgotten reformers out of the shadows.

Bibliography

This bibliography gathers together selected printed sources from all the chapters contained in this collection. For ease of reference, the material has been organized into two sections: contemporary sources printed up to 1900 and recent historiography and critical reception printed after 1900. For information about manuscript sources, unpublished theses and dissertations, and contemporary book reviews, please see the endnotes to individual chapters. Where different contributors have used multiple editions, the earliest edition only is given. For more details about the specific editions used by individual contributors, please consult the notes to their chapter.

Contemporary Sources to 1900

"Address of the Board of Managers of the New-York Society for the Promotion of Knowledge and Industry," *American Railroad Journal and Advocate of Internal Improvement*, June 8, 1833, 356–57.

Address to the People of Maryland: With the Constitution. Baltimore: Maryland State Colonization Society, 1831.

Anecdotes and Memoirs of William Boen. Philadelphia, 1834.

Armistead, Wilson. *Anthony Benezet.* London, 1859.

Ball, Martha. "Address of the Committee of the Fair, in Aid of the Massachusetts Abolition Society." Boston, n.p., 1843.

———. "Appeal of the Massachusetts Female Emancipation Society. Boston: n.p., 1842.

Banks, George Washington. *Orthodoxy Unmasked.* Philadelphia: G. W. Banks, 1829.

Barclay, Robert. *Apology for the True Christian Divinity.* London, 1678.

Benezet, Anthony. *A Caution and Warning to Great Britain and Her Colonies in a Short Representation of the Calamitous State of the Enslaved Negroes in the British Dominions. Collected from Various Authors, and Submitted to the Serious Considerations of All, and More Especially of Those in Power.* Philadelphia: Henry Miller, 1766.

———. *Notes on the Slave Trade.* Philadelphia, 1781.

———. *Observations on the Inslaving, Importing and Purchasing of Negroes, with Some Advice theron, Extracted form [sic] the Yearly Meeting Epistle of London for the Present Year.* Germantown, Pa., 1759.

————. *Observations on Slavery, Treatise Bound with Serious Considerations on Several Important Subjects viz., On War and Its Inconsistency with the Gospel and the Bad Effects of Spirituous Liquors.* 2nd ed. Philadelphia, 1778.

————. *The Plainness and Innocent Simplicity of the Christian Religion.* Philadelphia, 1782.

————. *Serious Considerations on Several Important Subjects, viz, on War and Its Inconsistency with the Gospel; Observations on Slavery, and Remarks on the Nature and Bad Effects of Spirituous Liquors.* Philadelphia, 1778.

————. *A Short Account of That Part of Africa Inhabited by the Negroes . . . and the Manner by Which the Slave-Trade Is Carried On.* Philadelphia, 1762.

————. *Short Observations on Slavery, Introductory to Some Extracts from the Writing of the Abbé Raynal on that Important Subject.* Philadelphia, 1781.

————. *Some Historical Account of Guinea, Its Situation, Produce, and General Disposition of Its Inhabitants, with an Inquiry into the Rise and Progress of the Slave Trade, Its Nature and Lamentable Effects.* Philadelphia, 1771.

Besse, Joseph. *A Collection of the Sufferings of the People Called Quakers.* 2 vols. London: L. Hinde, 1753.

Bisset, Robert. *The History of the Negro Slave Trade, in Its Connection with the Commerce and Prosperity of the West Indies, and the Wealth and Power of the British Empire.* 2 vols. London: S. Highley, et al., 1805.

Brissot de Warville, Jacques-Pierre. *Correspondance et papiers, précédés d'un avertissement et d'une notice sur sa vie,* edited by Claude Perroud. Paris: Librairie Alphonse Picard, 1912.

————. *Examen critique des voyages dans l'Amérique septentrionale de M. le marquis de Chastellux, ou Lettre à M. le marquis de Chastellux, Dans laquelle on réfute principalement ses opinions sur les Quakers, sur les Nègres, sur le Peuple, et sur l'Homme.* London, 1786.

Browne, Josias. "To the Friends of the Anti-Slavery Movement." Manchester: n.d, ca. 1853.

————. *To the Members of Anti-Slavery Societies: And All Friends of the Slave.* Manchester: n.d, ca. 1853.

Burritt, Elihu. "Twenty Reasons for Total Abstinence from Slave-Labour Produce." London: Unwin, ca. 1853.

The Cabinet; or Works of Darkness Brought to Light. Philadelphia: John Mortimer, 1825.

The Case of Our Fellow Creatures the Oppressed Africans. London, 1783.

Chastellux, François-Jean de. *Voyage de M. le chevalier de Chastellux en Amérique.* N.p., 1785.

Child, L. Maria. *Isaac T. Hopper: A True Life.* Boston: J. P. Jewett, 1854.

Clarkson, Thomas, *An Essay on the Impolicy of the African Slave Trade.* London: James Phillips, 1788.

————. *An Essay on the Slavery and Commerce of the Human Species, Particularly the African,* Translated from a Latin Dissertation, Which Was Honoured with the First Prize in the University of Cambridge, for the Year 1785. London: James Phillips, 1786.

———. *The History of the Rise, Progress, and Accomplishment of the Abolition of the African Slave-Trade by the British Parliament.* 2 vols. London: Longman, Hurst, Rees, and Orme, 1808.

———. *Memoirs of the Private and Public Life of William Penn.* 2 vols. London: Longman, Hurst, Rees, Orme, and Brown, 1813.

———. *A Portraiture of Quakerism, as Taken from a View of the Moral Education, Discipline, Peculiar Customs, Religious Principles, Political and Civil Economy, and Character of the Society of Friends.* 3 vols. London: Longman, Hurst, Rees, and Orme, 1806.

Cobbett, William, ed., *The Parliamentary History of England from the Earliest Times to the Year 1803.* 36 vols. London: Longman, 1815.

Colman, Lucy N. *Reminiscences.* Buffalo, N.Y.: H. L. Green, 1891.

Comly, John, ed. *Journals of the Lives, Religious Exercises, and Labours in the Work of the Ministry of Joshua Evans and John Hunt,* Vol. 10 of *Friends Miscellany.* Philadelphia: William Sharpless, 1837.

Cooper, Thomas. *Supplement to Mr Cooper's Letters on the Slave Trade.* Warrington: W. Eyres, 1788.

Correspondence between Oliver Johnson and George F. White. New York: O. Johnson, 1841.

Crèvecoeur, J. Hector St. John de. *Letters from an American Farmer and Sketches of Eighteenth-Century America,* edited by Albert E. Stone. Harmondsworth: Penguin Books, 1981.

———. *More Letters from an American Farmer: An Edition of the Essays in English Left Unpublished by Crèvecoeur,* edited by Dennis D. Moore. Athens: University of Georgia Press, 1995.

Crèvecoeur, Michel Guillaume Jean, dit Saint Jean de. *Lettres d'un cultivateur américain, écrites à W.S, Ecuyer, Depuis l'année 1770, jusqu'à 1781, Traduites de l'Anglois par ***.* Vol. 1. Paris: Cuchet, 1784.

Crèvecoeur, Robert de. *Saint-John de Crèvecoeur, sa vie et ses ouvrages 1735–1813.* Paris: Librairie des bibliophiles de Paris, 1833.

Crisp, Thomas. *Babel's Builders Unmasking Themselves: As Appears by the Following Paper from Barbadoes (Promoted by George for His Party, and Subscribed by Eighty Two of Them).* London, 1681.

[Curwen, Alice, and Thomas Curwen.] *A Relation of the Labour, Travail and Suffering of That Faithful Servant of the Lord Alice Curwen.* [London], 1680.

Description of Haydon's Picture of the Great Meeting of Delegates. London: Charles Reynell, 1841.

Douglass, William. *Annals of the First African Church in the United States of America, Now Styled the African Episcopal Church of St. Thomas.* Philadelphia, 1862.

Edmundson, William. *A Journal of the Life, Travels, Sufferings and Labour of Love in the Work of the Ministry. . . .* London, 1715.

Emmons, Sarah Hopper, ed. *Life of Abby Hopper Gibbons.* 2 vols. New York: G. P. Putnam, 1897.

Epistles from the Yearly Meeting of Friends. London, 1818.

Evans, Joshua. *A Journal of the Life, Travels, Religious Exercises, and Labours in the Work of the Ministry.* Byberry, N.J.: J. and I. Comly, 1837.

Extracts from the Minutes of the Yearly Meeting of Friends [Hicksite] *Held in Philadelphia.* Philadelphia: William Sharpless, 1830.

Forster, W. E. "Preface." In Thomas Clarkson, *Memoirs of the Public and Private Life of William Penn.* London: C. Gilpin, 1849.

Fox, George. *Gospel Family Order, Being a Short Discourse concerning the Ordering of Families, Both of Whites, Blacks, and Indians.* [London], 1676.

———. *The Heathens Divinity Set upon the Heads of All Christians, That Say, They Had Not Known That There Had Been a God, or a Christ, unless the Scripture Had Declared It to Them.* [London], 1672/1673.

———. *A Journal or Historical Account of the Life, Travels, Sufferings, Christian Experience, and Labour of Love.* 3rd ed., corr. London: Luke Hinde, 1765.

Garnet, Henry Highland. *Memorial Discourse.* Philadelphia: Joseph M. Wilson, 1865.

Gibbons, Phebe Earle. *Pennsylvania Dutch and Other Essays.* Philadelphia: J. B. Lippincott, 1882.

[Gibbons, William.], *Truth Advocated.* Philadelphia: Joseph Rakestraw, 1822.

Grégoire, Henri. *De la littérature des Nègres, ou Recherches sur leurs Facultés Intellectuelles, leurs Qualités morales et leur Littérature.* Paris: Maradan, 1808.

Griest, Ellwood. *John and Mary; Or, the Fugitive Slaves.* Lancaster, Pa.: Inquirer, 1873.

Harper, Ida Husted. *The Life and Work of Susan B. Anthony.* Indianapolis: Bobbs-Merrill, 1899.

Heyrick, Elizabeth. "Immediate, not Gradual Abolition; an Enquiry into the Shortest, Safest Means of Getting Rid of West Indian Slavery." London: n.p., 1824.

Hicks, Edward. *Memoirs of the Life and Religious Labors of Edward Hicks.* Philadelphia: Merrihew and Thompson, 1851.

Hicks, Elias. *Journal of the Life and Religious Labors of Elias Hicks.* New York, 1832.

———. *Observations on the Slavery of the Africans.* New York: Wood, 1811.

Hopper, Isaac T. *Narrative of the Proceedings of the Monthly Meeting of New-York.* New York: H. Ludwig, 1843.

Hutcheson, Francis. *A System of Moral Philosophy.* Edinburgh, 1755.

Lady, A [pseud.] *The Workwoman's Guide Containing Instructions to the Inexperienced in Cutting Out and Completing Those Articles of Wearing Apparel etc. Which Are Usually Made at Home; Also Explanations on Upholstery, Straw-Plaiting, Bonnet-Making, Knitting etc. "A Method Shortens Labour."* London: Simpkins, Marshall and Co., 1835.

Latrobe, John H. B. *African Colonization—Its Principles and Aims: An Address. . . .* Baltimore: 1859.

Lundy, Benjamin, ed. *Essays. Philanthropic and Moral, by Elizabeth Margaret Chandler: Principally Relating to the Abolition of Slavery in America.* Philadelphia: Lemuel Howell, 1836.

————. *The Poetical Works of Elizabeth Margaret Chandler: With a Memoir of Her Life and Character*. Philadelphia: Lemuel Howell, 1836.

Mann, James. *The Cotton Trade of Great Britain: Its Rise, Progress and Present Extent*. 1860. Reprint, London: Cass, 1968.

Mason, Isaac. *Life of Isaac Mason as a Slave*. Worchester, Mass., 1893.

Memorials concerning Deceased Friends. New York: W. J. Banner, 1848.

Montgomery, James. *The Abolition of the Slave Trade: A Poem, in Four Parts*. London: R. Bowyer, 1814.

A Narrative of the Early Life, Travels, and Gospel Labors of Jesse Kersey. Philadelphia: T. E. Chapman, 1851.

Pancoast, Charles Edward. *A Quaker Forty-Niner: The Adventures of Charles Edward Pancoast on the American Frontier*, edited by Anna Paschall Hannum. Philadelphia: University of Pennsylvania Press, 1930.

Pancoast, Henry S. *The Indian before the Law*. Philadelphia: Indian Rights Association, 1884.

Penn, William. *Judas and the Jews Combined against Christ and His Followers. . . .* London, 1673.

Raynal, Abbé G. Th. *Histoire philosophique et politique des deux Indes: Avertissement et choix de textes par Yves Bénot*. Paris: La découverte, 2001.

Richardson, Anna, and Henry Richardson. "The Beloved Crime. Who Are the Slaveholders?" Newcastle: n.p., ca. 1852.

————. "Conscience Versus Cotton, or the Preference of Free-Labour Produce." Newcastle: n.p., 1860.

————. "Free Labour Cotton: It Can Be Had." Newcastle: n.p., ca. 1851.

————. "A Revolution of Spindles." Newcastle: n.p., ca. 1851.

————. "There is Death in the Pot!" London: Gilpin, 1848.

Rous, John. *A Warning to the Inhabitants of Barbadoes: Who Live in Pride, Drunkennesse, Covetousnesse, Oppression and Deceitful Dealings; and also to All Who Are Found Acting in the Same Excess of Wickedness, of What Country Soever, That They Speedily Repent. . . .* [London, 1657].

Rowntree, John Stephenson. "Quakerism, Past and Present, Being an Inquiry into the Causes of Its Decline in Great Britain and Ireland." London: Smith, Elder and Co., 1859.

A School History of the Negro Race in America. 1891.

Sermon by George F. White . . . Delivered 12 Mo. 19th 1843 . . . at Cherry Street Meeting. Philadelphia: King & Baird, 1843.

A Short Account of the Manifest Hand of God That Hath Fallen upon Several Marshals and Their Deputies: Who Have Made Great Spoil and Havock of the Goods of the People Called Quakers in the Island of Barbadoes. . . . London, 1696.

The Slave; His Wrongs and Their Remedy. Newcastle, 1851–1856.

Smedley, R. C. *History of the Underground Railroad in Chester and the Neighboring Counties of Pennsylvania*. Lancaster, Pa.: The Era, 1883.

Stowe, Harriet Beecher. *A Key to Uncle Tom's Cabin*. Boston: John P. Jewett, 1853.

————. *Sunny Memories of Foreign Lands*. London: Sampson and Low, 1854.

————. *Uncle Tom's Cabin*, edited with an introduction and notes by Jean Fagin Yellin. New York: Oxford University Press, 1998.

Twain, Mark. *Life on the Mississippi* (1883) in *Mississippi Writings*. New York: Library of America, 1982.

Vaux, Robert. *Memoirs of the Life of Anthony Benezet*. Philadelphia, 1817.

Vokins, Joan. *God's Mighty Power Magnified*. London, 1691.

Wallace, George. *A System of the Principles of the Laws of Scotland*. Edinburgh, 1760.

Ward, Samuel Ringgold. *Autobiography of a Fugitive Negro*. London: John Snow, 1855.

White, George F. *Discourse at the Friends' Meeting House, Rose Street*. New York, n.d.

————. *Sermon by George F. White, of New York*. n.p., 1843.

————. *Sermon Delivered by George F. White, in Friends' Meeting House, Cherry Street, Philadelphia*. New York: Baker and Crane, 1843.

Whittier, John G. *The Writings of John Greenleaf Whittier*. 7 vols. Boston: Houghton Mifflin, 1889.

Wilberforce, Robert Isaac, and Samuel Wilberforce. *The Life of William Wilberforce*. 5 vols. London: John Murray, 1838.

Historiography and Reception from 1900

Abbott, Margaret Post, ed. *Post, Albertson, and Hicks Family Letters*. 2 vols. Portland, Ore.: Margaret Post Abbott, 2009–2010.

Alford, Violet. "Rough Music or Charivari." *Folklore* 70 (1959): 505–18.

Allen, Gay Wilson, and Roger Asselineau. *St. John de Crèvecoeur: The Life of An American Farmer*. New York: Viking, 1987.

Annual Reports of the American Society for Colonizing the Free People of Colour of the United States. New York: Negro Universities Press, 1969.

Anonymous. *La Révolution française et l'abolition de l'esclavage*. Vol. 6: *La Société des Amis des Noirs*. Paris: EDHIS, 1968.

Anstey, Roger. *The Atlantic Slave Trade and British Abolition, 1760–1810*. London: Macmillan, 1975.

Ash, James L., Jr. "'Oh No, It Is Not the Scriptures!' The Bible and the Spirit in George Fox." *Quaker History* 63, no. 2 (1974): 94–107.

Auslander, L. "Beyond Words." *American Historical Review* 110, no. 4 (2005): 1015–45.

Bacon, Margaret Hope. *Valiant Friends: Life of Lucretia Mott*. New York: Walker, 1980.

Bailey, Thomas A. *American Pageant: A History of the Republic*. 2nd ed. Boston: D. C. Heath, 1961.

Baldwin, Lewis V. *"Invisible" Strands in African Methodism*. Philadelphia: American Theological Library Association, 1983.

Barbé-Marbois, François, Marquis de. *Our Revolutionary Forefathers: The Letters of François, Marquis de Barbé-Marbois: During His Residency in the United States as Secretary of the French Legation,* translated and edited by Eugene Parker Chase. 1969. Reprint, Freeport, N.Y.: Books for Library Press, 1990.

Barber, L. H. Clark. *The Shoemaking Business of C. and J. Clark of Street, 1825–1950.* Somerset: C. and J. Clark, 1951.

Barton, Christopher P. "Antebellum African-American Settlements in Southern New Jersey." *African Diaspora Archaeology Network Newsletter,* December 2009. Available at: http://www.diaspora.illinois.edu/news1209/news1209-4.pdf.

Baum, Robert M. *Shrines of the Slave Trade: Diola Religion and Society in Precolonial Senegambia.* New York: Oxford University Press, 1999.

Baumgarten, L. *What Clothes Reveal: The Language of Clothing in Colonial and Federal America.* Williamsburg, Va.: The Colonial Williamsburg Collection, 2002.

Beard, Charles, and Mary Beard. *History of the United States.* New York: MacMillan, 1927.

Beaudry, M. C. *Findings: The Material Culture of Needlework and Sewing.* New Haven, Conn.: Yale University Press, 2007.

Bennett, William. *America: The Last Best Hope.* 2 vols. Nashville, Tenn.: Thomas Nelson, 2006.

Berlin, Ira. "American Slavery in History and Memory." In *Slavery, Resistance, Freedom,* edited by Gabor Boritt and Scott Hancock. 1–20. New York: Oxford University Press, 2007.

Billington, Louis. "British Humanitarians and American Cotton, 1840–1860." *Journal of American Studies* 11, no. 3 (1977): 313–34.

Blackett, Richard. *Building an Anti-Slavery Wall: Black Americans in the Atlantic Abolitionist Movement, 1830–1860.* Baton Rouge: Louisiana State University Press, 1983.

Block, Kristen. "Cultivating Inner and Outer Plantations: Property, Industry, and Slavery in Early Quaker Migration to the New World." *Early American Studies* 8, no. 3 (2010): 533–41.

Block, Kristen. *Ordinary Lives in the Early Caribbean: Religion, Colonial Competition, and the Politics of Profit.* Athens: University of Georgia Press, 2012.

Bolt, Christine, and Seymour Drescher, eds. *Anti-Slavery, Religion and Reform.* Folkstone, U.K.: W. Dawson, 1980.

Boorstin, Daniel. *The Americans: The Colonial Experience.* New York: Random House, 1958.

Bradley, A. Day. "Progressive Friends in Michigan and New York." *Quaker History* 52 (1963): 95–103.

Brathwaite, William C. *The Second Period of Quakerism.* Cambridge: Cambridge University Press, 1961.

Braude, Ann. *Radical Spirits: Spiritualism and Women's Rights in Nineteenth-Century America.* Boston: Beacon Books, 1999.

Brendlinger, Irv A. *To Be Silent Would be Criminal: The Antislavery Influence and Writings of Anthony Benezet.* Lanham, Md.: Scarecrow Press, 2007.

Broekhoven, Deborah van. "'Better than a Clay Club': The Organization of anti-Slavery Fairs, 1835–1860." *Slavery and Abolition* 19, no. 1 (1998): 24–45.

Bronner, Edwin. "Moderates in London Yearly Meeting, 1857–1873: Precursors of Quaker Liberals." *Church History* 59 (1990): 357–71.

Brookes, George S. *Friend Anthony Benezet.* London: Oxford University Press, 1937.

Brooks, George E. *Landlords and Strangers: Ecology, Society, and Trade in Western Africa, 1000–1630.* Boulder: Westview Press, 1993.

Brown, Christopher Leslie. *Moral Capital: Foundations of British Abolitionism.* Chapel Hill: University of North Carolina Press, 2006.

Bruns, Roger, ed. *Am I Not a Man and a Brother: The Antislavery Crusade of Revolutionary America 1688–1788.* New York: Chelsea House, 1977.

Bruns, Roger. "Anthony Benezet's Assertion of Negro Equality." *Journal of Negro History* 56 (1971): 230–38.

Bryden, Inga, and Floyd, Janet. *Domestic Space: Reading the Nineteenth Century Interior.* Manchester: Manchester University Press, 1999.

Burin, Eric. *Slavery and the Peculiar Solution: A History of the American Colonization Society.* Gainesville: University of Florida Press, 2005.

Burman, Barbara. *The Culture of Sewing: Gender, Consumption and Home Dressmaking.* New York: Berg, 1999.

Burrows, Simon. *Blackmail, Scandal, and Revolution. London's French Libellists, 1758–92.* Manchester: Manchester University Press, 2006.

Cadbury, Henry J. "Negro Membership in the Society of Friends." *Journal of Negro History* 20 (1936): 151–213.

Carey, Brycchan. "'The Power that Giveth Liberty and Freedom': The Barbadian Origins of Quaker Antislavery." *ARIEL: A Review of International English Literature* 38, no. 1 (January 2007): 27–47.

———. *British Abolitionism and the Rhetoric of Sensibility: Writing, Sentiment, and Slavery, 1760–1807.* Basingstoke, U.K.: Palgrave Macmillan, 2005.

———. *From Peace to Freedom: Quaker Rhetoric and the Birth of American Antislavery, 1657–1761.* New Haven, Conn.: Yale University Press, 2012.

———. "Inventing a Culture of Antislavery: Pennsylvania Quakers and the Germantown Protest of 1688." In *Imagining Transatlantic Slavery,* edited by Cora Kaplan and John Oldfield. 17–32. Basingstoke, U.K.: Palgrave Macmillan, 2010.

Carretta, Vincent. *Equiano the African: Biography of a Self-Made Man.* Athens: University of Georgia Press, 2005.

Carroll, Kenneth L. *John Perrot: Early Quaker Schismatic.* London: Friends' Historical Society, 1971.

Caughey, John, John Hope Franklin, and Earnest May. *Land of the Free: A History of the United States.* New York: Benzinger Brothers, 1966.

Chevignard, Bernard. *Michel Saint John de Crévecoeur.* Paris: Belin, 2004.

———. "St. John de Crèvecoeur in the Looking Glass: Letters from an American Farmer and the Making of a Man of Letters." *Early American Literature* 19, no. 2 (Fall 1984): 173–90.

———. "Une Apocalypse sécularisée: le quakerisme selon Brissot de Warville et St John de Crèvecoeur." In *Le facteur religieux en Amérique du nord,* edited by Jean Béranger. 49–69. Bordeaux: Institut d'etudes politiques de Bordeaux, 1981.

Clark, Roger. *Somerset Anthology: Twenty-Four Pieces by Roger Clark of Street 1871–1961.* York: Sessions, 1975.

Clegg, Claude A., III. *The Price of Liberty: African Americans and the Making of Liberia*. Chapel Hill: University of North Carolina Press, 2004.

Cockrell, Dale. *Demons of Disorder: Early Blackface Minstrels and Their World*. Cambridge: Cambridge University Press, 1997.

Cordwell, Justine, and Schwarz, Ronald. *The Fabrics of Culture: The Anthropology of Clothing and Adornment*. Paris: Mouton, 1979.

Crawford, Michael J. *The Having of Negroes Is Become a Burden: The Quaker Struggle to Free Slaves in Revolutionary North Carolina*. Gainesville: University Press of Florida, 2010.

Creighton, S. "'Slavery Is Sustained by the Purchase of Its Productions.' *The Slave; His Wrongs, Their Remedy*, Newspaper (1851–1856)" in Pallua, Ulrich, Knapp, Adrian and Exenberger, *(Re)Figuring Human Enslavement: Images of Power, Violence and Resistance*. Innsbruck: Innsbruck University Press, 2009.

Cugoano, Quobna Ottabah. *Thoughts and Sentiments on the Evil and Wicked Traffic of Slavery and Commerce of the Human Species,* edited by Vincent Carretta. New York: Penguin Classics, 1999.

Dailey, Barbara Ritter. "The Early Quaker Mission and the Settlement of Meetings in Barbados, 1655–1700." *Journal of the Barbados Museum and Historical Society* 39 (1991): 24–46.

Darley, Gillian. *Villages of Vision: A Study of Strange Utopias*. Nottingham: Five Leaves, 2007.

Darnton, Robert. *The Literary Underground of the Old Regime*. Cambridge: Harvard University Press, 1982.

Davidoff, Lenore, and Hall, Catherine. *Family Fortunes: Men and Women of the English Middle Class 1780–1850*. London: Routledge, 1992.

Davidson, Carlisle G. "A Profile of Hicksite Quakerism in Michigan, 1830–1860." *Quaker History* 59 (1970): 106–12.

Davis, David Brion. *Inhuman Bondage: The Rise and Fall of Slavery in the New World*. Oxford: Oxford University Press, 2006.

———. *The Problem of Slavery in the Age of Revolution, 1770–1823*. Ithaca, N.Y.: Cornell University Press, 1975.

———. *The Problem of Slavery in Western Culture*. Ithaca, N.Y.: Cornell University Press, 1966.

Densmore, Christopher. "'Be Ye therefore Perfect': Anti-Slavery and the Origins of the Yearly Meeting of Progressive Friends in Chester County, Pennsylvania." *Quaker History* 93 (2004): 28–46.

———. "From Hicksites to Progressive Friends: The Rural Roots of Perfectionism and Social Reform among North American Friends." *Quaker Studies* 10 (2006): 243–55.

———. "The Quaker Origins of the Women's Rights Convention." *Friends Journal* (July 1998): 26–28.

Diouf, Sylviane A. *Servants of Allah: African Muslims Enslaved in the Americas*. New York: New York University Press, 1998.

Dorigny, Marcel, and Bernard Gainot, eds. *La Société des Amis des noirs 1788–1799: Contribution à l'histoire de l'abolition de l'esclavage.* Paris: Editions de l'Unesco, Edicef, 1998.

Dorsey, Bruce. "Friends Becoming Enemies: Philadelphia Benevolence and the Neglected Era of American Quaker History." *Journal of the Early Republic* 18 (Autumn 1998): 395–428.

Drake, Thomas E. *Quakers and Slavery in America.* New Haven, Conn.: Yale University Press, 1950.

Drescher, Seymour. *Abolition: A History of Slavery and Antislavery.* Cambridge: Cambridge University Press, 2009.

———. *Capitalism and Antislavery: British Popular Mobilization in Comparative Perspective.* New York: Oxford University Press, 1987.

Edwards, Steve. *The Making of English Photography: Allegories.* Philadelphia: Pennsylvania State University Press, 2006.

Ehrard, Jean. *Lumières et esclavage: L'esclavage colonial et l'opinion publique en France au XVIIIè siècle.* Bruxelles: André Versaille, 2008.

Elson, Ruth Miller. *Guardians of Virtue: American Schoolbooks of the Nineteenth Century.* Lincoln: University of Nebraska Press, 1964.

Engel, Katherine Carté. "Religion and the Economy: New Methods for an Old Problem." *Early American Studies* 8, no. 3 (2010): 482–99.

Epstein, Terrie. "Adolescent Perspective on Racial Diversity in U.S. History: Case Studies from an Urban Classroom." *American Educational Research Journal* 37 (2000): 185–214.

Equiano, Olaudah. *The Interesting Narrative of the Life of Olaudah Equiano or Gustavus Vassa, the African,* edited by Robert J. Allison. New York: Bedford, 1995.

Farnie, David, and David, Jeremy. *The Fibre That Changed the World: The Cotton Industry in International Perspective 1600–1905.* Oxford: Pasold Research Fund and Oxford University Press, 2004.

Farrell, Stephen, Melanie Unwin, and James Walvin, eds. *The British Slave Trade: Abolition, Parliament and People.* Edinburgh: Edinburgh University Press, for the Parliamentary History Yearbook Trust, 2007.

Faulkner, Carol, *Lucretia Mott's Heresy: Abolition and Women's Rights in Nineteenth-Century America.* Philadelphia: University of Pennsylvania Press, 2011.

———. "The Root of the Evil: Free Produce and Radical Antislavery, 1820–1860." *Journal of the Early Republic* 27, no. 3 (2007): 377–405.

Fisch, Audrey. *American Slaves in Victorian England: Abolitionist Politics in Popular Literature and Culture.* Cambridge: Cambridge University Press, 2000.

Fitzgerald, Frances. *America Revised History Schoolbooks in the Twentieth Century.* Boston: Little, Brown, 1979.

Foner, Philip S., and George E. Walker, eds. *Proceedings of the Black State Conventions, 1840–1865,* Vol. 1: *New York, Pennsylvania, Indiana, Michigan, Ohio.* Philadelphia: Temple University Press, 1979.

Forbes, Ella. *But We Have No Country: The 1851 Christiana, Pennsylvania Resistance.* Cherry Hill, N.J.: Africana Homestead Library, 1998.

Forbush, Bliss. *Moses Sheppard: Quaker Philanthropist of Baltimore*. Philadelphia: J. B. Lippincott Company, 1968.

Foster, Helen Bradley. *"New Raiments of Self": African American Clothing in the Antebellum South*. Oxford: Berg, 1997.

Freehling, William W. "'Absurd' Issues and the Causes of the Civil War: Colonization as a Test Case." In *The Reintegration of American History: Slavery and the Civil War*. 138–57. New York: Oxford University Press, 1994.

———. *The Road to Disunion*. Vol. 2: *Secessionists Triumphant, 1854–1861*. New York: Oxford University Press, 2007.

Frey, Sylvia R., and Betty Wood. *Come Shouting to Zion: African American Protestantism in the American South and British Caribbean to 1830*. Chapel Hill: University of North Carolina Press, 1998.

Friedman, M. *Consumer Boycotts: Effecting Change through the Marketplace and Media*. New York: Routledge, 1999.

Frost, J. William. "George Fox's Ambiguous Antislavery Legacy." In *New Light on George Fox*, edited by Michael Mullett. 69–88. York, U.K.: Ebor Press, 1991.

———. "Quaker Antislavery: From Dissidence to Sense of the Meeting." *Quaker History* 101 (Spring 2012): 12–33.

———. *The Quaker Family in Colonial America: A Portrait of the Society of Friends*. New York: St. Martin's Press, 1973.

———, ed. *The Quaker Origins of Antislavery*. Norwood, Pa.: Norwood Editions, 1980.

Furneaux, Robin. *William Wilberforce*. London: Hamilton, 1974.

Gabriel, Ralph, and Mabel B. Casner. *Exploring American History*. New York: Harcourt, Brace, and Co., 1935.

Gandy, Mary. *Guide My Feet, Hold My Hand*. Canton, Mo.: M. G. Gandy, 1987.

Gara, Larry. *The Liberty Line*. Lexington: University of Kentucky Press, 1960.

Gerbner, Katharine. "Antislavery in Print: The Germantown Protest, the 'Exhortation,' and the Seventeenth-Century Quaker Debate on Slavery." *Early American Studies* 9 (2011): 552–75.

Gerona, Carla. *Night Journeys: The Power of Dreams in Trans-Atlantic Quaker Culture*. Charlottesville: University of Virginia Press, 2004.

Glickman, Lawrence. "'Buy for the Sake of the Slave': Abolitionism and the Origins of American Consumer Activism." *American Quarterly* 56, no. 4 (2004): 889–912.

———. *Buying Power: A History of Consumer Activism in America*. Chicago: University of Chicago Press, 2009.

Goggin, Maureen Daly, and Beth Fowkes Tobin. *Women and the Material Culture of Needlework 1750–1950*. London: Ashgate, 2000.

Goodman, Paul. *Of One Blood: Abolitionism and the Origins of Racial Equality*. Berkley: University of California Press, 1998.

Gragg, Larry. *The Quaker Community on Barbados: Challenging the Culture of the Planter Class*. Jefferson City: University of Missouri Press, 2009.

Green, James. "The Publishing History of Olaudah Equiano's *Interesting Narrative*." *Slavery and Abolition* 16 (1995): 362–75.

Greene, Dana, ed. *Lucretia Mott: Her Complete Speeches and Sermons*. New York: Mellon, 1980.

Gummere, Amelia Mott. *A Study in Costume*. Philadelphia: n.p., 1901.

Guyatt, Mary. "The Wedgwood Slave Medallion: Values in Eighteenth Century Design." *Journal of Design History* 13, no. 2 (2000): 93–105.

Hague, William, *William Wilberforce: The Life of the Great Anti-Slave Trade Campaigner*. London: HarperPress, 2007.

Hamm, Thomas. "Two Indiana Quaker Communities and the Abolition Movement." *Indiana Magazine of History* 88 (June 1991): 117–54.

Hamm, Thomas D. *God's Government Begun: The Society for Universal Inquiry and Reform, 1842–1846*. Bloomington: Indiana University Press, 1995.

———. "The Hicksite Quaker World, 1875–1900." *Quaker History* 89 (Fall 2000): 17–41.

Hamm, Thomas, April Beckman, Marissa Florio, Kirsti Giles, and Marie Hopper. "'A Great and Good People': Midwestern Quakers and the Struggle against Slavery." *Indiana Magazine of History* 100, no. 1 (March 2004): 3–25.

Hamm, Thomas D., David Dittmer, Chenda Fruchter, Ann Giordano, Janice Mathews, and Ellen Swain. "Moral Choices: Two Indiana Quaker Communities and the Abolition Movement," *Indiana Magazine of History*, 87, no. 28 (June 1991): 117–54.

Handler, Jerome S., and John T. Pohlmann. "Slave Manumissions and Freedmen in Seventeenth-Century Barbados." *William and Mary Quarterly* 41, no. 3 (1984): 390–408.

Hansen, Debra Gold. *Strained Sisterhood: Gender and Class in the Boston Female Anti-Slavery Society*. Amherst: University of Massachusetts Press, 1993.

Hargreaves, John, and Hilary Haigh, eds. *Slavery in Yorkshire: Richard Oastler and the Campaign against Child Labour in the Industrial Revolution*. Huddersfield, U.K.: University of Huddersfield Press, 2012.

Hewitt, Nancy A. *Women's Activism and Social Change: Rochester, New York, 1822–1872*. Ithaca, N.Y.: Cornell University Press, 1984.

Hirsch, Marianne. *Family Frames: Photography, Narrative and Post-Memory*. Cambridge: Harvard University Press, 2002.

Hochschild, Adam. *Bury the Chains: Prophets and Rebels in the Fight to Free an Empire's Slaves*. Boston: Houghton Mifflin, 2005.

Hockett, Homer C., "Review of *Charles Edward Pancoast: A Quaker Forty-Niner*," *Mississippi Valley Historical Review* 17, no. 4 (1931): 620–21.

Holmes, Richard. *The Age of Wonder: How the Romantic Generation Discovered the Beauty and Terror of Science*. New York: Pantheon Books, 2008.

Holton, Sandra Stanley. *Quaker Women, Personal Life, Memory and Radicalism in the Lives of Women Friends 1780–1930*. London: Routledge, 2007.

Hornick, Nancy Slacom. "Anthony Benezet and the African School: Toward a Theory of Full Equality." *Pennsylvania Magazine of History and Biography* 99 (1975): 399–421.

Horton, Scott, "The Forgotten Bicentennial." *Harper's Magazine*, December 31, 2007.

Iannini, Christopher. "'The Itinerant Man': Crèvecoeur's Caribbean, Raynal's Revolution, and the Fate of Atlantic Cosmopolitanism." *William and Mary Quarterly* 3rd ser. 41, no. 2 (April 2004): 201–34.

Ingle, H. Larry. *Quakers in Conflict: The Hicksite Reformation*. Knoxville: University of Tennessee Press, 1986.

Isichei, Elizabeth. *Victorian Quakers*. Oxford: Oxford University Press, 1970.

Jackson, Maurice. *Let This Voice Be Heard: Anthony Benezet, Father of Atlantic Abolitionism*. Philadelphia: University of Pennsylvania Press, 2009.

James, Sydney V. *A People among Peoples: Quaker Benevolence in Eighteenth-Century America*. Cambridge: Harvard University Press, 1963.

Janzen, John M. *Lemba, 1650–1930: A Drum of Affliction in Africa and the New World*. New York: Garland Publishing, 1982.

Jeffrey, Julie Roy. *Abolitionists Remember: Antislavery Autobiographies and the Unfinished Work of Emancipation*. Chapel Hill: University of North Carolina Press, 2008.

———. *The Great Silent Army of Abolitionism. Ordinary Women in the Antislavery Movement*. Chapel Hill: University of North Carolina Press, 1998.

Jennings, Judith. *The Business of Abolishing the British Slave Trade, 1783–1807*. London: Frank Cass, 1997.

Jones, Adam. *From Slaves to Palm Kernels: A History of the Galinhas Country (West Africa), 1730–1890*. Wiesbaden: Steiner, 1983.

Jordan, Ryan P. "The Dilemma of Quaker Pacifism in a Slaveholding Republic, 1833–1865." *Civil War History* 53, no. 1 (2007): 5–28.

———. "The Indiana Separation of 1842 and the Limits of Quaker Anti-Slavery." *Quaker History* 89 (Spring 2000): 1–27.

———. *Slavery and the Meetinghouse: The Quakers and the Abolitionist Dilemma, 1820–1865*. Bloomington: Indiana University Press, 2007.

Kantrowitz, Stephen. *More than Freedom: Fighting for Black Citizenship in a White Republic, 1829–1889*. New York: The Penguin Press, 2012.

Kashatus, William C. *Just over the Line: Chester County and the Underground Railroad*. Chester, Pa.: Chester County Historical Society in cooperation with the Penn State University Press, 2002.

Keen, Suzanne. "Quaker Dress, Sexuality and Domestication of Reform in the Victorian Novel." *Victorian Literature and Culture* 30, no. 1 (2002): 211–36.

Kendall, Joan. "The Development of a Distinctive Form of Quaker Dress." *Costume* 19 (1985): 58–74.

Kowaleski-Wallace, Elizabeth. *Consuming Subjects. Women, Shopping and Business in the Eighteenth Century*. New York: Columbia University Press, 1997.

Lapsanky, Emma, and Bacon, Margaret Hope, eds. *Benjamin Coates and the Colonization Movement in America 1848–1880*. University Park: Penn State University Press, 2005.

Lapsansky, Emma Jones, and Anne Verplanck, eds. *Quaker Aesthetics: Reflections on a Quaker Ethic in American Design and Consumption.* Philadelphia: University of Pennsylvania Press, 2003.

Larkin, Edward. "The Cosmopolitan Revolution: Loyalism and the Fiction of an American Nation." *NOVEL: A Forum on Fiction* 40, nos. 1/2 (Fall 2006–Spring 2007): 52–76.

Leach, Robert E., and Peter Gow. *Quaker Nantucket: The Religious Community behind the Whaling Empire.* Nantucket, Mass.: The Mill Hill Press, 1999.

Lemire, Beverly. *Fashion's Favourite: The Cotton Trade and the Consumer in Britain 1660–1800.* Oxford: Oxford University Press, 1991.

——, ed. *The Force of Fashion in Politics and Society.* London: Ashgate, 2010.

Lerner, Gerda. *The Grimké Sisters from South Carolina: Pioneers for Women's Rights and Abolition.* Rev. ed. Chapel Hill: University of North Carolina Press, 2004.

Levy, Barry. *Quakers and the American Family: British Settlement in the Delaware Valley.* New York: Oxford University Press, 1988.

Lopez, Claude-Anne. *Mon Cher Papa: Franklin and the Ladies of Paris.* New Haven, Conn.: Yale University Press, 1990.

Luna, Frederick A. de. "The Dean Street Style of Revolution: J. P Brissot, Jeune Philosophe." *French Historical Studies* 17, no. 1 (Spring 1991): 159–90.

Mack, Phyllis. *Heart Religion in the British Enlightenment.* Cambridge: Cambridge University Press, 2008.

——. *Visionary Women: Ecstatic Prophecy in Seventeenth-Century England.* Berkeley: University of California Press, 1992.

Maffly-Kipp, Laurie F. *Religion and Society in Frontier California.* New Haven, Conn.: Yale University Press, 1994.

Makris, G. P. *Changing Masters: Spirit Possession and Identity Construction among Slave Descendants and Other Subordinates in the Sudan.* Evanston, Ill.: Northwestern University Press, 2000.

Marietta, Jack. *The Reformation of American Quakerism, 1748–1783.* Philadelphia: University of Pennsylvania Press, 1984.

Mattingly, Carol. "Friendly Dress: A Disciplined Use." *Rhetoric Society Quarterly* 29, no. 2 (1999): 24–45.

Mayer, Henry. *All on Fire: William Lloyd Garrison and the Abolition of Slavery.* New York: St. Martin's Press, 1974.

McCauslin, Debra Sandoe. *Reconstructing the Past: Puzzle of a Lost Community.* Gettysburg, Pa.: For the Cause Productions, 2005.

McDaniel, Donna, and Vanessa Julye. *Fit for Freedom, Not for Friendship: Quakers, African Americans and the Myth of Racial Justice.* Philadelphia: Quaker Press of Friends General Conference, 2009.

McFeeley, William S. *Frederick Douglass.* New York: W. W. Norton, 1991.

McGarvie, Michael. *The Book of Street: A History from Earliest Times to 1925.* Buckingham: Barracuda Press, 1987.

McGowan, James. *Station Master on the Underground Railroad: Life and Letters of Thomas Garrett.* Jefferson, N.C.: McFarland, 2005.

McKelvey, Blake. *Rochester, the Water Power City.* Cambridge: Harvard University Press, 1945.

Meer, Sarah. *Uncle Tom Mania: Slavery, Minstrelsy, and Transatlantic Culture in the Nineteenth Century.* Athens: University of Georgia Press, 2005.

Mekeel, Arthur. *The Relation of Quakers to the American Revolution.* Washington, D.C.: University Press of America, 1979.

Micheletti, Michele. *Political Virtue and Shopping: Individuals, Consumerism and Collective Action.* Basingstoke, U.K.: Macmillan, 2003.

Midgley, Clare. *Feminism and Empire: Women Activists in Imperial Britain 1790–1865.* London: Routledge, 2007.

———. "Slave Sugar Boycotts, Female Activism and the Domestic Base of British Anti-Slavery Culture." *Slavery and Abolition* 17, no. 3 (1996): 137–62.

———. *Women against Slavery. The British Campaigns 1780–1870.* London: Routledge, 1992.

Miller, Joseph. "Retention, Reinvention, and Remembering: Restoring Identities through Enslavement in Africa and under Slavery in Brazil." In *Enslaving Connections: Changing Cultures of Africa and Brazil during the Era of Slavery,* edited by José C. Curto and Paul E. Lovejoy. 81–121. New York: Humanity Books, 2004.

Milligan, Edward. *Biographical Dictionary of British Quakers in Commerce and Industry 1775–1920.* York: Sessions, 2007.

Montesquieu, Charles de Secondat, Baron de. *The Spirit of the Laws.* Cambridge: Cambridge University Press, 1989; first edition Paris, 1748.

Moreau, Joseph. *Schoolbook Nation: Conflicts over American History Textbooks from the Civil War to the Present.* Ann Arbor: University of Michigan Press, 2004.

Morgan, Jennifer L. "'Some Could Suckle over their Shoulders': Male Travelers, Female Bodies, and the Gendering of Racial Ideology, 1500–1770." *William and Mary Quarterly* 54, no. 1 (1997): 167–92.

Morgan, Simon. *A Victorian Woman's Place: Public Culture in the Nineteenth Century.* London: Tauris, 2007.

Morison, Samuel Eliot, and Henry Steele Commager. *Growth of the American Republic.* 2nd ed. 2 vols. New York: Oxford University Press, 1937.

Moses, Wilson J. *Afroutopia: Roots of African American Popular History.* Cambridge: Harvard University Press, 1998.

Moulton, Phillips, ed. *Journal and Major Essays of John Woolman.* Richmond, Ind.: Friends United Press, 1971.

Muzzey, David. *History of the American People.* New York: Ginn and Co., 1927.

Muzzey, David Saville. *History of Our Country.* Boston: Ginn and Co., 1937.

Nash, Gary B. *First City: Philadelphia and the Forging of Historical Memory.* Philadelphia: University of Pennsylvania Press, 2002.

Nash, Gary B., and Jean R. Soderlund. *Freedom by Degrees: Emancipation in Pennsylvania and Its Aftermath.* New York: Oxford University Press, 1991.

Nash, Gary B, Charlotte Crabtree, and Ross Dunn. *History on Trial: Culture Wars and the Teaching of the Past.* New York: Alfred K. Knopf, 1997.

Nelson, Jack, and Gene Roberts, Jr. *The Censors and the Schools*. Boston: Little, Brown, 1963.

Newman, Richard S. *The Transformation of American Abolitionism: Fighting Slavery in the Early Republic*. Chapel Hill: University of North Carolina Press, 2002.

Novick, Peter. *That Noble Dream: The "Objectivity Question" and the American Historical Profession*. Cambridge: Cambridge University Press, 1988.

Nuermberger, Ruth Ketring. A. *The Free Produce Movement: A Quaker Protest against Slavery*. 1942. Reprint, New York: AMS, 1970.

O'Donnell, Elizabeth. "'There's Death in the Pot!' The British Free Produce Movement and the Religious Society of Friends, with Particular Reference to the North-east of England." *Quaker Studies* 13, no. 2 (2009):184–204.

Oldfield, John. *Popular Politics and British Anti-Slavery: The Mobilisation of Public Opinion against the Slave Trade 1787–1807*. Manchester: Manchester University Press, 1995.

Olmsted, Frederick Law. *The Cotton Kingdom: A Traveller's Observations on Cotton and Slavery in the Slave States 1853–1861*. 1861. Reprint, New York: da Capo, 1966.

Olwig, Karen Fog. "African Cultural Principles in Caribbean Slave Societies: A View from the Danish West Indies." In *Slave Cultures and the Cultures of Slavery*, edited by Stephen Palmié. 230–39. Knoxville: University of Tennessee Press, 1995.

Otter, Samuel. *Philadelphia Stories: America's Literature of Race and Freedom*. New York: Oxford University Press, 2010.

Palmer, Beverly Wilson, ed. *Selected Letters of Lucretia Coffin Mott*. Urbana: University of Illinois Press, 2002.

Parker, Rozsika. *The Subversive Stitch: Embroidery and the Making of the Feminine*. London: Women's Press, 1984.

Parker, William. "Account of the Christiana Riot." *Atlantic Monthly* 17 (Feb.–March, 1866): 152–66, 276–95.

Pickard, Samuel Thomas, ed. *Letters of John Greenleaf Whittier*. 3 vols. Cambridge: Harvard University Press, 1975.

Plank, Geoffrey. "The First Person in Antislavery Literature: John Woolman, His Clothes, and His Journal." *Slavery and Abolition* 30, no. 1 (2009): 67–91.

———. *John Woolman's Path to the Peaceable Kingdom: A Quaker in the British Empire*. Philadelphia: University of Pennsylvania Press, 2012.

Pointon, Marcia. "Quakerism and Visual Culture 1650–1800." *Art History* 20, no. 3 (1997): 397–431.

Prochaska, Frank. *Women and Philanthropy in Nineteenth Century England*. Oxford: Clarendon, 1980.

Punshon, J. *Portrait in Grey. A Short History of the Quakers*. 1984. Reprint, London: Quaker Books, 2006.

Quarles, Benjamin. *Black Abolitionists*. New York: Oxford University Press, 1969.

Raynal, Abbé G. Th. *Histoire philosophique et politique des deux Indes: Avertissement et choix de textes par Yves Bénot*. Paris: La découverte, 2001.

Rediker, Marcus, *The Slave Ship: A Human History*. London: Penguin, 2007.

Rhodes, Barbara, and William Wells Streeter. *Before Photocopying: The Art and History of Mechanical Copying, 1780–1938*. Newcastle, Del.: Oak Knoll Press, 1999.

Rhodes, Jane. *Mary Ann Shadd Cary: The Black Press and Protest in the Nineteenth Century*. Bloomington: Indiana University Press, 1998.

Rice, Howard Crosby. *Le cultivateur américain, étude sur l'œuvre de Saint John de Crèvecoeur*. Paris: Honoré Champion, 1933.

Rizzo, Dennis. *Parallel Communities: The Underground Railroad in South Jersey*. Charleston: History Press, 2008.

Rodney, Walter. *A History of the Upper Guinea Coast, 1545–1800*. Oxford: Clarendon Press, 1970.

Rose, Clare. *Clothing, Society and Culture in Nineteenth Century England*. 3 vols. London: Pickering and Chatto, 2011.

Rose, Mary, ed. *The Lancashire Cotton Industry: A History since 1700*. Preston: Lancashire County Books, 1996.

Rugg, Harold. *History of American Civilization, Economic and Social*. Boston: Ginn and Co., 1930.

———. *A History of American Government and Culture: America's March toward Democracy*. Boston: Ginn and Co., 1931.

Ryan, James Emmett. *Imaginary Friends: Representing Quakers in American Culture, 1650–1950*. Madison: University of Wisconsin Press, 2008.

Saar, Doreen Alavarez. "'Crèvecoeur's Thoughts on Slavery': Letters from an American Farmer and Whig Rhetoric." *Early American Literature* 22, no. 2 (Fall 1987): 193–203.

Sabine, George H., Arthur N. Holcombe, Arthur W. Macmahon, Carl Wittke, and Robert S. Lynd. *The Textbooks of Harold Rugg*. New York: American Committee for Democracy and Intellectual Freedom, 1942.

Sancho, Ignatius. *Letters of the Late Ignatius Sancho, an African*, edited by Vincent Carretta. New York: Penguin Books, 1989.

Sassi, Jonathan. "Africans in the Quaker Image: Anthony Benezet, African Travel Narratives, and Revolutionary-Era Antislavery." *Journal of Early Modern History* 10 (2006): 95–130.

———. "With a Little Help from the Friends: The Quaker and Tactical Contexts of Anthony Benezet's Abolitionist Publishing." *Pennsylvania Magazine of History and Biography* 135 (2011): 33–71.

Savelle, Max. *Foundations of American Civilization: A History of Colonial America*. New York: Henry Holt, 1942.

Sayre, Robert. *La modernité et son autre: Récits de la rencontre avec l'Indien en Amérique du Nord au XVIIIè siècle*. Bécherel: Les Perséides, 2008.

Slaughter, Thomas P. *Blood Dawn: The Christiana Riot and Racial Violence in the Antebellum North*. New York: Oxford University Press, 1991.

Soderlund, Jean R. *Quakers and Slavery: A Divided Spirit*. Princeton, N.J.: Princeton University Press, 1988.

Staudenraus, Philip J. *The African Colonization Movement, 1816–1865*. New York: Columbia University Press, 1961.

Stephens, William, "Diary," (1788–1836) in J. E. Clark, "From an Old Quaker Diary, William Stephens 1788–1836," *The Friend* (30 Oct. 1931): 991–93.

Stuart, Nancy Rubin. *The Reluctant Spiritualist: The Life of Maggie Fox*. New York: Harcourt, 2005.

Sussman, Charlotte. *Consuming Anxieties: Consumer Protest, Gender and British Slavery, 1713–1833*. Stanford: Stanford University Press, 2000.

Sutton, George Barry. *C. & J. Clark 1833–1903: A History of Shoemaking in Street, Somerset*. York: Sessions, 1979.

Sword, Kirsten. "Remembering Dinah Nevil: Strategic Deceptions in Eighteenth-Century Antislavery." *Journal of American History* 97 (September 2010): 315–43.

Taves, Ann. "Knowing through the Body: Dissociative Religious Experience in the African- and British-American Methodist Traditions." *Journal of Religion* 73, no. 2 (1993): 200–222.

Taylor, Lou. *The Study of Dress History*. Manchester: Manchester University Press, 2002.

Temperley, Howard. *British Antislavery 1833–1870*. London: Longman, 1972.

Thompson, E. P. *Customs in Common*. New York: New Press, 1991.

Thornton, John K. *Africa and Africans in the Making of the Atlantic World, 1400–1800*. 2nd ed. Cambridge: Cambridge University Press, 1998.

———. *The Kongolese St. Anthony: Dona Kimpa Vita and the Antonian Movement, 1684–1706*. Cambridge: Cambridge University Press, 1998.

Tolis, Peter. *Elihu Burritt: Crusader for Brotherhood*. Hamden, Conn.: Archon Books, 1968.

Tolles, Fredrick. "'Of the Best Sort, but Plain': The Quaker Esthetic." *American Quarterly* 11, no. 4 (1959): 484–502.

Tomlins, Christopher. *Freedom Bound: Law, Labor, and Civic Identity in Colonizing English America, 1580–1865*. Cambridge: Cambridge University Press, 2010.

Trusty, Emma Marie. *The Underground Railroad Ties that Bound Unveiled*. Philadelphia: Amed Literary, 1999.

Turner, Edward Raymond. *The Negro in Pennsylvania: Slavery-Servitude-Freedom*. Washington, D.C.: American Historical Association, 1911.

Twain, Mark. *Life on the Mississippi* (1883) in *Mississippi Writings*. New York: Library of America, 1982.

Tyler-McGraw, Marie. *An African Republic: Black and White Virginians in the Making of Liberia*. Chapel Hill: University of North Carolina Press, 2007.

Uglow, Jenny. *The Lunar Men: The Friends Who Made the Future, 1730–1810*. London: Faber, 2002.

Vincent, David. *Literacy and Popular Culture, England, 1750–1914*. Cambridge: Cambridge University Press, 1993.

Wagstaffe, H. M., ed. "Minutes of North Carolina Manumission Society 1816–1834." Special issue, *The James Sprunt Historical Studies* 22, nos. 1 and 2 (1934).

Walvin, James. *The Quakers: Money and Morals*. London: John Murray, 1997.

———. "The Slave Trade, Abolition, and Public Memory." *Transactions of the Royal Historical Society* 6th ser., 19 (2009): 139–49.

———, ed., *Slavery and British Society, 1776–1846*. London: Macmillan, 1982.

Ware, Vron. *Beyond the Pale*. London: Verso, 1992.

Whitman, T. Stephen. *The Price of Freedom: Slavery and Manumission in Baltimore and Early National Maryland*. Lexington: University Press of Kentucky, 1997.

Wildes, Harry Emerson. *William Penn*. New York: Macmillan, 1974.

Williams, Eric. *Capitalism and Slavery*. Chapel Hill: University of North Carolina Press, 1944.

Willmore, Dorothy E. *Peter Spencer's Movement: Exploring the History of the Union American Methodist Episcopal Church*. Wilmington, Del.: Village Printing, 1991.

Wilson, Ellen Gibson. *Thomas Clarkson: A Biography*. York: William Sessions, Ltd., 1989.

Wood, Marcus. *Blind Memory: Visual Representations of Slavery in England and America 1780–1865*. Manchester: Manchester University Press, 2000.

Woodson, Carter G. *The Negro in Our History*. Washington, D.C.: Associated Publishers, 1922.

———. *Negro Makers of History*. Washington, D.C.: Associated Publishers, 1928.

———. *The Story of the Negro Retold*. Washington, D.C.: Associated Publishers, 1935.

Yellin, Jean Fagan. *Harriet Jacobs: A Life*. New York: Basic Books, 2004.

———. *Women and Sisters: The Antislavery Feminists in American Culture*. New Haven, Conn.: Yale University Press, 1989.

Yellin, Jean Fagan, and John C. Van Horne, eds. *The Abolitionist Sisterhood: Women's Political Culture in Antebellum America*. Ithaca, N.Y.: Cornell University Press, 1994.

Zimmerman, Jonathan. *Whose America? Culture Wars in the Public Schools*. Cambridge: Harvard University Press, 2002.

Contributors

DEE E. ANDREWS is a professor of History at California State University, East Bay. She is the author of *The Methodists and Revolutionary America, 1760–1800* (Princeton University Press, 2000), winner of the Hans Rosenhaupt Memorial Book Award from the Woodrow Wilson National Fellowship Foundation. Her articles include "Religion and the Revolutionary War" in the new edition of Scribner's *Encyclopedia of the American Revolution* (2006) and "From Natural Rights to National Sins: Philadelphia's Churches Face Antislavery" in *Antislavery and Abolition in Philadelphia* (Louisiana State University Press, 2011). Her new work on abolitionist book history has been inspired by research on a larger project on Gradual Emancipation.

KRISTEN BLOCK is an associate professor of History at Florida Atlantic University, where she teaches courses on early America, colonial Latin America, and Atlantic history. Her first monograph, *Ordinary Lives in the Early Caribbean: Religion, Colonial Competition, and the Politics of Profit* (University of Georgia Press, 2012), is a comparative microhistorical study of Christianity in the early Spanish and British Caribbean. She has begun work on a second project, tentatively titled *Health, Disease, and the Spirit: Religion, Healing and the Colonial Body in the Early Caribbean*, on how people of different religious and ethnic origins conceptualized disease and its connection to spiritual health—both of the individual body and of the social body.

BRYCCHAN CAREY is a professor of English Literature at Kingston University in London. He is the author of *From Peace to Freedom: Quaker Rhetoric and the Birth of American Antislavery, 1658–1761* (Yale University Press, 2012) and *British Abolitionism and the Rhetoric of Sensibility: Writing, Sentiment, and Slavery, 1760–1807* (Palgrave, 2005). He is the editor with Peter Kitson of *Slavery and the Cultures of Abolition: Essays Marking the British Abolition Act of 1807* (Boydell and Brewer, 2007) and with Markman Ellis and Sara Salih of *Discourses of Slavery and Abolition: Britain and its Colonies, 1760–1838* (Palgrave, 2004). He is currently writing a book on the relationship between antislavery activism and the emergence of environmental consciousness.

CHRISTOPHER DENSMORE is a curator at Friends Historical Library. He is the author of *Red Jacket: Iroquois Diplomat and Orator* (Syracuse, 1999); coeditor of *Quaker Crosscurrents: Three Hundred Years of the New York Yearly Meetings* (Syracuse, 1995); author of journal articles including "Be Ye therefore Perfect: Anti-Slavery and the Origins of the Yearly Meeting of Progressive Friends in Chester County, Pennsylvania," *Quaker History* (2004), "The Dilemma of Quaker Anti-Slavery: The Case of Farmington Quarterly Meeting, 1836–1860," *Quaker History* (1993), and other articles in *New York History, Canadian Quaker History Journal, Quaker Studies, Journal of Long Island History,* and elsewhere. He is currently vice president of the Pennsylvania Abolition Society.

ANDREW DIEMER is an assistant professor of History at Towson University. He received his Ph.D. from Temple University in 2011. He is the author of "Reconstructing Philadelphia: African Americans and Politics in the Post-Civil War North," which appeared in the January 2009 issue of the *Pennsylvania Magazine of History and Biography*. He is currently revising a book manuscript on African American politics in Philadelphia and Baltimore during the nineteenth century.

J. WILLIAM FROST is the Emeritus Jenkins Professor of Quaker History and Research and former director of the Friends Historical Library, Swarthmore College. He is the author of *A Perfect Freedom: Religious Liberty in Pennsylvania, The Quaker Family in Colonial America, A History of Christian, Jewish, Hindu, Buddhist, and Muslim Perspectives on War and Peace*; coauthor of *The Quakers* and also *Christianity: A Cultural History*; and editor of *The Quaker Origins of Antislavery, The Keithian Controversy in Early Pennsylvania,* and *The Records and Recollections of James Jenkins*.

THOMAS D. HAMM is a professor of History and director of Special Collections at Earlham College in Richmond, Indiana, where he has taught since 1987. He is the author of, among other publications, *The Transformation of American Quakerism: Orthodox Friends, 1800–1907* (Indiana University Press, 1988) and *The Quakers in America* (Columbia University Press, 2003) and the editor of *Quaker Writings, 1650–1920* (Penguin Classics, 2011). His work on George F. White is part of a larger project on Hicksite Friends in the nineteenth century.

NANCY A. HEWITT is a distinguished professor of History and Women's and Gender Studies at Rutgers University, New Brunswick, New Jersey. Her work focuses on women's activism in the United States and beyond with a particular focus on the ways that religion, race, and class shape women's efforts. Her publications include *Women's Activism and Social Change: Rochester, New York, 1822–1872, Southern Discomfort: Women's Activism in Tampa, Florida, 1870s-1920s*, and most recently, the edited collection, *No Permanent Waves: Recasting Histories of U.S. Feminism*. She is currently writing a biography of nineteenth-century abolitionist and woman's rights advocate Amy Kirby Post.

MAURICE JACKSON teaches Atlantic, African American, Urban, and Jazz history at Georgetown University in Washington, D.C. Before that he worked as a community and human rights organizer, housepainter, longshoreman, and rigger. His *Let This Voice Be Heard: Anthony Benezet, Father of Atlantic Abolitionism* was published in 2009 (University of Pennsylvania). He is the coeditor of *African-Americans and the Haitian Revolution* (Routledge, 2010). Jackson wrote the liner notes to the Grammy Nominated Jazz CD by Charlie Haden and Hank Jones, *Steal Away: Spirituals, Folks Songs and Hymns* (1995) and to *Come Sunday* (2012), both by Verve (Paris). He has recently lectured in Turkey, Italy, Puerto Rico, and Qatar. He has had fellowships at the Kluge Center (Library of Congress), the Smithsonian Institution, and the Wood-row Wilson Center for International for Scholars. His "Washington, D.C.: From the Founding of a Slaveholding Capital to a Center of Abolitionism" appears in the *Journal of African Diaspora Archeology and Heritage* (2013). A 2009 inductee into the Washington, D.C., Hall of Fame, he is at work on *Halfway to Freedom: African Americans and the Struggle for Social Progress in Washington, D.C.*

ANNA VAUGHAN KETT teaches in the School of Humanities at the University of Brighton in the United Kingdom. She completed a Ph.D. in Design History in 2012 and is currently researching Quaker women, the Free Pro-duce Movement, and British women's activism against slave-grown cotton goods during the mid-nineteenth century. Current projects include further investigation into "free" cotton cloth produced in Manchester and Carlisle, and the work of the shoemaking Clark family of Street.

EMMA JONES LAPSANSKY-WERNER is a professor of History Emerita and curator of Special Collections, Haverford College, in Haverford, Pennsylvania. A University of Pennsylvania Ph.D. graduate (1975), her recent scholarly publications include *Quaker Aesthetics* (University of Pennsylvania Press, 2003, with Anne Verplanck), *Back to Africa: Benjamin Coates and the American*

Colonization Movement (Penn State University Press, 2005, with Margaret Hope Bacon. Paperback 2007). Her research interests include Quaker history, African American history, urban history, family history, and the intersections between these. She is currently engaged in two research projects: a history of a Bryn Mawr, Pennsylvania Quaker family; and a study of a mid-twentieth-century Philadelphia Quaker utopian community.

GARY B. NASH is a professor of History Emeritus at University of California, Los Angeles, where he also directs the National Center for History in the Schools. Specializing in Early American, African American, and Native American history, he has won the UCLA Teaching Award, the Faculty Research Lecture Award, and the Distinguished Emeriti Faculty Award. He served as president of the Organization of American Historians in 1994–1995. He has been deeply involved with the OAH/National Park Service Committee, was a member of the Second Century National Park Service Commission, and coauthor of the Park Service report, "An Imperiled Promise," on the practice of history in the NPS. Nash is an elected member of the American Academy of Arts and Sciences, the American Philosophical Society, the American Antiquarian Society, and the Society of American Historians. He is the author of many books on Early American history, most recently *Liberty Bell* (2010).

GEOFFREY PLANK is a professor of Early Modern History at the University of East Anglia. He is the author of *John Woolman's Path to the Peaceable Kingdom: A Quaker in the British Empire* (University of Pennsylvania Press, 2012), *Rebellion and Savagery: The Jacobite Rising of 1745 and the British Empire* (University of Pennsylvania Press, 2006), and *An Unsettled Conquest: The British Campaign against the Peoples of Acadia* (University of Pennsylvania Press, 2001). He is currently researching the seventeenth-century pacifist, vegetarian, antislavery reformer Thomas Tryon.

ELLEN M. ROSS is an associate professor and the chair of the Religion Department and a member of the Peace and Conflict Studies Committee at Swarthmore College, Swarthmore, Pennsylvania. She is president of the Friends Historical Association. She is author of *The Grief of God: Images of the Suffering Jesus in Late Medieval England* (Oxford University Press, 1997) and articles in the areas of the history of Christianity and Quaker Studies. She is writing a book on "compassion" in eighteenth- and nineteenth-century Quaker life and thought.

MARIE-JEANNE ROSSIGNOL is a professor of American Studies at University Paris, Diderot, France. She recently translated and edited William Wells Brown's slave narrative with Claire Parfait (*Le Récit de William Wells Brown, esclave fugitif, écrit par lui-même*, Presses universitaires de Rouen et du Havre, 2012). She has been working on a history of early American antislavery in an Atlantic perspective for some time and is currently working on an edited translation of Anthony Benezet's *Some Historical Account of Guinea* (1771) with Bertrand Van Ruymbeke and a team of French scholars.

JAMES EMMETT RYAN is a professor of English at Auburn University, where he teaches early American literature. His books include *Imaginary Friends: Representing Quakers in American Culture, 1650–1950* (University of Wisconsin Press, 2009) and *Faithful Passages: American Catholicism in Literary Culture, 1844–1931* (University of Wisconsin Press, 2012). His essays on American literature and culture have appeared in *American Quarterly, American Literary History, Religion and American Culture, Studies in American Fiction,* and *Leviathan.*

JAMES WALVIN OBE is the Emeritus Professor of History at the University of York. A historian with a long and distinguished career, he is the author of more than thirty books on slavery and abolition, including most recently *The Zong: A Massacre, the Law and the End of Slavery* (Yale University Press, 2011) and *Crossings: Africa, the Americas and the Atlantic Slave Trade* (Reaktion Books, 2013). He has also written several books on British social history, including *The Quakers: Money and Morals* (John Murray, 1998).

Index

abolitionism: American, 44, 47–52, 141–42, 143–44, 145–46; in eighteenth-century Britain, 5, 10, 114, 165–79, 195–96, 205; French, 10, 114, 180; Garrisonian, 37–38, 49, 62, 137; in nineteenth-century Britain, 5, 29, 76, 199, 219–20; in school textbooks, 209–24. *See also* antislavery

Abolition Society (UK). *See* Society for Effecting the Abolition of the Slave Trade

Act for Total British Abolition 1807, 177

Africa: in Anthony Benezet's writing, 9, 106, 110–11, 114, 115; evangelization, 34; religion, 93, 95; slavery in, 34–35, 47, 94, 111, 168, 183; Thomas Clarkson and, 166, 167–68, 203, 204, 205; trade, 62, 93–94, 98–99, 166. *See also* colonization schemes; individual nations and regions by name

African Free School, 107–8, 116, 118

African Methodist Episcopal Church, 108, 124, 131

African Methodist Episcopal Zion Church, 75–76

Africans, 9, 30, 89–90, 92–96, 106

Africans in America, 219

African Union Methodist Church, 122, 124, 125, 128, 129

agriculture, 21

alcohol, 21, 139, 152, 153. *See also* rum

Alexander I, 203

Allen, Richard, 108, 116, 219, 221

Allen, William, 194, 196, 199

Allinson, Samuel, 17

America: geographical region, 21, 62, 176. *See also individual colonies and states by name;* United States

American Abolition Society, 37

American Anti-Slavery Society, 44, 50, 75, 127

American Civil War, Quaker activity in lead up to, 5, 30, 44; Quaker activity during and after, 40, 82, 153; in school textbooks, 210, 211

American Colonization Society, 9, 36, 108, 135–37, 145

American Free Produce Association, 67

American Revolution, and slavery, 4, 112, 113; and British abolitionism, 29; Crèvecoeur and, 180, 187; and Quaker politics, 7, 35; role of African Americans in, 219; in school textbooks, 213, 215; and the slave trade, 6, 113

American Sunday School Union, 45–46

American War of Independence. *See* American Revolution

Anabaptists, 33

An Account of the European Settlements in America, 111

Angola, 93

animals, 15

Anthony, Susan B., 83

Antigua, 2

antiracism, 217

antislavery, 16, 25, 44, 136, 180. *See also* abolitionism

Anti-Slavery Reporter, The, 58

Aptheker, Herbert, 214, 217

Arch Street Meeting (Philadelphia), 141

Aristotle, 118n13

Association for the Study of Negro Life and History, 214

Auslander, Leora, 64

Austin, Anne, 89

Bailey, Thomas A., 215–6

Baltimore, MD, 36, 121–22, 138, 140–41

Baltimore Yearly Meeting, 43

Bancroft Prize, 217

Baptists, 18, 33, 75

Barbados, Quaker colonists in, 2, 89–94, 111; Africans in, 9, 23, 93–102, 111–12; George Fox visits, 2–3, 32, 89, 94, 96

Barbé-Marbois, François, Marquis de, 106

Barclay, Robert, 34

Barham Court, 170

Barker, Rachel, 49, 51

Barlow, Joel, 190

Barnes, Elizabeth, 97

Bartram, John, 184

Bath, UK, 171

BBC, 219

Beale, Howard, 217

Beard, Charles A., 211

Beard, Mary, 211

Beecher, Lyman, 152

Bell, John, 30

Benezet, Anthony: antislavery arguments, 4, 108–13; *A Short Account of That Part of Africa Inhabited by the Negroes*, 110, 111–12; campaigns to celebrate, 10, 221; death, 116–17; early life, 106–8; historiography and legacy, 5, 117–18, 219, 220; influence beyond Quakerism, 9, 106, 114–15, 188, 189; *Observations on Inslaving, Importing and Purchasing of Negroes*, 110; *Notes on the Slave Trade*,

113, 115; and the Philadelphia Yearly Meeting, 3, 108–9; in school textbooks, 214, 218; *Short Observations on Slavery*, 107–8; *Some Historical Account of Guinea*, 110, 111, 112, 114, 167–68; and Thomas Clarkson, 106, 114, 167–68, 177, 200

Benezet, Jean, 106–7

Benin, 111

Bennett, William, 218–19

Bergan County, NJ, 120–21

Berlin, Ira, 120, 131

Bible, 31–32, 39, 91, 92

Birmingham, UK, 60, 219

Birmingham Ladies' Negro's Friend Society, 61

Bisset, Robert, 198–99

Bob Jones University Press, 218

Boen, William, 1–2

Boorstin, Daniel, 216–17

Boston, MA, 61, 78, 79, 83, 151, 213

boycotts, 4, 48, 58–59, 60, 171. *See also* free produce movement

Brazil, 113

Brecher, Aaron, 15

Bridgetown, Barbados, 97, 98

Bridgetown Women's Meeting, 97, 100

Bridport, UK, 61

Bright, John, 66

Bright, Margaret, 66

Bringhurst, Deborah Ferris, 43

Brissot, Jacques (or Jean) Pierre de Warville, and Crèvecoeur, 10, 180, 182, 185–90, 192n32; and Anthony Benezet, 114, 117; and the Société des Amis des Noirs, 114, 188–89, 190, 196

Bristol, UK, 62, 171

British and Foreign Anti-Slavery Society, 60

British Empire: abolition and emancipation in, 6, 48–49, 80, 165–79, 198; imperial policy, 35

Clarkson, Thomas (*continued*): *History of the Rise, Progress, and Accomplishment of the Abolition of the African Slave-Trade*, 10, 195, 198–202; impact on Quaker antislavery, 10; legacy and reputation, 5, 194; *Memoirs of the Private and Public Life of William Penn*, 10, 195, 202–3, 204; relationship with Society of Friends, 194–95, 205; *Summary View of the Slave Trade*, 171–72; as writer and researcher, 168–70, 194–95, 196–203
Clarkson Anti-Slavery Society, 126
Clavière, Étienne, 114, 189, 190
Clay, Cassius, 145
Clay, Henry, 39–40
Cleggett, Benjamin, 80
clothing, undyed, 19; African, 155; as antislavery action, 56–58, 62–69; extravagant, 22, 23; rags, 23, 24. *See also* cotton; free labor cotton; wool
Coatesville, P.A., 123
coffee, 60
Coffin, Levi, 217, 220
Cold War, 210, 215–16
Coleman, Elihu, 3, 30
Coleridge, Samuel Taylor, 196, 204
Collins, Emily, 83
Collins, Priscilla, 26n1
colonization schemes, 9, 33, 36, 116, 135–48, 211. *See also* Africa, American Colonization Society
Columbia University, 211, 212
Comly, John, 18, 51
Commager, Henry Steele, 214
commerce. *See* trade
Committee of the Society for Effecting the Abolition of the Slave Trade. *See* Society for Effecting the Abolition of the Slave Trade
communism, 215, 216
Condorcet, Nicolas, Marquis de, 106, 114, 189, 190

Congo. *See* Kongo
Congregational Friends, 73, 76–77, 80–81
Congress (U.S.), 36, 108, 201
Connecticut, 61
Constantine, 33
cotton, 4, 5, 8–9, 59, 62. *See also* free labor cotton
Courier de l'Europe, 185, 186
Creek Indians, 212
Crèvecoeur, J. Hector St. John de, 10, 180–93
Cuffee, Paul, 36
Cugoano, Ottobah, 9, 106, 114, 205
Cumberland County, NJ, 120–21

Danish West Indies, 101
Darlington, Chandler, 126
Dartmouth College, 141
Davis, David Brion, 194
DeGarmo, Rhoda, 85n10
Delaney, Martin, 80
Delaware, 122, 124
Delaware County, PA, 125
Delaware Indians, 153
Denton Hollow, 124
Diderot, Denis, 191n9
Dillwyn, William, 196, 199
Dilwyn, Moses, 22
Douglas, Stephen A., 152
Douglass, Frederick, on cotton, 60, 71n31; activism, 75, 78; and Amy Kirby Post, 75, 77; in Pennsylvania, 127; in Rochester, 77, 78, 79–80; in school textbooks, 217, 218; unconvinced by spiritualism, 81. See also *Frederick Douglass's Paper*; *North Star, The,*
Douglass, Sarah Mapps, 140–41
Drake, Thomas, 5, 96, 103n15, 129
dreams, 20, 31
dress. *See* clothing
Dublin, Ireland, 171

Harvey, Isaac and Sarah, 220
Haslewood, Clayborne, 98
Haverford, PA, 203
Haverford College, 199
Haviland, Eleazar, 45
Haydon, Benjamin Robert, 194
Hayley, William, 204
Henry, Patrick, 106, 112
Hepburn, John, 3, 30, 33
Hertfordshire, 169, 201
Heyrick, Elizabeth, 29, 60
Hicks, Edward, 45
Hicks, Elias: compared with George
    Fox White, 44, 53; *Observations on
    the Slavery of the Africans*, 25; on
    paid ministers, 45; as Quaker leader,
    6, 8, 38, 46; relationship with Joshua
    Evans, 15, on trade, 25
Hicks, Rachel, 44, 49
Hicksite Quakers, 6, 37, 38, 43–55, 73,
    76–77
Hobbes, Thomas, 118n13
Hochschild, Adam, 194
Holmes, Richard, 195
Hooton, Martha, 98, 99, 101
Hopper, Edward, 36
Hopper, Isaac T., 49, 50, 51, 52, 221
Howard, Frederick, 5th Earl of Carl-
    isle, 174
Huguenots, 106, 190
Hume, David, 193n47
Hunt, John, 17, 25
Hutcheson, Francis, 109

Illinois, 152, 158
Impey, Catherine, 61
India, 22, 62
Indiana, 36
Indiana Yearly Meeting, 37, 50
Indian Rights Association, 162n7
Indians. *See* Native Americans
indigo, 60
Inner Light, Inward Light: and

antislavery, 30–31, 48, 108, 160; as
    Quaker inspiration, 6, 30, 40, 74, 90
Inspires de la Vaunage, 106
Isaiah, 3
Islam, 93–94, 115
Israel, 32–33

Jackson, John, 25, 49–50
Jackson, Mary, 122–23
Jackson, Thomas, 139
Jacobs, Harriet, 75, 81
Jamaica, 2, 111, 112, 176, 200
James II, 204
Janney, Samuel, 37
Jay, John, 106, 118, 187
Jefferson, Thomas, 190, 193n47, 211
Jeffrey, Julie Roy, 58
Johnson, Edward Austin, 222n5
Johnson, Oliver, 50
Johnson, Samuel, 221
Jones, Absalom, 108, 116, 219
Jordan, Ryan, 5, 162n1
Joshua, 91
Journal du Lycée de Londres, 185
Julye, Vanessa, 129

Kane, Elisha, 82
Kansas, 40, 61, 153
Kay, Ann, 26n1
Kedzie, Lemira, 83
Kelley, Abby, 38, 39, 75–76
Kennett Square, PA, 121, 124, 126
Kent, 170
Kentucky, 145, 152
Kersey, Jesse, 46
Ketcham, John, 75
Kimpa Vita, Beatriz, 95
King, Robert, 5
Kneass, William, 201
Kongo, 93, 95, 111

Lafayette, Gilbert du Motier, Marquis
    de, 181, 185, 190

108–9; Hicksite, 46, 51, 77; Progressive, 50; statements on slaveholding, 3, 4, 20; structure and organization, 6

Phillips, James, 169–70, 171, 186, 194, 195, 196

Phillips, Wendell, 217

Phipps, Joseph, 113

photography, 64

Pike, Rachel, 49

Piles, Robert, 31

Pinder, Richard, 89

Pitt, William, the Younger, 173, 174, 175

plainness, 22, 29, 38, 64–65

Plank, Geoffrey, 60

Pleasants, Robert, 112

Poole, William, 45

Portugal, 93

Post, Amy Foster, 74

Post, Amy Kirby, 9, 73–86

Post, Isaac, 73, 75, 79, 80–82, 85n7, 85n9

Post, Mary R., 46–47, 51, 52

Potter, Nathaniel, 77

Poughkeepsie, NY, 52

Presbyterians, 33, 37, 45, 75, 81

Privy Council, 174–75

Progressive Quakers: and abolitionism, 37, 50, 82; and Amy Kirby Post, 73, 74, 77, 78; British, 60, 63, 65; decline, 82; and John Greenleaf Whittier, 39; and spiritualism, 81

progressive revelation, 31–32

progressivism, 218, 223n36

prophecy, 18

proslavery, 49, 136, 152, 158–59, 174, 198

Proud, Robert, 202

providentialism, 218, 223n36

Psalms, 108–9

Puritans, 5

Purvis, Robert, 127, 221

Quakers: antislavery position attacked, 198; and Brissot, 186–88; British, 29, 59–61, 165–66, 167, 168, 169–72, 177; and Crèvecoeur, 180–93; debates about slavery, 7, 29, 33, 36–40, 152; evangelism, 89–92; in fiction, 30, 127–28, 130, 144–45, 182–85; hostile to abolitionism, 29–30, 37, 39, 48–52, 137; key terms and beliefs, 6–7, 30, 91–91; networks, 59, 60–61, 168, 169–70, 197; racial attitudes, 2, 5, 9, 127, 129–30, 153, 156–57; in school textbooks, 10, 209–24; as slaveholders, 1–3, 9, 73, 89; unofficially oppose slavery, 3, 16–17, 25. See also Society of Friends

Quarles, Benjamin, 217

quietism, 37, 38, 46

race, 130, 140, 142, 153–54, 156–57, 210. See also antiracism, racism

racism, 29, 40, 157, 214. See also antiracism, race

Rafferty, Max, 218

Ramsdell, Laura, 83

Randolph, John, 211

Ranters, 91

Rathbone, William, 168

rationalism, 37

Raynal, Guillaume: and Anthony Benezet, 106, 114; antislavery arguments, 184, 191n9; and Brissot, 186, 189; and Crèvecoeur, 181–82, 183, 185; on Quakers, 182

Reconstruction, 111, 114, 217

Rediker, Marcus, 12n23

Red Lion (church), 124

Religious Society of Friends. See Quakers; Society of Friends

repatriation. See colonization schemes

Republican Party, 136, 152

resistance to enslavement: local, 123; personal, 144; uprisings, 20, 32, 112, 113–14, 116, 176, 182. See also fugitive slaves

Rhode Island Historical Society, 220

rice, 60

Rice, Howard, Crosby, 181, 192n29

Richardson, Anna and Henry, 58, 62

Richmond, IN, 46
Rochdale, UK, 66
Rochester, NY, 73–74, 77–83
Rochester Monthly Meeting, 75, 76
Rochester Working Women's Protective Union, 78
Rock, John S., 151
Rogers, Rachel, 49
Roman Catholicism, 33, 91, 106
Rotch, Charity, 22
Royal African Company, 110
Rugg, Harold, 212
rum, 4, 15, 21, 25
Rush, Benjamin, 108, 109, 112, 118, 190
Russia, 203

Sacramento, CA, 160
Saint Domingue, 176, 189, 193n44, 196, 205
Salford, UK, 176
salt, 23
Sancho, Ignatius, 9, 114, 205
Sandiford, Ralph, 3, 25, 33, 214
Savelle, Max, 215
Scotland, 109–10
sculpture, 220
Seneca Falls Women's Rights Convention, 78, 80
Seneca Indians, 80
Serres de la Tour, Antoine, 185
Seven Years' War, 7, 16, 180
sex, 24, 83, 99–100
Shadd, Abraham, 126, 127
Sharp, Granville, 5, 6, 106, 169, 204
shaving, 22
Sheppard, Moses, 9, 135–48
Sierra Leone, 205
sin, 18, 19, 30, 47, 95
Slave; His Wrongs and Their Remedy, The, 58, 68
slavery: British reliance on, 68; Crève-coeur and, 183–84; George Fox White and, 47–48; profitability, 7–8;

in Quaker communities, 1–2, 4–5; in school textbooks, 211, 213; theoretical objections to, 109–10, 135. *See also* abolitionism; antislavery; emancipation; enslaved persons; slave trade
slaves. *See* enslaved persons
slave trade: abolition, 6, 36, 37, 176–77, 201; abolition commemorated in 2007, 219–20; effect on Africa, 34, 47, 111, 168, 183; growth of, 170; non-Quaker opposition to, 37, 112, 114–16, 165–79; post-abolition, 49; Quaker involvement in, 73, 108; Quaker opposition to, 3, 10, 29, 33–34, 106, 157. *See also* Middle Passage
Sloane, Sir Hans, 112
Smedley, R.C., 123, 126, 130
Smith, Adam, 110
Smith, Gerrit, 77
Smith, Joseph, 152, 154
Snodgrass, J. E., 122
Société des amis des noirs, 114, 188–89, 193n44
Society for Effecting the Abolition of the Slave Trade, 171, 172–74, 176, 188, 194, 195
Society of Friends: beliefs and key terms, 6–7; in Caribbean, 2, 89–105; corporate antislavery statements, 3–4, 171, 205; early history, 2, 89–91, 94; formal debates about slavery, 7; reformation of, 16–19, 25, 35, 43, 64, schism, 36–40. *See also* Hicksite Quakers; Orthodox Quakers; Progressive Quakers; Quakers
Society for the Relief of Free Negroes Unlawfully Held in Bondage, 113
Soderlund, Jean, 4
Somerset, 8, 56
Somerset v. Stewart, 6
South Africa, 111
South Carolina, 23, 113, 160

Wades Mill, UK, 169
Wallace, George, 110
Walvin, James, 219
Ward, Samuel Ringgold, 120, 121, 123–24, 126
Warrensburg, MO, 155
Warrington, Abraham, 18
Warrington, UK, 176
Warsaw, MO, 156–57
Washington, George, 81, 180
Waterloo, NY, 76
Watkins, William, 143
Watson's Annual Journal, 116
Webb, Elizabeth, 95
Webster, Daniel, 40
Wedgwood, Josiah, 68
Wedgwood, Ralph, 199
Weims, John, 61
Wellman, Judith, 84
Welsh, Herbert, 162n7
Wesley, John, 112
West Chester, PA, 126
Western New York Anti-Slavery Society, 74, 75, 79
West Haven, CT, 212
West Indies, slavery in, 20, 111–12, 113, 167, 184; Danish, 101; French views of, 184, 186; produce of, 21, 60, 62; Quaker opinions of, 33, 48–49, 111; Quaker settlers in, 35, 89–102; West-India Lobby, 174, 200. *See also* individual colonies and nations by name
Whig Party (U.S.), 39
White, George Fox, 8, 38–39, 43–55
Whitefield, George, 107, 112
Whittier, John Greenleaf, 39–40
Wilberforce, William: Anthony Benezet and, 106, 114; in British historiography, 5, 204; as parliamentary abolitionist, 172, 174, 176–77, 199
William Penn Charter School, 107
Williams, Eric, 7–8
Williamson, Passmore, 221

Wilmington, DE, 36, 43, 45, 121–22, 125
Wilmington College, OH, 220
Wingrave, John, 63–64, 65
Wisbech, UK, 169
women: antislavery activism, 54, 58–59, 75; domestic roles of, 62, 99–100, 209; enslaved, 99–100; in Quaker meetings, 49, 75, 76, 91, 96; rights of, 39, 73, 75, 77–78, 81; sexist attacks on, 49; sexuality, 83, 99–100; in school textbooks, 209, 216; suffrage, 38, 83
Woods, Joseph, 176
Woodson, Carter G., 214
Woodward, C. Vann, 217
wool, 19, 60
Woolman, John: and Anthony Benezet, 112, 189; arguments against slavery, 23, 30; and clothing, 60; compared with George Fox White, 48; and Joshua Evans, 15, 16–17; *Journal*, 31–32; legacy, 220; in school textbooks, 214, 215, 218; *Some Considerations on the Keeping of Negroes*, 3, 30; and Thomas Clarkson, 200; tone and rhetoric, 37; views on emancipation, 4, 8; views on trade, 25; Wordsworth, Dorothy, 196, 199
Wordsworth, William, 196, 199
World Alliance for Promoting International Friendship through Churches, 213
World Court League, 213
World Peace Foundation, 213
World War I, 40, 209, 210
World War II, 215
Wyandotte Indians, 153

Yale University, 212
Yearly Meeting of Congregational Friends, 76–77
York, UK, 171
Young Men's Colonization Society of Baltimore, 139–40

*The University of Illinois Press
is a founding member of the
Association of American University Presses.*

University of Illinois Press
1325 South Oak Street
Champaign, IL 61820-6903
www.press.uillinois.edu